Expert Perspectives
on Interventions for Reading

A Collection of Best-Practice Articles
from the International Dyslexia Association

Edited by Louisa C. Moats,
Karen E. Dakin, and R. Malatesha Joshi

The International Dyslexia Association
Baltimore, Maryland

The
International
DYSLEXIA
Association®

Promoting literacy through research, education, and advocacy.™

Expert Perspectives on Interventions for Reading
A Collection of Best-Practice Articles from the International Dyslexia Association
Edited by Louisa C. Moats, Karen E. Dakin, and R. Malatesha Joshi
Published by The International Dyslexia Association, Baltimore, Maryland

The International Dyslexia Association
Promoting literacy through research, education, and advocacy.™
Founded in Memory of Samuel T. Orton
The International Dyslexia Association
40 York Road, 4th Floor
Baltimore, MD 21204-5202
Telephone: (410) 296-0232
(800) ABC-D123
Fax: (410) 321-5069
www.eida.org

Book cover & interior design and composition by Brian Taylor, Pneuma Books

Publisher's Cataloging-In-Publication Data
(Prepared by The Donohue Group, Inc.)

Expert perspectives on interventions for reading : a collection of best-practice articles from
  the International Dyslexia Association / edited by Louisa C. Moats, Karen E. Dakin and
  R. Malatesha Joshi.

  p. ; cm.

  Most of the articles are from IDA's quarterly journal Perspectives on Language and Literacy.
  Includes bibliographical references.
  ISBN: 978-0-89214-067-1

  1. Reading—Remedial teaching. 2. Dyslexic children—Education. 3. Dyslexia. I. Moats, Louisa
Cook. II. Dakin, Karen E. III. Joshi, R. Malatesha. IV. Title: Perspectives on language and literacy.

LB1050.5 .E86 2012

          371.91/44   2011940477

Printed in the United States of America by Mid-Atlantic Design & Print, Inc.

Contents

Section 7

About the Editors

Louisa C. Moats, Ed.D., has been a teacher, psychologist, researcher, and graduate school instructor specializing in reading, language, and learning disabilities. She has written many books, book chapters, and articles on these topics, including *Basic Facts about Dyslexia & Other Reading Problems,* with Karen E. Dakin. Dr. Moats has served several terms on the National Board of the International Dyslexia Association (IDA), including a term as Vice President, since 1994. Currently she leads the Standards and Practices Committee of IDA and works as an educational consultant and developer of professional training materials for teachers.

Karen E. Dakin, M.Ed., has been a classroom and resource room teacher, reading specialist, independent school administrator, and Co-Director of the Learning Assessment Clinic at the Cleveland Clinic Foundation, Cleveland, Ohio. Ms. Dakin is co-author of *Basic Facts about Dyslexia & Other Reading Problems,* and she has been active in the IDA for over 30 years serving as a member of the IDA Board for the past 9 years, an At-Large Director, Vice President, and currently as Secretary. Ms. Dakin is an educational consultant in Shaker Heights, Ohio.

R. Malatesha Joshi, Ph.D., is Professor of Literacy Education, ESL, and Educational Psychology, at Texas A&M University where he teaches courses and conducts research in the areas of assessment and intervention of reading problems in monolingual and bilingual students. He has also conducted research on the content and pedagogical knowledge of pre-service, in-service, and teacher educators and is the editor of *Reading and Writing: An Interdisciplinary Journal.*

Contributors

Section 1

P. G. Aaron, Ph.D., Professor Emeritus, Department of Educational Psychology, Indiana State University

R. Malatesha Joshi, Ph.D., Professor of Literacy Education, ESL, and Educational Psychology, Texas A&M University

Stephanie Al Otaiba, Ph.D., Associate Professor of Special Education and Faculty Associate, Florida Center of Reading Research, Florida State University

Carol McDonald Connor, Ph.D., Assistant Professor, Florida State University, College of Education, and a research faculty, the Florida Center for Reading Research

Barbara Foorman, Ph.D., Francis Eppes Professor of Education and Director of Florida Center of Reading Research, Florida State University

Christopher Schatschneider, Ph.D., Professor of Psychology, Associate Director, Florida Center of Reading Research and Florida State University

Luana Greulich, Doctoral candidate, Florida State University, College of Education

Jessica Folsom Sidler, Doctoral candidate, Florida State University, College of Education

Joseph K. Torgesen, Ph.D., Professor Emeritus of Psychology and Education and Director Emeritus, Florida Center for Reading Research at Florida State University

Section 2

Judith R. Birsh, Ed.D., CALT, QI, Founder and formerly Director of the Multisensory Teaching of Basic Language Skills program, Teachers College, Columbia University

Suzanne Carreker, Ph.D., CALT-QI, Chief Officer of Programs, Neuhaus Education Center in Houston, Texas

Carol Tolman, Ed.D., National LETRS (Language Essentials for Teachers of Reading and Spelling) Trainer and contributing author, Literacy Consultant

Maryanne Wolf, Ph.D., Director of the Center for Reading and Language Research, Tufts University and Professor of Child Development, Eliot-Pearson Department of Child Development, John DiBiaggio Professor

Stephanie Gottwald, M.A., Assistant Director, Center for Reading and Language Research, Tufts University

Melissa Orkin, Doctoral student, Tufts University

Section 3

Benita A. Blachman, Ph.D., Trustee Professor of Education and Psychology, Syracuse University

Darlene M. Tangel, Ph.D., Adjunct Assistant Professor, School of Education, Syracuse University

Eileen Wynne Ball, Ph.D., Professor, Curry College Coordinator, Education Department

Rochella Black, M.S., Learning Disabilities and Early Childhood Specialist, formerly of the Northport-East Northport School District and the Syracuse City School District

Pamela Hook, Ph.D., Clinical Professor, Department of Communication Sciences and Disorders, School of Health and Rehabilitation Sciences, MGH Institute of Health Professions

Barbara Fink-Chorzempa, Assistant Professor at the State University of New York, New Paltz

Steve Graham, Ed.D., Curry Ingram Professor of Special Education and Literacy, Vanderbilt University

Karen Harris, Ed.D., Curry Ingram Professor of Special Education and Literacy, Vanderbilt University

Marcia Kierland Henry, Ph.D., Professor Emeritus, San Jose State University, Former President, IDA (1992-1996)

Section 4

Jan Hasbrouck, Ph.D., Vice Chairman, Gibson Hasbrouck & Associates, Wellesly, MA; Research Associate University of Oregon

Pamela Hook, Ph.D., Clinical Professor, Department of Communication Sciences and Disorders, MGH Institute of Health Professions

Sandra D. Jones, Ph.D., President, Hanson Initiative for Language and Literacy (HILL), affiliated with the MGH Institute of Health Professions

Marianne Meyer, M.A., NCSP, Neurobehavioral instructor in neuro-psychology, Wake Forest University School of Medicine, Retired.

Section 5

Nancy Hennessy, M. Ed., Educational Consultant, The Consulting Network

Kate Cain, B.Sc., D.Phil. Reader in the Department of Psychology, Lancaster University, United Kingdom

Steven A. Stahl (Deceased), Formerly Professor of Curriculum and Instruction, University of Illinois, Champaign

Danielle S. McNamara, Ph.D., Professor, Psychology Department and the Learning Sciences Institute, Arizona State University

Margaret G. McKeown, Ph.D., Clinical Professor of Education and Senior Scientist, Learning Research and Development Center, University of Pittsburgh

Isabel L. Beck, Ph.D., Professor Emerita, University of Pittsburgh

Ronette G. K. Blake, Research Coordinator at Children's Hospital of Pittsburgh

Gary A. Troia, Ph.D., CCC-SLP, Associate Professor of Special Education and a principal investigator with the Literacy Achievement Research Center, Michigan State University

Section 6

Charles Haynes, Ed.D., CCC-SLP, Professor and Clinical Supervisor, MGH Institute of Health Professions, Boston

Terrill Jennings, Fd.M., Founding teacher and Head of the Language Department Arts, Landmark's Elementary and Middle School, Manchester, Massachusetts

Dolores Perin, Ph.D., Associate Professor of Psychology and Education, Coordinator of Reading Specialist Program, Teachers College, Columbia University

Steve Graham, Ed.D., Curry Ingram Professor of Special Education and Literacy, Vanderbilt University

Bruce Saddler, Ph.D., Associate Professor, Department of Educational and Counseling Psychology Department, Division of Special Education, University at Albany

Suzanne Carreker, Ph.D., CALT-QI, Chief Officer of Programs, Neuhaus Education Center in Houston, Texas

Charles A. MacArthur, Ph.D., Professor in the School of Education, University of Delaware

Section 7

Donald D. Deshler, Ph.D., Williamson Family Distinguished Professor of Special Education and Director, Center for Research on Learning, University of Kansas

Michael F. Hock, Ph.D., Associate Research Scientist, University of Kansas, Associate Director The Center for Research on Learning

Hugh W. Catts, Ph.D., Professor and Chairperson, Department of Speech, Language, and Hearing, University of Kansas

Mary Beth Calhoon, Ph.D., Assistant Professor of Special Education, Department of Education and Human Services, Lehigh University

James McPartland, Ph.D., Professor of Sociology and Director, Center for Social Organization of Schools, Johns Hopkins University

Robert Balfanz, Ph.D., Research Scientist, Johns Hopkins University Center for Social Organization of Schools and Co-Director, Everyone Graduates Center

Nettie Legters, Ph.D., Research Scientist, Johns Hopkins University Center for Social Organization of Schools and Co-Director, Everyone Graduates Center

Rebecca J. Moak, Ph.D., Educator with local, state, national, and international experience in working with learners from middle school through graduate school

Tanya Shuy, M.Ed., Education Program Specialist, U.S. Department of Education, Office of Vocational and Adult Education, Division of Adult Education and Literacy

Peggy McCardle, Ph.D., MPH, Chief, Child Development and Behavior Branch, Director, Language, Bilingualism, and Biliteracy Program, National Institute for Child Health and Human Development (NICHD)

John R. Kruidenier, Ed.D., Consultant, Kruidenier Education Consulting, Horsham, Pennsylvania

Sherry Mee Bell, Ph.D., Associate Professor, University of Tennessee

Introduction

Louisa C. Moats

This anthology is a collection of many of the most practical and informative articles ever published by the International Dyslexia Association (IDA) on the most enduring and effective instructional practices for teaching children and adults who struggle with learning to read. Most of the articles are from IDA's *Perspectives on Language and Literacy,* a quarterly journal informed by the best minds in our field dedicated to finding research-based best practices for educators who provide services to students with dyslexia and other reading problems. The journal is managed by members of IDA's national board of directors who determine the most timely and helpful themes for each issue and recruit editors nationally recognized for their expertise and experience with a particular theme, as well as their ability to recruit other expert authors to write on the topic.

The articles selected for this anthology address a range of important topics beginning in Section 1 with those that frame the larger issues in intervention. P. G. Aaron and R. Malatesha Joshi demonstrate why a multi-component approach to instruction is likely to be the most effective. In addition, they summarize the evidence that not all reading disabilities are alike, and that interventions must be designed to match the characteristics of the student. Dyslexia is the most common type of reading disability, characterized by phonological processing, decoding, and spelling problems; it responds best to a structured language approach. However, some poor readers have primary difficulties with language comprehension and benefit from an approach that emphasizes vocabulary, fluency, and comprehension. Stephanie Al Otaiba, with her colleagues from the Florida Center for Reading Research, also shows that in public school settings, the most effective instruction varies according to the type and degree of learning difficulty. Finally, Joseph K. Torgesen summarizes the intervention studies up through 2005 documenting how many students can respond to research-based instruction and why it is so important to intervene early, in kindergarten and first grade.

Multi-component, structured language teaching is described in Section 2 by Judith Birsh, Suzanne Carreker, and Carol Tolman—three highly accomplished teacher educators. These timeless articles explain the essential principles of effective teaching—explicit, systematic, cumulative, multisensory, and linguistic—and provide an overview of the content of decoding, spelling, and reading instruction. This section also includes a concise summary of decades of research conducted by Maryanne Wolf and colleagues, supporting the value of a multi-component instructional approach for students with severe reading disabilities.

The next series of articles in Section 3 focuses on the related topics of spelling, phonological processing, morphological processing, and word recognition. Benita A. Blachman, Marcia Henry, and Pamela Hook all are or have been professors in language and literacy graduate programs, and are among the few who can link recommended practices to theory and evidence. Barbara Fink Chorzempa, Steve Graham, and Karen Harris, are leading experts on handwriting, spelling, and written composition; here, they emphasize the value of metacognitive strategy instruction in language teaching.

Section 4 on reading fluency includes three articles that together provide a comprehensive discussion of issues in fluency assessment and instruction. Benchmarks for oral reading fluency (Jan Hasbrouck), the relationship between fluency and comprehension (Pamela Hook), and validated techniques for slow readers (Marianne Meyer) are all addressed in these experts' articles.

The vocabulary and comprehension section of this anthology (Section 5) includes articles by leading authorities who are changing the way we think about comprehension problems. Kate Cain, a British researcher and author of many research studies, offers a view of comprehension subskills that helps explain the disparate ways in which comprehension breakdowns can occur. Margaret McKeown, Isabel Beck, and Ronette Blake offer argument and evidence that a strategic questioning approach to text reading pays off. The late Steven Stahl, a former student of Jeanne Chall at Harvard and strong proponent of vocabulary instruction, lends a light touch to the treatment of this topic. Danielle McNamara reminds us that good readers are strategic readers, and that poor readers can be taught effective approaches to text that in turn can be automatized. Finally, Gary Troia highlights the role of summary writing in fostering reading comprehension, offering specific tactics for content area reading teachers.

Articles on writing and writing instruction are also included in this anthology in Section 6. Topics cover foundation skills such as multisensory grammar (Suzanne Carreker) and sentence combining (Bruce Saddler)—a proven technique for fostering gains in sentence-level composition. Charles Haynes and Terrill Jennings show explicitly how spoken language and written language should interact and bolster one another in the classroom. Charles MacArthur shares expert advice on the use of assistive technology to support struggling writers, while Dolores Perin and Steve Graham provide a brief summary of their meta-analysis of effective writing instruction for students in grades 4–12.

Rounding out the collection is Section 7 on educational treatments for adolescents and adults with reading, writing, and language difficulties. This population is often underserved and certainly less well understood than the population of younger poor readers. Donald Deshler and his colleagues, who have studied adolescent students with learning disabilities for decades, emphasize that this age group can improve significantly with proper treatment. Rebecca Moak challenges several myths about adolescent literacy, confirming that most poor readers in adolescence can benefit and do need decoding instruction in addition to comprehension instruction. Mary Beth Calhoon also demonstrates that a novel linguistic approach to word analysis results, followed by fluency and comprehension instruction, results in significant gains in middle school students. John Kruidenier and colleagues report on federally funded research documenting the characteristics of interventions that do work with adult poor readers. James McPartland and colleagues delve into the conditions necessary to train teachers to effectively implement the programs and strategies that work.

About IDA

One of IDA's primary missions is to inform professionals, parents, and individuals with dyslexia about evidence-based and research-based interventions and treatments for students with language-based learning disabilities. Publications such as this anthology are an important way that IDA pursues this goal. A monthly newsletter, fact sheets posted on the website (downloadable at www.interdys.org), and a book series are also means for communicating with the membership and the general public. Conferences, including an annual national conference and many regional conferences sponsored by IDA's 45 branches, serve to educate as well. All of these efforts to improve the lives of individuals with dyslexia owe tremendous debt to the research and clinical communities represented in this book.

As this collection of articles documents, IDA's traditional focus on systematic and explicit teaching of language, reading, and writing has considerable support in current research. All ages can benefit from informed teaching of language structure delivered by a knowledgeable and skillful professional. Expert instruction offers the best hope for students who suffer with specific language learning difficulties. To advance the mission of IDA, the organization recently adopted a *Standards and Practices* document (downloadable at www.interdys.org outlining the knowledge, skills, ethical behavior, and supervised experience that should be required of licensed professionals who provide intervention services to students with reading difficulties of all kinds. As IDA moves ahead to recognize training programs and certify individuals who meet these standards, articles in this anthology should be on the reading list of trainees and mentors alike.

I wish to thank all of the expert contributors, board members, office staff, and my co-editors, Karen Dakin and Malt Joshi, and our editor, Denise Douce, for their leadership and tireless commitment to the work of the IDA.

Louisa Moats
April 4, 2011

This book is dedicated to Louisa Cook Moats, Ed.D., for her exceptional commitment to and work with struggling readers and their teachers and for her years of service to IDA, as Board member, Vice President, and contributor to IDA publications. Louisa's expertise, passion, and dedication guided the work on this anthology from the selection of its timeless articles to its publication and beyond by helping children, parents, and educators succeed in their pursuit of literacy.

Research Frameworks for Understanding Intervention with Dyslexia and Related Difficulties with Literacy Acquisition

R. Malatesha Joshi

According to the recent National Assessment of Educational Progress (NAEP, 2009), only about 38% of 4th grade students read fluently and in many low-income school districts, close to 70% of 4th grade students may not read fluently. To help poor readers become better readers, reading researchers have attempted to identify reading instruction that works. The three articles in this section discuss different instructional programs that have been explored. Joseph Torgesen, after reviewing several successful programs with disabled readers, concluded that explicit instruction using different programs provided significant improvement in both severely disabled (scoring below the 5th percentile) and moderately disabled (6th–16th percentile) poor readers, especially word-level reading skills. Unfortunately, as Dr. Torgesen noted, similar gains were not obtained with reading comprehension.

Stephanie Al-Otaiba and colleagues discuss different programs that could be used under the Response-to-Intervention (RTI) model. Peer-Assisted Learning Strategies (PALS), Tutor Assisted Intensive Learning Strategies (TAILS), Early Intervention in Reading, Responsive Reading Instruction, and Phonological Awareness Training plus Synthetic Phonics (PASP) all showed successful results in improving word-level reading skills. Reading comprehension, however, did not show similar gains. Dr. Al-Otaiba and her colleagues stress the need for a clear outline of RTI and the importance of teachers' knowledge of key linguistic concepts needed to teach literacy skills.

Since many of the earlier programs had shown significant improvement in word reading but not in reading comprehension to the same extent, P. G. Aaron and I provide comprehension strategies to students who had comprehension problems and decoding strategies to a group with decoding deficits. After 12 weeks of instruction, there was a significant improvement in reading comprehension and decoding in each of the groups. The authors of all three of these articles point out the importance of systematic and explicit instruction in both word-reading and comprehension skills by first identifying the weak component. Additionally, they stress the importance of a clear explanation of RTI and the need for teachers' knowledge of linguistic concepts to teach literacy skills.

Reading difficulties are not all alike. Although the majority of poor readers have phonologically-based decoding deficits, others are hampered by language comprehension problems that require a different approach. Practitioners can now rely on studies such as these to differentiate the needs of poor readers and to select approaches that match a student's profile of strengths and weaknesses.

Why a Component Model of Reading Should Drive Instruction

P. G. Aaron and R. Malatesha Joshi

The existence of the condition known today as learning disability (LD) was recognized almost 100 years ago when it was noticed that some children who apparently were intelligent experienced a great deal of difficulty in learning to read (Hinshelwood, 1895). In the United States, the physician Samuel Orton (1937) recognized this as an educational problem and recommended a phonology-oriented method of instruction to overcome reading difficulty. The recognition that this unexpected form of reading difficulty (i.e., dyslexia) is a legitimate disability is evident from the subsequent acceptance of the term learning disabilities, which was introduced by Samuel Kirk in 1963. The concept of LD gained official status in 1975 with the passing of the Education for All Handicapped Children Act. The designation of LD as a form of disability entitled individuals with reading problems to identification, remedial services, and accommodations. It became necessary, therefore, to develop an objective means of diagnosing LD.

Discrepancy Model

For several decades, LD in reading was defined in terms of average or above-average IQ but below-average reading scores. It appeared reasonable that a logical means of diagnosing LD would be to compare the IQ scores of children with their reading scores. If a significant discrepancy existed between these two scores, then a diagnosis of LD could be made. The child was then sent to the resource room for various amounts of time depending on the school's policy. This method of diagnosis, which appeared straightforward and objective, came to be referred to as the "discrepancy model-based procedure" and led to its wide acceptance and use in schools over the last 40 years.

Problems with the Discrepancy Model

As years passed, researchers took a close look at the validity and utility of the discrepancy model and, as a result, they found that the model failed to deliver on its promise (Aaron, 1997; Fuchs & Fuchs, 2006). There are many reasons for the lack of success of the discrepancy model of LD identification and instruction. Among these are the high pupil-teacher ratio in the LD resource rooms and the placing of children with LD along with children who have emotional and behavioral problems in the same resource room. Many research reports, however, indicate that the primary reason for the disappointing outcome of LD instruction is the unsystematic way children are taught in many of the resource rooms. More specifically, a strong rationale for the instructional methods used for teaching children with LD may be lacking because the discrepancy model does not provide the LD teacher guidelines for instruction. In a review study, Vaughn, Levy, Coleman, and Bos (2002) synthesized studies conducted on students with LD and reported that the quality of reading instruction was poor, with excessive time allocated to seatwork and filling out worksheets with limited time given to reading itself. Moody, Vaughn, Hughes, and Fischer (1998) also reported that the quality of reading instruction provided was not based on a skill-development approach, but was driven by the whole language philosophy. Teachers relied mainly on group work that disregarded individual differences. The instructional time was also spent on completing homework assignments rather than remediating students' language learning difficulties. These reviews can be summarized by stating that there has been a disconnect between diagnosis and instruction because the discrepancy model neither tells the teacher the precise nature of the child's reading problem nor provides guidelines for the most suitable form of instruction. This leads to a situation wherein all children with reading problems are treated alike and instruction is rarely intensive enough to remediate weaknesses.

Response to Intervention Model (RTI)

The observed limitations of the discrepancy model of LD have led researchers and educators to look for alternative approaches to the teaching of students who experience difficulty in learning to read and spell. One such approach that is receiving much attention in recent years is response to intervention (RTI). RTI is embedded in a multitiered model which comprises assessment, intervention, and progress monitoring. Even though RTI can be conceived to be in the form of more than one tier of service, the most frequently cited model has three tiers by which instruction is organized and delivered, depending on the nature and severity of students' problems. At Tier 1, the focus is on the implementation of comprehensive, effective, regular classroom instruction designed to prevent the emergence of reading disabilities. The appropriateness of the regular class instruction is accomplished by determining the proportion of children who are below benchmark performance for their grade level. If a large number of children are found to be poor readers and only a few are good readers, then the quality of instruction or appropriateness of the program or approach in use may be suspected. In that case, coaching for the teacher and adoption of other programs or methods may be indicated. When students are still at risk on screening measures, supplementary support services may be provided in small groups. This constitutes Tier 2. Those students who are far behind (Tier 3) are provided more intense and specialized instruction and its effect is measured. Those students who still remain unresponsive to instruction in spite of preventive intervention are further tested or their previous history reviewed. Based on the outcome of this evaluation, the students may be provided one-to-one instruction or referred to special education services.

As an alternative to the discrepancy model, RTI is believed to be promising and is being tried out in several school systems. The two attractive features of RTI are early identification of potential reading difficulties (instead of waiting to fail) and continuous monitoring of progress. Screening measures for early identification, when used in kindergarten, should use good predictors such as letter knowledge, phonemic awareness, rapid naming, nonsense word reading, and oral reading fluency. Many investigators have used curriculum-based measures (CBMs) for screening and progress-monitoring, rather than formal diagnostic tests. Children identified as being at risk are taught by strategies such as training in phonemic awareness, phonics, decoding, vocabulary development, and comprehension strategies.

Considering the youthfulness of RTI, it is not surprising that there are not numerous studies which test effectiveness. In a longitudinal study, Simmons, Coyne, Kwok, McDonagh, Harn, and Kameenui (2008) followed 41 children from kindergarten through the 3rd grade. The authors report that, based on both formal and informal measures, a majority of the children showed improvement in phonemic and alphabetic tasks in kindergarten and in comprehension by 1st grade. Denton, Fletcher, Simos, Papanicolaou, and Anthony (2007) report a series of studies where RTI has been used. When Tier 1 and Tier 2 instruction was applied, fewer than 7% of the children performed below average in one school and the percentage was less than 1% in another school. In one study, Lovett et al. (2008) found that RTI produced positive results with children who learn English as a second language.

Issues Concerning RTI

In spite of the strong advocacy for RTI, many unanswered questions remain. One of them is how is RTI different from what teachers normally do with their poor readers in the regular classroom? Is it not because the child had not responded favorably to instruction that the teacher referred the child for assessment and evaluation? According to Gerber (2005), RTI is simply urging the educational system to try harder and to invest more effort in students who are difficult to teach and manage. According to Kavale (2005), RTI simply reoperationalizes LD instead of redefining it. Furthermore, there are several variants of RTI, indicating that a consensus about the method of implementation of RTI has not yet emerged. Another question concerns the criteria for the determination of "satisfactory progress" before instruction is changed or special education eligibility is invoked.

An inspection of titles of published reports indicates that the focus of RTI is still identification of LD rather than the cause of the reading problem, the appropriate instructional procedure, and the means of management. In their book *Response to Intervention*, Brown-Chidsey and Steege (2006) note that RTI is particularly important for identifying reading, math, and writing deficits. According to Haager, Klingner, and Vaughn (2007), "RTI is the most promising method for *identifying* individuals with learning disabilities" (p. 5). Addressing the issues in RTI, Speece and Walker (2007) note that "RTI, in its many forms and at its heart, is presumably a method for *identifying* LD" (p. 298). In the past, the preoccupation of the discrepancy model has been with diagnosis of LD and its definition, rather than instruction and remediation, which has impeded the progress of special education. Berkeley, Bender, Peaster, and Saunders (2009) reviewed the development and implementation of RTI in 50 states and concluded that because of the lack of specificity in assessment and intervention, RTI "seems to hold a similar *trajectory* as the discrepancy model" (p. 94). The reason for the emphasis on identification and diagnosis is perhaps rooted in the fact that federal and state budget allocations are based on the number of pupils identified as having LD.

One of the special features of RTI is its claim to early identification. It was noted earlier that measures such as phoneme awareness, letter knowledge, and rapid naming could be used for early assessment. However, as Wagner (2008) notes, it is unlikely that children with learning disabilities can be identified much earlier as suggested by the RTI model than they are under the traditional discrepancy approach. Furthermore, there is no strong research evidence to show that measures such phonemic awareness, rapid naming, and nonsense word repetition administered at the kindergarten level can reliably predict future reading achievement beyond 1st grade level, after which reading itself becomes the best indicator of future outcomes. One of the measures often recommended and used in RTI is Dynamic Indicators of Basic Early Literacy Skills (DIBELS). In a recent study of 12,762 participants, Catts, Petscher, Schatschneider, Bridges, and Mendoza (2009) found that DIBELS predicted well only some aspects of later reading performance and that it tended to identify a large number of students who later became adequate readers. They suggest that, in the future, assessment procedures such as dynamic assessment may perform better than the ones currently available.

To summarize, we quote Wagner (2008) who has examined the RTI approach critically, "Although identification models based on response to instruction appear potentially promising, the notion that they represent real progress for identification and intervention for children with dyslexia should be considered to be a popular myth until evidence from rigorous evaluation is available" (p. 188).

If implemented as presented in the current literature, RTI still may relegate unresponsive children to "special education" without exploring what else could be done to improve their reading skill. In this respect, RTI may still not be the best vehicle for realizing the insights of reading research for the benefit of students at risk.

Component Model of Reading

The component model of reading (CMR) (see Aaron, Joshi, Boulware-Gooden, & Bentum, 2008, for complete description) differs from the other two models in its educational philosophy; it does not dichotomize poor readers into LD and non-LD categories. After all, reading skill falls on a continuum which makes the question, "Where do we draw the line between LD poor readers and non-LD poor readers?" a conundrum. Research studies show that poor readers labeled as having LD and children described as non-LD, garden variety poor readers do not differ in reading-related processes, and that their reading profiles are similar (Algozzine, 1985; Hallahan and Kauffman, 1994).

Another difference between CMR and the other models is that CMR takes the comprehensive view that reading difficulties are caused by several factors, including cognitive deficit. The noncognitive factors that affect reading achievement often are environmental and psychological in nature. In CMR, these three factors are referred to as *domains*. The three domains of CMR are 1) cognitive, 2) psychological, and 3) ecological. Each domain has its own components as shown in Table 1.1.1. The main goal of CMR is neither redesigning the definition of LD nor the implementation of such a definition. The ultimate goal of CMR is to identify the component (or components) that is the cause of reading difficulty (i.e., cognitive, psychological, or environmental) and design the most appropriate means of dealing with the cause. The cognitive domain of CMR is the focus of the present article and will be taken up last. We start with the psychological domain.

Table 1.1.1. **Components of the Cognitive, Psychological, and Ecological Domains of the Component Model of Reading (CMR)**

Cognitive Domain	Psychological Domain	Ecological Domain
Word recognition Comprehension	Motivation and interest Locus of control Learned helplessness Teacher expectation Gender differences	Home environment Culture and parental involvement Classroom environment Peer influence Dialect

Psychological Domain

The psychological domain includes components such as motivation and interest, locus of control, learned helplessness, learning styles, teacher expectation, and gender differences.

Locus of control and learned helplessness

These two factors are closely interrelated. Locus of control can be internal or external. When the student feels that outcomes are the consequences of his or her own control, locus is internal. In contrast, when the student feels the outcomes are due to chance or luck, or are under the control of others, locus is external. The best thing the teacher can do is to create opportunities for all children to be successful by adjusting demands according to the student's ability. Repeated failure results in an attitude of helplessness.

Teacher expectation

This term refers to inferences teachers make about students' *future* behavior and achievement based on what the teachers know about the students at *present*. Children pick up teachers' expectations and fulfill these expectations. Teachers will do well by being aware of their own expectations, keeping expectations unprejudiced, and giving importance to present performance rather than to past performances.

Gender differences

Even though not accepted by all educators, more boys are said to have reading problems compared to girls. These observed differences may be due to boys being prone to more behavioral problems than girls or due to some innate biological gender differences. The best way to avoid gender-based expectations is to be aware that results of gender studies deal with averages and not individuals. In every classroom, there are boys who excel in reading and writing; there are also girls who excel in math.

Ecological Domain

The ecological domain includes the following components: home environment and culture, parental involvement, classroom environment, peer influence, and dialect.

Home environment

It is rightly said that the home is the smallest school. A good proportion of academic achievement of students can be explained by the following factors: quantity and quality of reading materials in the home, number of pages read for homework, the educational level of parents, number of days absent from school, number of hours spent watching TV, and the presence of two parents in the home. Reading problems in the classroom can be minimized by making parents feel they and the teacher are part of the same team. This can be accomplished by involving parents in school-related projects and by holding regular parent-teacher-child conferences.

Classroom environment

Young children are quite active and become restless if they are made to sit in one place for a long time. The classroom, therefore, should be arranged to provide plenty of opportunities for movement and action. Interaction among children and between the teacher and the students can be facilitated by seating the students in a semicircle so that the distance between the teacher and the students is the same for all students.

Peer influence

The influence of peers on children's behavior is well recognized in the psychology literature. Flexible grouping of students can help children be exposed to a variety of classmates and not be influenced by a few, particularly those who have no interest in what is going on in the classroom.

Dialect

Dialect is a regionally or socially distinctive variety of language characterized by a particular accent, set of words, and even grammatical structures. It is useful to remember that a single dialect that is spoken by a majority of people comes to be recognized as the standard form of language. Thus, Standard English (SE), also referred to as Academic English (AE), is the dialect spoken by a majority of people, not that it possesses a set of superior linguistic features. Even though estimates of the number of English dialects spoken in the U.S. vary from 3 to 24, the most widely known non-standard English dialect is African American English (AAE). Sociolinguists who have studied AAE have concluded that AAE is a rule-governed system of communication. Linguists have concluded, therefore, though different from Standard English, AAE is not deficient.

Teachers should be aware of the fact that dialectical variations can result in variations in spelling and syntax. Some of these deviations can result in decoding difficulties and masquerade as symptoms of reading disability. Telling students that they have to use SE because that is the only way to succeed in life may not motivate them to use SE. In contrast, telling them that it is good to know SE because a majority of people in the country use it and that the textbooks are written in SE is likely to be a more agreeable proposition.

Cognitive Domain

The cognitive domain of the model has two components: word recognition and comprehension. Word recognition is made up of two processes, decoding and instant word recognition (i.e., sight word reading). Instant word recognition encompasses the speed factor which translates into fluency. Comprehension is a generic term used for both reading and listening comprehension.

In the cognitive area of reading, some children may have difficulty recognizing printed words, others in comprehending text, and still others may be poor readers because of their limited vocabulary. It is reasonable to expect instruction in word recognition to improve the performance of the first kind of readers, comprehension instruction to help the second kind of readers, and vocabulary instruction to help the third group of children. In line with this logic, CMR identifies the weak component that underlies reading difficulties and focuses the appropriate remedial instruction at the weak component.

The inspiration for the components of the cognitive domain of this model comes from a report by Gough and Tunmer (1986) who presented a "simple view of reading" by noting that the two most important constituents of reading are the ability to decode the written word and the ability to comprehend text. If a child cannot decode printed English, he cannot comprehend it; if a child cannot comprehend spoken English, he cannot comprehend written English either. At this point, it is legitimate to ask, "Is there evidence to show that CMR is effective?"

Validation study of the cognitive domain of CMR

In this section, the educational outcome of seven, one-year programs of diagnosis and instruction of reading disability based on CMR is compared with the results of the traditional discrepancy-based LD diagnosis and instruction carried out in resource rooms (see Aaron, et al., 2008, for the statistical details and a complete description of the study). The reading achievement scores of 330 children from grades 2 through 5 were used for comparing the relative effectiveness of instruction based on CMR with that of the traditional discrepancy model. Of these 330 children, 171 received remedial reading instruction based on CMR (treatment group) and the remaining 159 children received instruction in LD resource rooms in their respective schools (comparison group).

Treatment group

The 171 children in the treatment group were enrolled in a remedial program named READ (Reading for Excellence in Academic Development). The program is intended for children from grades 2 through 5 and is conducted at the College of Education, Indiana State University. During the month of July, starting from the year 1998, an announcement was placed in the local newspaper inviting parents who thought their children were at risk for reading problems to enroll their children in the READ program. Parents brought their children for 1 hour of instruction 4 days a week, for 1 semester. The children were taught in small groups of four to five by seven or eight graduate students who were enrolled in the school psychology program and had taken courses in reading. During every instructional session, the instructors and the supervisor (one of the authors) were available to the parents as they put into practice some of the components of the psychological domain of CMR. This involved explaining the nature of the child's reading problem to the guardian, the importance of reading to the child, and restricting distractions such as the TV at home. In addition, three parent-instructor-supervisor conferences were held during the semester and the nature and outcome of the pretests and the method of instruction used with each child were explained to the guardian. Parents were also supplied with books and encouraged to read them with the children.

Children in the treatment group were from 7 different cohorts taught during the course of 7 years. The children were administered standardized pretests and reading instruction was tied to the outcome of the pretests. Based on the nature of the reading component they were deficient in (word recognition or comprehension and vocabulary), 125 children in the treatment group received word recognition training; 46 children received reading comprehension strategy/vocabulary training. At the end of the semester, these children were administered posttests to compare performance of the children in the treatment to those in the comparison group (described below).

Comparison group

Children in the comparison group were from three different geographical regions of the U.S. (Oklahoma, Illinois, and Washington). The reading scores of children with LD before and after resource room instruction were obtained from special education files kept in their respective districts. These files covered a period of 6 years from 1998 through 2004. In the LD programs, the posttests were administered 3 years after the administration of the pretests. The LD programs reported here did not classify children on the basis of their weaknesses and target instruction at the weak areas. The teachers could give only general descriptions of their instructional procedures. The 15 LD teachers of the children in the comparison group used a variety of procedures to teach the children. Information obtained through interviews of the teachers indicated that most of the instructional time in the resource room was used for completing homework assignments; some of them said they used phonics. The number of children in the resource room with reading disability varied from 3 to 7. However, available information showed that all these children received instruction for at least 1 hour per day during the school days. The children in the comparison group were matched, grade by grade, with those in the treatment group on the basis of their pretest scores on reading-related tests.

Differential Diagnosis of Children in the Treatment Group
Identification of the weak component

If a child's listening comprehension was in the average range or higher, but the reading comprehension was lower, then the reading difficulty was most likely due to a weakness in the word recognition component. This diagnostic conclusion was confirmed by the child's below-average word attack and spelling scores. Children with weak word recognition received instruction in word recognition skills. In contrast, if the child had below-average scores on tests of both reading and listening comprehension, but had word-attack scores in the average range, then the impediment to reading was the weak comprehension and vocabulary component. Such children received instruction in comprehension/vocabulary strategies. Children who were deficient in both word recognition and comprehension skills were started off with word recognition skills training. If and when they attained sufficient word recognition skill, they were moved to the comprehension group. Often, children with below-average comprehension skills also have limited vocabulary. In the READ program, vocabulary training was provided as part of comprehension training since words encountered in context are more readily learned and retained than words learned in isolation.

Occasionally, we had some children who had reading comprehension scores that were higher than their listening comprehension scores. This is a profile that is opposite to the one seen in children with reading disability. Research shows that children with this type of profile invariably have difficulty with sustained attention. This is because listening is more attention-demanding than reading. Inconsistent attention was dealt with by requiring children to summarize in one or two sentences what they have read during strategy instruction. This strategy seems to minimize the attention problem of some children and has produced satisfactory results. In general, inconsistent attention has not been a major impediment to instruction, probably because of the small size of the reading groups.

Instructional Procedures
Word recognition training

As a starting point, children in the READ program who were placed in the word recognition group received phonemic awareness training. During the initial stages, the instructional procedure followed the steps recommended in the program *Phoneme Sequencing Program for Reading, Spelling, and Speech* (Lindamood & Lindamood, 1998). Following this, consonant sounds and vowel sounds were introduced using the multisensory approach. After this training, "The Writing Road to Reading" (Spalding & Spalding, 1990) was used for further training in word recognition. When the phonograms segment was completed, simple sentences using the previously learned words were constructed and children were asked to read them and copy them. Depending on the progress each child had made, he or she was introduced to simple decodable story books.

Comprehension training

Children in the comprehension training group were taught to use seven strategies that many researchers have found to be useful in promoting reading comprehension skills. Passages within the reading level of the children were used for comprehension training exercises. Simple stories that were less than two pages long and could be completed within the 45-minute session were preferred.

The seven strategies in this comprehension instruction were

1. Activate schema (What do I already know about this?)
2. Determine purpose (What am I reading this for?)
3. Stop and think (Am I understanding what I have read?)
4. Visualize (Are there maps and pictures that I should look at?)
5. Seek help (If I do not know a word, I should raise my hand.)
6. Ask a question (I should ask the teacher or the author a question.)
7. Summarize (Can I tell the story in one or two sentences?)

These seven comprehension strategies were written on blank sheets of paper and the children were asked to memorize and use them as they read. First, the instructor modeled the process of reading utilizing all seven strategies.

Following the modeling, one child in the group simulated the instructor and the other children were encouraged to be actively involved in commenting and seeking help. Over the years we have learned that children can learn to recite the seven comprehension strategies but fail to incorporate them when they read a story or a passage. In the READ program, modeling by the instructor was found to be the most effective way of overcoming this difficulty. This requires the instructor to model the use of the seven strategies before every new lesson was introduced.

Results

Statistical analysis of pre- and posttest scores showed that the treatment group that received the word recognition training made significant gains in their word attack scores as well as comprehension scores, which was greater than the gains seen in the LD group. The comprehension gains of children who received word recognition training are not surprising since the reading comprehension of these children was held back by their poor word recognition skills. In other words, poor word recognition skill functioned as a factor that limited reading comprehension of these children. Once the constraints of poor word recognition skill were removed, a concomitant improvement in reading comprehension occurred.

Statistical analysis of the data showed that the treatment group that received the comprehension strategy training made gains in their comprehension scores that were significantly higher than the comprehension gain scores of the LD group. Actually, the children in the LD resource rooms lost 1.77 comprehension standard scores. Children in the treatment group who were not identified as having word attack deficiency and, therefore, did not receive word recognition training did not improve their word attack scores. Children in LD resource rooms also did not significantly improve their word attack scores.

On the whole, the results indicate that instruction provided under the framework of CMR is more effective than the undifferentiated resource room LD instruction. Many other studies show that instruction in phoneme awareness and phonics improves word recognition skills. Correspondingly, many studies show that comprehension strategy training of weak readers improves reading comprehension. What is unique about CMR is that it combines these elements and provides a comprehensive system for the differential diagnosis and treatment of reading problems. The philosophy of CMR is that when properly instructed, all children can improve their reading skills, even if only to a small degree.

Limitations of CMR

Even though CMR has three domains, the cognitive domain is within the direct control of the classroom teacher in the sense the teacher can focus on word recognition skills, vocabulary, and comprehension. The classroom teacher can work with psychological components such as motivation, learned helplessness, and teacher expectation. Even though teachers control the classroom environment, other components such as home environment and peer influence are beyond their reach.

Conclusions

Prevailing approaches in teaching poor readers seem to give more importance to identifying and labeling children as having LD rather than identifying the source of the reading difficulty. Instead, why not give an etiological description of poor readers, for example, as having decoding weaknesses, comprehension difficulties, a limited vocabulary, a lack of interest, or an inadequate home environment? Taking this approach makes the specific reading difficulty the focus of instruction.

It is our belief that when systematically implemented, CMR-based instruction makes diffident readers more confident, nudges reluctant readers toward becoming avid readers, and scaffolds instruction to help poor readers become better readers. With CMR all children can make progress, albeit to varying degrees, and no child will be left behind uninstructed.

References

Aaron, P. G. (1997). The impending demise of the discrepancy formula. *Review of Educational Research, 67*, 461–502.

Aaron, P. G., Joshi, R. M., Boulware-Gooden, R., & Bentum, K. (2008). Diagnosis and treatment of reading disabilities based on the component model of reading: An alternative to the discrepancy model of learning disabilities. *Journal of Learning Disabilities, 41*, 67–84.

Algozzine, B. (1985). Low achiever differentiation: Where is the beef? *Exceptional Children 52*, 72–75.

Berkeley, S., Bender, W. N., Peaster, L. G., & Saunders, L. (2009). Implementation of responsiveness to intervention: A snapshot of progress. *Journal of Learning Disabilities, 42*, 85–95.

Brown-Chidsey, R., & Steege, M. (2006). *Response to intervention*. New York: Guilford Press.

Catts, H. W., Petscher, Y., Schatschneider, C., Bridges, M. S., & Mendoza, K. (2009). Floor effects associated with universal screening and their impact on the early identification of reading disabilities. *Journal of Learning Disabilities, 42*, 163–176.

Denton, C. A., Fletcher, J. M., Simos, P. G., Papanicolaou, A. C., & Anthony, J. L. (2007). An implementation of a tiered intervention model: Reading outcomes and neural correlates. In D. Hager, J. Klinger, & J. Vaughn (Eds.), *Evidence-based reading practices for response to intervention* (pp. 107–137). Baltimore: Paul Brookes.

Fuchs, D., & Fuchs, L. S. (2006). Introduction to response to intervention: What, why, and how valid is it? *Reading Research Quarterly, 41*, 93–99.

Gerber, M. M. (2005). Teachers are still the test: Limitations of response to instruction strategies for identifying children with learning disabilities. *Journal of Learning Disabilities, 38*, 516–524.

Gough, P., & Tunmer, W. (1986). Decoding, reading, and reading disability. *Remedial & Special Education, 7*, 6–10.

Haager, D., Klingner, J., & Vaughn, S. (Eds.). (2007). *Evidence-based reading practices for response to intervention*. Baltimore: Paul Brookes.

Hallahan, D. P., & Kauffman, J. M. (1994). Toward a culture of disability in the aftermath of Deno and Dunn. *Journal of Special Education, 27*, 496–508.

Hinshelwood., J. (1895). Word-blindness and visual memory. *The Lancet, 21*, 1564–1570.

Kavale, K. A. (2005). Identifying specific learning disability: Is responsiveness to intervention the answer? *Journal of Learning Disabilities, 38*, 553–562.

Lindamood, P., & Lindamood, P. (1998). *Phoneme sequencing program for reading, spelling, and speech*. Austin, TX: PRO-ED.

Lovett, M. W., De Palma, M., Frijters, J., Steinbach, K., Temple, M., Benson, N., et al. (2008). Interventions for reading difficulties: A comparison of response to intervention by DLL and EFL struggling readers. *Journal of Learning Disabilities, 41*, 333–352.

Moody, S. W., Vaughn, S., Hughes, & M. T., Fischer, M. (1998). Broken promises: Reading instruction in resource rooms. *Learning Disability Quarterly, 64*, 211–215.

Orton, S. (1937). *Reading, writing, and speech problems in children*. New York: W. W. Norton.

Simmons, D. C., Coyne, M. D., Kwok, O., McDonagh, S., Harn, B. A., & Kame'enui, E. J. (2008). Indexing response to intervention: A longitudinal study of reading risk from kindergarten through third grade. *Journal of Learning Disabilities, 41*, 158–173.

Spalding, R. B., & Spalding, W. T. (1990). *The writing road to reading*. New York: William Morrow.

Speece, D. L., & Walker, C. Y. (2007). What are the issues in response to intervention research? In D. Haager, J. Klinger, & S. Vaughn (Eds.), *Evidence-based reading practices for response to intervention* (pp. 287–301). Baltimore: Paul Brookes.

Vaughn, S., Levy, S., Coleman, M., & Bos, C. (2002). Reading instruction for students with LD and EBD. *Journal of Special Education, 36*, 2–13.

Wagner, R. (2008). Rediscovering dyslexia: New approaches for identification and classification. In G. Reid, A. J. Fawcett, F. Manis, & L. S. Siegel (Eds.), The *Sage Handbook of Dyslexia* (pp.174–191). Thousand Oaks, CA: Sage Publications.

Identifying and Intervening with Beginning Readers Who Are at Risk for Dyslexia
Advances in Individualized Classroom Instruction

Stephanie Al Otaiba, Carol McDonald Connor, Barbara Foorman, Christopher Schatschneider, Luana Greulich, and Jessica Folsom Sidler

Researchers have demonstrated that students with dyslexia share a phonological linguistic deficit (Catts, Fey, Zhang, & Tomblin, 1999; Shaywitz, Fletcher, & Holahan, 1999). This deficit may be "unexpected," but it manifests very early when children have difficulties in learning about letters, sounds, rhymes, and language relative to their peers with similar home literacy experiences. When these early difficulties persist, they strongly predict which students are likely to develop difficulties with reading accuracy, fluency, and comprehension. Researchers have shown us that we could greatly reduce reading disabilities if we identified (accurately and early) children who are at risk for reading difficulties, and if we provided those children with evidence-based instruction immediately. Converging findings from over four decades of psychological and educational research show which instructional methods help most children learn to read (National Reading Panel, 2000).

It is encouraging, therefore, that general and special education policy (namely the Reading First Initiative of the No Child Left Behind Act and the reauthorization of the Individuals with Disabilities Act) allow school districts to "use a process that determines if the child responds to scientific, research-based intervention as a part of the evaluation procedures" for learning disabilities. The goal of using such a process, known as Response to Instruction or Intervention (RTI) is to eliminate ineffective reading instruction as a cause of reading difficulties. Further, this RTI process could alleviate the need for children at risk for reading difficulties to wait to receive reading intervention services until they have demonstrated a relatively severe and unexpected discrepancy relative to their intelligence (IQ-achievement discrepancy). Thus, with RTI, early intervening services are provided for struggling beginning readers before they fall farther and farther behind their peers and show severe discrepancies between their reading and cognitive abilities.

Prevention is far more powerful than remediation, so we are optimistic about RTI; at the same time we share concerns expressed by parents, practitioners, and fellow researchers that there are not yet a set of RTI "standard operating procedures." Our purpose in addressing *Perspectives on Language and Literacy* readers is not to provide a comprehensive guide to RTI, but to share our considerable research experience helping schools who are beginning to implement RTI, particularly emphasizing the early grades where the research is most strong. The research on early intervention is particularly compelling, so we are sharing the vision of what can happen at the early grades when all students receive the benefit of early intervention.

It is also important to provide intervention to older students, who desperately need, but too often do not receive, the intensive remedial multicomponent instruction necessary to help them read grade-level texts. In this article, we do not directly address RTI for older students with more severe reading or writing disabilities, but other authors do.

First, we describe an overview of the RTI implementation process. Next, we illustrate from our own research ways to maximize resources within beginning reading instruction. Then, we discuss implementation issues related to identifying children who need additional intervention. We conclude with some additional considerations and solutions.

An Overview: What Is the RTI Process?

Keeping in mind that there are many different models and that no specific model (or even RTI) is mandated, we describe RTI as a multitier system or problem-solving process that begins with Tier 1, or primary classroom instruction. The idea of RTI is not new, and the problem-solving process has been used in states such as Iowa since the 1980s. The goal of Tier 1 is for all students to receive evidence-based and well-implemented reading instruction for about 90 minutes per day. Generally speaking, Tier 1 should help the majority of children read on grade level and is more effective when children's individual differences in language and literacy skills are considered (i.e., instruction is differentiated).

Tier 2 interventions are provided to children who did not make adequate gains when they received high quality Tier 1. Tier 2 or secondary interventions are typically provided 3–5 days a week in a small group format as a supplement to Tier 1. Depending on resources, these Tier 2 interventions might be delivered by classroom teachers, well-trained and supervised paraprofessionals, or Title 1 tutors; or children might be pulled from more than one classroom for small group interventions led by reading specialists, speech and language pathologists, or other interventionists. Then, students still not catching up to their peers receive Tier 3 tertiary interventions. Ideally, Tier 3 is carefully individualized based upon student assessment data and is provided in even smaller groups of 1 to 3 students, with greater intensity or "dosage" by the most highly skilled interventionist. A goal of the process is for children to move across tiers as they need to; ideally a majority would catch up to peers and be able to return to the classroom. Then, only students with the most chronic and persistent reading difficulties would receive special education services.

Clearly, the roles of specialized reading interventionists are expanded within the RTI process. They help implement early screening for identification of students at risk for reading difficulties, and then collaborate with and train general education teachers to provide the strongest beginning reading instruction to those children. In addition, when primary instruction does not help children catch up to their peers, reading interventionists help match children's assessed needs to resources (interventions and interventionists). Thus, interventionists, in conjunction with school leaders, examine what intervention programs are available and what additional interventions or professional development is needed, which children are likely to benefit from which program, and what levels of expertise and professional development are needed to faithfully implement an intervention.

How is responsiveness or unresponsiveness typically defined?

Currently, there is no clear consensus about defining responsiveness within RTI. However, research can guide schools in designing the process, selecting specific screening measures, and creating decision rules about moving children to another tier (more or less intensive) and also for accurately and efficiently determining eligibility for special education. Fuchs and Deshler (2007) discuss several methods that schools could utilize: benchmarks, slope discrepancy (slower growth rate relative to peers), dual discrepancy (low performance and slow growth relative to peers), or normalization. We are currently conducting research on the efficacy of a dynamic RTI model, where children are moved to Tier 2 or even Tier 3 immediately based on achievement scores, rather than waiting to see what happens. Then, their growth rates are monitored to ensure they receive enough of the optimal intervention to achieve grade-level reading targets.

When screening children to determine who should receive intervention, schools may compare initial performance on a curriculum-based measure, such as oral reading fluency, relative to a benchmark or cut-point. An alternative, particularly in kindergarten, is to wait for 6–8 weeks to compare growth on such a measure relative to a peer group or to evaluate both initial risk status and growth. It is vital to establish the *treatment validity*, or implementation effectiveness within each Tier. As Fuchs and Deshler (2007) remind us, RTI can only be tested in the context of generally effective instruction and interventions. "Without validated instruction (implemented with fidelity by practitioners), RTI cannot be a valid method of disability identification or early intervention" (p. 134).

Keeping in mind that most RTI research has been conducted within the kindergarten–second-grade window, most researchers suggest a guideline that if Tier 1 is effectively implemented, then 80% or more students would be on grade level. Effective Tier 2 would help at least 10–15% more students to reach grade level. Effective Tier 3 would then help most remaining students to significantly improve their rate of growth. However, these guidelines may be overly ambitious for older students with persistent reading disabilities such as dyslexia. A "valid treatment" for these students would likely be individualized and may also involve accommodations. Hence, within special education, there is a need for ongoing progress-monitoring data to be used as a tool for problem solving to tailor intervention to strengths and weaknesses. In addition, normalization methods could be used to judge adequate end-of-year outcomes. For example, scoring below the 30th percentile on a normed test of reading achievement would be considered inadequate RTI. This would be helpful to gauge the degree to which a multitier process is helping children catch up to national or local norms.

Maximizing Resources: What Rates of Success Could Be Achieved through Effective Primary Beginning Literacy Instruction in Tier 1?

Research has shown that effective primary classroom teachers can reduce the percentage of children who do not perform on grade level to about 5–7%, or about one child in a 20-child classroom (Al Otaiba & Fuchs, 2006; Foorman, Brier, & Fletcher, 2003; Mathes, et al., 2005). This success rate is for the beginning stages of reading instruction, which reflects that prevention of reading difficulties is far easier than the remediation of reading disability. Notably, in these and other studies conducted mostly in kindergarten through second-grade classrooms, this rate of success or responsiveness has been achieved when teachers: 1) implemented an evidence-based literacy curriculum, 2) used universal screening and ongoing monitoring of student progress toward a targeted goal, and 3) delivered a dynamic mix of whole class and differentiated small group instruction, as well as adequate time to practice skills independently. Ensuring that Tier 1 is generally effective is important; otherwise, if too many children need secondary or tertiary intervention due to weak primary instruction, any RTI system will be too strained to provide intensive resources.

A strong foundation: An evidence-based core literacy curriculum

Tier 1 instruction begins with an evidence-based core literacy curriculum that scaffolds explicit code-focused instruction in phonological awareness, phonics, and decoding strategies (NRP, 2000). The curriculum should also support meaning-focused instruction to improve students' fluency, vocabulary, and reading comprehension skills. No one expects a single core curriculum to fit the needs of all children, so we have found that teachers appreciate guidance in selecting additional materials that are consistent with classroom instruction and are also evidence-based (e.g., Florida Center for Reading Research (FCRR) activities, http://www.fcrr.org/curriculum/SCAindex.shtm).

We have also learned through our descriptive and correlational research that the amount of instructional time varies greatly across classrooms and schools. School leaders play an important role in scheduling and protecting instructional time. Specifically, a daily uninterrupted block of primary instruction lasting between 45 to 120 minutes, with much of that time dedicated to differentiated instruction using small groups, is associated with stronger student reading achievement (Connor, Morrison, Fishman, & Schatschneider, 2008; Connor, Morrison, Fishman, Schatschneider, & Underwood, 2007; Connor et al., 2009; Pressley et al., 2001; Taylor & Pearson, 2004; Wharton-McDonald, Pressley, & Hampston, 1998).

Problem solving within Tier 1: Individualizing based upon progress-monitoring data

We have conducted several observational and experimental studies (pre-K through 3rd grade) related to kindergarten primary Tier 1 instruction. Within these studies, we have found that the least effective teachers appear almost compelled to follow a core curriculum in lockstep format and to deliver mainly whole group instruction, with some individual seatwork (worksheets, mostly) in their classrooms. If they do instruct in small groups, all children receive the same materials, rather than instruction that is matched to their proficiency level. Thus, many of these teachers may teach to a particular skill set (i.e., most often teaching to the middle) and so are not likely to help children who begin school with lower skills to catch up to the middle. Further, when the level of instruction is beyond these vulnerable children, their engagement or on-task behavior is greatly reduced.

By contrast, we also observed very effective Tier 1 instruction that succeeds in helping the vast majority of children read on grade level. Such instruction is systematic, but it is also tailored to student needs. So what does that look like? Collectively, over the past 4 years, we have trained over a hundred kindergarten and 1st grade teachers, through thoughtful reflective professional development, to use data to create dynamic, differentiated, flexible, small group instruction. An exciting new technological tool, Assessment to Instruction, or A2i, developed by Carol Connor uses child data to specify how many minutes a day of what type of instruction children need to reach the end-of-year, grade-level target (Connor et al., 2007; http://isi.fcrr.org).

Because small group instruction is more effective minute for minute than whole class instruction (Connor, Morrison, & Slominski, 2006), our professional development focuses on helping teachers plan and manage small group instruction and incorporate child-managed centers. In particular, the data-based A2i tool helps teachers target how many minutes a day they need to work with their lowest ability group who needs the most scaffolding. The tool also suggests different groupings for meaning versus code-focused instruction and allows teachers to create flexible groups. For example, if Johnny needs 30 minutes of small group instruction, he may come to the teacher table during 2–15 minute segments of explicit, code-focused instruction that is highly interactive with the teacher actively working with him, while the other children in his group are working in centers, with a peer or a paraprofessional. This approach is a more precise, but still dynamic, way of thinking about instruction than just saying the child needs more phonics instruction and assigning phonics worksheets or seatwork for extra practice.

A2i is dynamic in that it allows each child's data to be updated so that teachers can reformulate their groups based on assessment results, or based on changes in available resources (e.g., parent volunteer, student teacher, and more time from the special education teacher). The ability to adapt instructional strategies is important because what is successful depends on students' language and literacy skills (child-by-instruction interactions) and on the desired outcome (e.g., word reading, reading comprehension, or vocabulary).

Using classwide peer tutoring to supplement individualization of Tier 1

One particularly well-researched classwide peer tutoring program is Peer-Assisted Learning Strategies or PALS. Peer tutoring can double or triple students' reading practice time, their opportunities to respond, and their engagement in literate language. Converging findings across a number of randomized controlled studies demonstrate that children who participate in PALS show significantly more improved reading achievement across kindergarten to 6th grade (Fuchs, Fuchs, Mathes, & Simmons, 1997). PALS also led to improved reading skills within 1st grade Hispanic children, regardless of their English proficiency (Calhoon, Al Otaiba, Greenberg, Kin, & Avalos, 2006).

PALS is a Tier 1 supplement to primary reading instruction in that classroom lessons are presented by the teacher, and children then practice the taught skills with peers. Sessions typically last for 20–30 minutes 3 to 4 times per week usually across the school year. Teachers are directed to use data to assign children to dyads and to change partnerships about every 6 to 8 weeks depending on data. Teachers may use letter naming or oral reading fluency scores to rank order their students. At kindergarten, they might initially pair the very weakest performing child with the strongest child, or they may prefer to divide the class in half and pair the top performer in the top half with the bottom performer in the top half. Although the skills emphasized within PALS sessions vary by grade level, they incorporate code and some meaning-focused activities. For example, in kindergarten, lessons include sound play or phonological awareness activities and beginning letter-sound relationships; then in 1st and 2nd grade, as children learn to decode, fluency and comprehension play a larger role.

Fuchs and colleagues also examined the impact of 1 versus 2 years of PALS to a no-PALS condition (Al Otaiba & Fuchs, 2006). Of the 227 students who participated in intervention for 1 or 2 years (in kindergarten only, 1st grade only, or kindergarten and 1st grade), only about 7% were unable to reach the mean literacy scores of peers in the treatment group. A much higher proportion (25.35%) of the 71 control students did not reach this criterion. Unfortunately, nearly all of these unresponsive kindergartners were also unresponsive to 1st grade PALS. Thus, it is likely that if PALS did not meet their needs, these children should have been provided a more intensive Tier 2 intervention. Indeed, in a 3rd grade follow-up study, we found that all but one of the children who had been nonresponsive to kindergarten intervention had been identified as reading disabled and had received IEP goals in reading. These nonresponsive students had much lower scores than their responsive peers on several measures that are associated with reading disability including vocabulary, rapid naming, problem behavior, and verbal memory.

Using paraprofessionals, adult tutors, and adult volunteers to supplement individualization of Tier 1

Growing evidence supports the efficacy of supplementary programs provided by paraprofessionals, Title 1 and other tutors, and adult volunteers (e.g., community members and college students) (Al Otaiba & Foorman, 2008; Foorman & Al Otaiba, 2009). Some schools may consider this intensity to represent Tier 2 rather than Tier 1.

Features associated with effective programs include

1. a reading specialist or expert-provided training and supervision to tutors,
2. a tutoring program consistent with the classroom instruction,
3. high quality materials and engaging books,
4. monitoring of students' progress, and
5. delivery with sufficient intensity.

Increasing intensity and dedicating time for tutoring are vital. We learned that significantly stronger effects are found when tutoring occurs 4 days a week versus 2 days a week. This issue of intensity or *dosage*, was directly addressed in a randomized control trial by Al Otaiba, Schatschneider, and Silverman (2005), which tested the effects of a scripted tutoring program *Tutor-Assisted Intensive Learning Strategies (TAILS)*. *TAILS* provides scripted instructional routines for code-focused instruction (i.e., roughly 20 minutes of phonological awareness and phonics intervention) and also included meaning focused instruction (i.e., 10–15 minutes of dialogic book reading strategies to build language and listening comprehension) (Beck, McKeown, & Kucan, 2005; Lonigan, Anthony, Bloomfield, Dyer, & Samwel, 1999). The TAILS direct instruction format was consistent with the primary core reading program used in each classroom. Tutors in all three conditions were well trained and supervised (i.e., they had weekly visits and modeling or coaching by research staff) to support implementation fidelity, that is, the accuracy with which tutors implemented *TAILS* components.

This study was conducted in four high poverty schools. We screened all the kindergartners to select children who began school with very low letter naming (less than 2 letters correct per minute) or letter-sound naming scores (less than 3 letter sounds). Nearly all the children (over 80%) were African American and received free and reduced lunch. To control for the classroom reading instruction children received, we randomly assigned children within classrooms to three conditions. In the first condition, students were read storybooks in a group of three; in the second condition, students were individually tutored using *TAILS* for 2 days per week; and in the third condition, students were also individually tutored, but for 4 days a week. Tutors were observed regularly using checklists that assessed whether they implemented *TAILS* with fidelity; on average they did so the majority of the time.

We found that dosage was very important; students in the 4-day *TAILS* condition showed greater growth on word reading, word attack, and passage comprehension than students in either the 2-day or control condition on three reading measures. (Effect sizes favoring students in the 4-day versus control condition were large and educationally important: .79, .90, and .83, on word identification, passage comprehension, and basic reading skills, respectively.) This means that kindergartners in the 4-day condition outperformed the other students by almost a standard deviation. Helping children at risk by intervening early, and with adequate intensity, was highly successful and most students in the 4-day condition read on grade level at the end of the year. This study is an example of a low cost and high reward supplement to Tier 1 instruction.

What Are Success Rates When Students Receive Additional Tiers of More Intensive Early Interventions?

While there is strong empirical evidence demonstrating the effectiveness of intervention, there is less research on the efficacy of a multitier system. In fact, the stronger multitier studies have been implemented by research staff rather than classroom teachers and paraprofessionals (for a review see Al Otaiba & Torgesen, 2007). Two studies inform us about possible success rates, judged in terms of "normalization" (defined as grade-level reading scores by the end of the study).

The first study is salient because it demonstrates that more than one type of Tier 2 intervention, combined with effective Tier 1 classroom instruction, resulted in remarkably few 1st graders reading below grade level. Mathes and colleagues (2005) designed a study to compare Tier 1 classroom reading instruction with Tier 1 instruction *plus* one of two types of supplemental interventions delivered to small groups of three children. Researchers had screened children at the end of kindergarten to select those who performed in the bottom 30th percentile and then randomly assigned children within classrooms to the three conditions. To ensure that Tier 1 was generally effective, researchers trained teachers to use data to support reading instruction. Both of the Tier 2 interventions were intensive, lasting for 40 minutes daily over a period of 30 weeks; these were conducted by certified teachers who were hired and trained by the researchers (i.e., not by the children's classroom teachers). Implementation fidelity was strong.

The first intervention, *Early Interventions in Reading* (Mathes, Torgesen, Menchetti, Wahl, & Grek, 2004), provided code-focused instruction that followed a prescriptive scope and sequence of lessons that were standard for all children. The second intervention, *Responsive Reading Instruction* (Denton & Hocker, 2005), followed a problem-solving approach to tailoring intervention to individual student's strengths and weaknesses. The programs also differed slightly in that *Early Interventions* emphasized phonics relative to other skills and, in contrast, *Responsive* allocated more time to text reading and writing. Students who received either intervention (effects were similarly strong for both groups) outperformed the Tier 1-only group. By the end of 1st grade, if we extrapolated findings to the general population, the proportion of students who could not read on grade level would be reduced to about 0.2% in the *Early Interventions* condition and to 1.5% in the *Responsive* condition.

The second study, conducted by Torgesen and colleagues (1999), is noteworthy because it showed that well-trained paraprofessionals can successfully supplement intervention without an adverse impact on intervention fidelity or child outcomes. In January of their kindergarten year, children were randomly assigned to a no-treatment control condition (i.e., one of three one-to-one tutoring groups). Tutoring was conducted 20 minutes daily for 4 days a week and lasted through 2nd grade with approximately 47 total hours provided by teachers and 41 by paraprofessionals. The tutoring groups differed primarily in the explicitness with which phonics was taught. The most explicit program provided *phonological awareness training plus synthetic phonics (PASP)*, which consisted of explicit instruction in phonological awareness using voiced cues plus extensive decoding practice. The second, *embedded phonics*, also consisted of instruction in explicit phonics but also trained sight words and emphasized reading and writing connected text. The third, *regular classroom support*, consisted of tutorial assistance for the reading instruction provided in the regular classroom.

By the end of the study, students in the *PASP* group outperformed the other three groups on tests of decoding and also outperformed the control group and the regular class support group on a word reading measure. However, all four groups performed similarly on a measure of reading comprehension. Once again, if we extrapolate findings to a similar school population, if all students could participate in this sustained multitier process, 98% of children could be expected to attain grade-level word-level reading by the end of 2nd grade.

Other Considerations and Solutions

Researchers are discovering that one reason some children may have more difficulty learning to read is that they have difficulty with self-regulation. In fact, the comorbidity between reading disability and attention deficit disorder has been well-documented. Self-regulation is the ability to stay on a task, follow directions, understand how others feel, to control feelings of anger and frustration, and to switch from one task to another when required. Difficulties with self-regulation may occur because these students have trouble making the most of learning activities, are easily distracted, don't get along with classmates, and have difficulty following directions. Teachers report that children with poor self-regulation tend to have more behavior problems and weaker social skills than children with strong self-regulation (Connor, Cameron et al., in review). Having a greater number of children with poor self-regulation in the class can make it increasingly difficult for teachers to provide effective instruction and have an impact on student outcomes.

Running a highly organized classroom, providing very clear directions for projects and activities children are to complete, and providing structured opportunities to work with peers appear to improve children's self-regulation (Bodrova & Leong, 2006; Connor, Cameron, et al., in review). Classroom routines that are daily and ongoing are also very important, for example, using the same order of activities and signal to indicate that children are to change activities each day. Again, it is also important to prominently display the task or organizational chart so that children can operate independently and find out what group they are supposed to be in and what activity that group is supposed to be completing. The more children know what is expected of them, what they are supposed to be doing, and where they are supposed to be, the better they attend to the learning opportunities at hand. Avoiding disruptions, such as loudspeaker announcements and other people entering the classroom, also helps children with weaker self-regulation stay on task. Also, it is important to teach in a highly interactive and engaging manner (Guthrie et al., 2004).

Because much of the research on reading is so new, many teachers do not have knowledge about key concepts such as phonological awareness, phonics rules, comprehension strategies, and administering and using assessment. In one study on teacher knowledge (Piasta, Connor, Fishman, & Morrison, 2009), many teachers could correctly answer only about half of the multiple choice items (e.g., how many phonemes are in the word *box*). However, the better teachers did on this assessment, the more effective was their explicit decoding instruction. In other words, their students made greater reading skill gains, on average, than did the students of teachers who scored lower on the survey. For teachers who answered about half of the items correctly, their decoding instruction had no effect on students' reading gains. Unfortunately, when teachers answered less than half of the items correctly, the more they taught explicit decoding, the worse were their students' reading skill gains. This is because they were teaching the concepts incorrectly. For example, one teacher said the word *above* had the short *a* sound even though the *a* in *above* represents the schwa sound, not the short *a* sound as in *cat*.

Teacher knowledge about how to administer assessments and translate results into intervention is foundational for RTI success. The key to improving teacher knowledge is rigorous preservice training and targeted practice-based professional development. Accomplishing this goal would require hiring new teachers from programs where they receive excellent preparation and providing high quality, ongoing professional development. All teachers need relatively expert knowledge of the structure of language, and many benefit from coaching to learn more about how to apply this knowledge to explicitly teach it to students who enter their classrooms with a range of reading abilities.

In summary, RTI models have tremendous promise to insure high quality and effective literacy instruction for all children. Although not without challenges, districts are finding that RTI provides an avenue for systemic reform and opportunities for classroom teachers, special educators, reading specialists, and other professionals to leave their silos behind and work together to meet the needs of children who are struggling to become proficient readers.

References

Al Otaiba, S., & Foorman, B. (2008). Early literacy instruction and intervention. *Community Literacy Journal 3.1*, 21–37.

Al Otaiba, S., & Fuchs, D. (2006). Who are the young children for whom best practices in reading are ineffective? An experimental and longitudinal study. *Journal of Learning Disabilities, 39*(5), 414–431.

Al Otaiba, S., Schatschneider, C., & Silverman, E. (2005). Tutor assisted intensive learning strategies in kindergarten: How much is enough? *Exceptionality, 13*(4), 195–208.

Al Otaiba, S., & Torgesen, J. (2007). Effects from intensive standardized kindergarten and first grade interventions for the prevention of reading difficulties. In S. R. Jimerson, M. K. Burns, & A. M. Van der Heyden (Eds.), *The handbook of response to intervention: The science and practice of assessment and intervention* (pp. 212–222). New York: Springer.

Beck, I. L., McKeown, M. G., & Kucan, L. (2005). Choosing words to teach. In E. H. Hiebert & M. L. Kamil (Eds.), *Teaching and learning vocabulary: Bringing research to practice* (pp. 209–222). Mahwah, NJ: Lawrence Erlbaum Associates.

Bodrova, E., & Leong, D. J. (2006). Self-regulation as a key to school readiness: How early childhood teachers can promote this critical competency. In M. Zaslow & I. Martinez-Beck (Eds.), *Critical issues in early childhood professional development* (pp. 203–224). Baltimore: Paul H. Brookes.

Calhoon, B., Al Otaiba, S., Greenberg, D., King, A., & Avalos, A. (2006). Boosting the intensity of reading instruction for culturally diverse first grade students: The promise of peer-assisted learning strategies. *Learning Disabilities Research and Practice, 21*(4), 261–272.

Catts, H. W., Fey, M. E., Zhang, X., & Tomblin, J. B. (1999). Language basis of reading and reading disabilities: Evidence from a longitudinal investigation. *Scientific Studies of Reading, 3*, 331–361.

Connor, C. M., Cameron, C. E., Phillips, B., Travis, Q. M., Glasney, S., & Morrison, F. J. (in review). Teachers' Participation in an Individualized Instruction Intervention and Children's Literacy and Behavioral Regulation Growth.

Connor, C. M., Morrison, F. J., Fishman, B., & Schatschneider, C. (Eds.). (in press). *Assessment and instruction connections: The implications of child X instruction Interactions effects on student learning:* Rowman & Littlefield Education.

Connor, C. M., Morrison, F. J., Fishman, B. J., Schatschneider, C., & Underwood, P. (2007). The early years: Algorithm-guided individualized reading instruction. *Science, 315* (5811), 464–465.

Connor, C. M., Morrison, F. J., & Slominski, L. (2006). Preschool instruction and children's literacy skill growth. *Journal of Educational Psychology, 98*(4), 665–689.

Connor, C. M., Piasta, S. B., Fishman, B., Glasney, S., Schatschneider, C., Crowe, E., et al. (2009). Individualizing student instruction precisely: Effects of child by instruction interactions on first graders' literacy development. *Child Development, 80*(1), 77–100.

Denton, C. A., & Hocker, J. K. (2005). *Responsive reading instruction: Small-group reading intervention for grade 1.* Longmont, CO: Sopris West.

Foorman, B. R., & Al Otaiba, S. (2009). Reading remediation: State of the art. In K. Pugh and P. McCardle (Eds.), *How children learn to read: Current issues and new directions in the integration of cognition, neurobiology and genetics of reading and dyslexia research and practice* (pp. 257–274). New York: Psychology Press.

Foorman, B. R., Brier, J. I., & Fletcher, J. H. (2003). Interventions aimed at improving reading success: An evidenced-based approach. *Developmental Neuropsychology, 24*(23), 613–639.

Fuchs, D., & Deshler, D. (2007). What we need to know about responsiveness to intervention (and shouldn't be afraid to ask). *Learning Disabilities Research & Practice, 22*(2),129–136.

Fuchs, D., Fuchs, L. S., Mathes, P. G., & Simmons, D. C. (1997). Peer-assisted learning strategies: Making classrooms more responsive to diversity. *American Educational Research Journal, 34*(1), 174–206.

Guthrie, J. T., Wigfield, A., Barbosa, P., Perencevich, K. C., Taboada, A., Davis, M. H., et al. (2004). Increasing reading comprehension and engagement through concept-oriented reading instruction. *Journal of Educational Psychology, 96*(3), 403–423.

Lonigan, C. J., Anthony, J. L., Bloomfield, B. G., Dyer, S. M., & Samwel, C. S. (1999). Effects of two shared-reading interventions on emergent literacy skills of at-risk preschoolers. *Journal of Early Intervention, 22*(4), 306–322.

Mathes, P. G., Denton, C. A., Fletcher, J. M., Anthony, J. L., Francis, D. J., & Schatschneider, C. (2005). The effects of theoretically different instruction and student characteristics on the skills of struggling readers. *Reading Research Quarterly, 40*(2), 148–182.

Mathes, P. G., Torgesen, J. K, Menchetti, J. C., Wahl, M., & Grek, M. K. (2004). *Early Intervention in Reading*. (Teacher guides, daily lessons materials, and student activity books for first-grade reading intervention). Columbus, Ohio: SRA/McGraw-Hill.

National Reading Panel. (2000). *Teaching children to read: An evidence-based assessment of the scientific research literature on reading and its implications for reading instruction* (No. NIH Pub. No. 00-4769). Washington DC: U.S. Department of Health and Human Services, Public Health Service, National Institutes of Health, National Institute of Child Health and Human Development.

Piasta, S. B., Connor, C. M., Fishman, B., & Morrison, F. J. (2009). Teachers' knowledge of literacy, classroom practices, and student reading growth. *Scientific Studies of Reading, 13*(3), 224–248.

Pressley, M., Wharton-McDonald, R., Allington, R., Block, C. C., Morrow, L., Tracey, D., et al. (2001). A study of effective first-grade literacy instruction. *Scientific Studies of Reading, 5*(1), 35–58.

Shaywitz, S. E., Fletcher, J. M., Holahan, J., et al. (1999). Persistence of dyslexia: The Connecticut Longitudinal Study at adolescence. *Pediatrics, 104*, 1–9.

Taylor, B. M., & Pearson, P. D. (2004). Research on learning to read—at school, at home, and in the community. *Elementary School Journal, 105*(2), 167–181.

Torgesen, J. K., Wagner, R. K., Rashotte, C. A., Lindamood, P., Rose, E., Conway, T., & Garvan, C. (1999). Preventing reading failure in young children with phonological processing disabilities: Group and individual responses to instruction. *Journal of Educational Psychology, 91*, 579–593.

Wharton-McDonald, R., Pressley, M., & Hampston, J. M. (1998). Literacy instruction in nine first-grade classrooms: Teacher characteristics and student achievement. *Elementary School Journal, 99*(2), 101–128.

Acknowledgements

This work was supported by (a) a Multidisciplinary Learning Disabilities Center Grant P50HD052120 from the National Institute of Child Health and Human Development, (b) a Predoctoral Interdisciplinary Research Training Grant R305B04074 from the Institute for Education Science, (c) grants R305H04013 and R305B070074, "Child by Instruction Interactions: Effects of Individualizing Instruction" from the U.S. Department of Education, Institute for Education Sciences, and (d) by grant R01HD48539 from the National Institute for Child Health and Human Development. We acknowledge our project staff and the teachers and students participating in our projects. Requests for more information should be sent to Stephanie Al Otaiba, Florida Center for Reading Research, 227 N. Bronough St., Suite 7250, Tallahassee, FL 32301. Email: alotaiba@fcrr.org

Remedial Interventions for Students with Dyslexia
National Goals and Current Accomplishments

Joseph K. Torgesen

More than at any time before in our history, educators at the local, state, and national levels are focusing on the challenge of helping all children acquire proficiency in reading. The energy and direction behind this focus comes from a number of sources, with one of the most important being changes in society that are requiring ever higher levels of literacy in order to successfully enter and progress within the job market in our country. In a recent and influential consensus report about reading and reading instruction, the writers began with the introductory comment, "Current difficulties in reading largely originate from rising demands for literacy, not from declining absolute levels of literacy" (Snow, Burns, & Griffin, 1998, p.1). It is widely acknowledged that these increasing demands for higher levels of literacy in the workforce require that we do better than we have ever done before in teaching all children to read well.

Another source of motivation for the current focus on improving reading skills of students in the United States comes from heightened awareness that relatively large numbers of students in this country are struggling to become proficient readers by 4th grade. This heightened awareness is largely the result of the widely publicized results from the National Assessment of Educational Progress (NAEP), which has been administered to 4th and 8th grade students since 1971. A part of this test has been stable over almost a 30-year period, and Figure 1.3.1 shows how extremely stable student performance in reading has been over that period of time. On the 2003 assessment, 37% of all 4th graders performed below the basic level, which indicates that they do not have sufficient reading skills to adequately support grade-level work that involves reading. Equally alarming is the fact that poor and minority students perform much more poorly on this test than national averages. For example, 60% of African American students performed below the basic level, while 55% of poor students (those who qualify for free or reduced price lunch) also performed at that level.

Another important stimulus for the currently intense focus on reading instruction in the United States is the No Child Left Behind Act of 2002, which requires that the reading proficiency of all students be examined by a comprehensive reading assessment at the end of 3rd grade. An important feature of this law is that schools must report their progress in teaching children to read in a way that disaggregates the performance of poor and non-poor, minority and non-minority, and handicapped and non-handicapped students. Schools are evaluated within this law by the reading gains of students in all these separate groups so that they now must actively address the needs of all students. This law, and the sanctions that result from poor performance within its provisions are influencing district and school-level administrators to ask questions like "What works to improve performance for which students?" and "How much improvement can we expect for which students?" with greater frequency than ever before.

Figure 1.3.1.   **Trends in Average Scale Scores for the Nation in Reading**
Note: Performance is indicated in standard score units which represented performance on the same scale each year the test was administered

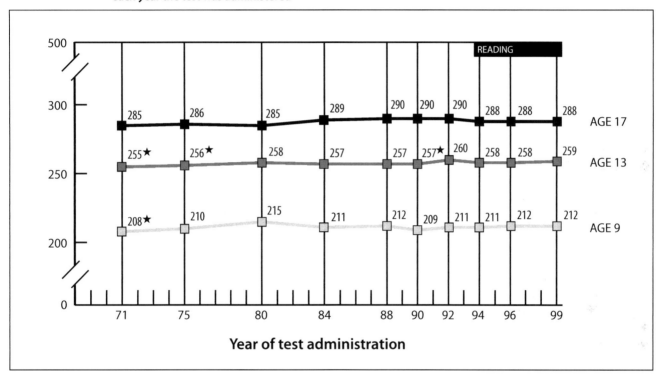

A final significant report that is raising new questions for educators in the field of special education is the report of the President's Commission on Special Education (2002). One of the most significant statements in this report, which is consistent with the general philosophy of the No Child Left Behind Act, is that, "The ultimate test of the value of special education is that, once identified, children close the gap with their peers" (p. 4). The report suggested that one of the most serious problems for special education programs as they are currently implemented is that they tend to stabilize the level of student's academic impairments rather than remediate them.

What is meant by "closing the gap"?

If special education is to respond to the challenge of the president's commission to "close the gap" between the academic performance of students receiving special education and their grade-level peers, it is important to have a clear understanding of what is meant by this phrase. For example, one interpretation for children with reading disabilities is that it means *narrowing* the gap between a student's current level of performance and grade-level reading skills. This requires instruction and support that can accelerate the growth of reading ability, and the best objective evidence that sufficient acceleration is taking place to narrow the gap is a change in the student's standard score or percentile rank on a valid and well-standardized measure of reading. Standard scores are an excellent metric for determining the "success" or " failure" of interventions for children with reading disabilities because they describe the child's relative position within the distribution of reading skills in a large standardization sample. If standard scores improve, it means the child has narrowed the gap with age- or grade-level peers. By the same token, if standard scores stay the same over time, or decrease, it means that the reading gap has remained stable or increased.

A second, and more stringent meaning for the phrase "closing the gap" involves bringing a student's reading skills to *within grade-level standards*. For children with reading disabilities, this will always involve an *acceleration of development* over a *sufficient period of time*. The most important and widely accepted grade-level standards in reading always involve reading comprehension. Grade-level standards in other reading skills such as phonemic decoding or text reading fluency are a means to an end, with the end being the ability to accurately construct the meaning of grade-level text.

Increasingly in the United States, whether or not the reading skills of struggling readers meet grade-level standards will be determined by their performance on a group administered measure of reading comprehension. As we think about the challenges of working to "close the gap" through special interventions for children with reading disabilities, it is important to understand the reading, language, and cognitive skills required for good performance on these tests and how these skills might change with age. Recently, my colleagues and I at the Florida Center for Reading Research (Schatschneider, et al., 2004) undertook a study of the reading portion of Florida's Comprehensive Assessment Test (FCAT) in order to answer two broad questions: 1) what reading, language, and cognitive skills are most important in accounting for individual differences in performance on the test at grades 3, 7, and 10; and 2) what are the areas of greatest difficulty for students who struggle on the test at various ages?

State-level accountability measures in reading are not all alike, and the FCAT has two features that may present special challenges to many students with reading disabilities. First, it was specifically created to place high demands on "higher level thinking skills" such as verbal reasoning and inference making. The proportion of questions requiring "higher order thinking skills" increases from roughly 30% in 3rd grade to 70% in 10th grade. Second, the FCAT requires students to read relatively long passages before asking them to answer questions about the text they have just read. The average length of passages in 3rd, 7th, and 10th grade is 325, 820, and 1,000 words, respectively. Although the test does not have strict time limits, passages of this length place special demands on reading fluency. At 4th grade, the standards set for "grade-level" performance on the FCAT are roughly equivalent to the NAEP test. For example, in 2003, 37% of 4th grade students in Florida performed below basic on the NAEP, while 40% of 4th graders performed below grade level on the FCAT.

In conducting this study, we gave a 2-hour battery of language, reading, non-verbal reasoning, and memory tests to approximately 200 children in 3rd, 7th, and 10th grade who were randomly selected within three locations across the state. We worked to identify a sample that would be roughly representative of the overall student population in Florida.

At 3rd grade, oral reading rate was the dominant factor in accounting for individual differences in performance on the FCAT, with the fluency factor accounting for 56% of the variance, the verbal knowledge/reasoning factor accounting for 44%, and the nonverbal reasoning and working memory factors accounting for 25 and 14% of the variance, respectively. At 7th grade, fluency and verbal knowledge/reasoning were equally dominant in accounting for variance on the FCAT, and at 10th grade, verbal knowledge/reasoning was the dominant factor (52% of the variance) with fluency (32% of the variance) being second, and the other variables being less important. The findings for 10th grade do not mean that reading fluency is no longer important for good performance on the test. Rather, they mean that the level of thinking and verbal knowledge required for good performance on the test have now become so high that many children struggle on the test because they cannot meet these demands. Although the fluency levels of students who performed at level 1 on the test were still substantially lower than those performing at level 5 (130 versus 199 words per minute on FCAT passages), they were apparently high enough that fluency was not as important a factor in limiting their performance on the FCAT as it was in 3rd grade.

Performance on the FCAT is categorized in five levels (1–5), with level 3 being considered grade-level performance. Students must perform at level 2 or higher on the FCAT to be eligible for promotion from 3rd to 4th grade, and they must also attain a given level of proficiency on the test in order to be eligible for a regular high school diploma. Table 1.3.1 presents the average performance levels on a number of our tests for students who performed at each of the levels on the FCAT in 3rd grade. The most striking finding from Table 1.3.1 is the extremely low performance of students at level 1 on measures of reading fluency. When we asked the students to read FCAT-level passages orally, level 1 students read them at half the rate of students who performed at the average level on the FCAT, and they achieved an average reading fluency score at the 6th percentile on a nationally standardized measure of reading fluency. These findings concerning the problems in reading fluency manifest by students performing at level 1 on the FCAT were particularly troubling to us because of our knowledge about difficulties in reading fluency for children with reading disabilities.

Table 1.3.1.   **Average Performance of 3rd Grade Students on Measures of Reading and Verbal Ability Who Achieved Different Levels of Proficiency on the FCAT**

Skill/Ability	FCAT Performance Level				
	1	2	3	4	5
	(47)*	(26)	(54)	(63)	(17)
Words per Minute on FCAT	54	92	102	119	148
Fluency Percentile[1]	6th	32nd	56th	78th	93rd
Phonemic Decoding[2]	25th	45th	59th	74th	91st
Verbal knowledge/reasoning[3]	42nd	59th	72nd	91st	98th

* *Numbers in parenthesis are the sample size at each performance level on the FCAT.*
[1] *Fluency was measured with the Gray Oral Reading Test (4th ed.) (Wiederholt & Bryant, 2003).*
[2] *Phonemic Decoding Efficiency was measured with the Test of Word Reading Efficiency (Torgesen, Wagner, and Rashotte, 1999).*
[3] *Verbal knowledge/reasoning were measured with the Vocabulary and Similarities subtests of the Wechsler Abbreviated Scale of Intelligence (Wechsler, 1974).*

We turn now to an assessment of our current knowledge about effective remedial procedures or "special education" for older students with reading disabilities.

What do we know about "closing the gap" for students with reading disabilities?

In order to aggregate data across studies to answer questions about the power of currently available interventions, we need a common metric that can be applied across studies. One such metric can be calculated by dividing the amount of gain in standard score units by the number of hours of instruction that are provided, so rate of growth is expressed as the number of standard score points gained per hour of instruction. Of course, this metric depends on the common use across studies of standardized measures that have the same standard deviation, but there are a number of studies that have used measures similar enough to allow rough comparisons to be made. As mentioned earlier, if standard scores improve as a result of intervention, it means that the intervention is sufficiently powerful to "close the gap," at least in the sense that the student's reading skills are becoming more like their nondisabled peers.

Table 1.3.2 reports these growth rates for phonemic decoding, untimed word reading accuracy, and passage comprehension for eight samples of students with reading disabilities who began the intervention with word-level reading scores below the 5th percentile. The number in parenthesis represents the final level of achievement in each area at the end of the study expressed as a percentile ranking for the group as a whole.

It should be noted from the beginning that the endpoints presented for passage comprehension are likely to be overestimates of the reading comprehension of students with reading disabilities, when compared to their performance on group-administered measures of reading comprehension that require students to read much longer passages. Unfortunately, none of these studies reports the performance of students before and after intervention on State accountability measures like the FCAT. Not all scores are represented for each study because standardized measures were not provided in all three areas of reading skill for all samples.

Table 1.3.2.   **Growth Rates and Ending Points for Samples of Reading Disabled Students Who Began the Intervention Below the 5th Percentile (SS=75) in Word Reading Ability**

Authors (date)	Phonemic Decoding	Word Identification	Passage Comp.
Alexander, et al., 1991	.32* (45th)**	.19 (21st)	
Lovett, et al., 1994		.13 (2nd)	.14 (5th)
Wise, et al., 1999	.30 (35th)	.24 (13th)	.14 (36th)
Torgesen, et al., 2001	.41 (39th)	.20 (12th)	.12 (27th)
Torgesen, et al., 2001	.30 (25th)	.21 (10th)	.15 (29th)
Lovett, et al., 2000	.24 (14th)	.18 (5th)	.16 (6th)
Lovett, et al., 2000	.30 (14th)	.20 (5th)	.18 (4th)
O'Connor & Wilson, 1995	.23 (35th)	.18 (9th)	.17 (14th)
Torgesen, et al., 2004	.18 (39th)	.07 (16th)	.07 (19th)

Decimal numbers represent growth in standard score units per hour of instruction. Thus, the value .32 means that this intervention produced growth in phonemic decoding ability at the rate of .32 standard score points per hour of instruction. For each 10 hours of instruction, the students gained 3.2 standard score points on the measure of phonemic decoding ability.

**Numbers in parenthesis represent the average final status of students in terms of percentile rank. Percentile ranks are reported here rather than standard scores because their meaning is more commonly understood. Percentile scores are not appropriate for measuring growth rates because they are not an interval scale like standard scores.*

Each of the studies reported in Table 1.3.2 will be briefly described in order to provide background for interpreting the effects that are reported. All studies had in common the fact that they selected students to participate in the research primarily because they were experiencing word-level reading difficulties. Most of the students in these studies had general ability estimates in the average range but were severely impaired in their ability to read text accurately and fluently. This focus on students with phonemic decoding and reading accuracy problems is consistent with the research-based definition of dyslexia that is most widely accepted among clinicians and researchers in the field (Lyon, 1995).

The study by Alexander, Anderson, Heilman, Voeller, and Torgesen (1991) provided 65 hours of 1:1 instruction to students with an average age of 10 years, 8 months at the beginning of the study. Students were provided explicit and systematic instruction in phonemic awareness and phonics using the instructional program developed by Patricia Lindamood and her husband Charles and named *Auditory Discrimination in Depth* (Lindamood & Lindamood, 1984). A more recent edition that is essentially the same program is named the *Lindamood Phoneme Sequencing Program for Reading, Spelling, and Speech (LiPS)* (Lindamood & Lindamood, 1998).

The second study listed in Table 1.3.2 (Lovett, Borden, Lacerenza, Benson, & Brackstone, 1994) provided 35 hours of instruction with the children being taught in groups of two. The average age of these students at the beginning of the study was 9 years, 7 months, and they were a very severely disabled sample. For example, the students in this study began the intervention with average standard scores on the Word Identification subtest of the *Woodcock Reading Mastery Test* (Woodcock, 1987) of 66.7. The method used to teach the students was a modification of the *Reading Mastery* program which provides direct instruction in phonemic decoding, with an emphasis on achieving mastery and fluency.

The study by Wise, Ring, and Olson (1999) provided 40 hours of both 1:1 and 1:4 instruction to students with an average age of 8 years, 9 months. This study employed a combination of teacher delivered instruction using the Lindamood method and computer administered instruction that provided extensive practice in reading text with the computer providing support for reading accuracy.

The next study (Torgesen, et al., 2001) used two different instructional approaches with a sample of students with an average age of 9 years, 10 months. Both approaches explicitly taught phonemic awareness and phonics, but they had quite different instructional emphases. Students who were randomly assigned to the condition using the Lindamood method spent 85% of their time learning and practicing articulatory/phonemic awareness and phonemic decoding and encoding skills in single word activities (activities that did not involve reading meaningful text), 10% of their time learning to fluently recognize high-frequency words, and only 5% of their time reading meaningful text. Children in the other instructional condition, labeled Embedded Phonics (EP), spent 20% of their time on phonemic awareness and phonemic decoding activities involving single words, 30% of their time learning high frequency "sight words," and 50% of their time reading meaningful text with teacher support. This latter approach was labeled Embedded Phonics because students received a significant proportion of their instruction in phonemic decoding strategies in the context of error correction and discussion of word reading strategies while they were reading meaningful text. It should be emphasized that this approach did provide explicit and direct instruction in the phonemic decoding skills the students were lacking. In both approaches, the students were taught 1:1, and received 67.5 hours of instruction delivered in two 50-minute sessions every day for 8 weeks. The only difference in outcome between the two approaches that was statistically reliable was that the students receiving the Lindamood approach showed stronger growth in phonemic decoding skills during the instructional period.

Lovett, et al. (2000) also reported outcomes from two equally successful instructional approaches with children with severe reading disabilities who had an average age of 9 years, 8 months at the beginning of the study. The instruction in both approaches was offered in groups of three students, who were taught in 60-minute sessions for a total of 70 hours of instruction. The two approaches investigated in this study differed primarily in the order in which the various elements of the instructional program were taught. Students who produced the first outcome for the study listed in Table 1.3.2 received 35 hours of explicit phonics instruction first, followed by 35 hours of instruction in four different word reading strategies (i.e., looking for familiar "embedded words," using analogies to known words, breaking off affixes, and vowel flexibility). Students whose outcomes are presented next in Table 1.3.2 received just the opposite sequence of instruction.

The next to last study (O'Connor & Wilson, 1995) reported the effects of about 60 hours of instruction provided 1:1 to students ranging from the 3rd to 8th grades. The instruction was provided 1:1 by teachers newly trained in the use of the Wilson Reading System (Wilson, 1988). A potential limitation of this study is that the pre- and posttest measures were collected by the teachers who provided the instruction.

The final study in Table 1.3.2 (Torgesen, et al., 2004) provided 133 hours of 1:1 and 1:2 instruction to students with an average age of 9 years, 10 months. This study examined the effects of adding fluency oriented practice at various stages to the Lindamood program. However, this manipulation had no noticeable effect on student outcomes, so the results from both instructional conditions are combined in this presentation. The students also received 25 hours of instruction in reading comprehension delivered in groups of two students using a program called *Visualizing and Verbalizing for Language Comprehension and Thinking* (Bell, 1991).

Several aspects of the data reported in Table 1.3.2 are worthy of specific discussion. First, there is remarkable consistency in the rates of growth for phonemic decoding skills, word reading accuracy, and passage comprehension skills reported across the studies, except for the last study reported. The similarities in growth rate between the LiPS and EP conditions in the Torgesen, et al. (2001a) study, along with the consistencies across other studies that did not use the Lindamood method, suggests that, given the right level of intensity and teacher skill, it may be possible to obtain strong positive rates of growth using a variety of approaches to direct instruction in reading. The most obvious conclusion from these rates of growth is that current interventions, when properly applied, are sufficiently powerful to narrow the reading gap for students with severe reading disabilities in these three areas of reading skill.

Another point to note from Table 1.3.2 is that growth rates for phonemic decoding skills are consistently higher than they are for word reading accuracy and passage comprehension. Not only the substantial growth rate, but also the essential "normalization" of phonemic decoding skills reported in a number of these studies indicates that even children with severe difficulties in the phonological domain can acquire productive and generative phonemic decoding skills if they are taught with intensity and skill.

The final point of interest from Table 1.3.2 is that the ending points for students in the ability to accurately identify real words are consistently low across these studies. Of the three measures reported, Word Identification is most highly correlated with text reading fluency, and for samples like this, standard scores on the Word Identification test are usually substantially higher than standard scores on tests of reading fluency (Torgesen, Rashotte, & Alexander, 2001). Of all the studies reported in Table 1.3.2, the two reported by Torgesen, et al. are the only ones that reported standard scores for fluency. The standard scores for Word Identification at the end of the intervention in the first study (2001) were 82 and 80, the corresponding scores for fluency were 75 and 72. These latter standard scores convert to percentile ranks of 5 and 3, respectively. In the second study (2004), the ending percentile rank for accuracy was the 16th, but the corresponding score for fluency was the 3rd percentile.

What about students who begin the intervention with slightly stronger reading abilities? Table 1.3.3 presents growth rates for students who had scores on a measure of word reading accuracy between the 6th and 16th percentiles at the start of the intervention.

Truch (1994) provided 80 hours of 1:1 instruction to students with an average age of 12 years. The instructional program followed in this study was Auditory Discrimination in Depth (Lindamood and Lindamood, 1984). The second study by Truch (2003) worked with a slightly older group of students (12 years, 10 months) and used the Phono-Graphix (McGuiness, McGuiness, & McGuiness, 1996) method to provide instruction 1:1 for a total of 80 hours.

Table 1.3.3. **Growth Rates and Ending Points for Samples of Reading Disabled Students Who Began the Intervention with Word Reading Skills Between the 6th and 16th Percentile**

Authors (date)	Phonemic Decoding	Word Identification	Passage Comp.
Truch 1994		.21 (32nd)	
Truch, 2003		.19 (48th)	
Torgesen, et al., 2003	.29 (55th)	.16 (25th)	.24 (35th)
Torgesen, et al., 2003	.23 (77th)	.19 (39th)	.19 (39th)

The two samples reported on by Torgesen, Rashotte, Alexander, Alexander, & MacPhee (2003) were both taught using the Spell Read P.A.T. program (MacPhee, 1998). Instruction to students in these samples was provided in groups of four, and they were 12 years old when instruction began. The first sample received an average of 51 hours of instruction while the second sample received 100 hours of instruction.

The findings reported in Table 1.3.3 are similar to those for Table 1.3.2 except that the ending points are higher, which would be expected since the students began the intervention with stronger reading skills. For the two samples that also had standard scores for fluency (Torgesen, et al., 2003), the ending points for fluency were substantially lower than those for word reading accuracy. Whereas the two samples ended the intervention with reading accuracy scores at the 25th and 39th percentiles, their corresponding percentile scores for fluency were 7 and 8.

Table 1.3.4 presents average growth rates and final status for students from both Table 1.3.2 and Table 1.3.3 who began the intervention with different levels of reading skill. One thing that is immediately clear from Table 1.3.4 is that the rates of growth for word-level skills are very similar for the severely and moderately disabled students. The same cannot be said for reading comprehension, where the growth rate for moderately impaired students was substantially larger than for the severely impaired students. Given the differences in both beginning and ending points between these two groups in their word-level skills, I would speculate that the greater growth in comprehension (if this proves to be a reliable finding in future research) for the moderately impaired students is primarily the result of the fact that they are beginning to move into a region of growth in word-level skills that enables them to more readily take advantage of their relatively strong language comprehension skills, and to profit from whatever comprehension instruction was provided during the interventions.

Table 1.3.4.   **Growth Rates and Final Status for Students Who Begin Reading Interventions at Different Levels of Word Reading Ability**

Beginning Level	Phonemic Decoding	Word Identification	Passage Comp.
Below the 5th percentile	.28 (29th)	.18 (9th)	.14 (14th)
Between the 6th and 16th percentile	.26 (66th)	.19 (29th)	.21 (36th)

It is also clear from Table 1.3.4 that although we have clear evidence from research that we understand the instructional conditions that need to be in place to *narrow* the gap between the reading skills of moderately and severely reading disabled students and their nondisabled peers, we have yet to demonstrate that we know how to *close* the gap. This latter statement is particularly true in the area of reading fluency. Only a small number of studies reported standardized measurement of reading fluency, but from those that did, it is clear that this is the reading skill that is most resistant to intervention if the goal is to close the gap between disabled readers and their grade-level peers. For example, for children who began the intervention with word-level reading skills below the 5th percentile, the average fluency level at the end of the intervention was the 4th percentile. For students who began between the 6th and 16th percentile in word-level skills, the average percentile rank for fluency at the end of the study was 7.5. If these fluency rates are representative of the broad range of interventions reported in Tables 1.3.2 and 1.3.3, this will make it difficult for students like those in these studies to perform well on State-level reading accountability measures such as the Florida Comprehensive Reading Test. It seems important for future intervention studies not only to provide a standardized assessment of reading fluency, but also to monitor the progress of the students receiving the intervention on group administered measures of reading comprehension that require students to read lengthy passages before they respond to questions about meaning.

Factors that Affect Rate of Growth and Final Status in Intervention Studies

One conclusion from the previous analysis is that use of a metric that focuses on the amount of growth in standard score units per hour of instruction is a potentially useful way to evaluate intervention outcomes both in research and practice. For practical purposes, such a metric could easily be used in a cost/benefit analysis that focused on identifying the benefits from a given amount of investment in instruction. Although a metric like this may be useful in describing impacts within a given set of instructional conditions, it must be used with caution when comparing results across studies. A number of factors can influence both growth rates and final status after an intervention is completed that are independent from the nature of the actual instructional program used. These factors range from obvious things such as the particular measure of word reading accuracy that was used to more subtle things such as the hours of intervention that were provided. For example, in our studies, we find that estimates of word reading accuracy are consistently higher when a measure of text reading accuracy (such as the *Gray Oral Reading Test*) is used rather than a measure of single word reading accuracy (such as the Word Identification subtest from the *Woodcock Reading Mastery Test*).

The particular test used to assess word reading accuracy affects the estimate of final status more than it does the estimate of growth rate. For example, in the Torgesen, et al. (2001a) intervention study, posttest standard scores for word reading accuracy as measured by the Woodcock were 82.4 and 80.5 for the LiPS and EP programs, respectively. In contrast, posttest scores for word reading accuracy from the Gray (Wiederholt & Bryant, 1992) were 89.4 and 87.5, respectively. The higher scores for the Gray undoubtedly reflect the student's ability to use passage-level context as an aid to more accurate identification of words (Share & Stanovich, 1995).

Another factor that is likely to influence the estimate of growth rate obtained within any single study is the number of hours of intervention that were provided. Truch (2003) has recently documented that rate of gain may decelerate quite rapidly for intensive interventions after the first 12 hours of the intervention. In his study, 80 hours of intensive instruction using the *Phono-Graphix* method (McGuinness, McGuinness, & McGuinness, 1996) were provided to 202 students ranging in age from 6 years old to over 17 years old. For students ranging in age from 10–16, the average gains per hour of instruction for single word reading accuracy was .74 standard score points per hour of instruction for the first 12 hours of instruction. For the next twelve hours, the rate was .11, and for the final 56 hours, it was .10 standard score points per hour. Although this study did not calculate standard scores for their phonemic decoding measure, the findings were similar, but expressed in terms of grade-level units per hour of instruction. For phonemic decoding, the growth rate for the first 12 hours of instruction was .25 grade-level units per hour of instruction, for the next 12 hours it was .07, and for the final 56 hours, it was .04. This deceleration in growth rate across time within intensive interventions is probably part of the explanation for the particularly low growth rates observed in the 133-hour intervention study reported by Torgesen, et al. (2003a). However, another factor may have also been operating in this latter study to moderate the growth rates that were observed.

This study was conducted in the same school district, and within many of the same schools, as a previously reported (Torgesen, et al., 2001a) study of intensive interventions. In spite of the fact that children in the second study received twice as much instruction as those in the first study, they actually improved less in text reading accuracy and comprehension than the first group. Since both the first and second groups had received very similar interventions and had been selected by the same criteria, the most likely explanation for this unexpected finding is that the latter group had more severe reading disabilities than the first one. Our primary evidence for this assertion is that the special education classes from which the children were selected had improved substantially during the three years that intervened between the selections of the two samples. It was actually more difficult to find students who read poorly enough to meet our selection criteria when we selected the second sample than it was when we identified children for the first study. Teachers who had worked in both studies also noticed immediately that the second group was "much more difficult to teach" than children in the first sample.

This finding introduces an important moderating variable that must be kept in mind when looking at the results of intervention studies. The actual reading impairment a child shows at any point is always the result of an interaction between the child's degree of disability and the strength of instruction that has already been provided. Children with a mild reading disability who are provided only weak instruction (in the regular classroom or in a special education setting) will show larger reading impairments when tested than will children with the same degree of reading disability who have had stronger instruction. In fact, if the instruction received by this latter group was sufficiently strong, they might not even qualify to be part of the study! By the same token, children who remain severely reading impaired within a strong instructional environment are likely to have a more serious reading disability than those who have remained impaired after receiving only weak instruction. Thus, if researchers select their intervention samples from among children who have already received a good dose of appropriate and reasonably intensive instruction, the children in those samples will be more difficult to teach than children who are selected by the same reading criteria from a weaker instructional environment. This moderating factor raises the clear possibility that, if schools are successful in organizing instruction to provide powerful support for the initial acquisition of reading skills in young children (Foorman & Torgesen, 2001; Torgesen, 2002), growth rates for students in special education may not show the improvement one might expect, even with better models of intervention.

This latter point is important in thinking about the rates of improvement we might expect from effective special education within schools that operate a well developed "three tier" system of intervention for students with learning difficulties. Within such a system, students first receive explicit and responsive classroom instruction, and if they do not respond well within that environment, they are to receive a secondary level of intervention that provides more powerful and explicit instruction focused on their specific needs (Vaughn, et al., in press). Finally, if this more powerful secondary level of intervention is not successful in "closing the reading gap" for these students, they will be referred for a tertiary intervention, which is sometimes considered to be synonymous with special education (Gresham, 2002). This method for identifying students with reading disabilities theoretically has the potential to identify for special education only students who have not profited from effective instruction in the first and second tiers. If these earlier tiers are sufficiently powerful, it will dramatically reduce the number of students requiring tertiary intervention, but it will also identify a group of students who may show relatively slow rates of change, even under very powerful instructional conditions.

Conclusions and Future Directions

At the beginning of this article, I discussed two possible meanings of the phrase "closing the gap" for students with reading disabilities. In one of the meanings, the word "closing" is synonymous with "narrowing" while in the other meaning the word "closing" means the same thing as "eliminating." Using these two synonyms, the intervention research reviewed in this article can be summarized in the following way: we currently have available reading interventions that can *narrow* the gap between older students with reading disabilities and their nondisabled peers, but we have not yet demonstrated that we understand the conditions required to *eliminate* this gap. We can come closest to eliminating the gap in the area of phonemic decoding skills, which has traditionally been seen as an area of particular difficulty for students with reading disabilities (Share & Stanovich, 1995, Torgesen, 1999). Eliminating gaps in this area is important, because it provides children with reading disabilities a new level of access to text, and it is one of the critical skills required for reading independently.

For severely disabled readers (those who begin the intervention with word-level skills below the 5th percentile), rates of growth in word reading accuracy are generally stronger than for reading comprehension, but final status for reading comprehension skills at the end of the intervention is generally higher than scores for word reading accuracy. The most likely explanation for this finding is that the samples of children with reading disabilities used in current research have broad verbal ability and language comprehension skills that are roughly in the average range. Thus, because of their good general comprehension skills, these students can often "fill in the gaps" to build reading comprehension by relying on their background knowledge and reasoning ability. In a sense, they compensate for their weak word-level reading abilities by relying on their more strongly developed language comprehension skills (Stanovich, 1984). What is currently unknown is whether children with reading disabilities who receive effective remediation as we currently understand it will improve significantly in their performance on the kinds of "high stakes" reading accountability measures currently being used in the United States to evaluate both individual student progress and the effectiveness of school programs. These accountability measures of reading are different from the measures of reading comprehension that have typically been used in intervention research in that they involve longer passages and more complex questions about the meaning and interpretation of text. Future intervention studies with older students should include as one of their outcome measures a test of reading comprehension that is more similar to widely used State accountability measures than the individually administered tests that have been used previously.

Particularly troubling at this point are the outcomes from intervention research with older students in the area of reading fluency. The effective interventions that have been used thus far have had little impact on either narrowing or eliminating the gap in reading fluency between students with disabilities and their nondisabled peers. Given what we know about the importance of reading fluency in explaining individual differences in performance on group administered tests of reading comprehension like the Florida Comprehensive Assessment Test, this finding suggests an immediate need for more research on ways to accelerate reading fluency as part of an intervention program for older struggling readers. If our previous analysis of this problem is correct (Torgesen, et al., 2001), closing the gap in this area represents a formidable problem for practitioners and researchers. Although promising techniques for reducing the fluency gap are available (Hiebert, 2004; Levy, 2001; Meyer & Felton, 1999), there is no evidence currently available that these techniques can produce "normalization" of fluency in children who have struggled in learning to read for several years. Wolf and her colleagues (Wolf, Miller, & Donnelly, 2000) are currently investigating interventions specifically targeted on fluency issues that extend considerably beyond word-level problems, but as yet there are no reports of findings available from these studies.

As a final point for future research, it seems important to plan studies that include sufficient instructional time so that we can obtain better answers as to whether it is possible to eliminate the gap between the reading skills of older students with reading disabilities and their nondisabled peers. It is possible to obtain evidence about the ability of interventions to *narrow* the gap within a relatively short period of time, but *elimination* of the gap requires powerful instruction over a sufficient period of time to close the gap. Given the evidence provided earlier (Truch, 2003) on the decelerating effects of interventions as the number of intervention hours increase, we should avoid directly extrapolating findings from short-term studies in estimating long-term growth. In other words, we should not assume that if 60 hours of an intervention produces a given growth rate in terms of standard score points per hour of intervention, that extending that particular intervention for another 60 or 100, or 200 hours will completely close the gap. We will only discover the conditions necessary to eliminate reading deficiencies when we actually include enough instructional time to accomplish the feat empirically.

References

Alexander, A., Anderson, H., Heilman, P. C., Voeller, K. S., & Torgesen, J. K. (1991). Phonological awareness training and remediation of analytic decoding deficits in a group of severe dyslexics. *Annals of Dyslexia, 41,*193–206.

Bell, N. (1991). *Visualizing and verbalizing for language comprehension and thinking.* San Luis Obispo, CA: Gander Publishing.

Foorman, B., & Torgesen, J. K. (2001), Critical elements of classroom and small-group instruction to promote reading success in all children. *Learning Disabilities Research and Practice, 16,* 203–212.

Gresham, F. M. (2002). Responsiveness to intervention: An alternative approach to the identification of learning disabilities. In R. Bradley, L. Danielson, & D. Hallahan (Eds.), *Identification of learning disabilities: Research to practice* (pp. 467–519). Mahwah, NJ: Lawrence Erlbaum Associates.

Hiebert, E. (2004). Effects of daily reading of information text on young reader's fluency. Presented as part of a symposium titled "Informational Text and Young Readers: Findings from Research" at the International Reading Association Annual Convention, May 5, 2004 in Reno-Tahoe, NV.

Levy, B. A. (2001). Moving the bottom: Improving reading fluency. In M. Wolf (Ed.), *Dyslexia, fluency, and the brain.* (pp. 357–382). Parkton, MD: York Press.

Lindamood, P., & Lindamood, P. (1998). *The Lindamood Phoneme Sequencing Program for Reading, Spelling, and Speech.* Austin, TX: PRO-ED.

Lindamood, C. H., & Lindamood, P. C. (1979). *Lindamood Auditory Conceptualization Test.* Austin, TX: PRO-ED.

Lindamood, C.H., & Lindamood, P.C. (1984). *Auditory Discrimination in Depth.* Austin, TX: PRO-ED.

Lovett, M. W., Borden, S. L., Lacerenza, L., Benson, N. J., & Brackstone, D. (1994). Treating the core deficits of developmental dyslexia: Evidence of transfer of learning after phonologically- and strategy-based reading training programs. *Journal of Educational Psychology, 30,* 805–822.

Lovett, M. W., Lacerenza, L., Borden, S. L., Frijters, J. C., Steinbach, K. A., & DePalma, M. (2000). Components of effective remediation for developmental reading disabilities: Combining phonological and strategy-based instruction to improve outcomes. *Journal of Educational Psychology, 92,* 263–283.

Lyon, G. R. (1995). Towards a definition of dyslexia. *Annals of Dyslexia, 45,* 3–27.

MacPhee, K. (1998). *Spell Read P.A.T.* Charlottetown, Canada: Spell Read P.A.T. Learning Systems.

McGuinness, C., McGuinness, D., & McGuinness, G. (1996). Phono-Graphix: A new method for remediating reading difficulties. *Annals of Dyslexia, 46,* 73–96.

Meyer, M. S., & Felton, R. H. (1999). Repeated reading to enhance fluency: Old approaches and new directions. *Annals of Dyslexia, 49,* 283–306.

O'Connor, J., & Wilson, B. (1995). Effectiveness of the Wilson Reading System used in public school training. In C. McIntyre & J. Pickering (Eds)., *Clinical studies of multisensory structured language education.* Salem, OR: International Multisensory Structured Language Education Council.

Schatschneider, C., Buck, J., Torgesen, J. K., Wagner, R. K., Hassler, L., Hecht, S., & Powell-Smith, K. (2004). A multivariate study of factors that contribute to individual differences in performance on the Florida Comprehensive Reading Assessment Test. Technical Report # 5, Florida Center for Reading Research, Tallahassee, FL.

Share, D. L., & Stanovich, K. E. (1995). Cognitive processes in early reading development: A model of acquisition and individual differences. *Issues in Education: Contributions from Educational Psychology, 1,* 1–57.

Snow, C. E., Burns, M. S., & Griffin, P. (1998). *Preventing reading difficulties in young children.* Washington, DC: National Academy Press.

Stanovich, K. (1984). The interactive-compensatory model of reading: A confluence of developmental, experimental, and educational psychology. *Remedial and Special Education, 5,* 11–19.

Torgesen, J. K. (1999). Phonologically based reading disabilities: Toward a coherent theory of one kind of learning disability. In R. J. Sternberg & L. Spear-Swerling (Eds.), *Perspectives on learning disabilities.* (pp. 231–262). New Haven: Westview Press.

Torgesen, J. K. (2002). The prevention of reading difficulties. *Journal of School Psychology, 40,* 7–26.

Torgesen, J. K., Alexander, A. W., Alexander, J., Voeller, K., Conway, T., Wagner, R. K., & Rashotte, C. A. (2004). Accuracy oriented vs. Accuracy plus fluency interventions: A study of intensive instruction with older students with severe reading disabilities. Unpublished manuscript, Florida Center for Reading Research, Tallahassee, FL.

Torgesen, J. K., Alexander, A. W., Wagner, R. K., Rashotte, C. A., Voeller, K., Conway, T., & Rose, E. (2001a). Intensive remedial instruction for children with severe reading disabilities: Immediate and long-term outcomes from two instructional approaches. *Journal of Learning Disabilities, 34,* 33–58.

Torgesen, J. K., Rashotte, C. A., Alexander, A., Alexander, J., & MacPhee, K. (2003). Progress towards understanding the instructional conditions necessary for remediating reading difficulties in older children. In B. Foorman (Ed.), *Preventing and remediating reading difficulties: bringing science to scale* (pp. 275–298). Parkton, MD: York Press.

Torgesen, J. K., Rashotte, C. A., & Alexander, A. (2001). Principles of fluency instruction in reading: Relationships with established empirical outcomes. In M. Wolf (Ed.), *Dyslexia, fluency, and the brain* (pp. 333–355). Parkton, MD: York Press.

Truch, S. (1994). Stimulating basic reading processes using Auditory Discrimination in Depth. *Annals of Dyslexia, 44,* 60–80.

Truch, S. (2003). Comparing remedial outcomes using LiPS and Phono-Graphix: An in-depth look from a clinical perspective. Unpublished manuscript. Calgary, Alberta, Canada: The Reading Foundation.

U.S. Department of Education Office of Special Education and Rehabilitative Services (2002). A new era: Revitalizing special education for children and their families. Washington, DC: Government Printing Office.

Vaughn, S., Linan-Thompson, S., Wanzek, J., Rodriguez, K., Sanderson, C., Cavanaugh, C., Roberts, G., Elbaum, B., & Torgesen, J. (in press). Effectiveness of tier I and tier II reading interventions for at-risk kindergarten students, *Exceptional Children*

Wiederholt, J. L., & Bryant, B. R. (1992). *Gray Oral Reading Tests—III.* Austin, TX: PRO-ED.

Wiederholt, J. L., & Bryant, B. R. (2003). *Gray oral reading tests—4th edition.* Austin, TX: PRO-ED.

Wilson, B. (1988). *Wilson Reading System.* Wilson Language Training: Milbury, MA: Wilson Language Training.

Wise, B. W., Ring, J., & Olson, R. K. (1999). Training phonological awareness with and without explicit attention to articulation. *Journal of Experimental Child Psychology, 72,* 271–304.

Wolf, M., Miller, L., & Donnelly, K. (2000). Retrieval, automaticity, vocabulary elaboration, orthography (RAVE-O): A comprehensive, fluency-based reading intervention program. *Journal of Learning Disabilities, 33,* 375–386.

Woodcock, R.W. (1987). *Woodcock Reading Mastery Tests-Revised.* Circle Pines, MN: American Guidance Service.

The Principles of Multi-Component, Structured Language Teaching

Louisa C. Moats

The next four articles together constitute a pocket bible on how to teach students with specific language difficulties. Expert teacher trainers and scholars, Judith Birsh and Suzanne Carreker, concisely articulate the essence of multisensory structured language teaching—skilled teaching that combines listening, speaking, reading, and writing. The prototypical lesson format, refined by a consensus of practitioners over decades, originated with Samuel T. Orton and Anna Gillingham in the 1930s. The classic lesson has stood the test of time because it addresses many layers of language structure that contribute to fluent reading and writing, and because it incorporates systematic, cumulative practice in every subskill that, woven together, will culminate in reading comprehension.

In Carol Tolman's overview, specific linguistic concepts are enumerated and categorized. Her charts nicely summarize the phoneme, grapheme, rime, syllable, and morpheme constituents of English that students must be taught. In addition, she summarizes the key principles necessary for strong implementation of vocabulary, fluency, and comprehension instruction. Her "working smarter, not harder" motto was adopted only after years of discovering that passion is not all that distinguishes an effective teacher: Knowledge, skill, and research-based practices must also be in the mix.

Maryanne Wolf and colleagues report another in a long line of "gold standard" studies on a multi-component approach that has achieved meaningful gains with the very poorest readers. The instruction deliberately fosters metacognition and linguistic analysis at several levels within a lesson. The "serious word play" they endorse is deeply grounded in scientific studies of the reading brain at work, as well as empirical evidence that the instruction produces better results than unidimensional methods.

Practitioners who study the guidance of these experts will recognize that reading instruction is a complex undertaking. A well-crafted lesson teaches language organization incrementally, systematically, and explicitly, often with multisensory techniques. Practitioners should also be reassured that the content of instruction (language) can be learned and that even the most challenged students, when appropriately taught, can progress.

What Is Multisensory Structured Language?

Judith R. Birsh

Learning to read, write, and spell are cognitive linguistic tasks. Extensive research over the last decade has shown that teaching in these basic cognitive linguistic areas must include a language-based approach that is direct, systematic, explicit in content, and addresses the following foundational skills: phonemic awareness, phonics, fluency, vocabulary study, comprehension strategies, (NRP, 2000), spelling (Moats, 2006), and writing (Berninger & Amtmann, 2004), with an emphasis on accuracy and automaticity in every aspect. This kind of instruction is especially mandated for those who are at risk or are struggling to learn to read. For many students, learning to read is a painstaking process. They need every step of the way made crystal clear in order to fill in the gaps in their knowledge.

Beginning early in the 20th century, long before the use of sophisticated brain imaging techniques to illuminate the reading pathways, multisensory instruction formed the basis of treatment for diverse groups of students with reading difficulties (Moats & Farrell, 2005). We now know much more about the brain through work in the neurosciences. Brain imaging has allowed scientists to follow the pathways used in reading in both children and adults. As the science of reading has evolved, however, there has been a great deal of research on what causes reading disability and how to define it. What has not progressed at the same pace is sound, experimental research on treatment and instructional practices such as multisensory techniques. The absence of such evidence has not prevented educators from routinely prescribing and implementing multisensory practice combined with a structured language curriculum with their most severely dyslexic students. In fact, there has been a strong and growing interest in such techniques, with many teachers and administrators eagerly changing classroom practice to include explicit examples of simultaneous multisensory experiences in their reading instruction.

This description of multisensory structured language (MSL) has four purposes. The first is to explain what MSL is, using the typical lesson plan format as the framework for the discussion. The second is to propose reasons, from clinical and classroom experiences, why MSL seems to work with children and adults with dyslexia and other reading challenges. The third part will look briefly at some experimental research that uses programs that contain components of MSL and work well with a variety of groups. The last part will describe the new initiative from the International Dyslexia Association (IDA) on research into MSL.

A Potent and Powerful Pairing: Multisensory Teaching and Learning with a Structured Language Curriculum

Many experienced teachers who work with students with dyslexia and related learning difficulties teach the scientifically based components of reading instruction, using a multisensory structured language program to insure learning of the cognitive linguistic concepts necessary for successful reading acquisition.

"Multisensory teaching is not lights, camera, action," as one teacher has said. Multisensory teaching and learning is a form of direct instruction of the phonologic, morphemic, semantic, and syntactic layers of language. Multisensory strategies simultaneously involve visual, auditory, tactile-kinesthetic sensory systems, and/or articulatory-motor components while linking listening, speaking, reading and writing; this means it directly involves students in seeing, hearing, saying, and writing during instruction. For example, to teach a vowel sound, the teacher emphasizes visual awareness of the teeth, tongue and lips positions, and the kinesthetic feel of the sound in the throat while simultaneously having the student name the letter along with a key word to reinforce the sound/letter association. After instruction, direct application of the sound/symbol correspondences to reading and spelling are practiced using a variety of skills such as letter matching, blending words with the new sound, and analyzing words with the sound for spelling.

In their daily lessons, teachers deliberately and systematically incorporate many multimodal opportunities to hear, see, say, and move, while following a carefully organized and sequenced approach to language structure. Students handle a wide variety of manipulatives such as sound cards, sound boards, pocket charts, letter tiles, three-dimensional alphabets, dry-erase boards, blackboards, pencil grips, index cards, story and information books, notebooks, and many styles of writing implements and textured surfaces to write on. New knowledge is accumulated, based on what has already been previously learned and then maintained for daily review and practice in future lessons. The power behind these strategies resides in the pairing of multisensory teaching and learning with the structured language curriculum.

Lesson Planning Is at the Heart of Multisensory Teaching and Learning

The salient features of what makes a lesson multisensory will be highlighted in the routines of a typical MSL lesson. "The core content for instruction is the carefully sequenced teaching of the structure and use of sounds, syllables, words, sentences, and written discourse." (Moats & Farrell, 2005). The lesson plan format includes a progression of structured, scientifically based, (NRP, 2000) language activities. The essential components are rotated through carefully planned lessons on a daily basis with differing emphases according to the needs of the students. In each section of the lesson, teachers pay close attention to how they are going to involve different sensory systems to reinforce the learning in brief and varied routines that motivate students and hold their attention. It is common for MSL trained teachers to engage their students actively in question-response-feedback cycles.

Essence of a Multisensory Structured Lesson Plan

The plan for an MSL lesson includes a specific order of activities taught for a prearranged period of time so that all components of the structure of language are included each time the teacher meets with students. Conscious multisensory procedures using the student's eyes, ears, hands, and mouth help to link the sound, sight, and feel of the spoken language to the printed language on the page. (Adapted from Birsh & Schedler, 2005.)

The multisensory lesson plan formats of the programs based on the original Orton-Gillingham approach have many common features. Programs that are similar in structure and philosophy have been developing since the 1970s. They adhere to the principles learned from research studies and clinical experiences with input from many allied professionals from the fields of education, psychology, neuroscience, medicine, and speech-language pathology (Birsh, 2005).

Programs accredited by The Alliance for Accreditation and Certification of Structured Language share the philosophy that effective MSL includes instruction that is explicit, systematic, cumulative, direct, and sequential. Some MSL programs are derived from the original Orton-Gillingham approach and bear the name of their authors, such as Slingerland, Sonday, Spalding, and Wilson (For more programs see Baker Hill, 2005, p. 609; Henry, 2005). Many emphasize different content areas of reading-related skills, depending upon the needs of the students they are designed to serve. This is reflected in the lesson plans of each program, which are variations on the same theme. Furthermore, programs based on the Orton-Gillingham approach present the building blocks of written language in a sequence that addresses phonemic awareness, sound–symbol relationships, phonics, syllable types, structural analysis, spelling, fluency, vocabulary, comprehension, composition, and handwriting.

Daily lessons typically include the following discrete components of language, which are modified for each student or group and for different levels of instruction. All components do not appear every day. They are rotated through the weekly lesson plans to help students develop fast, accurate decoding, automatic recognition of familiar words and sight words, and fluent reading of text, spelling proficiency, comprehension, and writing.

- Alphabet sequence and letter naming
- Phonemic awareness activities including segmenting and blending
- Review of sound–symbol associations, learned in previous lessons using letter decks and key words to aid memory
- Spelling dictated sounds to integrate reading and spelling
- Introduction of new letter/sound associations and language concepts, and/or review of previously introduced concepts
- Reading phonetically regular words in lists and sentences with letter patterns already taught, and developing automatic recognition of high-frequency sight words to build automaticity

- Vocabulary study including Greek and Latin layers focusing on morphology and syllabication
- Reading controlled and/or decodable text to develop fluency
- Spelling and writing words and sentences from dictation using words from reading practice
- Handwriting practice, with explicit instructions in letter formation
- Comprehension and listening strategies for use with connected text
- Oral language practice and written composition

The structured lesson plans used in MSL intervention target these specific skill components with the ultimate goal of increasing accuracy and fluency through sufficient practice and synthesizing these skills for effective comprehension and written expression. The lesson plan in Figure 2.1.1 provides an example.

Figure 2.1.1.   **Lesson Plan Example with Multisensory Components**

1. **Alphabet/Phonological Awareness**
Students touch and name the letters of the alphabet in sequence (tactile/auditory) Echo, discriminate and tap out individual sounds in spoken words. (auditory/ kinesthetic)

2. **Handwriting**
Students name and trace the letter *d* three times while listening to guided stroke description. (auditory/kinesthetic)

3. **Reading Deck Review**
Students name previously learned letters and give the keywords and sounds. (visual/auditory)

4. **Spelling Deck Review**
Students listen to previously learned sounds, repeat sounds, and write letters with index finger on tabletop. (auditory/ kinesthetic)

5. **Concept Introduction**
Teacher provides multisensory introduction of a language concept using guided discovery of sound, with letter, key word, and feeling of mouth positions, reinforced with sky writing, handwriting on paper, reading the sound, and spelling the sound. (auditory/visual/tactile and kinesthetic)

6. **Reading Practice**
Students build words with syllable cards, blending syllables into words. (kinesthetic/visual/auditory)

7. **Spelling**
Students review the rule for doubling the final consonant (the Floss Rule) and checkpoints: 1) one syllable, 2) short vowel, and 3) final /f/, /l/, or /s/. Spell words: Look and listen; echo the word; write naming the letters; proofread. (auditory/kinesthetic/visual)

8. **Extended Reading/Writing**
Goal is accuracy, fluency, and comprehension. Students read aloud from connected decodable text with controlled vocabulary geared to the students' level. Students write sentences using vocabulary they have been reading and spelling. (visual/auditory, kinesthetic)

9. **Oral Language Practice**
Students practice expanding sentences orally starting with basic simple sentences and use cards to represent parts of speech in sentences. (auditory, visual, kinesthetic)

10. **Listening**
Teacher reads expository texts of interest to students at their level of comprehension. Uses comprehension strategy such as think-aloud K-W-L, a structured graphic organizer (Marzola, 2005). (auditory/kinesthetic/visual)

From Carreker, S. (1998). *Basic language skills: Concept manual, book one* (p. iv). Bellaire, TX: Neuhaus Education Center. Adapted with permission.

What May Make Multisensory Instruction Effective

As the science of reading has evolved, there has been a great deal of research on reading development, aspects of reading instruction, and what causes reading disability. What has not progressed at the same pace is sound, experimental research with empirical evidence lending theoretical support to specific multisensory instructional practices for reading-related disorders.

Despite long-term use of multisensory techniques by experienced practitioners for students with reading difficulties and the number of well-established instructional programs incorporating them as central to their design, very little is actually known about the efficacy of multisensory instruction. "Although devoted practitioners emphasize the significance of the multisensory component as pivotal for student success, it is perhaps this component that is least understood…" (Moats & Farrell, 2005).

Moats and Farrell (2005), however, provide some insights into why MSL is effective in language learning. Careful to note the lack of empirical evidence to support the power of the approach, they, nevertheless, see some theoretical support coming from the science of cognition and neuroscience. This is not familiar territory for most teachers. However, because of the emerging popularity and current adoption of multisensory activities for intensive instruction and within the classroom, many will want to know the theoretical basis for these activities.

Three different areas of research offer support for multisensory instruction. The first area is in the nature of memory; the second area comes from the neurosciences; and the third, from the nature of learning (Moats & Farrell, 2005).

Research concerning short and long-term memory finds that the neural networks are temporarily activated during new learning. Focusing on specific pieces of information holds learners' attention when control processes are used. For example, "selective attention, attentional shift, and employment of strategies for remembering such as verbal rehearsal or use of imagery are features of working memory as well" (Moats & Farrell, 2005). Selective attention is the ability to attend to certain stimuli while ignoring other stimuli, and working memory involves putting ideas on hold while working on other ideas or taking in new information. Storage mechanisms that store small pieces of speech information and graphic or print information are active in working memory. In a study cited by Moats and Farrell, (Mousavi, Low, & Sweller, 1995), it was found that integrating in working memory what is being learned is more easily done when the material is physically conjoined through both the visual and auditory modalities. For children who show evidence of phonological disability with difficulty in sorting out speech sounds and storing them accurately in phonological memory, improvement in phoneme awareness, reading, and spelling came as a result of working on the "articulatory features of the phonemes and phoneme sequences in words" (Moats & Farrell, 2005) combined with the written representations (Gillon, 2003).

Functional neuroimaging has allowed researchers to understand how reading takes place in the brain and how language is processed there. Reading involves multiple sites and has multiple systems for processing the symbols into sounds. Dyslexia is manifested by a disruption in these language systems, which leads to phonological weaknesses. The phonologic weakness occurs "At the lowest level of the language system," and in turn impairs decoding (Shaywitz, 2003). In fact, there are two neural systems for reading: one for word analysis in the parieto-temporal region and the other for automatic, rapid responses localized in the occipitotemporal area that is used by skilled readers for rapid word recognition. Low phonological processing skills are the result of left hemisphere posterior processing anomalies typical of children with dyslexia (Birsh, 2005). This means that individuals with dyslexia have difficulty accessing and manipulating the sound structure (phonemes) of spoken language. Such a deficit prevents easy and early access to letter-sound correspondences and decoding strategies that foster accurate and fluent word decoding and recognition.

Although these differences affect the ability to read, neural systems for reading are malleable and highly responsive to effective reading instruction. In their research using functional magnetic resonance imaging to study the effects of a systematic phonics-based intervention with 6- to 9-year-old children, Shaywitz and Shaywitz (2004) found evidence of plasticity of neural systems for reading. The changes in the brain made these readers comparable to good readers. "Teaching matters and can change the brain" (p. 931).

It is possible that people with dyslexia can compensate for this neural disruption with the help of multisensory components within the lesson taught. Moats and Farrell (2005) propose that when alternative circuits are engaged to circumvent those that are weak for developing phonological processing skills by activating sensorimotor pathways when using "fingertips, hand, arm, whole body, and/or vocal; speech apparatus during symbolic learning, that circuits for word recognition are more easily accessed and established" (p.32).

The third area of support for MSL comes from clinical evidence of successful instructional approaches over the years. In working with students with learning difficulties, clinicians and classroom teachers have found that the most successful interventions are carefully constructed with special attention to linking old and new information, reinforcement of what they know through multiple opportunities for practice and review, and the use of ready responses between teachers and students along with acknowledged specific strategies for solving linguistic conundrums. Active learning is the key concept. Teachers accomplish this by using a conscious set of metacognitive strategies to group, rearrange, and transfer topics of information using a common language to refer to, for example, types of syllables, steps in a story map, or ways to spell the sound /o/. Moats and Farrell (2005) also suggest that creating mnemonic strategies such as using key words, chunking, rhyming, visualizing, and grouping related facts tends to help students remember better than when given ready-made ones. In addition, students who use verbal rehearsal while working remember more and are more accurate. Using a motoric response while learning something new leads to better attention to detail and better retention of what is being learned.

Teachers See Benefits of MSL

Experienced teachers and clinicians have known about the benefits of MSL for a long time. Most importantly, structured lesson planning ensures that teachers include all levels of language in the same session as well as ample opportunities to incorporate instances of multisensory instruction. Because of the variety of modalities and media, and the consistency of the approach, teachers experience enthusiastic interaction with their students, helping them establish a positive rapport.

MSL is based on teachers using a well-defined scope and sequence so that there is systematic introduction of new information in small steps for the precise teaching of skills (Cox, 1992). This feature promotes the use of guided discovery through Socratic questioning to learn new language concepts based on what the students already know. "When students make a discovery, they understand and connect the new learning to prior knowledge" (Carreker, 2005). The guided discovery instructional process is an essential aspect of MSL; one that sets it apart from whole language instruction and balanced literacy. The basic steps in multisensory guided discovery teaching can be used at every level of language instruction. Here is an example of how it can be put into practice:

- The teacher reads words aloud that contain a common element, with the student repeating each example. (auditory/kinesthetic)
- Students discover the new language element that sounds the same in each word.
- Students then see the words written on the board. (visual)
- Students discover the common element in each of the words by looking at it (visual) and its position. (visual)
- Students say out loud what they have discovered. (auditory/kinesthetic)
- The teacher makes a card with the new element to add to a review deck. At the same time, the students name the element, spell it, give it a key word to aid recall, and assign a meaning to it if it is an affix, for example. They then add the information to their language notebook. (visual/auditory/ kinesthetic/tactile)

In place of rote memorization, teachers and students engage in metacognitive dialogues about pertinent strategies. Teachers and students develop together a consistent language about concepts that need to be taught directly. For example, in the Wilson Reading System (Wilson, 2002), questioning techniques are used throughout the lesson after introducing new material to assure that the student has understood. Students justify their choice of strategies based on what they have just learned. Such terminology as *digraph, blend, syllable*, and *schwa sound* gives students and teachers a common vocabulary to discuss new concepts, review what they have learned, and make corrections themselves.

Multisensory Teaching and Learning from the Students' Point of View

From the students' point of view, MSL lessons fit their need for structure, limits, and an anxiety-free atmosphere in which to learn. Students do not like surprises or last-minute changes that can confuse them and affect their performance. The agenda of the lesson plan is often displayed using words and symbols for the activities listed. Students and teacher refer to this schedule as the lesson progresses. There is less anxiety because the daily presentation of activities occurs in the same order so students know what to expect and when. MSL lessons adhere to a daily structure to ensure that students feel secure in knowing that the lesson is stable and predictable, and that it is designed for their success. Student attention is better focused because the activities rotate rapidly, none lasting more than about 10 minutes. Students are frequently surprised at the fast pace and amount accomplished at the end of the session. By verbalizing, generalizing, comparing, and contrasting language elements, their active participation increases as they build the structure of language for themselves (Birsh & Schedler, 2005).

Visual reminders in the form of procedure charts are frequently used for laying out the steps for spelling, making letter shapes, punctuation reminders, or story maps to prompt students to use strategies they have learned without the necessity of verbal repetition from the teacher.

Careful planning guarantees that all aspects of language are practiced and integrated systematically, based on an organized curriculum. This seamless presentation assures students that the basic skills needed to become skilled readers are not presented in a disjointed, disconnected way. Students participate in short, intensive, interactive activities that integrate reading, writing, and spelling. What they read, they write; what they write, they read; what they read, they spell. They are learning while using all pathways to learn in every lesson.

Grasping written language concepts presents difficulties, especially when attention is a problem. Therefore, activities are short and focused with small steps taken in sequence, at first easy and then more difficult. With the rapid changing of learning modalities (visual, auditory, and tactile/kinesthetic) and media, teachers keep the lesson interesting. Students learn to accept and even anticipate variety within the structure (Tucker, 2003).

Necessary repetition builds toward mastery while all taught concepts are maintained in the lessons (Wilson, 2002). New learning and practice with prior learning are well balanced. Review is automatically built in for purposes of fluency and automaticity of the essential components of reading and writing.

As students gain mastery of the sub skills, teachers continue to introduce new content in the curriculum sequence. Some students take longer to reach mastery during remediation. However, the strong organization of well-planned MSL lessons often helps students improve their memory over time and thus have better retrieval of information. Furthermore, teachers find that these techniques engage their students while encouraging them to think about the structure of language in ways that may have been inherently difficult for them.

Research Studies Use Intensive, Systematic, Structured Language Instruction for Children and Adults

There are a number of recent studies that show that following intensive, systematic, structured language teaching with many instances of multisensory elements incorporated into the programs, children and adults with reading disabilities demonstrated normalized brain patterns to aid their word recognition (Blachman, Schatschneider, Fletcher, & Clonan 2003; Eden, et.al., 2004; Shaywitz, 2003; Simos et al., 2002). However, the research does not support within the research protocols the multisensory components of structured language lessons emphasized by teachers who use MSL. This lack of evidence, in light of what is already known about the science of reading, has provided a challenge to adherents of MSL to seek evidence to support their use of such principles of instruction. Moats and Farrell (2005) put these concerns into perspective:

> Although many of the programs incorporating these strategies have been effective according to clinical reports, the specific contribution of the multisensory component to the overall success of those programs has not yet been thoroughly documented or explained through rigorous manipulation of instructional conditions and subsequent measurement of outcomes. Current reading research, however, does offer strong support for the content and overall approach of MSLE programs because they address language processing skills necessary for both decoding and comprehension. (p. 29)

IDA's Initiative on Research in Multisensory Teaching and Learning

Recognizing the need first for a consensus on a definition of multisensory teaching and learning and its theoretical frameworks based on scientific evidence, IDA has created the Multisensory Instruction Research Initiative to stimulate scientific investigation into how the components of multisensory teaching and learning might or might not enhance the learning of reading-related skills. This initiative has adopted scientific investigation of multisensory teaching and learning in literacy acquisition as its major agenda.

Although the value of its clinical and classroom use has been known for over 75 years for students with dyslexia and other struggling readers, the true nature of its efficacy and an understanding of its individual components and subcomponents have yet to be given scientific scrutiny. Studies on the multisensory aspects of the interventions and remediation work with students are needed to provide the missing evidentiary link. In other words, studies are needed to determine the value of the multisensory aspect of the MSL approach when combined with evidence-based instruction that directly and explicitly addresses the multiple components of oral and written language in an integrated, systematic, and cumulative approach with various populations of learners including those with dyslexia. The new grant program will provide funds for research projects focused on multisensory instruction. For information on this initiative go to the IDA web site at www.interdys.org

In summary, research supports the general conclusion that knowledge of the structure of language, systematically and explicitly taught and learned within a complete lesson framework that focuses on fluency, is important for beginning and struggling readers. However, there is no scientific evidence behind the multisensory component, emphasized by practitioners of multisensory structured language education, and central to programs derived from the principles of Orton-

Gillingham instruction. Yet, its efficacy has been demonstrated over and over again for students with dyslexia and other struggling learners in independent and public school contexts as well as in clinical settings (Joshi, Dahlgren, & Boulware-Gooden 2002). The need for discovering what Dr. Gordon F. Sherman, chair of the Multisensory Instruction Research Initiative, calls "the mysteries of multisensory teaching and learning" in light of the broad implications for instruction in this nation's public schools, which have come to rely on evidence-based instruction, brings a new urgency to the Multisensory Instruction Research Initiative at IDA.

The principles of multisensory teaching and learning rest on a bedrock of decades of clinical and classroom experience as the approach of choice for reading instruction for students with dyslexia. The emphasis on the basic language components of a comprehensive program along with the application of direct, intensive, and systematic instruction parallels the consensus derived from the science of reading on what and how to teach reading to beginners and those struggling to learn. The future promises new knowledge and information based on scientific evidence that will test the efficacy of the multisensory components deemed essential in multisensory teaching and learning.

References

Baker Hill, H. (2005). Appendix B, materials and sources. In J. R. Birsh (Ed.), *Multisensory teaching of basic language skills* (2nd ed., pp. 609–611). Baltimore: Paul H. Brookes.

Berninger, V., & Amtmann, D. (2004). Preventing written expression disabilities through early and continuing assessment and intervention for handwriting and/or spelling problems: Research into practice. In H. L. Swanson, K. Harris, & S. Graham (Eds.), *Handbook of research on learning disabilities.* New York: Guilford Press.

Birsh, J. R. (2005). Research and reading disability. In J. R. Birsh (Ed.), *Multisensory teaching of basic language skills* (2nd ed., pp. 1–22). Baltimore: Paul H. Brookes.

Birsh, J. R., & Schedler, J. F. (2005). Planning multisensory structured language lessons and the classroom environment. In J. R. Birsh (Ed.), *Multisensory teaching of basic language skills* (2nd ed., pp. 187–211). Baltimore: Paul H. Brookes.

Blachman, B. A., Schatschneider, C., Fletcher, J. M., & Clonan, S. M. (2003). Early reading intervention: A classroom prevention study and a remediation study. In B. R. Foorman (Ed.), *Preventing and remediating reading difficulties: Bringing science to scale* Timonium, MD: York Press.

Carreker, S. (2005). Teaching reading: Accurate decoding and fluency. In J. R. Birsh (Ed.), *Multisensory teaching of basic language skills* (2nd ed., pp. 213–255). Baltimore: Paul H. Brookes.

Cox, A. R. (1992). *Foundations for literacy: Structures and techniques for multisensory teaching of basic written English language skills* Cambridge, MA: Educators Publishing Service.

Eden, G. F., Jones, K. M., Cappell, K., Gareau, L., Wood, F. B., Zeffiro, T. A,…Flowers, D. L. (2004). Neural changes following remediation in adult developmental dyslexia. *Neuron, 44*, 411–422.

Gillon, G. T. (2003). *Phonological awareness: From research to practice.* New York: Guilford Press.

Henry, M. K. (2005). *Framework for informed reading and language instruction: Matrix of Multisensory structured language programs*. Baltimore: The International Dyslexia Association.

Joshi, R. M., Dahlgren, M., & Boulware-Gooden, R. (2002). Teaching reading in an inner city school through a multisensory teaching approach. *Annals of Dyslexia, 52*, 229–242.

Marzola, E. S. (2005). Strategies to improve reading comprehension in the multisensory classroom. In J. R. Birsh (Ed.), *Multisensory teaching of basic language skills* (2nd ed., pp. 377–412). Baltimore: Paul H. Brookes.

Moats, L. C. (2006). How spelling supports reading. *American Educator, 29*, 12–22, 42–3.

Moats, L. C., & Farrell, M. L. (2005). Multisensory structured language education. In J. R. Birsh (Ed.), *Multisensory teaching of basic language skills* (2nd ed., pp. 23–41). Baltimore: Paul H. Brookes.

Mousavi, S. Y., Low, R., & Sweller, J. (1995). Reducing cognitive load by mixing auditory and visual presentation modes. *Journal of Educational Psychology, 87*, 319–334.

National Reading Panel (2000). *Teaching children to read: An evidence based assessment of scientific research literature on reading and its implications for reading instruction.* Washington, DC; National Institute of Child Health and Human Development. Publication No. 004754): Washington, DC: Government Printing Office.

Neuhaus Education Center. *Basic language skills: Therapy for dyslexia*, (1998). Bellaire, TX: Author.

Shaywitz, S., (2003). *Overcoming dyslexia: A new and complete science-based program for reading problems at any level.* New York: Alfred A. Knopf.

Shaywitz, S. E., & Shaywitz, B. A. (2004). Neurobiologic basis for reading and reading disability. In P. McCardle & V. Chhabra (Eds.), *The voice of evidence in reading research* (pp. 417–442). Baltimore: Paul H. Brookes.

Simos, P. G., Fletcher, J. M., Bergman, E., Breier, J. I., Foorman, B. R.,...Papanicolaou, A.C. (2002). Dyslexia-specific brain activation profile becomes normal following successful remedial training. *Neurology, 58,* 1203–1213.

Tucker, V. (2003). *Planning multisensory structured language lessons.* Manuscript in preparation.

Wilson, B. (2002). *Wilson reading system instructor manual* (3rd ed.). Milbury, MA: Wilson Language Training.

Teaching the Structure of Language through Seeing, Hearing, and Doing

2.2

Suzanne Carreker

Many teachers and practitioners have long believed in multisensory instruction even though research has yet to validate this kind of teaching. These same teachers and practitioners firmly believe in directly teaching the structure of language, which research has confirmed to be efficacious (National Reading Panel, 2000). The fundamental question is whether it is the engagement of multiple senses, or the teaching of the structure of language, or the combination of the two that makes the instruction effective. In view of the research, and in deference to the time-honored practices of multisensory structured language education, this article presents activities that explicitly teach the structure of language and engage multiple senses.

The activities are divided into three categories—the phonology of language, the orthography of language, and the semantics of language. The activities in the first category promote the understanding of the *phonology* or sound structure of language. These activities aid emergent and struggling readers in learning that spoken words are made up of sounds, which are mapped onto letters in printed words. The second category of activities promotes the understanding of the *orthography* or letter patterns of the language. Once students understand that spoken words are made up of sounds, they need to know exactly how those sounds are represented in printed words so they can read unfamiliar words. They also need to learn how to deal with words that have more than one syllable. The activities in this category develop rapid word recognition, which enables students to read words quickly and maintain their attention to the meaning of the text they are reading. Activities in the final category promote the *semantics* or the meaning of language, so students can understand what they are reading. Even before students are able to read text independently, these activities can be used as listening comprehension activities. The activities in all three categories promote reading success.

The Phonology of Language

A student's success with reading is dependent upon his or her knowledge of the sound structure of language. Ultimately, the student must be able to segment words into their constituent phonemes or sounds. Before teaching a student to segment words into sounds, it is helpful if he or she understands that spoken sentences are made up of words and that spoken words can be made up of syllables.

Word Awareness

To build a student's sense of "wordness," an understanding of where one word ends and the next word begins in a spoken sentence, the teacher sits beside the student and lays out four blocks or counting tokens in a row. The teacher dictates a four-word sentence (e.g., *The brown dog ran.*) and touches a counter for each word in the sentence, starting with the counter on the far left of the row. The student repeats the sentence as he or she touches a counter for each word in the sentence. The teacher removes the counter in the row that represents the last word in the sentence. The teacher says, "Now you will say part of the sentence. Say the sentence again and touch a counter as you say each word. One word will be left off." The student says the sentence again, touching a counter for each word, and leaves off the last word (e.g., *The brown dog*). The activity continues until only one counter is left. The student says, "The," as he or she touches the remaining counter.

The teacher dictates other sentences and uses the same sequence. The number of words in the sentences can vary from two to six. Initially, the teacher uses sentences with only one-syllable words and gradually includes two- and three-syllable words in the sentences. The student moves only one counter for a word with more than one syllable such as *children, number*, and *hamburger*.

Awareness of Syllables

Awareness of syllables at an oral level later helps the reader perceive the division of words in print and can be developed with this activity. The student makes fists with both hands and places them at the shoulders. The teacher dictates a compound word (e.g., *sidewalk*). The student repeats the word. The student says the word again in syllables. He or she drops the left fist to waist-level as he or she says the first syllable (e.g., *side*) and drops the right fist to waist-level as he or she says the second syllable (e.g., *walk*). The teacher dictates another compound word. When the student is comfortable with compound words (e.g., *flashlight, inside, baseball, football, airplane, cupcake, driveway*), the teacher dictates two-syllable words (e.g., *magnet, basket, market, number, monster, dentist, winter*). This activity can be done in whole group instruction.

Segmenting Words into Sounds

The teacher lays out three one-inch blocks in a row in front of the student. The teacher dictates a word with two or three sounds (e.g., *at, is, mat, set, lip, shop, luck*). The student repeats the word. The student says the word again slowly and moves one block for each sound in the word. When the student is finished, he or she sweeps a pointer finger under the blocks and says the word quickly. The teacher asks, "How many blocks did you move?" The student touches and counts the blocks that were moved. The teacher then asks, "How many sounds are in the word?" The student answers. When the student is comfortable segmenting words with two and three sounds, the teacher adds more blocks and dictates words with more sounds (e.g., *last, sent, slip, drop, plant, split*).

In whole group instruction, students can count the number of sounds in a word using their fingers. They make a fist. Beginning with the thumb, they hold up a finger for each sound in a word. When students have segmented the word, they sweep the pointer finger of the other hand across the raised fingertips and say the word quickly. The teacher asks how many fingers they are holding up, and how many sounds are in the word.

The Orthography of Language

The word *orthography* comes from the Greek language and means *correct* (ortho) *writing* (graphy). In short, orthography deals with how spoken words are represented in print. Individual sounds in spoken words can be represented with one letter or a group of letters in printed words. Explicit, systematic instruction of sound-symbol correspondences provides students with the means of sounding out an unfamiliar word and helps students establish letter patterns and words in memory, which provides the foundation for rapid word recognition. Knowledge of syllable types, spelling patterns, and morphemes (i.e., prefixes, suffixes, roots) further supports rapid word recognition; this frees students' attention from the word level to the meaning of the text.

Syllable Types

Most words in English can be categorized as one syllable type or as a combination of six different syllable types—closed, open, vowel-consonant-*e*, vowel pair or team, vowel-*r* or *r*-controlled, and consonant-*le*. These syllable types have distinctive patterns that cue students to the vowel sound within a syllable. For example, a *closed syllable* ends in one vowel and at least one consonant (e.g., *at, bet, fist, stop, crunch*). The vowel is short and is coded with a breve, a curved diacritical mark (˘) that is placed over the vowel.

Introduction of a Syllable Type

Each syllable type is introduced with an auditory and a visual discovery as illustrated with the introduction of a closed syllable.

Auditory Discovery: The teacher dictates five to seven words that are closed syllables (e.g., *at, add, pet, list, drop, brunch*). The teacher dictates the words one at a time. Students repeat each word after the teacher. When all the words have been dictated, the teacher asks, "What sounds the same about all the words? Think about the vowel sounds." Students discover that all the words have short vowel sounds.

Visual Discovery: The teacher writes the discovery words on the board and asks, "What looks the same in all these words? How do they end?" Students discover that all the words end in one vowel and at least one consonant. The teacher and students formulate a definition of a closed syllable such as the one mentioned above.

Definitions and Hand Movements for Syllable Types

After the introduction of each syllable type, students periodically review the syllable types by stating the definitions with hand movements.

Closed Syllable: "A closed syllable ends in <u>one vowel</u>…" [Students hold up the pointer finger of the left hand and then make a *v* with the pointer and middle fingers of the left hand.] "…and at least <u>one consonant.</u>" [Students hold up the pointer finger of the left hand and then cup the left hand to make it look like a *c*.]
    "The <u>vowel</u>…" [Students make a *v* with the pointer and middle fingers of the left hand.] "…is <u>short</u>." [Students pull the *v* straight down vertically about six inches.] "Code it with a <u>breve</u>." [With the right hand, students draw a breve over the *v*.]

Open Syllable: An *open syllable* ends in only one vowel (e.g., *he, she, hi, go, no*). The vowel is long and is coded with a macron, a flat diacritical marking (¯) that is placed over the vowel. The definition of this syllable type can be reinforced with the following hand movements:
    "An open syllable ends in only <u>one</u>…" [Students hold up the pointer finger the left hand.] "…<u>vowel</u>." [Students make a *v* with the left hand.] "The vowel is <u>long</u>." [Students slide the *v* horizontally to the right about six inches.] "Code it with a <u>macron</u>." [With the right hand, students draw a macron from left to right over the *v*.]

Vowel-consonant-e Syllable: A *vowel-consonant-e syllable* ends in one vowel, one consonant, and a final *e* (e.g., *name, these, five, rope, cube*). The *e* is silent and is crossed out. The vowel is long and is coded with a macron. The definition and hand movements for this syllable type are as follows:
    "A vowel-consonant-e syllable ends in <u>one vowel</u>…" [Students hold up the pointer finger of the left hand and then make a *v* with the left hand.] "…<u>one consonant</u>…" [Students hold up the pointer finger of the left hand and then make a *c* by cupping the left hand.] "…and a <u>final *e*</u>." [Students hold up the pointer finger of the left hand and then make an

American Sign Language *e* (Humphries, Padden, & O'Rourke, 1994) by placing the left thumb across the palm of the left hand and the tips of the four fingers along the thumb.] "The *e* is <u>silent</u>." [Students place the pointer finger of the left hand on their lips.] "<u>Cross</u> it out." [With the right hand, students draw a diagonal "cross out" line from left to right.] "The vowel is <u>long</u>." [Students make a *v* with the left hand and slide it to the right about six inches.] "Code it with a <u>macron</u>." [With the right hand, students draw a macron from left to right over the *v*.]

Vowel Pair (Team) Syllable: A *vowel pair* or *team syllable* has two adjacent vowels (e.g., *paint, see, boat, head, out, pause, zoo*). Because the familiar adage, "When two vowels go walking, the first one does the talking," is reliable only about 45% of the time (Adams, 1990), students need to learn each vowel pair individually. Students can review the syllable type with this definition and these hand movements:

> "A vowel pair syllable has <u>two</u>..." [Students make a *v* with the pointer and middle fingers of both hands and hold up the *v*'s shoulder's width apart.] "...<u>adjacent</u> vowels." [Students move the *v*'s together in front of them.] "Treat each <u>pair</u>..." [Students cup their hands, with palms up.] "...with <u>loving care</u>." [Students gently rock their hands back and forth.]

Vowel-r (r-controlled) Syllable: A *vowel-r* or *r-controlled syllable* has a single vowel that is followed by an *r* (e.g., *car, her, stir, short, church*). The vowel sound in this syllable type is unexpected; the syllable looks like a closed syllable, but the vowel in the syllable is not short. Students must learn each vowel-r combination individually. The good news is that *er*, *ir*, and *ur* are pronounced /er/ in accented and unaccented syllables. The combination *ar* is pronounced /ar/ in an accented syllable (e.g., *art, park, market, sparkle*) and /er/ in an unaccented syllable (e.g., *mustard, dollar*). The combination *or* is pronounced /or/ in an accented syllable (e.g., *for, short, border, portrait*) and /er/ in an unaccented syllable (e.g., *doctor, odor*). Students can remember this syllable type with this definition and these movements:

> "A vowel-r syllable has an <u>r</u>..." [Students cross the middle and the pointer fingers of the left hand to make an American Sign Language *r* (Humphries et al., 1994).] "...after the <u>vowel</u>." [Students make a *v* with the left hand.] "The vowel makes an..." [Students pause and then snap their fingers.] "...<u>unexpected</u> sound."

Consonant-le Syllable: A *consonant-le syllable* appears in the final position of a word (e.g., *bum**ble**, can**dle**, ta**ble**, ma**ple***). This combination of letters constitutes a syllable even though there is no sounded vowel. The identification of the consonant-*le* syllable helps students perceive the syllables within the word and where the word will divide. It also helps students determine the placement of the accent as the accent usually falls on the syllable before the consonant-*le* syllable. These are movements for the consonant-*le* syllable:

"A consonant-*le* syllable is coded with a <u>half-bracket</u>." [With the right hand, students draw a half-bracket ( )).] "The <u>accent</u>..." [With the right hand, students draw an accent mark from right to left.] "...falls on the syllable before."

Syllable Type Cards

The teacher prepares a deck of index cards that contains words or syllables that represent the syllable types that have been previously introduced. In addition to word lists, sentences, and connected text that contain the previously introduced syllable types, the deck of cards can be used to review the syllable types.

Syllable Sort – Students sort the deck of cards by syllable type. When the cards have been sorted into separate stacks, students take turns reading the syllables in each stack of cards.

Concentration – The teacher provides students with a stack of cards that contains equal numbers of different syllable types. Students shuffle the cards. They lay the cards face down in rows. Player One turns over two cards and identifies and reads the syllables on the cards. If there is a match of syllable types (e.g., *lip, fast*), the player keeps the cards and another player takes a turn. If there is not a match (e.g., *no, need*), the player replaces the cards and another player takes a turn. The player with the most cards wins.

Quick I.D. – The teacher shuffles the deck of cards and designates a syllable type for students to identify, for example, an open syllable. The teacher quickly flashes the cards. Students say "yes" and clap if a card contains an open syllable and say "no" if it does not contain an open syllable.

Spelling

English orthography has rules about what letters can appear in certain positions, what letter combinations can occur, and what letters can double. Teaching and calling attention to the patterns and rules of orthography helps students spell words correctly and increases their rapid recognition of words.

Cheer for Seven Brave Letters

There are seven letters in English orthography that never or rarely double. Students can learn this cheer for these brave letters that are not afraid to stand alone (Carreker, 2005):

h, k

y, j

v, w, x

Never or rarely double in real

English words.

Arm movements such as these can be added to the cheer:

1. Students make a fist with the right hand and raise it over the head as they say, "*h.*" They do it again as they say, "*k.*" The raised fist connotes the tallness of these two letters.

2. Students make a fist with the left hand and thrust it toward the ground as they say, "*y.*" They do it again as they say, "*j.*" The downward motion of the fist connotes the tails of these two letters.

3. Students make fists with both hands and place them knuckles to knuckles at chest level, with elbows bent and forearms parallel to the floor. Students pull the fists apart horizontally as they say, "*v.*" They place their fists together and pull them apart again as they say, "*w.*" They do it one more time as they say, "*x.*" The level forearms connote the baseline that these letters rest upon.

4. Students make fists with both hands. They cross their arms and place them on the chest as they say, "Never or rarely…." They then uncross their arms and hold them parallel with elbow bent as they say, "…double in real English words."

The Doubling Rule and the Four-Leaf Clover

A useful rule for students to learn is the Doubling Rule, which states that when a base word ends in one vowel, one consonant, one accent, the final consonant of the base word is doubled before adding a suffix that begins with a vowel (i.e., a vowel suffix). There are four checkpoints to the Doubling Rule: 1) one vowel, 2) one consonant, 3) one accent, and 4) a vowel suffix. If all the checkpoints are present, students know to double the final consonant before adding the suffix. If any checkpoint is missing, students know to just add the suffix.

To remember the checkpoints, students use a manipulative four-leaf clover (Carreker, 2002; see Figure 2.2.1). Each leaf of the clover has a checkpoint for the Doubling Rule, and the stem has the word *double* written on it. A clover is printed for each student. Students cut the pieces apart and line them up in random order at the top of their desks. The teacher writes a base word, a plus sign, and a suffix on the board (e.g., *shop + ing, run + er, hop + ed, red + ish, begin + er, omit + ed*). Students look at the base word and begin to build the four-leaf clover. If the base word ends in one vowel, one consonant, and one accent, they move the leaves with 1V, 1C, and 1' to the middle of their desks and arrange them into a clover. Students look at the suffix. If the suffix begins with a vowel, they move the last leaf. Because all the checkpoints are present, students place the

Figure 2.2.1. **Four-Leaf Clover for Reviewing the Checkpoints of the Doubling Rule**

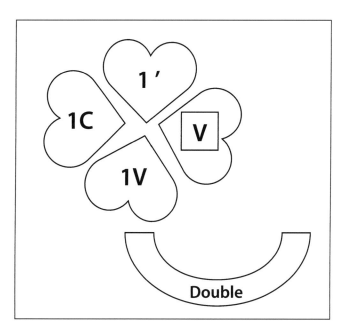

stem at the base of the clover. Students write the derivative on a piece of paper, doubling the final consonant of the base word before adding the suffix. If any of the leaves had been missing (e.g., *cup + ful, camp + ed, wait + ing, open + er*), students would know not to double the final consonant of the base word. As students think about the Doubling Rule, they will also need to think about letters that never or rarely double. For example, what will students do with *fax + ing*?

Morphology

With knowledge of morphemes (prefixes, roots, and suffixes) or meaningful word parts, students can unlock the meanings of unfamiliar words, and they can read and spell multi-syllabic words that contain these word parts.

Derivative Web

A derivative web is used to introduce the definitions of derivatives with useful word parts as well as the word parts that constitute the derivatives (Carreker, 2004; see Figure 2.2.2). Students write a derivative (e.g., *portability*) at the top of an unlined, landscaped piece of paper. They draw a circle with about a four-inch diameter in the center of the paper. They draw six smaller circles that radiate from the large center circle.

In the center circle, students write the origin, the word parts and their meanings, and the definition of the word. For example, *portability* is from Latin and

Figure 2.2.2.   **A Derivative Web**

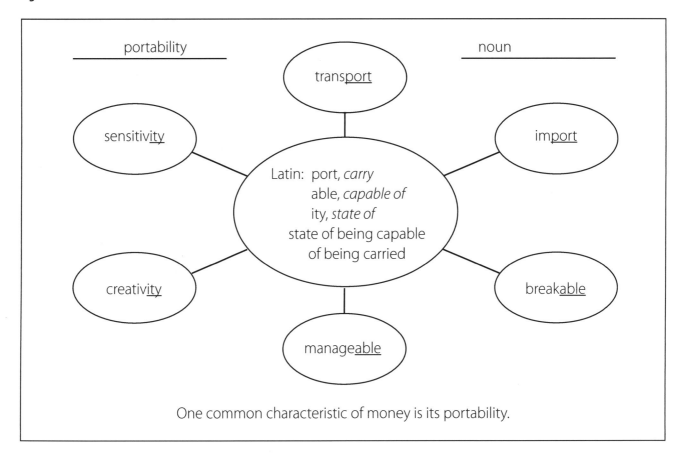

contains three word parts: *port* meaning *carry*, *able* meaning *capable of*, and *ity*, meaning *state of*. The definition of *portability* is *the state of being capable of being carried*. Students connect the word parts in the derivative to words they already know. In two of the smaller circles, students write two derivatives that contain *port* (e.g., *transport*, *import*). In two other circles, students write two derivatives that contain *able* (e.g., *breakable*, *manageable*). In the remaining two circles, students write two derivatives with *ity* (e.g., *creativity*, *sensitivity*). Students write a sentence with the word *portability* at the bottom of the paper.

Word Part Bingo

The teacher provides each student with a grid that contains 25 squares, 15 counters, and a list of 12 roots, 12 prefixes, and 12 suffixes. Students write *FREE* in the center square. Students choose eight of each kind of word part and write them in the remaining 24 squares in random order. The teacher prepares slips of paper with the definitions of all the word parts and places them in a container (e.g., *pre* means *before*).

To play, the teacher draws a slip of paper from the container and reads the definition. If students have the word part that matches the definition in one of the squares on their grid, they cover the square with a counter. The goal is to cover five squares horizontally, vertically, or diagonally.

The Semantics of Language

Comprehension is the main goal of reading. Accurate and fluent reading facilitates students' comprehension but does not guarantee it. Just as with decoding, students need explicit instruction in comprehension. One important skill that needs to be taught is summarization. Listed below are two activities that teach students how to summarize narrative text (Carreker, 2004).

Wh-Question Cards

After students have read a short story (see Figure 2.2.3), they prepare five cards with the questions: Who? What? When? Where? Why? They write one question on each card. They line the cards up along the left-hand side of their desks in the order listed below. With a partner, students answer each question orally:

Who?—Students name the characters (e.g., a lion and a mouse).

What?—Students state all the events of the story in order and then determine the most important event, the one event that allows the story to end as it does (e.g., the mouse saves the lion).

When?—Students state the time(s) in which the events take place (e.g., one afternoon).

Where?—Students state the place(s) in which the events take place (e.g., on the savanna).

Why?—Students state the reason why the most important event happens (e.g., the mouse is returning a favor).

As students answer each question, they move the card from the left-hand side of their desks to the right-hand side of their desks. When all the cards have migrated to the right-hand side of their desks, students rearrange their cards in this order: Who? When? Where? What? Why? This order will aid the summarization of the passage in three sentences: 1) The story is about [Who?], 2) It takes place [When?] [Where?], and 3) [What happens?] because [Why?] (e.g., the story is about a lion and a mouse; it takes place one afternoon on the savanna; the mouse saves the lion because he is returning a favor.)

Figure 2.2.3.   **A Narrative Text**

The Lion and the Mouse

The tall savanna grass fluttered in the slight breeze as a great lion slept. While he slept, something ran across his paw. The lion awoke to see a small mouse nibbling on a seed of grass.

The lion scooped up the mouse in his paw and opened his fierce-looking mouth. Before the lion could eat it, the mouse cried, "Please, let me go. I will be glad to return the favor someday." The lion roared with laughter at this thought. But because he was still sleepy and not very hungry, the lion let the mouse go.

Later that afternoon, the lion awoke and felt hungry. He went to look for food. Soon, he was caught in a net. He tried to get free, but the lion could not break the ropes. The lion roared.

The mouse heard him and ran to see what the matter was. Seeing the great lion caught helplessly in the net, the small mouse said, "I am glad that I can now return the favor." Then the mouse gnawed the ropes and the lion was soon free.

"I may be meek, but even I can be of help to the mighty," said the mouse. The lion and mouse were forever friends.

From Carreker, S. (2004). Developing metacognitive skills: Vocabulary and comprehension (p. 37). Bellaire, TX: Neuhaus Education Center. Adapted by permission.

Summary with a Piece of Rope

Instead of using the Wh-Question Cards or in addition to the cards, students can summarize a narrative text (see Figure 2.2.3) by using a piece of rope that is about three feet long to identify the five parts of the plot.

1. *Exposition*—The *exposition* of a plot lays out the initial facts of the story—the characters, settings, what the characters are doing, and the complication that

ignites the conflict that will fuel the action of the story. Students hold the rope straight and state the exposition (e.g., the characters are the lion and the mouse, the setting is one afternoon on the savanna, the lion is sleeping and the mouse is nibbling on a seed of grass, the complication is that the mouse runs across the lion's paw).

2. *Rising Action*—Once the complication is introduced, the action in the story becomes more intense. This is called the *rising action*. Students tie a loose knot and begin to recount the events. With each event, they pull the knot tighter and tighter (e.g., the lion captures the mouse; the mouse pleads with the lion to let him go; the lion lets the mouse go; the lion takes a nap; the lion awakes and goes to find food; the lion gets caught in a net, the lion roars).

3. *Climax*—At the *climax*, the action is most intense, and the knot is pulled as tightly as possible. At this point, fate intervenes or a character acts (e.g., the mouse comes to save the lion), makes a decision, changes, or realizes the conflict.

4. *Denouement*—After the climax, the tension eases. This is the *denouement*, which means *to separate the knot*. The conflict that fueled the action is heading toward resolution. Students slowly loosen the knot as they recount the events after the climax (e.g., the mouse gnaws the ropes; the lion is freed).

5. *Resolution*—The *resolution* is the point in the story where the conflict is solved. Students hold the rope straight and state the ending of the story (e.g., the mouse and the lion are forever friends).

Summary

It may be some time before research definitively corroborates the value or the role of multisensory instruction. In the meantime, teachers and practitioners can use activities such as the ones presented in this article that explicitly teach the structure of language, engage multiple senses, and promote reading success by making sure that all bases are covered!

References

Adams, M. J. (1990). *Beginning to read: Thinking and learning about print.* Cambridge: The MIT Press.

Carreker, S. (2002). *Scientific spelling.* Bellaire, TX: Neuhaus Education Center.

Carreker, S. (2004). *Developing metacognitive skills: Vocabulary and comprehension.* Bellaire, TX: Neuhaus Education Center.

Carreker, S. (2005). Teaching spelling. In J. R. Birsh (Ed.), *Multisensory teaching of basic language skills* (2nd ed.). Baltimore: Paul H. Brookes.

Humphries, T., Padden, C., & O'Rourke, T. J. (1994). *Basic course in American sign language.* Carrollton, TX: T. J. Publishers.

National Reading Panel (2000). *Teaching children to read: An evidence based assessment of scientific research literature on reading and its implications for reading instruction.* Washington, DC: National Institute of Child Health and Human Development.

Working Smarter, Not Harder

What Teachers of Reading Need to Know and Be Able to Teach

2.3

Carol Tolman

IN my 27 years of involvement in public education, I have never met a teacher that did not care deeply about each and every one of his or her student's reading skills. As a special education teacher within elementary, middle, and high school settings, I, along with my peers, spent countless hours and sleepless nights preparing and delivering lessons with the hope of improving students' reading skills. As I worked harder, I watched my students' reading skills improve at a frustratingly slow rate; however, their progress never completely reached the grade level for which they strove. In searching for the answers to student reading success, I was left with the continual feeling that there was something more that could be done. Yet, even with over two decades of experience and the title of M.Ed., I could not identify what was missing in my reading instruction. Having not learned what I needed to know in my first two degrees, I was determined not to let that same mistake happen again. Consequently, before I began my doctoral work, I queried numerous national reading experts in an attempt to identify what I needed to learn.

Over time, I came to understand that I had been missing a fundamental understanding of the scope and sequence of skills necessary to include within effective reading instruction. The often-quoted "five core components" of reading, including phonemic awareness, phonics, fluency, vocabulary, and comprehension, are inarguably crucial components. Until I studied this field in an in-depth manner, however, it was not always clear to me exactly what skills should be included within these components. Along with this is the necessary knowledge of exactly what we mean by these components, how these skills are translated throughout the grade levels and what components should be emphasized, with what intensity for which students. For example, we know that an emphasis on teaching decoding at the word level, including the skills of phonological awareness, phonics, and fluency, should be emphasized in grades K–3 in order to provide an accurate and automatic foundation for all future reading practices. Advanced word study is important to include beyond grade 3, especially for continued reading success at the multisyllable word level. A strong emphasis on phonemic awareness and phonics within the early grades, supported by fluency, is reflected in the following scope and sequence

> "While vocabulary and comprehension are truly the ultimate goals of reading, the teaching of phonemic awareness, phonics, and fluency are steps that must be in place to meet the ultimate goal of comprehension."

of skills for teaching reading. While vocabulary and comprehension are truly the ultimate goals of reading, the teaching of phonemic awareness, phonics, and fluency are steps that must be in place to meet the ultimate goal of comprehension.

One issue to consider is the older poor reader who does not decode words accurately and/or automatically. Older poor readers must also be taught the prerequisite skills necessary for reading before they are able to move beyond to a deep understanding of what they read. Teachers must layer a strong foundation in reading at the word level for these students, or these students will continually build their reading skills on a rocky foundation.

The information and understanding I have gained in the field of reading has enabled me to "work smarter, not harder" to increase the reading skills of students. I share the following outlines of these skills in the hopes that you too, can use this knowledge to improve student reading achievement at all levels. We *can* make a difference in the lives of so many students!

Phonological Awareness

What it is: A student's awareness of how spoken words consist of sounds.

When to teach: Focus on pre-kindergarten, kindergarten, and first grade. Taught beyond grade 1 for those students who have not mastered this skill.

Young children typically enter kindergarten with the ability to articulate words. They hear and produce, however, only connected streams of speech. To the average kindergarten student, "Once upon a time" sounds like one big, long word. Over time and with proper instruction, students must become aware of increasingly smaller units of speech, until they are able to identify and manipulate the individual phonemes, or speech sounds, of the English language. Instruction in phonological awareness follows a scope and sequence from easier, larger units of spoken segments of words to smaller, individual spoken sounds within words. Instruction is done without letters, focusing solely on the sounds of the language. One way to think of this is that you can do phonological awareness activities "in the dark." While there are more levels of phonological awareness than are listed here, the following outline includes those levels found to be most connected to student progress in reading and spelling.

Teaching Phonological Awareness

Phonological awareness is an over-arching, superordinate term referring to a student's awareness of units of sounds that comprise our spoken language. The phonological awareness skills listed in Figure 2.3.1 should be taught in frequent, distributed lessons throughout kindergarten and 1st grade; for example, do activities daily for 5 to 15 minutes rather than twice per week for 30 minutes. Keep in mind that these skills should be mastered as a foundational skill for reading and spelling, and as such must be taught to older poor readers who exhibit weaknesses in this skill area.

Figure 2.3.1. **Phonological Awareness Skills**

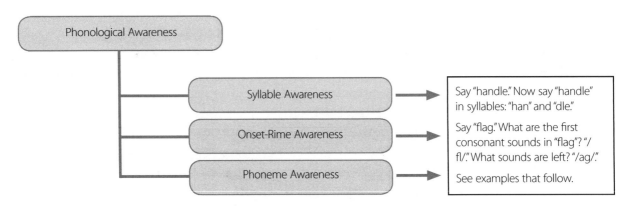

Table 2.3.1. **Phonological Awareness Examples**

Type	Definition	Examples
Syllable Awareness	Syllable awareness refers to a student's ability to orally segment words into spoken syllables, with each spoken syllable containing a vowel sound.	Say the word *"window."* Now clap the syllables in this word: *"win" "dow."*
Onset – Rime Awareness	Onset-rime awareness refers to a student's ability to orally segment a word into its component parts, to include the onset, or initial consonant sound or sounds, followed by the rime, or the vowel and every sound that comes after it.	Say the word *"splat."* What are the first consonant sounds (the onset)? *"/spl/."* What sounds are left (the rime)? *"/at/."*
		Say the word *"spat."* What are the first consonant sounds? *"/sp/."* What sounds are left? *"/at/."*
		Say the word *"sat."* What is the first consonant sound? *"/s/."* What sounds are left? *"/at/."*

Phoneme Awareness

The phoneme, or individual speech sound, is the level at which you ultimately want students to be able to identify, categorize, and manipulate speech sounds. While the individual speech sound is abstract in that we do not speak in individual sounds, students need to utilize this skill in order to later map these individual sounds to letter and letter patterns when ready for phonics in their reading and spelling instruction. Figure 2.3.2 and Table 2.3.2 show examples of phoneme awareness activities, from easier to more difficult:

Figure 2.3.2.   **Phenome Awareness Activities**

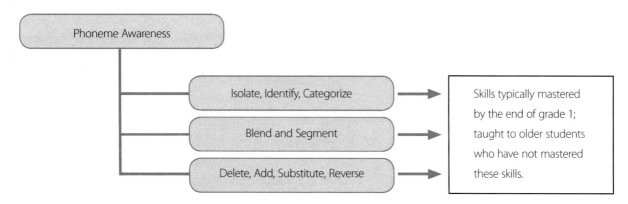

Table 2.3.2.   **Phoneme Awareness Examples**

Phoneme Isolation	What is the first speech sound in the word? What is the last speech sound in the word? What is the second speech sound in the word?	fast /f/ flash /f/ spark /s/ tax/s/ please/z/ trapped /t/ shout /ou/ blond /l/ trap /r/
Phoneme Identity	What is the first speech sound in these words? What is the last speech sound in these words?	giraffe, jar, jaunt /j/ stem, comb, autumn /m/
Phoneme Categorization	What word does not belong here?	ceiling, kite, sister kite apple, egg, avalanche egg
Phoneme Blending	Blend the following sounds to make a word.	/s/ /ou/ /n/ /d/ /z/ sounds /th/ /or/ /n/ thorn
Phoneme Segmenting	What are the sounds in the word "switch"? What are the sounds in the word "phone"?	/s/ /w/ /i/ /ch/ /f/ /oe/ /n/
Phoneme Deletion	Say *"climb."* Now say *"climb"* without /c/. Say *"flinch."* Now say *"flinch"* without /l/.	lime finch
Phoneme Addition	What word would you have if you added /**sh**/ to the beginning of "out"? What word would you have if you added /**z**/ to the end of *"bog"*?	shout bogs
Phoneme Substitution	Say *"splat."* Change /**t**/ to /**sh**/. What word would you get? Say *"browse."* Change /**z**/ to /**n**/. What word would you get?	splash brown
Phoneme Reversal	Say *"skit."* Now say the sounds in the word *"skit"* backwards Say *"church."* Now say the sounds in the word *"church"* backwards.	ticks church

Table 2.3.3. **Phonics / Word Study**

		Phonics is a fundamental component of reading instruction for all children, not just those with reading difficulties. It is the lifeline for those students who do not readily interpret the alphabetic principle, and assists those good readers with improving both their fluency and spelling skills. Phonics skills begin with a student's ability to identify letter names both accurately and fluently and continue with the subsequent mapping of these letters onto sounds for the reading and spelling of words. Beginning phonics skills are to be mastered from K through grade 2, with more advanced phonics concepts introduced and taught from grade 3 and beyond. Table 2.3.4 shows examples of skills to be included within comprehensive phonics instruction, from easier to more difficult skills.
What it is:	Mapping of letters to sounds	
	Analyzing the structure of how a word is spelled	
When to teach:	Beginning phonics from kindergarten through grade 2	
	Advanced phonics concepts in grade 3 and beyond	
	Taught at any grade for those students who have not mastered these skills	

Table 2.3.4. **Comprehensive Phonics Instruction Skills**

Note: Letters within two slash marks refer to the sound of the letter, not the letter's name.

Mapping of Letters to Sounds	Examples		
Knowledge of the names of the letters of the alphabet, both accurately and fluently.			
Mapping single consonant sounds with their most common letter representations.	p for /p/	b for /b/	m for /m/
	f for /f/	t for /t/	d for /d/
	n for /n/	s for /s/	z for /z/
	l for /l/	r for /r/	k for /k/
	c for /k/	g for /g/	j for /j/
	w for /w/	h for /h/	
Mapping initial blends, which are two or three consonant sounds together in a word.			
- Initial blends with two consonant sounds	st-	sm-	sn-
	qu-	sl-	sp-
	sc-	sk-	bl-
	cl-	fl-	gl-
	pl-	br-	cr-
	dr-	fr-	gr-
	pr-	tr-	sw-
	tw-		
	Note that qu- represents two consonant sounds, /k/ and /w/, even though we think of the letter *u* as a vowel, and that this represents two sounds, not one.		

- Initial blends with three consonant sounds:	spr	str	scr	spl		
- Final blends with two consonant sounds:	-mp	-nd	-sk	-st	-ft	-lk	-ld

Mapping single consonant sounds with their more complex letter representations		

(Table 2.3.4 continued on next page)

Table 2.3.4. **Comprehensive Phonics Instruction Skills** *(continued)*

Note: Letters within two slash marks refer to the sound of the letter, not the letter's name.

Mapping of Letters to Sounds	Examples			
Digraphs: two letters that represent one speech sound that is usually different from the sounds for either of the two letters.				
- Sounds that are different from either letter	sh for /sh/	ch for /ch/	ng for /ng/	ph for /f/
	th for /th/ (unvoiced, as in the word *think*)			
	th for /th/ (voiced, as in the word *then*)			
- Sounds that are the same as one of the sounds in the digraph	wh for /w/			
Trigraphs: three letters that represent one sound	tch for /ch/		dge for /j/	
Silent letter patterns	kn for /k/	mb for /m/		gn for /n/
	mn for /n/		pn for /n/	
Orthographic patterns	ck for /k/ at the end of a single syllable word with a short vowel sound (*stick*)			
	doubling the –f, -s, -l, or –z at the end of a single syllable word with a short vowel sound (*staff, kiss, pull*, and *fizz*)			
	the sound for the letter *c* changes to /s/ when followed by the letters *i, e*, or *y* (*city, cents, cyst*)			
	the sound for the letter *g* sometimes, but not always, changes to /j/ when followed by the letters *i, e*, or *y* (*gist, gentleman, gymnasium*, but not in the words *gift* or *get*)			
	su, -ge, or si used to represent the consonant sound /zh/, as in the words *pleasure, montage*, and *vision*			
	The letter *x* represents different sounds depending on where it is within a word. *X* sounds like /z/ at the beginning of a word or syllable, but sounds like the two sounds of either /k/ /s/ or /g/ /z/ within the middle of a word. *X* takes on the sounds /k/ /s/ at the end of a word.			

Once you have explored the consonant sounds and their letter patterns, review the vowel sounds and the letters and letter patterns in Table 2.3.5 that represent these sounds. Teach students the most common letter patterns first, moving gradually to more complex, less frequent spelling patterns for these vowel sounds.

Table 2.3.5. **Vowel Sounds and Letter Patterns**

Note: Letters within two slash marks refer to the sound of the letter, not the letter's name.

Letter Patterns	Examples		
Single letters for vowel sounds	a for /a/	e for /e/	ea for /e/ (bread)
	i for /i/	y for /i/ (gym)	o for /o/	u for /u/
Each of the individual vowel letters *a, e, i, o,* and *u* can represent their long vowel sound, and single letters can also represent long vowel sounds.	a for /ā/ in vacation		e for /ē/ in revisit
	y for /ē/ in happy		i for /ē/ in linguini
	i for /ī/ in bicycle		y for /ī/ in cry
	o for /ō/ in potato		u for /ū/ in tsunami
Vowel teams, or letter combinations to represent a single vowel sound	The long vowel sound /ā/ represented by the letters *ai, ay, ei, eigh, ey, ei*		
	The long vowel sound /ē/ represented by the letters *ee, ea, ie*		
	The long vowel sound /ī/ represented by the letters *igh, ie*		
	The long vowel sound /ō/ represented by the letters *oe, oa, ow*		
	The long vowel sound /ū/ represented by the letters *u, oo* (moon), *ew* (new), *ue* (clue)		

(Table 2.3.5 continued on next page)

Table 2.3.5. **Vowel Sounds and Letter Patterns** *(continued)*

Note: Letters within two slash marks refer to the sound of the letter, not the letter's name.

Letter Patterns	Examples
Diphthongs, or vowel sounds that seem to slide in your mouth, giving you the feel of two movements. These are, however, classified as one speech sound.	oi / oy: use *oi* at the beginning or middle of a syllable
	use *oy* at the end of a word or syllable
	ou / ow: use *ou* at the beginning or middle of a syllable
	use *ow* at the end of a word or syllable

Notes:
1. Some programs classify /ī/ as a diphthong. Some programs classify /ū/ as a diphthong. Technically, this is one sound that does not make two mouth movements, as heard in the word *blue*.
2. Some programs may classify the /ū/ sound, as found in the word *butane*, as one sound; here the letter u actually represents the same sound as the *oo* in *moon*, and there is a hidden glide /y/ before this vowel sound. The sounds in the word *butane* are /b/ /y/ /ū/ /t/ /ā/ /n/.
3. The important point is to teach all the sounds of the English language, mapping letters and letter patterns in a direct, systematic manner using a scope and sequence that corresponds to the frequency of spelling pattern used within the English language.

Table 2.3.6. **Mapping Letter Patterns**

Letter Patterns	Examples
R-controlled vowel sounds	*er*, *ir*, and *ur* used to spell the sound /er/ as in the words *her*, *mirth*, and *church*
The consonant letter *r* affects the sound of the preceding vowel so much that they become unitized into one speech sound	*or* used to spell the sound /or/ as in the word *port*
	ar used to spell the sound /ar/ as in the word *charm*

Once students have become accurate and fluent in their ability to decode (read) and encode (spell) many of the previously listed consonant and vowel rules within single syllables, teachers can begin building student knowledge at both the single and multisyllable word levels. Compound words such as *playground* and *cowboy* are introduced. Following are more advanced phonics skills, to include work at the morpheme and syllable levels and expanding to the topic of word origin as a way to categorize and understand the reasoning behind many of the letter patterns used in the English language.

Syllables

Syllables are taught to aid students in their ability to pronounce and spell multisyllable words. In general, most programs introduce the six syllable types outlined in Table 2.3.7. While there may be slight variations in the way in which syllables are taught within different programs, the most important point to consider is whether syllables are included within phonics instruction.

Table 2.3.7.　　　**Syllable Instruction**

Syllable Type	Definition	Examples		
Closed Syllables	A syllable that ends in a consonant sound or sounds; the vowel sound is short. Introduce this syllable type first, as it accounts for approximately 50% of the syllable types in text.	stomp	<u>cap</u> / tain	
		re / <u>sist</u>	<u>rip</u> / ple	
Vowel-Consonant-e Syllables	A syllable that includes a vowel followed by one consonant and the silent letter –*e* Teach this syllable type second, as it is found in many words and is a common spelling pattern for long vowel sounds.	bite	com / <u>pete</u>	
		re / <u>bate</u>	e / <u>mote</u>	
Open Syllables	A syllable that ends with a single vowel letter that represents a long vowel sound	so	<u>mo</u> / ment	<u>cre</u> / a / tion
Vowel Team Syllables	A syllable that includes a vowel sound that is made up of more than one letter. The sound of the vowel can be either long, short, or diphthong.	boil	<u>pleat</u> / ed	<u>pow</u> / der
Consonant-le Syllables	A syllable that ends with a consonant that is followed by the letters –*le*	puz / <u>zle</u> bum / <u>ble</u>	bot / <u>tle</u> peo / <u>ple</u>	
Vowel-r Syllables	A syllable that includes a vowel letter followed by the letter *r*, where the vowel and the *r* act as one unitized sound	***birth*** <u>***pur***</u> / pose	re / ***port*** ***farm*** / ing	

Morphemes

The smallest meaningful unit of a word is a morpheme. Understanding words at the morphemic level allows students to get to the meaning of words accurately and quickly.

A morpheme can be as short as one letter, as in the letter *s* to mark the plurality of a word. Examples: start<u>s</u>　frog<u>s</u>

A morpheme can consist of letter combinations that contain meaning, as in roots, prefixes, and suffixes within words.

Examples of underlined morphemes: <u>pre</u> <u>dic</u> <u>tion</u>　<u>un</u> <u>like</u> <u>ly</u>　<u>con</u> <u>form</u>

Word Origin

Directly teaching the origin of English language letter patterns aids students' understanding of how these words are spelled, increasing their ability to spell and read fluently and readily gain meaning from what they read. Word origins typically included within reading instruction include:

Table 2.3.7.   **Word Origin Instruction**

Word Origin	Definition	Examples	
Anglo-Saxon	One of the oldest influences on the English language that has permeated throughout many years, Anglo-Saxon influences have an impact on many of the single syllable function words and nouns that name our common objects. This influence accounts for the use of digraphs, vowel teams, r-controlled vowels, and many simple syllable patterns. While these words are found within the earliest of words, they frequently do not follow the expected phoneme-grapheme mappings we expect in English words.	mother	have
		head	water
		love	eye
Latin	One of the most prevalent influences on the English language, Latin is responsible for the construction of words that contain a root, along with the addition of a prefix and/or suffix.	construction	absolutely
		premeditated	reconstitute
Greek	Influences that have an impact on words typically associated with the areas of mathematics, science, and philosophy, words with Greek origins typically consist of a combination of roots connected to make a word.	polymorphous	atmosphere
		technophobe	philanthropic

Vocabulary

- *What it is:* A student's lexicon, or internal dictionary, of knowledge of word and phrase meanings.

- *When to teach:* Vocabulary skills are taught in both direct and indirect ways throughout all grade levels; in actuality, throughout life! Early on, students learn vocabulary directly and indirectly through exposures to words in conversations and read-alouds. By approximately 3rd grade students gain much of their new vocabulary knowledge through exposure to print. The importance of teaching students to decode both accurately and fluently by the end of 3rd grade supports vocabulary development, since print exposure is crucial for students' continual vocabulary development. If unable to decode grade level text, students should be encouraged to listen to taped readings or have others read aloud to them in order to continue to increase exposure to challenging vocabulary words.

- *Its impact:* Vocabulary knowledge aids the reading process at multiple levels. For example, vocabulary knowledge is a strong support for reading comprehension. Those students who are good decoders tend to have strong vocabulary knowledge and can use both decoding and vocabulary knowledge to aid in fluent, accurate reading comprehension. Additionally, while a student may have strong decoding skills, if he or she is unable to connect a word to its appropriate meaning, comprehension is continually compromised.

- *What to consider:* While there is an urgent need for continued research efforts to identify effective, research-based vocabulary practices, the National Reading Panel (NRP) outlined major points to consider for vocabulary instruction. A summary of these findings is included below:
  1. Teach vocabulary in multiple ways, not just with one method.

2. Provide many exposures to a vocabulary word in a wide variety of contexts.

3. Encourage active interactions between students and the vocabulary, making words come alive in students' speech and writings.

4. Directly explain how word knowledge fits into the bigger picture of language comprehension.

5. When confronted with unknown words within a reading passage, teach these words directly to students.

6. Pay attention to and foster the indirect ways in which vocabulary growth can occur, such as through conversations, use of words at home and with peers, or through discussions of readings. Most of a student's vocabulary knowledge is gained through multiple, indirect exposures over time, as the sheer volume of the number of words to know is too large to teach directly.

There is no one agreed-upon list of words to teach for vocabulary development. When choosing words to teach directly, focus on those words that will be most useful in students' lives. The following resources address best practices for choosing and instructing vocabulary.

Fluency

- *What it is:* The ability to gain deep meaning from what you read while using a limited amount of time.

- *When to teach:* All throughout reading instruction, especially starting in mid-1st grade, with a focus on students who do not meet grade level fluency benchmarks.

- *Its impact:* Fluency is the glue that holds word reading together and enables students to focus on comprehension. When fluent, students use the sound/symbol code automatically to decode words, allocating much of their memory capacities to the job of thinking about what they are reading.

- *What to consider:* Students may need fluency work at the subword, word, phrase, or sentence levels as well as practice at connected text levels. To date, the following practices have been found to be most effective in increasing student fluency rates:
  - Guided oral reading in small groups is sufficient for the average and above-average reader.
  - Systematic, explicit practice is needed for the dysfluent reader, but take care to identify why each student is dysfluent. Some may appropriately need fluency work, while others may continue to struggle with either phonological awareness, phonics, or both skill areas as the reason for their dysfluent reading. When poor decoding is the cause of dysfluent reading, instruction must include remediation in the affected area(s) of decoding along with fluency practice.
  - Read out loud to students to model appropriate rate and prosody.
  - For fluency practice, use texts that are at a student's instructional or frustration

level, making sure that a knowledgeable reader listens and provides continued feedback on accuracy.

- Require repeated readings of selections (up to three times per passage).
- Group students in pairs, alternating oral reading between each.
- Drill students on frequently found words in our language, writing each word on a 3 X 5 card and having them practice reading them daily until mastered.
- Keep track of student progress by charting correct word per minute scores (WCPM). When appropriate, have students chart their own progress to monitor their growth.
- Encourage the use of proper prosody, including phrasing and intonation, when reading.
- Give the message that comprehension, not speed, is the most critical factor when reading. To that end, let students know that you will be asking them to think about and tell you about what they just read.

Reading Comprehension

- *What it is:* The ability to understand what you read at a "deep" level.

- *When to teach:* Throughout all grades, and throughout one's lifetime! Improving reading comprehension never stops.

- *Its impact:* Oral language and vocabulary development are crucial support skills to reading comprehension. With the ultimate goal of understanding what one reads, reading comprehension has an impact on reading at its core and is the whole point of reading.

- *What to consider:* Special attention should be given to students of low socio-economic levels, students with English as a second language, and students who do not learn to decode on grade level by the end of third grade, as these groups are typically at-risk for low vocabulary and comprehension skills.

The teaching of reading comprehension goes far beyond the use of a list of strategies to aid comprehension. It is an ever-evolving, flexible process that is not linear in nature. The RAND Report (2002) identifies four major factors that contribute to reading comprehension. These include:

1. The Reader

   A student's ability to decode the words on the page, both with accuracy and fluency, has an impact on how well he or she will comprehend what is being read. Reading comprehension cannot occur if a student is continually struggling to decode. Read-alouds to young children, continuing until they can decode grade-level materials, assist in exposing these students to academic language structures. The practice of reading grade level texts aloud is equally important for older poor readers, who continually need immersion in more difficult texts in order to hear complex vocabulary and sentence structures crucial to comprehension at an advanced level.

2. The Text

Much about the text can be controlled by a teacher, and text factors frequently have an impact on reading comprehension. A teacher's pre-reading of the text in preparation for students' comprehension difficulties is a major factor in assisting student comprehension. For example, the difficulty of vocabulary knowledge, complexity of sentence structures, and organization of paragraphs all have an impact on a student's ability to make sense of what is being read. Teachers can help students understand such text difficulties through the use of strategies such as questioning the author, completing graphic organizers, asking clarifying questions, making predictions and inferences, using graphic organizers, and/or visualizing what is being read. A combination of these strategies is most helpful rather than the use of one in isolation.

3. The Task

What teachers ask students to do contributes to how thoroughly a student understands the text, which in turn can affect students' motivation to read. When at all possible, make connections to students' prior knowledge and personal life in order to create an atmosphere of interest and involvement with reading. Connecting the reason for reading with an intrinsic, internally motivating goal for students will aid in their continued processing at a deep level.

4. The Context

The context within which students live has an impact on their involvement with reading, and along with this, their motivation to read. Do the student's community and family support the importance of reading? Can teachers reach out to foster a love of reading beyond the classroom? Is there a social culture and reinforcement for reading? While most of these factors are beyond a teacher's control, one can create a nurturing, safe, exciting environment within the classroom to explore reading at many levels. Providing group interactions around reading texts fosters a celebration of reading, a love of learning, and a deep motivation to comprehend what is read well beyond the surface level.

In conclusion, it is my hope that this article provides you with an overview of skills to consider in the teaching of reading for all students, good and poor readers alike. In addition to the five major components of phonemic awareness, phonics, fluency, vocabulary, and comprehension, it is important to further our understanding of reading research and keep abreast of recent developments in the field. Like the act of reading comprehension itself, learning about the teaching of reading never stops!

Teacher preparation is at the core of student reading success. With a proper foundation in the skills of reading, teachers no longer have to guess or hope that their students' reading skills improve. We now have the information to track student reading progress from early on in an objective way, identifying those students at-risk for reading failure and providing appropriate instructional support for all. The LETRS (Moats, 2004) training materials provide in-depth teacher knowledge through the attendance of a series of workshops, supported by modules of text that extend information regarding each topic area. In addition, I have included references that continue to assist teachers in their quest for best practices for "working smarter, not harder" to improve all students' reading skills.

References

General

Birsh, J. R. (Ed.). (2005). *Multisensory teaching of basic language skills*. (2nd ed.). Baltimore: Paul H. Brookes. A thorough review of many of the components of reading, including both the "what" and the "why" of each component.

Moats, L. C. (2004). *LETRS: Language essentials for teachers of reading and spelling*. Longmont, CO: Sopris West Educational Services.

Phonological Awareness

Gillon, Gail T. (2004). *Phonological awareness: From research to practice*. NY: Guilford Press. A thorough, well-written text including both theory and practice.

Phonics/Word Study

Blevins, W. (1998). *Phonics from A to Z: A practical guide*. NY: Scholastic.

Blevins, W. (2001). *Teaching phonics and word study in the intermediate grades: A complete sourcebook*. NY: Scholastic. Practical teachers' guides that outline both the skills of phonics as well as best practices to teach them. *Phonics from A to Z* focuses on grades K–3, while *Teaching phonics and word study* focuses on grades 3–8.

Henry, M. K. (2003). *Unlocking literacy: Effective decoding and spelling instruction*. Baltimore: Paul H. Brookes. A thorough guide to all components of phonics, including the advanced word study necessary for teachers of upper elementary, middle school, and high school settings.

Vocabulary

Beck, I. L., McKeown, M.G., & Kucan, L. (2002). *Bringing words to life: Robust vocabulary instruction*. New York: Guilford Press. An especially teacher-friendly text containing activities and exercises to teach vocabulary well, focusing on students in K–3.

National Institute of Child Health and Human Development (2000). Report of the National Reading Panel: An evidence-based assessment of the scientific research literature on reading and its implications for reading instruction: Washington, DC:NICHD. See www.nationalreadingpanel.org for more information. A panel of experts reviewed scientifically-based reading research efforts to make solid recommendations for teacher practices; the five core areas of phonological awareness, phonics, vocabulary, fluency, and comprehension were identified. An important read for all teachers involved with the teaching of reading at any level.

Stahl, S. A. (1999). Vocabulary development. In J. Chall (Ed.). *From reading research to practice; A series for teachers*. Cambridge, MA: Brookline Books. An academic discussion of vocabulary research, containing valuable information concerning the number of words to teach, and when to teach them.

Vocabulary and the child with learning disabilities. (Winter 2002). Stahl, S. A. (Ed.) *Perspectives*. Baltimore: International Dyslexia Association. A thorough, practical guide for teaching vocabulary at all grade levels, including best practices and activities to use for increased vocabulary learning.

Fluency

Hasbrouck, J. E., & Tindal, G. (2005, January). Behavioral Research & Teaching. *Oral Reading Fluency: 90 Years of Assessment* (BRT Technical Report No. 33), Eugene, OR.

Hook, P. E., & Jones, S.D. (2002 Winter). The importance of automaticity and fluency for efficient reading comprehension. *Perspectives*. Baltimore: International Dyslexia Association.

Stahl, S. A. (2004). What do we know about fluency? Findings of the National Reading Panel. In P. McCardle & V. Chhabra (Eds.), *The voice of evidence in reading research* (pp. 187–211). Baltimore: Paul H. Brookes.

Comprehension

Beck, I. L., McKeown, M. G., Hamilton, R. L., & Kucan, L. (Eds.) (1997). *Questioning the author: An approach for enhancing student engagement with text*. Newark, DE: International Reading Association. A teacher-friendly resource outlining ways to interact with text to build student metacognition and increase reading comprehension.

Carlisle, J., & Rice, M. S. (2003). *Reading comprehension: Research-based principles and practices*. Baltimore: York Press. A review of what we know about reading comprehension to date, and how we know it.

RAND Reading Study Group (2002). *Reading for understanding: Toward a research and development program in reading comprehension*. A panel of experts reviewed what research told us what we know, and do not know, about best practices in reading comprehension to date. This RAND report identifies both best practices and considerations as well as where we need to go from here in our research efforts.

Serious Word Play
How Multiple Linguistic Emphases in RAVE-O Instruction Improve Multiple Reading Skills

Maryanne Wolf, Stephanie Gottwald, and Melissa Orkin

For many elementary-school children the achievement of reading with fluent comprehension—that is, the ability to read quickly and accurately enough to understand and think about text—remains an essential, but elusive goal. The most used intervention for these children involves "repeated reading" methods, where children read the same text several times till accuracy and fluency are achieved. Proponents of repeated reading make several important assumptions about these *implicit* methods: 1) fluency represents the end result of decoding instruction; 2) fluency gains on practiced texts generalize to new texts; 3) repeated exposures teach new vocabulary words and reinforce orthographic patterns; and 4) fluency gains advance comprehension. Growing evidence from several research directions indicates that these assumptions do not hold for many struggling readers.

In this article, we present an overview of a very different intervention for fluent comprehension, the RAVE-O program, based on a developmental, multicomponent model of fluent comprehension. The assumptions underlying RAVE-O share with repeated reading methods the goals of teaching new vocabulary and reinforcing orthographic pattern knowledge, but have explicit emphases on these and additional major linguistic systems such as syntactic knowledge and morphological processes. Indeed, we argue that the fallacies in past assumptions about indirect reading instruction (i.e., it teaches basic phonological knowledge and decoding principles through exposure and immersion in texts) extend to instruction for fluent comprehension in children with reading difficulties.

Research Background

The first body of evidence comes from research in the cognitive neurosciences regarding how the brain learns to read in typical development and fails to read in children with reading disabilities (Pugh, Sandak, Frost, Moore, & Mencl, 2005; Wolf, 2007). An examination of the young reader's first "reading circuit" illustrates the many components involved—from visual pattern recognition systems to varied cognitive and linguistic systems (Tan, Spinks, Eden, Perfetti, & Siok, 2005; Sandak, Mencl, Frost, & Pugh, 2004). Multiple linguistic systems are essential to understand the many dimensions contained within a spoken or written word: phonology, morphology, syntax, semantics, and pragmatics, with orthography necessary for written words. Each system activates discrete areas of the brain when we read.

A leitmotiv in this research and RAVE-O is that *everything* the child knows about oral language contributes to the development of written language.

To bring the multiple emphases in the RAVE-O program to life, we would like you, the reader, to analyze what you know about any single word. In the process, you'll have a bird's eye perch from which to view many of the different linguistic systems important to reading and oral language. Consider the word *duck*. First, the reader begins to process visual features of letters and of the word's shape and to discern the size, shape, and spacing of each symbol. Discerning meaningful visual symbols is an evolutionarily adaptive ability that has developed over thousands of years of token-based economies, hieroglyphic drawings, and other early writing systems (Wolf, 2007). The ability to store representations of visual patterns and connect that information to linguistic knowledge and writing conventions provides the foundation for an individual's orthographic knowledge (Wolf, 2007). During reading, children use their orthographic knowledge to discriminate between letters and recognize common letter patterns in their language. The ability to rapidly identify visual chunks in words (e.g., vowel digraphs, consonant blends, and morpheme units) ultimately increases the speed of reading.

To read *duck*, orthographic knowledge must become automatically connected to corresponding sound or phoneme-based knowledge. The individual visual symbols, *d*, *u*, *c*, and *k*, carry virtually no meaning until paired with their analogous sounds. The alphabetic principle—beginning with the cognitive understanding that each visual letter corresponds to a sound—underlies children's capacity to learn their language's sound-symbol correspondences. To read the word *duck*, children must recognize each symbol, connect the corresponding sounds or phonemes, and blend them together to form the word.

In the process, they utilize the repertoire of skills we call phonological processes. The phonological awareness and proficiency required to segment and blend phonemes in words is honed over hours of explicit instruction and repeated practice. Extensive research confirms the effectiveness of direct sound-symbol instruction on the development of phoneme awareness and decoding skills (Adams, 1990; Lundberg, 1991; Stanovich, 1991; Torgesen et al., 1999). This evidence demonstrates that children benefit most when common structures of sounds are explicitly taught, particularly when special attention is paid to distinctions between onsets, such as *d*, rimes, such as *uck*, and syllable patterns (Goswami & East, 2000). Instruction which provides this phonological foundation alongside multiple exposures to common orthographic patterns results in more efficient word recognition.

Phonological and orthographic knowledge are not the only linguistic components key to reading fluency. Rich semantic knowledge both plays a significant role in children's reading comprehension and impacts fluent word recognition. Semantic knowledge refers both to the size of a vocabulary, and also to the strength and depth of individual word knowledge (Frishkoff, Collins-Thompson, Perfetti, & Callan, 2008). Think of the multiple meanings of the word *duck*. When functioning as a noun, it represents a web-footed, swimming bird; as a verb, it means to avoid. In fact, a great many of the most common children's words have more than one meaning. The more knowledgeable children are about a word, its multiple meanings, and various pragmatic and syntactic contexts of use, the more rapidly the word is processed during reading (Locker, Simpson & Yates, 2003). As a result, children can move into more sophisticated text-level reading with greater fluency and thus, have more time for understanding. In short, the semantic system not only affects the speed of accessing the word, but also has an impact on the deeper comprehension of text.

The implications of this conclusion are significant. Investigations into "word poverty" (Moats, 2000) and the effects of impoverished word environments have demonstrated the significant and long-term impact of a child's vocabulary size on his or her reading comprehension (Stanovich, 1985). Moats (2001), for example, estimates that there is a significant word gap between lower and higher income children who enter 1st grade. The significance of this finding is brought home by Biemiller (2005) who found that kindergarten children with a vocabulary in the bottom 25% remain behind in vocabulary and comprehension into middle school and often beyond.

Related to both semantic and orthographic knowledge is the least studied linguistic component of reading—morphological awareness—which refers to the conventions that govern word formation, and the ways in which roots and affixes create new word meanings. For example, adding the suffix morpheme *s* to the root *duck*, creates the plural noun *ducks*; adding *ing* creates the present participle *ducking*; adding *ed* creates the past verb form *ducked*. Such morphological knowledge also provides disambiguating syntactic information (e.g., *ed* rapidly clarifies that *ducked* is the verb form). In addition, because the role a word has in sentence structure helps determine its meaning, this collective morphosyntactic information aids comprehension.

Morphological awareness is particularly important in English, which is a *morphophonemic* language that represents both morphemes and phonemes in its spelling. Words that are irregularly spelled no longer seem as arbitrary in their spelling when children understand their morphemic roots. For example, the word *muscle* connects this seemingly irregularly spelled word to its basic roots. In so doing, it illumines the semantic relationships among words like *muscle*, *muscular*, and *musculature* (see Chomsky & Halle, 1968). From this perspective, by conveying semantic, syntactic, and orthographic information, morphological knowledge contributes to the development of spelling, faster word recognition, and fluent comprehension.

Another less emphasized component in fluency intervention concerns syntactic knowledge. Knowledge of how words are used within different grammatical or syntactic contexts is essential for the child's fluency and comprehension, along with a variety of increasingly sophisticated sentence constructions and literary conventions.

In sum, what does the young human brain learn to do when it reads a single word? It uses an exquisitely precise visual system to recognize letters and familiar *letter patterns*; it connects this information to the stored, corresponding *phonemes*; and almost simultaneously, it connects this same information to the *meaning(s)* of the word, to its *grammatical* uses, the potential *morphemes*, and how this word is used in social contexts (i.e., *pragmatic* knowledge). Most importantly, the brain must retrieve, connect, and integrate all this information in a fraction of a second to have time to comprehend the word in text.

RAVE-O Intervention

The RAVE-O program is an innovative reading program whose purpose is to teach the young reading brain how to build up and connect all these sources of visual, cognitive, and linguistic information and rapidly retrieve them during reading. Based on theoretical accounts of reading fluency and comprehension (Wolf & Katzir-Cohen, 2001), the program attempts to simulate what the brain does when it tries to read a single word with fluency and comprehension. RAVE-O's basic premise is that the more the child knows about a word (i.e., phonemes, orthographic patterns, semantic meanings, syntactic and pragmatic uses, and morphological roots and affixes), the faster the word is decoded, retrieved, and comprehended. RAVE-O is not so much a wholly new program, as it is the application of some best teaching practices and some newly-designed practices to systematically address multiple linguistic, cognitive, and affective systems.

Each week children learn all the relevant phonological, orthographic, semantic, and syntactic content for a small group of core words and learn to make explicit connections across these linguistic systems. Making these connections is key to re-enacting what the brain's "reading circuit" does. For example, with the word *jam*, the instructor first reviews the individual phonemes, /j/ + /a/ + /m/, and then teaches the child to find the chunks in *jam*: that is, the *rime* (the part of the syllable that consists of the vowel and any consonants that come after the vowel) (/am/) and the *onset* or beginning consonant (/j/). This step consolidates sound-level knowledge and connects it to letter patterns. In turn, this knowledge is immediately connected to the semantic base. The word *jam* possesses at least three common meanings and can be used in different syntactic contexts (as noun and verb). Moreover, *jam* can be easily changed by the addition of different morphemes (e.g., jams, jamming, unjammed) to show how words can change but still have their root visible. The uniqueness of RAVE-O is that explicit attention is given to learning and connecting each of the five major linguistic components in every word, in every unit.

The overall structure of the RAVE-O curriculum emphasizes systematic instruction with a repeating format within each unit and each individual lesson. The general movement is from accuracy to speed: from the multicomponential introduction of words, through activities that build accuracy in letter-pattern and word recognition, to building speed and understanding in ever increasing levels of complexity in words and connected text. Games and activities exemplify the progression from activities that emphasize accuracy of retrieval early in the unit to speed of retrieval by the end of the unit. For example, a variety of activities and games are used to enhance the child's ability to connect multiple linguistic processes. *Spelling-Pattern Cards* are small color-coded cards that are divided into starters, rimes, and affixes and teach phoneme patterns and morphemes. *Speed Wizards* is a set of computerized games designed to reinforce these same sets of processes at different levels of complexity and three speeds of recognition. *Word Webs* is a regularly recurring semantic exercise that provides a simple, visual way of illustrating how words are interconnected and that gives visual images to aid memory. All of these game-like activities offer whimsical means to teach children to connect individual phonemes, to orthographic units, to meanings, to uses. In turn, these connections facilitate rapid decoding and comprehension processes and improve spelling along the way.

A range of metacognitive strategies (called *Magic Tricks*) enables children to segment the most common orthographic and morphological units in words. The tricks are quick, often humorous mnemonics that teach key strategies about words. For example, the strategy called "Ender Benders" helps children quickly recognize common morpheme endings that "bend" (i.e., change) the word's meaning. The "Think Thrice" comprehension trick is a set of three comprehension strategies to enhance the child's prediction, comprehension-monitoring, and analytical and inferential skills.

Within every unit, fluent comprehension for connected text is addressed through metacognitive comprehension strategies implemented with a series of specially written RAVE-O *Minute Stories*. The stories' controlled vocabulary incorporates the phonemic and orthographic patterns, multiple meanings, and varied syntactic contexts of core words. The *Minute Stories* are multipurpose vehicles for facilitating more automatic rates within phonological, orthographic, syntactic, and semantic systems at the same time that they reinforce connections across these systems. In the process, the stories build overall fluency and comprehension skills. An important affective dimension in these stories is that the content provides a platform for exploring feelings struggling readers often have about learning to read.

Although these tricks and emphases on word play may appear deceptively fun-filled, what we hope to achieve with them is very serious. Children who are struggling readers need to learn the interconnected nature of words, and they usually don't. These strategies are elaborated in the weekly lessons for the teachers and provide a foundation for many of the most important comprehension skills used in all later learning. The end goal of RAVE-O, therefore, is ultimately not about how rapidly children read, but about *how well they understand and enjoy what they read.*

Summary of Results

The effects of RAVE-O with struggling readers have now been studied for 10 years in three research contexts: 1) a pull-out intervention during the school day; 2) an intensive summer-school remediation program; and 3) an after-school intervention. In each of these studies, RAVE-O is combined with a systematic phonological analysis and blending program (such as SRA Reading Mastery or Orton-Gillingham) and taught to small groups of four children.

Recent results come from a three-city, federally funded (National Institute for Child Health and Human Development), randomized treatment-control study. In this study, children who represented the most impaired readers in grades 2 and 3 were randomly assigned to four treatment conditions and were controlled for socioeconomic status (SES), race, and IQ. Each group received 70 hours of treatment throughout the school year. Each of the sessions had one-half hour with a phonological decoding program. RAVE-O and another theoretically multidimensional treatment (PHAST; see Lovett's extensive work in references) went beyond a phonological approach to include different multidimensional emphases in the second half-hour. Specifically, PHAST employed multiple emphases on phonological, orthographic, and morphological processes, as well as distinctive metacognitive strategies for word identification and comprehension.

We compared the effects of the four types of treatment on an extensive battery of tests on all aspects of reading—from accuracy and fluency in word attack to comprehension—and on many language measures. When compared to a control group receiving a math treatment, the RAVE-O group and the PHAST group outperformed the control group on every measure. When compared to a group who received only the systematic phonological analysis and blending treatment, the RAVE-O and PHAST groups again proved better on every measure. When compared to PHAST, RAVE-O made similar significant gains on standardized measures of decoding, and superior gains on the GORT-3 Oral Reading Quotient, a combined fluency and comprehension score, and on measures of vocabulary and semantic flexibility (see overview in Morris, Lovett, Wolf, et al., submitted 2009). In other words, students who received instruction in programs that emphasized multiple dimensions of linguistic knowledge, performed equally well or better on every word attack and word identification measure (the specific emphases of the more unidimensional decoding treatment). RAVE-O also outperformed all other treatments in vocabulary and the GORT fluency-comprehension measure.

The theoretical implications of these outcome data are critical. The premise of RAVE-O is that the plural linguistic emphases will enhance decoding, as well as vocabulary and comprehension. The fact that RAVE-O spent far *less* time on specific decoding skills and yet made comparable or superior gains in word attack and word identification to programs that spent more of their instructional time on these skills is compelling evidence supporting the theoretical premise of RAVE-O: the more the child knows about a word, the faster and better the word will be decoded and understood.

In addition, and very importantly, this NICHD study demonstrated that impaired reading children could make significant gains in reading regardless of initial SES, race, or IQ factors (Morris et al., submitted 2009; Wolf et al., 2009). The latter set of results cannot be overemphasized. It suggests that despite these known impediments to achievement, the two multidimensional interventions produced similar gains in children from privileged and unprivileged backgrounds regardless of IQ level or race. This result directly answers the question whether the linguistic demands in RAVE-O are too heavy for children in poverty or for children with lower cognitive aptitudes.

In fact, these results point to the success and the importance of explicit emphases on the multiple dimensions of language in our interventions. They also raise the issue of assessing and knowing the needs of each individual child before deciding what type of intervention is most appropriate. There are no silver bullets or one best program. Future analyses by our NICHD group will examine differential treatment response by subtype. Understanding research on different forms of remediation—what works best for which child and when—is like having a "tool-box" from which to create better-tailored teaching. It is not that many of our children can't learn to read; it is that we haven't found the right ways to teach them. The onus is upon us, their teachers, not the children, to find ways that work. Within that context, our collective findings underscore that explicit teaching of multiple linguistic systems propels our teachers and our students.

References

Adams, M. J. (1990). *Beginning to read: Thinking and learning about print*. Cambridge, MA: MIT Press.

Biemiller, A. (2005). Size and sequence in vocabulary development: Implications for choosing words for primary grade vocabulary instruction. In A. Heibert & M. Kamil (Eds.), *Teaching and learning vocabulary: Bringing research to practice* (pp. 223–242). Mahwah, NJ: Erlbaum.

Chomsky, N., & Halle, M. *Sound Pattern of English*. New York: Harper and Row, 1968. Reprint. Cambridge, MA and London: The MIT Press, 1991.

Frishkoff, G. A., Collins-Thompson, K., Perfetti, C. A., & Callan, J. (2008). Measuring incremental changes in word knowledge: Experimental validation and implications for learning assessment. *Behavioral Research Methods 40*(4), 907–925.

Goswami, U., & East, M. (2000). Rhyme and analogy in beginning reading: Conceptual and methodological issues. *Applied Psycholinguistics, 21*, 63–93.

Locker, L. Jr., Simpson, G. B., & Yates, M. (2003). Semantic neighborhood effects on the recognition of ambiguous words. *Memory & Cognition, 31*(4), 505–515.

Lovett, M. W., Borden, S. L., DeLuca, T., Lacerenza, L., Benson, N. J., & Brackstone, D. (1994). Treating the core deficits of developmental dyslexia: Evidence of transfer-of-learning following phonologically- and strategy-based reading training programs. *Developmental Psychology, 30*(6), 805–822.

Lovett, M. W., Lacerenza, L., & Borden, S. L. (2000). Putting struggling readers on the PHAST track: A program to integrate phonological and strategy-based remedial reading instruction and maximize outcomes. *Journal of Learning Disabilities, 33*(5), 458–476.

Lovett, M. W., Lacerenza, L., Borden, S. L., Frijters, J. C., Steinbach, K. A., & Palma, M. D. (2000). Components of effective remediation for developmental reading disabilities: Combining phonological and strategy-based instruction to improve outcomes. *Journal of Educational Psychology, 92*(2), 263–283.

Lundberg, I., & Höien, T. (1991). Initial enabling knowledge and skills in reading acquisition: Print awareness and phonological segmentation. In D. J. Sawyer & B. J. Fox (Eds.), *Phonological awareness in reading: The evolution of current perspectives* (pp. 73–95). New York: Springer-Verlag.

Moats, L. (2000). *Speech to print: Language essentials for teachers*. Baltimore, MD: Paul H. Brookes.

Moats, L. C. (2001). Overcoming the language gap. *American Educator, 25*(2), 4–9.

Morris, R., Lovett, M., & Wolf, M. (submitted 2009). Treatment effects of multidimensional approaches to reading intervention in children with reading disabilities.

Pugh, K. R., Sandak, R., Frost, S. J., Moore, D., & Mencl, W. E. (2005). Examining reading development and reading disability in English language learners: Potential contributions from functional neuroimaging. *Learning Disabilities Research & Practice, 20*(1), 24–30.

Sandak, R., Mencl, W. E., Frost, S. J., & Pugh, K. R. (2004). The neurological basis of skilled and impaired reading: Recent findings and new directions. *Scientific Studies of Reading, 8*(3), 273–292.

Stanovich, K. E. (1985). Explaining the variance in reading ability in terms of psychological processes: What have we learned? *Annals of Dyslexia, 35*, 67–96.

Stanovich, K. E. (1991). Changing models of reading and reading acquisition. In L. Rieben & C. A. Perfetti (Eds.), *Learning to read: Basic research and its implications* (pp. 19–31). Hillsdale: Erlbaum.

Tan, L. H., Spinks, J. A., Eden, G. F., Perfetti, C. C., & Siok, W. T. (2005). Reading depends on writing in Chinese. *Proceedings of the National Academy of Sciences, 24*, 8781–8785.

Torgensen, J., Wagner, R., Rashotte, C., Rose, E., Lindamood, P., Conway, T., et al. (1999). Preventing reading failure in young children with phonological processing disabilities: Group and individual responses to instruction. *Journal of Educational Psychology, 91*(4), 579–593.

Wolf, M., & Katzir-Cohen, T. (2001). Reading fluency and its intervention. *Scientific Studies of Reading (Special Issue on Fluency), 5*, 211–238.

Wolf, M. (2007). *Proust and the squid: The story and science of the reading brain*. New York: Harper Collins.

Wolf, M., Barzillai, M., Gottwald, S., Miller, L., Spencer, K., Norton, E., et al. (2009). The RAVE-O Intervention: Connecting Neuroscience to the Classroom. *Mind, Brain, and Education, 3*(2), 84–93.

3

Phonological Awareness, Word Recognition, and Spelling

Marcia Henry

Section 3 focuses on the importance of instruction in phonological awareness, word recognition (decoding), and spelling (encoding) for children with specific learning disabilities. Recent and current research show that children who do not master the alphabetic code and with it, reading and spelling competence, often first show deficits in phonological awareness followed by difficulty learning to read and spell.

In the first article in this section, Benita Blachman, Darlene Tangel, Eileen Ball, and Rochella Black describe an 11-week phoneme awareness training conducted by kindergarten teachers, followed by a 1st grade reading program (extended to 2nd grade in some cases) for children in the treatment group. Children receiving this multisensory instruction exhibited a significant advantage in reading at the end of 1st and 2nd grades.

In the next article, Pamela Hook grounds spelling instruction within the context of writing processes in the early grades. She illustrates classic multisensory strategies for phoneme awareness, alphabetic spelling, and structural analysis (morphology) based on four kinds of words in English orthography (i.e., words regular for reading and for spelling, words regular for reading but not for spelling, rule- or generalization-based words, and irregular words.

Barbara Chorzempa, Steve Graham, and Karen Harris discuss their work with the Center to Accelerate Student Learning (CASL) in this section's third article. They developed and tested a sequence of instructional techniques that significantly enhanced spelling performance in second graders in four urban schools.

In the final article in this section, I stress the etymology (origins) of English words. As most English words stem from Anglo-Saxon, Latin, or Greek languages, I provide characteristics of words in each origin and emphasize the importance of learning the morpheme patterns (e.g., prefixes, suffixes, and roots), especially as children move beyond one syllable words as they progress in the upper grades.

Because phonological awareness, word recognition, and spelling all play important roles in early literacy, this section holds critical interest for reading educators. Each article contains strategies based on current research findings that will be useful for teachers and tutors in general and special education settings.

Combining Phonological Awareness and Word Recognition Instruction

Benita A. Blachman, Darlene M. Tangel, Eileen Wynne Ball, and Rochella Black

Many recent studies have shown that instruction in phoneme awareness helps children acquire early reading and spelling skills. Phonological awareness instruction, combined with instruction that connects the phonological segments to letters, enables more children to master early decoding than programs that lack these components. Practice with phoneme segmentation, blending, and manipulation also enhances early spelling and accelerates the rate at which children learn to read new words in text. Children who learn how print maps to speech and who can apply that knowledge in kindergarten or 1st grade are more likely to become good readers than children who remain dependent on contextual guessing strategies. This article describes the specific techniques we have used to obtain significant improvements in reading with low-income, inner-city children (Blachman, Ball, Black, & Tangel, 1994; Blachman, Tangel, Ball, Black, & McGraw (1999).

The first phase of our project involved an 11-week intervention carried out by kindergarten teachers; the second phase examined the effects of a follow-up 1st grade reading program that emphasized explicit, systematic instruction in the alphabetic code. At the end of both 1st and 2nd grades, treatment children outperformed control children in phonological awareness, letter-sound knowledge ,and word recognition. Control children were taught with the Scott Foresman basal reading program, with workbooks and trade books as supplements. The instructional procedures described below were associated with superior outcomes for children in the treatment group.

Kindergarten Intervention Program

The 11-week kindergarten phoneme awareness training program conducted by the teachers and their assistants was adapted and expanded from an earlier 7-week version of this program (Ball & Blachman, 1988). Each 15- to 20-minute lesson consisted of three parts: a) say-it-and-move-it phoneme segmentation activities; b) segmentation-related activities; and c) letter name and letter sound training. The segmentation activities incorporated suggestions found in the phoneme awareness literature (e.g., Bradley & Bryant, 1983; Elkonin, 1973; Liberman & Shankweiler, 1979). The say-it-and-move-it activities were designed to teach children to segment words into phonemes. Children were taught to move disks from the top half of an 8 1/2 by 11 inch card to the bottom half to represent the phonemes in one-, two-, and three-phoneme items. First, children learned to say and represent single sounds (e.g., /i/), then repeated sounds (e.g., /i/ /i/), then two phoneme items (e.g., *it*), and finally three phoneme items (e.g., *lip, sun*).

Initially, continuous sounds were used in the initial position to reduce the distortion of the sounds in the segmentation activity. During the fourth week of instruction, one or two letters (beginning with the letter *a*) were put on the tiles of only those children who had mastered both the name and sound of the letter. The letters were selected from among the eight letters introduced during the intervention (*a, m, t, i, s, r, f, b*). The children who were ready for the letter tiles could use a combination of letter tiles and blank tiles, or they could continue to use all blank tiles to segment a word. During the eighth week of instruction, children who had mastered several letter names and sounds were given enough letter tiles to produce a consonant-vowel-consonant real word (e.g., *bit*) during the segmentation activities. Thus, during the final 3 weeks of instruction (during the last twelve, 20-minute lessons), selected children were exposed to a small pool of real words. The children in each group who had not mastered letter names and sounds continued to use blank tiles throughout the intervention.

The segmentation-related activities included activities involving various degrees of segmentation. For example, a sound categorization task that was similar to the task used by Bradley & Bryant (1983) was included in this part of the lesson. In this task, children were asked to group words on the basis of rhyme or alliteration. In another segmentation-related activity, modeled after Elkonin (1973), children were given booklets containing pictures of objects representing simple consonant-vowel-consonant words (e.g., *fan, sit, lip*). Underneath each picture was a series of boxes representing the number of phonemes in the word. Children learned to say the word slowly and simultaneously move a disk to the appropriate box to represent each phoneme in the word.

A third part of each lesson involved direct instruction in letter names and letter sounds. The results of previous phoneme awareness training studies suggest that phoneme awareness instruction may have a greater influence on early reading and spelling when connections are made between the sound segments of the word and letters representing those segments (Blachman, 1989; Bradley & Bryant, 1983). Eight letters were included in our intervention, *a, m, t, i, s, r, f, b*. These letters were selected because combinations of these letters generate a significant number of real words, using the consonant-vowel-consonant pattern. Illustrated alphabet cards were used to reinforce initial sounds. For example, the *r* card had a picture of a red rooster in red running shoes and the *t* card showed two teenagers talking on telephones. Children also played a variety of games (e.g., Bingo) to reinforce sound-symbol associations.

Grade 1 Reading Program

The 1st grade reading program for the treatment children (described below) was provided in place of and not in addition to the basal reading program used with other children in this district. The length of each lesson (30 minutes) was consistent with the length of time both treatment and control classroom teachers reported spending with each of their reading groups. Children receiving the treatment approach, when compared to the control group, did not receive any extra time devoted to reading instruction in 1st grade.

Treatment children began the 1st grade year with a review of the phoneme awareness and letter sound activities presented in kindergarten. To help teachers accommodate individual differences, guidelines for the 1st grade reading program were prepared at three different levels. One level was for groups needing minimal review of the kindergarten activities (1 to 2 weeks at the beginning of the school year). One level was for groups needing a longer review period (4 to 6 weeks), and another level was for children needing an extensive review and gradual transition to the 1st grade reading program (about 12 weeks). In addition to phoneme segmentation activities and games used during kindergarten, the 1st grade review and transition phase included introducing all letter sounds (not just the eight sounds introduced during the kindergarten program), using selected workbook pages for the first time for additional practice connecting letters to sounds, and learning some high frequency words that would appear in the early readers (e.g., *I*, *to*, *said*). Following the review and transition phase, the 1st grade reading program for the treatment children consisted of a daily, 30-minute, five-step reading program (adapted from Blachman, 1987) that continued to reinforce phoneme awareness skills and emphasize the alphabetic code.

Although groups began the 1st grade five-step reading program at different times in 1st grade (depending on the number of weeks spent in phonological awareness and sound-symbol review activities), once the five-step program began, the group followed the steps described below:

1. Each lesson began with a brief and quick-paced (1 to 2 minutes) review of sound-symbol associations learned in previous lessons and the introduction of new sound-symbol correspondences. For this part of the lesson, teachers utilized a sound pack (set of cards) containing each of the graphemes (letters and letter clusters) being reviewed. To highlight the vowels, vowel letters were printed in red.

2. The second step in the program was instruction in phoneme analysis and blending skills. To avoid the pitfalls of the letter-by-letter blending strategy that teachers often use, a blending technique adapted from Englemann (1969) was utilized. In the typical approach used to teach blending, children are taught to attack an unknown word by sounding it out letter-by-letter (e.g., /b/ /a/ /t/) and then blending it to produce the word. However, it is impossible with this approach to recover the original word, *bat*, regardless of how quickly the child tries to blend the sounds together (Liberman & Shankweiler, 1979). The Engelmann procedure avoids much of the distortion that comes with trying to produce sounds in isolation. Children were taught to pronounce as a single unit a consonant (continuant) followed by a vowel. To begin, the teacher represented this strategy on the board as shown in Figure 3.1.1:

Figure 3.1.1.   **Strategy Representation**

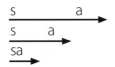

The teacher pointed to the first letter, and the child was taught to produce that letter's sound and hold the sound until the teacher's finger reached the second letter. When her finger touched the second letter, the second sound was produced and held. With each successive practice opportunity, the length of time between sounds was decreased until the two sounds were pronounced as a single unit. By adding final consonants (initially, stop consonants) and pronouncing the whole word, a set of real words was built (e.g., *sat*, S*am*). Words containing new short vowels also were introduced in this manner. Depending on the needs of the group, this activity was used for a few days or a few weeks and then eliminated from the lessons.

A second phoneme analysis and blending technique was used throughout the 1st grade year to help children learn to synthesize sounds without resorting to letter-by-letter blending. Adapted from a technique suggested by Slingerland (1971), each child used a small pocket-chart, which we called a "sound board," to manipulate letters and form words. Consonants and vowels previously mastered by the children were written on individual letter cards and placed in the top pocket. First, the teacher pronounced a word, such as *fat*, emphasizing the medial vowel sound. Then, children repeated the word, listened for the vowel sound, and selected the appropriate vowel grapheme card (vowels were color coded) from the top pocket and placed it in the lower pocket. The teacher then repeated the word and asked the child to select the letter that represented the first sound in the word and place it in the appropriate position (in front of the vowel) in the bottom pocket. The teacher pronounced part of the word saying, "Now we have *fa*. Our word is *fat*. What is the last sound we hear in *fat*?" The child then selected the *t* and placed it at the end of the word. The whole word was then read either by an individual child or by the group.

Once the child was successful representing words in this fashion, phoneme manipulation was introduced. For this task, the child might be asked to change *fat* to *fan* and, when new vowels were mastered, change *fan* to *fin*. A later lesson might require changing *fin* to *shin* and, eventually, as new syllable types were introduced on the sound board, changing *shin* to *shine*.

3. The third activity in this five-step plan gave children the opportunity to develop more automatic recognition of words that they had practiced previously on the sound board. Once they could construct and accurately read a pool of phonetically regular words on the sound board, these words were put on flash cards and the children practiced reading them quickly. High frequency words that have to be memorized, such as *said*, were selected from stories the children would be reading and were also introduced at this time. These words were written in a different color. For approximately 2 to 3 minutes daily, children prac-

ticed reading both phonetically regular words and irregular, high frequency words. The goal of this quick-paced activity was to build automaticity.

4. Next, children engaged in 10 to 15 minutes of reading connected text. Children read phonetically controlled readers from the Primary Phonics series published by Educators Publishing Service, and selected stories from the Scott Foresman basal reading series used throughout the school district. (None of the other materials, such as workbooks, from the Scott Foresman series were used.) Each classroom also had trade books for independent reading at other times during the day, and children went to the school library for additional reading materials. Although the materials used during the 30-minute reading lesson were consistent across treatment groups, treatment teachers were free to use whatever books they thought appropriate for the rest of the day. There was considerable variation across classrooms.

5. The last step of each lesson included a short writing to dictation activity. Generally, four to six words and a sentence were dictated. Teachers dictated words drawn from word lists that were practiced on the sound boards or words encountered in the phonetically controlled readers. Children were directed to print vowel headings at the top of each dictation page (e.g., *a* and *i*, or later, ai, oa, ea). These headings represented the particular vowel sounds that were the target sounds for that day's lesson. The dictation activity gave teachers an opportunity to evaluate student progress on the target sounds for the day. The dictation notebooks became a record of student growth over the 1st grade year, as both students and their teachers could review the progress that was made as students progressed from writing and reading simple closed syllable words (e.g., *ham*) to more complex patterns (e.g., *hike, rain*).

By the time children completed the program, they had been introduced to words representing all six syllable types, including closed (*fat, flat*), final e (*cake, shine*), open (*me, cry*), vowel team (*pain, teach, crawl*), vowel + r (*burn, start*), and consonant le (*bottle, table*). Although the focus of many of the early activities was on developing accurate and automatic word recognition skills, vocabulary development and comprehension were not neglected. Teachers were encouraged to make sure that children knew the meaning of all words they were asked to read or spell, and comprehension of stories was developed using a variety of strategies (e.g., re-tellings, making predictions). As the children progressed through the program and were able to recognize more words, more time in each lesson was devoted to reading new stories and rereading old ones. To continue to stay within the time allocated for reading groups, it was suggested to teachers that they begin to alternate the use of the sound board and dictation, using the sound board 2 days per week and dictation 3 days per week. This allowed more time for reading connected text.

We found that children who participated in our phonological awareness program in kindergarten, followed by a 1st grade reading program (extended to grade 2 for some children) that built on this awareness and emphasized explicit instruction in the alphabetic code, demonstrated a significant advantage in reading at the end of grades 1 and 2. Our findings reinforce the conclusions of many researchers that during the early stages of reading acquisition, "instruction that facilitates both phoneme awareness and alphabetic coding is vitally important to success" (Vellutino, 1991, p. 442).

Acknowledgements

This article is adapted from Blachman et al. (1994) and Blachman et al. (1999). The research was funded by a grant from the National Center for Learning Disabilities.

References

Ball, E. W., & Blachman, B. A. (1988). Phoneme segmentation training: Effect on reading readiness. *Annals of Dyslexia, 38*, 208–225.

Blachman, B. A. (1987). An alternative classroom reading program for learning disabled and other low achieving children. In R. Bowler (ed.) *Intimacy with language: A forgotten basic in teacher education* (pp. 49–55). Baltimore, MD: Orton Dyslexia Society.

Blachman, B. A. (1989). Phonological awareness and word recognition: Assessment and intervention. In A. G. Kamhi & H. W. Catts (eds.) *Reading disabilities: A developmental language perspective* (pp. 133–158). Boston: College-Hill Press.

Blachman, B. A., Ball, E. W., Black, R. S., & Tangel, D. M. (1994). Kindergarten teachers develop phoneme awareness in low-income, inner-city classrooms: Does it make a difference? *Reading and Writing: An Interdisciplinary Journal, 6*, 1–18.

Blachman, B. A., Tangel, D. M., Ball, E. W., Black, R. S., & McGraw, C. K. (1999). Developing phonological awareness and word recognition skills: A two-year intervention with low-income, inner-city children. *Reading and Writing: An Interdisciplinary Journal* (pp. 239–273).

Bradley, L., & Bryant, P. (1983). Categorizing sounds and learning to read: A causal connection. *Nature, 30*, 419–421.

Elkonin, D. B. (1973). U.S.S.R. In J. Downing (ed.), Comparative reading (pp. 551–580). New York: MacMillan.

Engelmann, S. (1969). Preventing reading failure in the primary grades. Chicago: Science Research Associates.

Liberman, I.Y., & Shankweiler, D. (1979). Speech, the alphabet, and teaching to read. In L. B. Resnick & P. A. Weaver (eds.), *Theory and practice of early reading, Vol.2* (pp. 109134). Hillsdale, NJ: Lawrence Erlbaum Associates.

Slingerland, B. H. (1971). *A multisensory approach to language arts for specific language disability children: A guide for primary teachers*. Cambridge, MA: Educators Publishing Service.

Vellutino, F. R. (1991). Introduction to three studies on reading acquisition: Convergent findings on theoretical foundations of code-oriented versus whole-language approaches to reading instruction. *Journal of Educational Psychology, 83*, 437–443.

Transcription Processes Related to Spelling
Intervention Strategies

Pamela E. Hook

Writing is a complex process involving functions related to planning, translating, and reviewing (Hayes & Flower, 1980). Berninger and Swanson (1994) have defined translation processes as involving transcription (spelling, punctuation, and handwriting) and text generation (language formulation and memory). Difficulties in these transcription processes interfere with efficient and coherent written formulation (McCutchen, 1995). The focus of this article is on transcription issues related to spelling. Prerequisites for spelling include the abilities to
- analyze and sequence the sounds in syllables and words (phonemic awareness)
- map letter patterns on to sound patterns (alphabetic spelling)

- retrieve the motor patterns to form the letters that represent the word
- recall specific orthographic patterns (orthographic retrieval)

Phonemic awareness pertains to phonological awareness of the sound structure of one's language at the single phoneme level and the abilities to segment, blend, and manipulate those sounds. Phonemic awareness is different from *phonics*, an instructional approach that emphasizes letter-sound correspondences in the teaching of reading and spelling. *Orthography* is the total writing system of a language and also refers to specific spelling patterns.

Uta Frith's (1985) theory of spelling development highlights the changing importance of phonological and orthographic processing skills as children acquire automaticity in spelling. She notes that children learn to spell alphabetically (through the analysis of speech sounds and the application of phonics) before they learn to spell orthographically. Spelling is more difficult than reading in that it requires retrieval of orthographic patterns, while reading relies on recognition of those patterns.

It is more difficult to learn to spell English than languages with more transparent orthographies (more direct letter-sound correspondence) such as Spanish. Thus, English instruction requires more emphasis on developing strong orthographic representations. In general, instructional programs that have been found to be most effective for children with language learning difficulties are characterized by
- explicit teaching of concepts;
- systematic and structured sequence;
- multisensory presentation (involving visual, auditory and tactile/kinesthetic modalities); and
- extensive opportunities for review and practice.

> " It is more difficult to learn to spell English than languages with...
> more direct letter-sound correspondence..."

Programs sharing these characteristics are often referred to as *multisensory structured language (MSL)* approaches.

In order for teachers to develop a systematic approach to teaching spelling, it can be helpful to think of four kinds of words in English orthography:

Type 1: regular for reading and for spelling (e.g., *dig*, *sprint*)– unambiguous spelling to sound relationship

Type 2: regular for reading but not for spelling (e.g., *boat*–could be *bote*, *plain*–could be *plane*)–unambiguous for reading but ambiguous for spelling

Type 3: rule or generalization based (e.g., *planning* = doubling rule; *back*, *badge*, *batch* = based on -ck, -tch, -dge generalization)

Type 4: irregular [e.g., *beauty* (note: most of this word is regular – only eau is irregular)]

Students must learn to recall all four types of words automatically in order to be effective spellers; thus, techniques for developing strong orthographic representations for each type of word are essential. Type 2 words (ambiguous: *rain, light*) and Type 4 (irregular: *friend*) for spelling place much more strain on the orthographic memory system as well as the lexical association system because there are no rules governing their spelling. For example, in order to know if the spelling is *pain* or *pane*, or to know that *friend* is spelled with *ie*, requires one to memorize the orthographic pattern in relationship to its meaning.

Spelling Type 1 Words: Regular for Reading and for Spelling (e.g., *dig*, *sprint*)

Because English orthography is semi-alphabetic in nature, there are many words that are Type 1 (regular for reading and spelling). In early stages, skills in reading and spelling develop in parallel: if a word is regular for spelling, it is also regular for reading. These words can be spelled through the application of alphabetic strategies (letter-sound correspondence). Thus, teaching of reading and spelling can go hand in hand. When word Types 2 and 3 are introduced (ambiguous; rule based for spelling but regular for reading), learning to read often moves at a faster pace and ultimately reach a higher level than spelling.

Phonemic Awareness

In order to learn alphabetic spelling skills, students must develop phonemic awareness (See Figure 3.2.1). A strong base in phonemic awareness allows for the development of alphabetic spelling and ultimately, orthographic spelling (the ability to spell words automatically as wholes). For many students phonemic awareness develops naturally, beginning in the preschool years and continues to develop in a synergistic manner with sound-symbol skills with the introduction of phonics in kindergarten and 1st grade. Some students, however, have difficulty developing phonemic awareness and need to be taught this skill in a structured and systematic way.

There are many techniques designed to teach phonemic awareness but, for the purposes of discussion, I will focus on two here. The Russian psychologist, David Elkonin, devised a technique for developing phoneme awareness that specifically addresses segmentation and blending skills. It first uses tokens to represent sounds, then, once sound-symbol correspondence has been established, the instructor can move to letters representing those sounds (i.e., phonics). The student segments the word or word part into sounds (phonemes) while moving a token down to a segmented line or series of boxes for each sound in the word. While running her finger under the tokens, the student then reblends the sounds and pronounces the word. (See Figure 3.2.2.)

Figure 3.2.1.   **Development of Spelling**

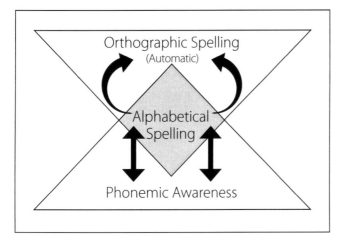

Figure 3.2.2.   Say-It-and-Move-It

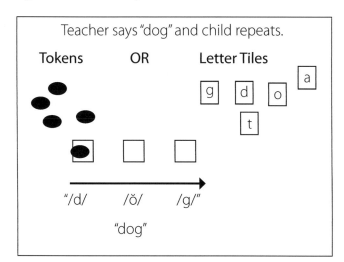

Teacher says "dog" and child repeats.

Tokens   OR   Letter Tiles

"/d/   /ŏ/   /g/"

"dog"

This "Say-It-and-Move-It" activity can be systematically adjusted to represent words of increasing phonemic complexity (e.g., multi-syllabic words for syllable segmentation, or individual words or word parts for segmentation at the phoneme level [VC, CVC, CCVC, CCVCC, and CCCVC]) depending on an individual student's abilities. Say-It-and-Move-It is an example of a classic phonemic awareness teaching method that employs all the aspects of multisensory structured language techniques: explicit training of segmentation and blending, systematic and sequenced instruction, ample opportunity for practice, and multisensory delivery (involving motor movement as well as visual and auditory processing). (One of our students had the highly successful strategy of pasting pictures of Leonardo DiCaprio on the tokens for a fourteen-year-old girl.) Words for Say-It-and-Move-It can be taken from texts that the children are reading or that will be read to them. In addition, word parts (sometimes referred to as *pseudo-words* or *nonsense syllables*) can be used to further increase phonemic awareness skills. Word parts can be particularly helpful in working with older students who may otherwise over-rely on orthographic knowledge of simple CVC words to help them complete the task.

A second technique often employed to increase phonemic awareness uses chains of words or word parts that vary in only one phoneme (e.g., ip ➔ ap ➔ tap ➔ pat ➔ past ➔ pats). This technique is based on the kinds of errors that struggling readers and spellers often make: substitutions, additions, reversals, omissions, and transpositions. Activities train the student to monitor exact correspondence between auditory and visual patterns. Students manipulate colored blocks (or letters, once letter-sound correspondence has been introduced) to make changes in the visual pattern where they hear the changes in the auditory pattern. (For example, for spelling, the teacher says, "If that says *ip*, make it say *ap*" and the student would change the colored blocks to represent the change in auditory pattern.) A number of published programs contain systematic use of this technique (e.g., Lindamood & Lindamood, 1998; Telian, 2001; Clark-Edmunds, 1998).

Alphabetic Spelling

Although phonemic awareness is not the same thing as phonics (one being auditory in nature and the other involving letter-sound correspondence), interventional training methods that combine phonemic awareness with direct instruction in how letters map on to sounds (phonics) are more effective than phonemic awareness instruction alone (Ball & Blachman, 1991). Although phonemic awareness is critical for developing alphabetic spelling strategies, a direct link to letter-sound correspondence is important.

The order in which letter-sound correspondences should be taught varies from one program to another but a structured sequence is essential for a student who struggles. Many programs first teach high frequency letters that are not visually or auditorily similar to avoid unnecessary confusions (e.g., *s, t, m* will be easier than *b, d, p* in that the fomer are both visually and auditorily distinct). However, other programs choose a sequence based on how sounds are produced in the mouth and therefore would present *p/b* and *t/d* early on because the sounds that these letters represent vary in only one aspect, voicing. Thus, it is not one particular order that is necessary but instead a consistent systematic sequence that is important.

A common technique employed by multisensory structured programs is the use of tactile kinesthetic cues to aid in recall of letter-sound correspondences. These programs often use techniques such as tracing on a rough surface or sky writing to help solidify the associations between the auditory, visual, and tactile-kinesthetic modalities. See Gillingham A. and Stillman B. (1997) for an in-depth discussion of this type of approach. Other programs use tactile-kinesthetic cues from the tongue and lips to help students identify what their mouth is doing when producing sounds (See Lindamood & Lindamood, 1998; Telian, 2001; Weiss-Kapp, 2005). They organize sounds into "minimal pairs" based on similarities in articulation and varying only in voicing (for example, /p/-/b/, /d/-/t/, or /k/-/g/) or other characteristics as being "nose" sounds (/m/-/n/-/ng/). This develops strong awareness of the phonological structure of spoken language, which is key for spelling.

Many programs use mnemonics to help children learn letter-sound correspondences. Orton Gillingham based programs often use a key word with a picture to aid recall of these associations. For example, children learn to respond with the letter name, keyword, and sound in response to a card showing the letter and picture (i.e., they would say, "/o/, octopus, /ŏ/" in response to the letter card for *o* to develop associations for the short sound of *o*). Other programs (Telian, 2001; Weiss-Kapp, 2005) use stories, pictures, mouth shape cues, and voicing characteristics to help with memory. For example, in the *Lively Letters* program, letters are grouped by articulatory characteristics and become individuals with personalities: when introducing the consonant pairs *b* and *p*, to avoid problems with reversals, the students are told that the line always comes first (reading from left to right), reminding them to first put their lips together and then puff them out; the *b* is described as having a circle down low like a little baby who makes lots of noise (voiced), while the *p* is described as a tall mother with the circle up high, telling her baby to be quiet (unvoiced). (See Figure 3.2.3.)

Alphabetic strategies do not, however, end with learning letter-sound correspondence—the

Figure 3.2.3.   **Meaningful Story Cards**

Telian, *Lively Letters*, 2001

application of this knowledge to reading and spelling words is critical. Once some sound-symbol correspondences have been taught, students are asked to read and spell words using those letters. Type 1 words (regular for reading and spelling) can be presented and practiced.

Many MSL programs present spelling patterns based on six syllable types: closed (not), open (no), silent e (note), vowel combination (moat), r controlled (part), and consonant-le (noble). Moats (2000) provides an in-depth discussion of these syllable types, and Carreker (1992) as well as Moats and Rosow (2003) provide examples of a systematic scope and sequence. Open and closed syllables are generally regular for reading and spelling but other syllable types are ambiguous for spelling (Type 2 words). For example, /tāl/ can be written *tail* or *tale* depending on the meaning and /gōt/ could be written as *goat* or *gote* and still be consistent with English orthographic patterns. Students with adequate phonemic awareness and orthographic memory are able to invoke these associations automatically, with little or no conscious effort. However, students with poorly developed phonemic awareness and weak orthographic memory have difficulty seeing, hearing, and remembering these patterns and benefit enormously from systematic instruction in the structure of English orthography and how it maps onto English phonology.

Spelling Type 2 Words: Regular for Reading but Ambiguous for Spelling (e.g., *boat*–could be *bote*)

One way to teach ambiguous words (Type 2) is to combine associative verbal learning strategies and visualizing and verbalizing techniques. This strategy capitalizes on the often stronger ability of the student with learning disabilities to remember meaningful information (concept images) than to recall arbitrary non-meaningful letter strings (symbol images). When utilizing a visual associative spelling technique, students semantically associate words with similar orthographic patterns (*ai* words versus *a-e* words: *sail, pail, tail, mail,* etc. /*sale, pale, tale, male,* etc.); students form a meaningful visual image and describe the image verbally (e.g., a visual image of a little girl named *Gail* who is carrying a *pail* at the beach with her dog—she looks at the ocean and sees a *sail* boat on the water—she starts to run and steps on the dog's *tail*—this causes *pain* so he walks with a funny *gait* …"). This strong visual image enables them to recall the correct spelling of a set of orthographically similar words associated with their image. Fischer (1999) has developed a similar technique in which students draw pictures of their images.

> "…for spelling multi-syllable words…awareness of the morphological structure of language has proven to be helpful."

Spelling Type 3 Words: Rule or Generalization Based

Many words in English follow orthographic rules that can be very helpful for learning to spell Type 3 words. Several of these rules revolve around the vowel sounds, particularly short vowels. For example, the spelling of *chatting, stitch, lodge,* and *smack* involves the application of rules or generalizations related to single syllable words with short vowels; these words contain an extra consonant after the single short vowel. Armed with the four most common spelling rules [f-l-s-z (muff, tell, mass, buzz); doubling (run +ing = running); drop e (skate + ing = skating); change y (candy + es = candies)] and a handful of generalizations [when to use –ke versus –ck (back/bake); -ge versus –dge (rage/badge); –ch versus –tch (ranch/ batch)], students can spell a large number of words that would otherwise elude them. Most of the MSL programs have systematic presentations of these orthographic rules.

Spelling Type 4 Words: Irregular (e.g., *beauty*)

Typical MSL strategies for increasing orthographic memory important for irregular words are tracing or writing while naming letters. Fading of letter cues while copying, simultaneously naming letters and then ultimately writing from memory (busy: b _ sy, b_ _ y, b _ _ _, _ _ _ _, _____) can also strengthen the orthographic representation. In addition, "air writing" may be employed to create an afterimage to enhance memory; the students then close their eyes and attempt to answer orthography-specific questions such as, "What is the fourth letter in *their*?" (Bell, 1997).

Irregular words can also be approached through strategies that involve: 1) over articulating words to help access correct spelling (e.g., Wednesday = wed nes day or February = feb ru ary); 2) grouping words with the same root where the silent letter is actually pronounced (e.g., two/twice; sign/signal; bomb/bombard; column/ columnist; mnemonic/amnesia; crumb/crumble): or 3) creating meaningful associations (e.g., the princi*pal* is your *pal*).

Structural Analysis

Alphabetic spelling is heavily dependent on awareness of the structure of language at the level of phonology. However, for spelling multisyllable words (more than one or two syllables), awareness of the morphological structure of language has proven to be helpful. This involves understanding prefixes, stems and suffixes (the meaningful units of language or morphemes) and rules that govern the spelling of multi-syllabic words. While there are extremely large numbers of syllables, there is a finite number of prefixes, stems, and suffixes. These recur in many words (e.g., *export, import, transport; repeat, reflect, retract*) and also have meaning (*ex* means *out of* and *port* means *to carry*); thus, the task of creating orthographic representations to aid spelling is easier and the study of morphology can also be used to enhance vocabulary knowledge.

Many programs divide English words based on their origin, Anglo-Saxon, Latin, or Greek. Anglo-Saxon based words tend to be higher frequency and deal with everyday life *(helpfully, forgetful)*, while Latin-based words are often associated with government or law *(constitution, transportation, structure)* and Greek with math, science, and the theater *(biology, parallel, proscenium)*. Often words evolving from these different languages have specific spelling patterns related to prefixes, stems, and suffixes. For example, in a word like *contemptuous*, although the prefix *con* and much of the root *tempt* is regular for spelling, other parts of the word are quite difficult. Thus, knowing that the word comes from Latin, the spelling of the suffix *ous* will be accessible as will the representation of the /ch/ sound as *t* followed by *u* (ligatured tu). The *u* in this case is a "connective"–in Latin based words connectives *u* and *i* connect the suffix with the root (*i* says /ee/ and *u* says its long sound)–e.g., familial, continuous. With this knowledge, what seemed an impossibly complex word becomes quite manageable.

Another example of how strategies related to morphological structure can be helpful is the rule that explains why there are two *l's* in the word *illustrate*. To enhance pronunciation, the last letter of the prefix (i.e., *in*) changes to the first letter of the stem *(lustr)*. It is easier to say "illustrate" than "inlustrate" and the change is marked orthographically. This rule also allows students to recognize that *il* is in fact the prefix *in* meaning *in* or *into*. There are also specific spelling patterns that are characteristic of words that have evolved from different languages. For instance, that Latin-based words do not contain the letter *k*; or, knowing that the word *psychology* comes from Greek, students can understand that it is spelled with the Greek root *psych* (related to the mind) and the suffix *ology* (the study of) and are thus not surprised that the vowel sound /i/ is spelled with a *y* and that /k/ is spelled with *ch* since these patterns are common in Greek words. In addition, Greek-based words have other characteristics; for example, /f/ is spelled *ph* (physical, autograph), -*cian* is used to signify a person (physician, magician) and many Greek words have to do with science (chlorine, pachyderm, chemist). See Henry (1995) and Steere, et al., (1988) for systematic sequences for teaching structural analysis strategies.

Conclusions

Spelling English can seem an insurmountable task for students who struggle with underlying processing skills related to transcription (phonemic awareness and orthographic memory). However, strategies for strengthening these skills and systematic instruction in the structure of English orthography can be quite helpful. Students presented with this information often remark, "If only someone had shown me this before."

References

Ball, E., & Blachman, B. (1991). Does phoneme awareness training in kindergarten make a difference in real world recognition and spelling development? *Reading Research Quarterly, 26*, 46–66.

Bell, N. (1997). *Seeing Stars.* San Luis Obispo, CA: Gander Educational Publishing.

Berninger, V., & Swanson, H. (1994). Modifying Hayes and Flower's model of skilled writing to explain beginning and developing writing. In J. S. Carlson (Series ed.) & E. C. Butterfield (Vol. Eds.), *Advances in cognition and educational practice, Vol. 2: Children's writing: Toward a process theory of the development of skilled writing.* Greenwich, CT: JAI Press. 57–81.

Carreker, S. (1992). *Scientific Spelling.* Houston, TX: Neuhaus Education Center.

Clark-Edmands, S. (1998). *Specialized Program Individualizing Reading Excellence (SPIRE).* Kennebunk, ME: Progress Learning, Inc.

Fischer, P. E. (1999). *Concept Phonics.* Farmington, ME: Oxton House.

Frith, U. (1985). Beneath the surface of developmental dyslexia. In L. Patterson, J. Marshall, & Coltheart (Eds.), *Surface dyslexia* (pp. 301–303). London: Erlbaum.

Gillingham, A., & Stillman, B. (1997). Remedial training for children with specific disability in reading, spelling, and penmanship (Orton Gillingham). Cambridge, MA: Educators Publishing Service.

Hayes, J., & Flower, L. (1980). Identifying the organization of writing processes. In L. W. Gregg & E. R. Steinberg (eds.), Cognitive processes in writing. Hillsdale, NJ: Erlbaum. 3–30.

Henry, M. (1995). *WORDS: Patterns of success in reading & spelling*. Austin, TX: Pro-Ed.

Lindamood, C., & Lindamood, P. (1998) *The Lindamood Phoneme Sequencing Program (LiPS)*. Columbus, OH: SRA Division, Macmillan/ McGraw-Hill.

McCutchen, D. (1995). Cognitive Processes in children's writing development and individual differences. *Issues in Education: Contributions from Educational Psychology, 1*, 2:123–160.

Moats, L. (2000). *Speech to print: Language essential for teachers.* Baltimore: Paul H. Brooks.

Moats, L., & Rosow, B. (2003). *Spellography.* Longmont, CO: Sopris West.

Steere, A., Peck, C., & Kahn, L. (1988). *Solving language difficulties.* Cambridge, MA: Educators Publishing Service.

Telian, N. (2001) *Lively Letters.* Stoughton, MA: Telian-Cas Learning Concepts, Inc.

Weiss-Kapp, S. (2005), *WKRP: Reading by the rules.* Arlington, MA: Dearborn Academy.

Strategies for Teaching Spelling to Students with Learning Disabilities

Barbara Fink Chorzempa, Steve Graham, and Karen R. Harris

Learning to write is a complex process, involving the development of a host of writing skills and processes as well as knowledge about writing and the topics of writing (Graham, in press). Some of these skills, processes, and knowledge must be learned to the point where they can be executed with little conscious effort, whereas others, such as planning and evaluation, require thoughtful and reflective application (Bos & Vaughn, 1994). Although we do not fully understand all of the mechanisms involved in the development of skilled writing, research during the past two decades has identified two areas of development that are especially problematic for struggling writers, including students with learning disabilities. One, these students often experience difficulty mastering the strategic processes underlying skilled writing, including planning, monitoring, evaluating, revising, and so forth (Graham, in press). Two, the acquisition of skills such as handwriting and spelling, which must be learned to the point of near automaticity, present a considerable challenge for many of these children (Graham, 1990). Problems mastering basic text transcription skills, such as spelling and handwriting, can be particularly troublesome for beginning writers and children with learning disabilities. Having to devote considerable attention to how to form letters or spell words correctly minimizes the cognitive resources available for carrying out other important writing processes, such as content generation, planning, and revising, which also exert considerable demands on attention as well (Graham, 1990; McCutchen, 1996; Scardamalia, Bereiter, & Goleman, 1982).

In this article, we concentrate on just one part of the writing disabilities puzzle — enhancing the spelling performance of young struggling writers. While this singular focus is not enough to overcome a writing disability in most cases, it is an essential element for students who experience difficulty mastering this skill. First, a writer's message can be blurred or misconstrued because of spelling errors, as exemplified by this primary grade student's statement: "My mom makes the best choklit mouse." Second, perceptions about writing competence can be influenced by a child's poor spelling. As Marshall and Powers (1969) found, students' papers with more spelling miscues were assigned lower marks for writing quality than papers with few or no spelling errors. Third, a child's development as a writer can be constrained due to early problems with spelling. These difficulties may lead young children to avoid writing; cultivating a mindset that they cannot write (Berninger, Mizokawa, & Bragg, 1991; Graham, 1999). Finally, the influence of spelling difficulties extends beyond writing, as knowledge obtained through learning how to spell enhances the ability to read words (Adams, 1990).

<blockquote>"Problems mastering basic text transcription skills, such as spelling and handwriting, can be particularly troublesome for beginning writers and children with learning disabilities."</blockquote>

The instructional program described here was designed to strengthen the spelling development of the weakest spellers, including students with learning disabilities, in second grade classrooms in four urban schools. The instruction was provided as a supplement (or in addition to) the spelling instruction children were already receiving in the regular classroom. Our goal was to teach students basic spelling words, skills, and strategies in order to improve their spelling, writing, and reading performance.

The CASL Spelling Program

As part of our work with the Center to Accelerate Student Learning (CASL), a federally funded grant involving Vanderbilt University, Columbia, and the University of Maryland, we developed and tested an instructional program designed to teach children common sound/letter combinations (e.g., consonants, blends, digraphs), spelling patterns or phonic generalizations involving short and long vowels, and frequently used rimes that fit these patterns (Graham, Harris, & Fink Chorzempa, 2002). The instructional program consists of 48 twenty-minute lessons divided into 8 units; each unit focuses on two or more spelling patterns reinforcing knowledge of short vowels sounds, long vowel sounds, or both (see Table 3.3.1).

For each unit, the six lessons follow a set pattern that includes seven different activities. Students are engaged in a word-sorting activity (Graham, Harris, & Loynachan, 1996) during the first lesson of each unit. This activity helps students learn the pattern or generalization emphasized in the unit. For example, in unit 4, students sort words into categories that fit the pattern for CVC-type words that contain the short vowel sound /o/ (e.g., *not*) and for CVCe-type words containing the long vowel sound of /o/ (e.g., *note*).

Unit Spelling Patterns

1. Short vowel sound for /a/, /e/, and /i/ in CVC type words
2. Short vowel sound for /o/ and /u/ in CVC type words
3. Short vowel sound for /a/ in CVC type word. Long vowel sound for /a/ in CVCe type words
4. Short vowel sound for /o/ in CVC type word. Long vowel sound for /o/ in CVCe type words
5. Short vowel sound for /i/ in CVC type word. Long vowel sound for /i/ in CVCe type words
6. Short vowel sound and /ck/ at the end of monosyllabic words. Long vowel sound and /ke/ at the end of monosyllabic words
7. Adding the suffix **ed** to monosyllabic words with a short vowel or long vowel sound
8. Adding the suffix **ing** to monosyllabic words with a short vowel or long vowel sound

The lesson begins by having the teacher place a master word card for each category next to each other, pronouncing each master word. Next, the teacher says the word again, this time emphasizing the target feature. The students are then asked how the master words are similar and different. Students' attention is directed to critical features, such as the different sound the vowel makes in each of the master words and the silent /e/ in the CVCe master word.

The teacher then begins modeling the process of sorting other word cards with the CVC and CVCe pattern (with the vowel *o*) under the appropriate master word. First the students are told they are going to be looking at other words and deciding in which category they should place each word, with the goal of trying to figure out why the letter *o* makes the short /o/ sound in *not* and the long /o/ sound in *note*. From a pack of 12 cards (with an equal number of words that fit each pattern), the teacher draws a card and pronounces the word, emphasizing the target feature. The teacher thinks aloud about where to place the word and then places it under the appropriate category. This is modeled for the students until students understand the process, and then they are encouraged to place the remaining words in the appropriate categories, thinking aloud as they do so. If an error occurs, the teacher shares his or her thoughts on where to place the word and then moves the card into the appropriate category.

After all the cards are placed, students are asked to derive a generalization from the patterns, with the teacher providing assistance as needed. (The term *generalization* is used instead of *rule* because a *rule* to children is something that should not be broken. However, in the English language there are many exceptions and thus the term *generalization* is more accurate.) Once the generalization or pattern is established, students are asked to generate their own words, write them on a blank card, and place them in the correct category. If an exception word is generated and misplaced (e.g., *love* is placed in the CVCe category), a new category is started, using a question mark to designate this category. This helps to teach or reinforce (depending on a student's background knowledge) that there are exceptions to the patterns or generalizations.

If time remains in the first lesson, students repeat the word sort with a peer, including words they generated themselves. The lesson concludes with the teacher asking students to search for words that fit the target patterns when reading and writing at other times during the day (activity two). Students share any words they've located in lessons two through five.

During the second lesson of each unit, four activities are completed. First, students participate in a 2-minute phonics warm-up activity designed to improve their skills in correctly identifying the letter(s) corresponding to sounds for short vowels, consonants, blends, and digraphs (activity three). After the warm-up activity, the generalization for the current unit is reviewed, and students are asked to share words they found in their reading and writing that fit the pattern.

Also during lesson two, each student is assigned a list of eight spelling words to study over the course of the unit, emphasizing the patterns in that unit (activity four). These words should be words that are common in students' writing (see Graham, Loynachan, & Harris, 1993, for a list of these words). Once the words are assigned, each student practices the words using a procedure called "graph busters." This involves the students using a taught strategy to spell their words and then graphing the number of words written correctly. The strategy involves the following steps: 1) say the word and study the letters; 2) close your eyes and say the letters; 3) study the letters again; 4) write the word three times without looking at it; and 5) check the spellings and correct any mistakes. During subsequent lessons (lessons three and five), graph busters is used for students to equal or beat their previous score.

For the last activity of lesson two, students participate in a word building activity (activity five) in which a rime (e.g., op) corresponding to one of the features or patterns (e.g., short /o/ sound) is introduced. The teacher first models how to build words by adding onset cards (containing either a consonant, blend, or digraph) to this rime, and then students are asked to identify real and nonsense words using these cards. The students work together to identify as many real words as they can, using approximately 18 onset cards of which at least 10 make a real word.

Procedures during lesson three are identical to those in lesson two, the only exception being that a new rime is introduced during the word building activity. Lesson four is also similar to lesson two. The only differences involve the introduction of a new rime during the word building activity and the use of a game instead of "graph busters" as the study procedure for the assigned spelling words. The procedures for the games are as follows. First, students work in pairs to play a game (e.g., Tic-Tac-Toe), requiring the children to produce the correct spelling of a word to complete a move. To play, each student is given his or her partner's spelling list and the partner reads one of the words for the student to spell. The child can either spell the word orally or write the word on paper. If the spelling is correct, the child is permitted to make a move; but if the word is not spelled correctly, the partner reads the correct spelling and the student writes the correct spelling. The student does not move until spelling a word correctly on the first try.

For lesson five, there are only two differences in the basic format established in lesson two. First, the teacher can decide to use either "graph busters" or the game format to facilitate the study of the assigned spelling words. This option is provided to teachers because some students may need the stronger review provided by graph buster before they take the unit test. The second difference occurs during the word building activity, as students work in pairs to generate as many words as they can using the three rimes and onset cards introduced during lessons two, three, and four.

On the final lesson of the unit, lesson six, students complete a unit test to determine if they have mastered the eight words they studied during the course of the unit (activity six). After taking the test, students correct any misspelled words and then graph their performance on the eight spelling words they studied. If they correctly spell all eight words, they set a goal to do as well on the next unit test. If one or more words are missed, students are encouraged to set a goal to do better on the next unit test and record this on the graph as well. If a goal for the unit test is met, the teacher places a big star on the graph. To conclude this lesson, a brief review of the word patterns or generalizations presented in prior units is conducted using the rimes emphasized during those units (activity seven). If time permits, the phonics warm-up activity is completed as well.

Expected Student Outcomes

Graham et al. (2002) tested the effectiveness of this spelling program with 54 second-grade children who were experiencing difficulties learning to spell, many of whom also had problems learning to read and write. Forty percent of these students had also been identified as having a disability (i.e., learning disability, attention deficit hyperactivity disorder, developmental disability, behavior disorder, and speech or language problems).

Performance of the children receiving the supplemental spelling instruction was compared to 2nd-grade students in a control condition who received math instruction from the same teachers. Students participating in the spelling program made greater gains in spelling, sentence writing skills, and reading word attack skills immediately following instruction. Improvements in word recognition skills were also made by students with the weakest word reading skills at the start of the study.

Current practices in literacy reflect the need for systematic, explicit instruction in phonics; it is our belief the same holds for spelling. If problems with writing fluency in the primary grades lead toward writing difficulties in the upper grades as Berninger and her colleagues (Berninger et al., 1991) suggest, then supplemental spelling programs such as the one we have described may become necessary for children with spelling and learning difficulties. If you are interested in obtaining the manual for the CASL program, please contact Steve Graham at steve.graham@ vanderbilt.edu

References

Adams, M. (1990). *Beginning to read: Thinking and learning about print.* Cambridge, MA: MIT Press.

Berninger, V., Mizokawa, D., & Bragg, R. (1991). Theory-based diagnosis and remediation of writing disabilities. *Journal of School Psychology, 89,* 57–*97*.

Bos, C., & Vaughn, S. (1994). *Strategies for teaching students with learning and behavior problems, 3rd ed.* Needham Heights, MA: Allyn and Bacon.

Graham, S., (in press). Writing. In P. Alexander & P. Winne (Eds). *Handbook of educational psychology*. Mahwah, NJ: Erbaum.

Graham, S. (1990). The role of production factors in learning disabled students' compositions. *Journal of Educational Psychology, 82,* 781–791.

Graham, S., (1999). Handwriting and spelling instruction for students with learning disabilities: A review. *Learning Disability Quarterly, 22,* 78–98.

Graham, S., Harris, K. R., & Fink Chorzempa, B. (2002). Contribution of spelling instruction to the spelling, writing, and reading of poor spellers. *Journal of Educational Psychology, 94,* 669–686.

Graham, S., Harris, K. R., & Loynachan, C. (1996). The directed spelling thinking activity: Applications with high frequency words. *Learning Disabilities Research and Practice, 11,* 34–40.

Graham, S., Loynachan, C., & Harris, K. R. (1993). The basic spelling vocabulary list. *Journal of Educational Research, 86,* 363–368.

Marshall, J., & Powers, J. (1969). Writing neatness, composition errors, and essay grades. *Journal of Educational Measurement, 6,* 97–101.

McCutchen, D. (1996). A capacity theory of writing: Working memory in composition. *Educational Psychology Review, 8,* 299–325.

Scardamalia, M., Bereiter, C., & Goleman, H. (1982). The role of production factors in writing ability. In M. Nystrand (Ed.), *What writers know: The language, process, and structure of written discourse* (pp. 173–210). New York: Academic Press.

3.4

Spelling Instruction in the Upper Grades
The Etymology/Morphology Connection

Marcia Kierland Henry

IN their review of reading research, McCardle and Chhabra (2004) state, "In international comparison, U. S. children do not on average perform badly in the early years; if international comparisons are taken as our guide, the reading crisis is one of adolescent literacy, not one of first-to-fourth-grade literacy" (xx). I believe the same might be said for spelling. Teachers are often ambivalent about spelling. On one hand they bemoan the poor spelling of many students, and on the other hand they ask if it is really important for children to learn to spell accurately. I often hear statements such as "Why bother teaching spelling? Students can use the spell checkers on their computers as they write." Yet, with over 10 million websites listed as dealing with *spelling*, and over one third of those listed under *spelling instruction*, (www.Google.com, March, 2005) one assumes that spelling is important to many people.

The focus of this article is spelling instruction in the upper elementary and secondary grades. Experience over four decades, along with current research on spelling, provides evidence for the efficacy of teaching the structure of English orthography (the spelling system) as well as the etymology (the word origin) of many words (Hanna, Hodges, & Hanna, 1971; Henderson, 1990; Henry, 1988, 2003). Word structure includes the many patterns available to students such as letter-sound correspondences, syllable types, and morphemes (the compound words, prefixes, suffixes, bases, and roots). Word origins reflect historical events in language. English words come primarily from Anglo-Saxon, Latin, and Greek origins. Knowing the differences in words from these origins provides a logical basis for teaching spelling.

I've always been fascinated with the end of school year national spelling bee. The moderator gives a student a word such as *physiologist*. Then the student may ask the moderator to pronounce the word again, and may ask the origin of the word, the part of speech, and the definition. Let's consider why knowing the origin and part of speech would be especially helpful in a word like *physiologist*. When told that the word is of Greek origin, the learned student will know to spell the /f/ with ph and the /ĭ/ with y as that is what happens in most Greek-based words. Knowing the word is a noun provides the clue to the final suffix. The student will choose –ist knowing the schwaed suffix is spelled –ist as a noun (e.g., *chemist, pianist, dentist, physiologist*) and –est as an adjective (e.g., *greenest, fastest, slowest, happiest*).

The Role of Etymology

Lederer (Personal correspondence, 2004) estimates that 25% of English words are the short, common, everyday Anglo-Saxon words, often with Germanic and Norse influence, that we use about 65% of the time in our speaking and writing. The Latin-based words make up about 50% of English words; these are usually poly-syllabic words containing prefixes, roots, and suffixes. Approximately 10% of our English words come from the Greek language.

Anglo-Saxon Layer of Language

The first words taught are generally from the Anglo-Saxon layer of language. These are the common, short, down-to earth, everyday words found in primary grade text. These words can be phonetically regular such as *cat, stamp, check*, and *spoil*, or irregular (usually in the vowel spelling) such as *do, done, only, want*, and *friend*. Students need to learn the common spellings for consonants, consonant blends, consonant digraphs, short and long vowels, -r and -l controlled vowels, and vowel digraphs. They also begin to learn the specific terminology applied to graphemes and phonemes.

Latin Layer of Language

Latin-based words, the majority of words in English, are generally polysyllabic; they are the more sophisticated words found in upper elementary and secondary literature and expository text. Latin is the basis for the Romance languages spoken in France, Italy, Spain, Portugal, and Rumania. Latin roots are generally affixed to make words such as *informing, disrupted, conventional*, and *incredulous*. These words contain the same letter-sound correspondences found in Anglo-Saxon based words. Happily those vowel digraphs that are problematic for many spellers occur infrequently in Latin-based words. However, the schwa (ə), the neutral vowel in an unaccented syllable, is often found in the unaccented prefixes and suffixes. The schwa is a problem for most poor spellers, as any vowel may be schwaed.

Greek Layer of Language

Students begin to read Greek-based words in their science and math textbooks around the 3rd grade. These words, like the Latin, use most of the phonics patterns found in Anglo-Saxon words. Several unique letter-sound correspondences must be introduced for the Greek-based words. These include the *ph* for /f/ as in *photograph*, the *ch* for /k/ as in *chromosome*, and the *y* as /ĭ/ as in *physiology* or the *y* as /ī/ in *hydrogen*. Less common spellings such as *pn* for /n/ in *pneumonia*, *rh* for /r/ in *rhinoplasty*, and *pt* for /t/ in *pterodactyl* may also be taught to older students.

The Role of Morphology

Morphemes are the smallest unit of meaning in words. Just as phonemic awareness is important for reading and spelling, those students with morphemic awareness appear to be better spellers (Carlisle, 1987). Although many students develop morphemic awareness without instruction, students with specific reading disabilities often do not.

Anglo-Saxon Morpheme Patterns

Anglo-Saxon base words can either compound or affix. Children learn to combine two short Anglo-Saxon base words to read and spell words like *catfish, lamppost*, and *sailboat*. The first affixes found in text are the inflectional suffixes such as plural *–s*, past tense *–ed*, and adjective or noun *–er*. Additional suffixes and prefixes should be taught to expand the number of words students can read and spell accurately. Students learn that since affixes are often unstressed, the schwa sound is prevalent in prefixes and suffixes. Prefixes taught first since they are added to Anglo-Saxon base words include *in-, un-, mis-, dis-, non-, mid-, fore-, re-, de-, pre-,* and *a-*. Suffixes taught in the early grades include *-s, -es, -ed, -ing, -ly, -er, -en, -est, -less, -ness,* and *-ful.*

Teachers begin instruction by asking children to spell words where suffix addition rules (see Carreker, 2005) are unnecessary. For example: *help, helped, helps, helping, helper, helpful, unhelpful, helpfulness, helpless, helplessness;* or *spell, spelled, speller, spelling, misspell, misspelled, respell, respelling*. They then move on to teach the rules for adding suffixes to words ending in vowel consonant (e.g., *big, sad*), silent final *e* (e.g., *slide, blame*), and *y* (e.g., *try, copy*).

Latin Morpheme Patterns

The Latin word roots are usually perfectly phonetic. Third and fourth graders who know consonant and vowel patterns are ready to learn common roots like *rupt, struct, spect, tract, cred, form, port,* and *fer.* Many of the Latin roots have two, three, or four variants (e.g., *scrib/script, spec/spect, mit/miss, duc/duce/duct, tend/ tens/tent,* and *viv/vivi/vit/vita.*

Additional prefixes and suffixes need to be taught to accompany Latin roots. The major prefixes, in addition to those listed earlier, include *trans-, ab-, ambi-, ante-, anti-, bene-, circum-, ex-, inter-, intra-, intro-, mal-, multi-, pro-,* and *se-.* In addition, several prefixes (called assimilated or chameleon prefixes) have several variants depending on the first letter of the root. For example, *in-,* meaning *in* or *not,* changes to *il-*before roots beginning with an *l* (e.g., *illegible*), to *ir-*before roots beginning with *r* (e.g. *irregular*), and to *im* before roots beginning with *m, b,* and *p* (e.g., *immature, imbibe, imported*). Similar changes occur in the prefixes *con-,* meaning *together* or with; *sub-,* meaning *under* or *below;* and *ad-,* meaning *to* or *toward.* (See Henry, 2003, for additional information.)

Suffixes added to Latin word roots must also be taught systematically. These include *tion-, -sion, -cian, -ture, -ent, ence, -age, -ate, -ous, -or, -ar -ist, -ive, -al, -ible, -ize, -ify,* and *-ity.*

Greek Morpheme Patterns

Many Greek-based words will be found in student's math and science texts. Greek combining forms, or roots, usually compound two word parts of equal stress and importance as in *autograph, hydrometer, telephone, philosophy,* and *monologue.* Affixes may be added to these combining forms as in *photography, photographer,* and *philanthropist.* Important Greek combining forms to teach include: *phon/photo, graph/gram, auto, tele, ology, micro, meter, therm, bio, scope, hydro, biblio, crat/cracy, geo, metro, polis, dem, cycl, derm, hypo, hyper, chron, chrom, phys, psych, techni, lex, path, poly, gon, sphere,* and the number prefixes.

Instruction

As students learn the common Latin roots and Greek combining forms, I encourage teachers to purchase or make drill cards for these word-parts. The cards can be used as visual and auditory drills to achieve automaticity in identifying the morphemes. This automaticity will assist in achieving fluency as students read words containing these morphemes in context. During auditory drills the teacher pronounces the root or affix and the students write the morpheme as they say letter names or sounds.

Present the affixes and roots systematically. Once a few have been introduced teachers can generally present several roots at a time. (See Henry, 2003; Henry & Redding, 2002.) Ask students to generate words containing the target roots you

> " ...learning the frequently used morphemes not only helps students' spelling, but also provides strategies for decoding and for enhancing vocabulary. "

are teaching, provide numerous opportunities to read and spell words, phrases, and sentences containing the target morphemes. As they read their textbooks, see if students can identify words from the various layers of language. The words in Figure 3.4.1 were selected from 3rd and 4th grade social studies textbooks.

Notice how the Anglo-Saxon words both compound (*homestead, redcoat*) and affix (*neighborhood, imprinted, westward, hardship*). The Latin-based words affix to roots with specific meanings such as *port*, to *carry* (*transportation, imported, exported*), and *dict*, to *say* (*dictate, prediction, dictatorship*).

Greek-based words combine two and even three root forms (e.g., *hemi + sphere, demo + cracy, auto + bio + graph*).

Figure 3.4.1. **Textbook Words**

Anglo-Saxon	Latin	Greek
homestead	irrigation	hemisphere
neighborhood	transportation	democracy
imprinted	manufacturing	bicentennial
westward	segregation	meteorology
redcoat	dictatorship	autobiography
hardship	reconstructionist	philanthropist

Teachers should articulate carefully as they dictate spelling words. Students will benefit from using the following process in spelling multisyllabic words:

- Repeat the word dictated by the teacher
- Count the number of syllables
- Say each syllable as the word is written
- Sound out each syllable, if necessary
- Reread the word, phrase, or sentence to check

The Friday Spelling Test

Many teachers feel beholden to the weekly spelling test. Teachers often tell me that parents wouldn't like it omitted. I suggest that teachers design their own spelling test. This alleviates the situation I find in many spelling materials. For example, in one frequently used 5th grade spelling series, a typical lesson included the following words: *straight, favor, sleigh, reins, great,* and *praise*. Note that all these words contain different spellings for /ā/. Most children learn to memorize each word in lists such as this. Henderson (1990) reminded us that while memory plays a role in learning to spell, it does not play the only role. Many children practice words during the week and pass the Friday test, only to be unable to spell them a week or two later.

In contrast, I recommend that teachers select several patterns that they have been teaching in the previous several weeks. Children in the primary grades might be taught final *–ck* and *–tch*. I would tell my students that they will have to think hard about when to use *–ck* and *–tch* in the 15 spelling words that will contain the /k/ and /ch/ sounds. I don't give them the list, but I do review the rule that we use *–ck* when the /k/ sound comes directly after a short vowel at the end of a one syllable word. Similarly, we use *–tch* when the /ch/ comes directly after a short vowel at the end of a one syllable word. The words dictated on Friday might include: *stick, pluck, strike, beak, crock, stroke, flake, stretch, lunch, crutch, stitch, peach, coach,* and *pitch*.

The other 10 words for the spelling test can be words that the students study both at school and at home. However, these words should be relevant to what is being read and written. They may be place names found in geography, or names of people in the literature they are reading. They could be non-phonetic words (often called rote memory words or irregular words) such as *foreign, ocean,* and *colonel*. As students read *Esperanza Rising* (Ryan, 2000) they might be asked to spell Spanish proper nouns such as *Esperanza , Josefina,* and *Aguacalientes*. Other Spanish words such as *campesinos* and *tamales,* along with English words such as *monotonous* and *ritual,* could be added. Words such as *immigration* and *accustomed* would support the learning of chameleon prefixes.

Poor handwriting compounds the spelling problem. While I encourage the use of the computer for compositions, reports, and essays, I believe that upper level students need to learn to use cursive writing. As you teach new roots and affixes, provide models for student to trace and copy in cursive writing. The kinesthetic act of writing supports the spelling-memory of the student.

Conclusion

Learning the common prefixes, suffixes, Latin roots, and Greek combining forms supports Venezky's Principle 6: "Visual identity of meaningful word parts takes precedence over letter-sound simplicity" (Venezky, 1999, p. 6, 197). This statement implies that the morpheme will often be spelled the same even though its pronunciation changes. Examples of this change include *know-knowledge, athlete-athletic, insane-insanity, electric-electricity, sign-signal, breath-breathe,* and *divine-divinity*. Venezky calls this the "...morphophonetic level in the translation from spelling to sound" (p. 197).

Even though the sound changes, the morpheme identity is preserved. In closing, I agree completely with Templeton and Morris (2002) as they refer to spelling instruction based on how words work. They conclude:

> Instructional emphasis is placed on the explorations of patterns that can
> be detected in the sound, structure, and meaning features of words—as
> opposed to the single-minded focus on learning how to spell the 5,000
> plus most frequently occurring words in writing or particular words that
> may be problematic for individual students (p. 103).

Remember, too, that learning the frequently used morphemes not only helps students' spelling, but also provides strategies for decoding and for enhancing vocabulary.

References

Carlisle, J. F. (1987). The use of morphological knowledge in spelling derived forms by learning-disabled and normal students. *Annals of Dyslexia*, *37*, 90–108.

Carreker, S. (2005). Spelling instruction: Foundation of reading and ornament of writing. *Perspectives on Language and Literacy*, *31(3)*, 23–25.

Hanna, P. R., Hodges, R. E., & Hanna, J. S. (1971). *Spelling: Structure and strategies*. Boston: Houghton Mifflin.

Henderson, E. H. (1990). *Teaching spelling* (2nd ed.). Boston: Houghton Mifflin.

Henry, M. K. (1988). Beyond phonics: Integrated decoding and spelling instruction based on word origin and structure. *Annals of Dyslexia*, *38*, 259–275.

Henry, M. K. (2003). *Unlocking literacy: Effective decoding and spelling instruction*. Baltimore: Paul H. Brookes.

Henry, M. K., & Redding, N. C. (2002). *Patterns for success in reading and spelling*. Austin, TX: PRO-Ed.

McCardle, P., & Chhabra, V. (2004). *The voice of evidence in reading research*. Baltimore: Paul H. Brookes.

Ryan, P. M. (2000). *Esperanza Rising*. New York: Scholastic.

Templeton, S., & Morris, D. (2002). Theory and research into practice: Questions teachers ask about spelling. *Reading Research Quarterly*, *34*, 102–112.

Venezky, R. (1999). *The American way of spelling*. New York: Guilford Press.

Fluency in Basic Skills

Marianne Meyer

By now, reading fluency is acknowledged as an important component of a balanced reading program, but it deserves attention, as well, as a topic by itself because slow, inaccurate readers often experience frustration and may avoid reading altogether. Furthermore, comprehension, one of the main goals of reading, is often compromised by dysfluency.

So what is fluency? At its simplest, *fluency* is the rate and accuracy of oral reading or proficiency in word recognition. Other characteristics sometimes included in the definition are smoothness and automaticity of oral reading; rapid, accurate decoding; correct prosody; and anticipatory ability.

Note that the authors of all of the articles in this section emphasize the importance of early screening, assessment, and intervention when fluency problems are detected. Why? Because research has shown that fluency among the poorest readers is notoriously difficult to improve the older a child becomes.

This section of the anthology begins with an article by Jan Hasbrouck who presents a straight forward, teacher-friendly, easy-to-implement method using curriculum-based measurement (CBM) to assess fluency within the classroom setting. This screening or *benchmark* assessment requires measuring rate and accuracy in one-minute intervals on unpracticed, grade-level material, often using several passages. Using data from an impressively large group of 255,000 students in grades 1–8, Drs. Hasbrouck and Tindal (2006) provide norms for the fall, winter, and spring of each grade level. Importantly, for the teacher and clinician, Dr. Hasbrouck also provides guidelines on when teachers should be concerned. Student reading rates +/- 10 words below the 50th percentile should be given a "yellow flag," a practical rule of thumb indicating to the teacher the need for careful observation and possible further assessment.

Pamela Hook and Sandra Jones use their clinical experience to provide useful, specific fluency techniques with the goal of helping students develop efficient reading comprehension. Beginning at the "word level" and proceeding to the "text level," they explain the underlying reason for each technique, creating a coherent framework for teachers. They detail each technique, among them teaching the six syllable types, using symbol imagery, practicing pattern recognition, developing intonation for meaning, chunking and scooping text, and anticipating what comes next in text.

My article, which is based on an earlier one written with Rebecca Felton (1999), looks at the research and history of Repeated Reading (RR), the most commonly used fluency intervention. Traditional RR, in which a student reads a passage aloud until the desired rate of reading (measured in words per minute) is reached, has several variations. This article reports efficacy research on various RR techniques with different populations. Based on the research, 10 concise principles of RR fluency training are enumerated. Finally, three new innovative approaches to improve fluency in elementary through college-age students are discussed.

These three articles provide a good foundation for understanding the major issues and developments in fluency practice and research. However, there continues to be much to be learned in this critical and developing area. Researchers, practitioners, and educational publishers alike are providing more and more relevant material for teachers. The job of the teacher is to use these three articles as a basis for deciding which materials are valid and useful to their students.

Using Oral Reading Fluency as a Benchmark Assessment

Jan Hasbrouck

Curriculum-based measurement (CBM) has a research base that extends over 25 years (see "Progress Monitoring Within a Multitiered Prevention System" by Lynn S. Fuchs and Doug Fuchs in the spring 2007 issue of IDA's *Perspectives on Language and Literacy*) to support its use by teachers to identify students who may need extra help with basic academic skills and to monitor their progress as they receive instruction. CBM for reading, or CBM-R, is a valuable set of procedures that can be used by teachers and specialists to make decisions about students' progress—or lack of progress—in reading.

The act of reading involves processing phonological (phoneme awareness), orthographic (decoding skills), semantic (vocabulary), and context (background knowledge) information through the application of decoding, word recognition, and fluency skills to understand the meaning of written text. The research on CBM-R indicates that results from these quick, fluency-based measures, when administered using a set of standardized procedures, can be interpreted as an accurate indicator of overall skill level in the complex process of reading, not just as an indicator of the development of the fluency component of reading.

> "...current research strongly suggests that early intervention can prevent most reading difficulties."

CBM-R involves assessing students' oral reading fluency by measuring *words read correctly per minute* or *WCPM*. Educators use these procedures in two ways to monitor their students' progress. One procedure is to assess students three times per year and compare the resulting scores to a benchmark score. This procedure, commonly called screening or benchmarking, ensures that all students make sufficient academic progress over the course of the school year to stay on-track for future skill development. If a student's score does not reach the expected benchmark at any point, teachers know to take a careful look to determine if that student might benefit from extra instructional assistance.

A second form of CBM-R is typically used only with students who are already receiving extra assistance with their reading at a supplementary (Tier 2) or intensive (Tier 3) level that would include many students with dyslexia. This form of progress monitoring involves using CBM-R procedures as frequently as once a week. Teachers and specialists graph students' oral reading fluency scores and then use those graphs to evaluate the effectiveness of each student's instructional program.

Defining Benchmarking

Benchmarking is widely used in elementary schools across the country to find students who need extra assistance with reading. Student progress is monitored from fall to winter to spring by having individual students read aloud one, two, or three unpracticed passages at their grade level for 1 minute to a teacher or other trained examiner. The number of passages varies depending on the assessment instrument. Students in kindergarten and the first half of 1st grade read aloud from lists of letter names and letter sounds for 1 minute. Other benchmarking measures have students identify phonemic elements of words presented verbally.

Most schools using benchmarking procedures administer the assessments to every student, despite skill level. This approach ensures that students do not "fall between the cracks" and miss the assistance they need with their reading. This is especially important for students with dyslexia because current research strongly suggests that early intervention can prevent most reading difficulties.

How to Administer Benchmarking Assessments

During the administration of benchmarking assessments, the examiner listens for errors. Each word that is mispronounced, substituted for another word, or omitted is counted as one error. If a student hesitates on a word for more than 3 seconds, that is considered an error. Errors that are self-corrected, words that are read correctly but repeated, and words that are inserted by the student are not counted as errors. A passage score is determined by subtracting the total number of errors from the total number of words read in 1 minute. The resulting score is reported as WCPM. If two or three passages were administered, a final score would be calculated as either the average (mean) or the middle score (median) of the scores. This final score is then compared to a benchmark.

How to Interpret Benchmarking Scores

Some commercially available benchmarking tools such as *DIBELS* (Dynamic Indicators of Basic Early Literacy Skills) and *AIMSweb* have established their own recommended benchmarks by compiling scores from students. Other benchmarking tools, such as *The Reading Fluency Benchmark Assessor,* use the oral reading fluency norms compiled by Jan Hasbrouck and Gerald Tindal (Hasbrouck & Tindal, 2006) (see Figure 4.1.1).

Benchmark scores are calculated by comparing the performance of a group of students on a benchmarking assessment to their future performance on a comprehensive standardized assessment. A benchmark is determined to be the score that predicts which students will likely pass these comprehensive tests. For example, the benchmark score for the DIBELS assessment in the spring of 1st grade is 40 WCPM. This benchmark means that a student reading at least 40 WCPM on the DIBELS 1st grade passage in the spring will likely go on to do well with learning to read and to pass reading assessments in the future. If a student does not reach that benchmark of 40 WCPM, that student will probably need some extra assistance with reading. Additional assessments may also be necessary to determine why this student is falling behind.

Figure 4.1.1.   **WCPM = Word Count Per Minute**

GRADE	PERCENTILE	FALL WCPM	WINTER WCPM	SPRING WCPM
	90		81	111
	75		47	82
1	50		23	53
	25		12	28
	10		6	15
	90	106	125	142
	75	79	100	117
2	50	51	72	89
	25	25	42	61
	10	11	18	31
	90	128	146	162
	75	99	120	137
3	50	71	92	107
	25	44	62	78
	10	21	36	48
	90	145	166	180
	75	119	139	152
4	50	94	112	123
	25	68	87	98
	10	45	61	72
	90	166	182	194
	75	139	156	168
5	50	110	127	139
	25	85	99	109
	10	61	74	83
	90	177	195	204
	75	153	167	177
6	50	127	140	150
	25	98	111	122
	10	68	82	93
	90	177	195	204
	90	180	192	202
	75	156	165	177
7	50	128	136	150
	25	102	109	123
	10	79	88	98
	90	185	199	199
	75	161	173	177
8	50	133	146	151
	25	106	115	124
	10	77	84	97

The Hasbrouck and Tindal (2006) oral reading fluency norms can be used to make similar decisions. These norms were compiled from the WCPM scores of over 255,000 students from across the country, each of whom was given a benchmarking assessment using the standardized CBM-R procedures (unpracticed, grade-level passages read aloud for 1 minute). These norms simply describe the oral reading performance of a very large number of students who read a wide variety of passages. Hasbrouck and Tindal recommend using the 50th percentiles on their chart for benchmarking decisions. If a student's WCPM score is within 10 +/- of the 50th percentile score in the fall, winter, or spring, a teacher can assume that that student is likely on track with reading. A WCPM score more than 10 words below the 50th percentile may indicate that the student is having difficulty with his or her reading and further actions may need to be taken. To be extra vigilant about these important decisions, Hasbrouck and Tindal recommend that WCPM scores that fall in the range between 5 and 10 words below the 50th percentile be considered a "yellow flag" for a student. A student with a WCPM in this range may be on the way to having difficulty with reading and should be observed carefully during instruction.

The following case provides a useful example of the screening decision process. Jessica is in 2nd grade. Her teacher administered a fluency-based benchmarking assessment to each of her students in February to determine if they were making sufficient progress in reading at the midpoint in the school year. She followed standardized procedures and used three different second-grade-level passages that had not been previously read by any of her students for this screening. Jessica's scores on the three assessments were 63, 57, and 59 WCPM. The teacher compared Jessica's median score of 59 WCPM to the Hasbrouck and Tindal (2006) second grade winter scores. The score of 59 WCPM falls 13 words below the 50th percentile score of 72 WCPM, but is 17 words above the 25th percentile score of 42 WCPM. This result indicates that Jessica may not be making adequate progress in reading. Further assessment is warranted to verify this conclusion, in addition to examining Jessica's performance in daily reading lessons and independent work. The teacher realized that Jessica was showing increased reluctance to read, and when called upon to read aloud or answer questions, she often made errors, read with hesitation, or seemed confused by the text. Jessica's teacher decided to investigate further, by conducting one-to-one, second-grade-level skills assessments with Jessica.

Concerns About Benchmarking

Some educators have expressed very strong concerns about benchmarking assessments. How can such a short—60 second—measure, of only one, isolated reading skill—fluency—be used to determine a student's progress in the highly complex linguistic act of reading? (Hamilton & Shinn, 2003). This concern is certainly legitimate and can be addressed in two ways: first, by considering logically the purpose of benchmarking, and second, by examining the research base supporting these assessments.

Purpose of Benchmarking

Educators use oral reading fluency in much the same way that physicians use thermometers. Both are measures that provide a quick "score" that has scientifically proven reliability and validity; that is, when either benchmarking assessments are used to measure student performance (WCPM), or a thermometer is used to measure body temperature (Fahrenheit or Celsius), both provide "scores" that are consistent, accurate, and useful. Moreover, in both cases, the score obtained is compared to a calculated benchmark that is then used as an indicator of general "wellness" (on-track for reading) or "illness" (may need some extra assistance with reading).

Even when using such a precise tool, physicians understand that body temperature does not tell the whole story. If a man comes to an emergency room with a serious injury to his leg, it is likely that one of the first things that will happen is that someone will take his temperature. If it turns out to be in the normal range, the man will not be sent home, because the medical staff is trained to treat body temperature as only one, single indicator of health or wellness. On the other hand, if this same man had a body temperature of 103.7 degrees Fahrenheit, a doctor would not rush him off to surgery to remove his gallbladder. Along with the leg injury, this person may have something else happening in his body. A thermometer reading does not say what is wrong, only that something is wrong. It is only an indicator that the physician should look carefully for a variety of possible causes. In much the same way, it is important for educators to understand that benchmarking assessments provide a score that can be used to indicate academic progress, but professional judgment is necessary for interpreting the score and deciding how to respond.

Research Base

Benchmarking is supported by 25 years of research. The article "Progress Monitoring Within a Multitiered Prevention System" by Lynn and Doug Fuchs, in the spring 2007 issue of *Perspectives on Language and Literacy*, provides an overview of the research base in CBM that provides strong scientific support for using benchmark assessments for making decisions about students' progress in reading. Educators who are concerned about using these assessments should review this research to understand why benchmarking assessments were developed and how to interpret them.

Summary

Oral reading fluency measures have a well-established role in the assessment of students for various purposes. One way to use these measures is for screening a large number of students to determine which ones have achieved a "benchmark" or a certain level of performance, and which students have not yet achieved that level of skill development. When the students who are lagging behind have been identified, appropriate interventions can be determined as quickly as possible. It is vital that as professional educators— teachers and administrators—we understand the tools available for making key decisions about our students. Quick, efficient, and accurate benchmarking assessments can help us find potentially struggling readers as quickly as possible and respond with appropriate instruction. Benchmarking is certainly one important tool that should be in the professional repertoire of every teacher who works with students with dyslexia and other reading problems.

Resources for CBM-R, Benchmarking, and Progress Monitoring

- *DIBELS* (Dynamic Indicators of Basic Early Literacy Skills), http://dibels.uoregon.edu
- EasyCBM System, http://easycbm.com
- Edformation (2004). *AIMSweb* progress monitoring and assessment system, http://www.edformation.com/
- National Center on Student Progress Monitoring, http://www.studentprogress.org
- Read Naturally (2002). Reading Fluency Benchmark Assessor and Reading Fluency Progress Monitor, http://www.readnaturally.com
- Shinn, M. R. (Ed.). (1989). Curriculum-based measurement: Assessing special children. NY: Guilford.
- Shinn, M. R. (Ed.). (1998). Advanced applications of curriculum-based measurement. NY: Guilford.

References

Hamilton, C., & Shinn, M. R. (2003). Characteristics of word callers: An investigation of the accuracy of teachers' judgments of reading comprehension and oral reading skills. *School Psychology Review*, *32*(2), 228–240.

Hasbrouck, J. (2006). Putting fluency in perspective. *Balanced Reading Instruction*, *13*, 9–22.

Hasbrouck, J., & Tindal, G. A. (2006). Oral reading fluency norms: A valuable assessment tool for reading teachers. *The Reading Teacher*, *59*(7), 636–644.

The Importance of Automaticity and Fluency for Efficient Reading Comprehension

Pamela E. Hook and Sandra D. Jones

The reading process involves two separate but highly interrelated areas—word identification and comprehension. It is well established that difficulties in automatic word recognition significantly affect a reader's ability to efficiently comprehend what they are reading (Lyon, 1995; Torgesen, Rashotte, & Alexander, 2001). Even mild difficulties in word identification can pull attention away from the underlying meaning, reduce the speed of reading, and create the need to reread selections to grasp the meaning. Many students who struggle to learn to read are able, with appropriate instruction, to compensate for initial reading problems by becoming accurate decoders but fail to reach a level of sufficient fluency to become fast and efficient readers. Thus, the development of techniques for improving automaticity and fluency is critical. Although the research is clear that a systematic alphabetic approach to teaching beginning and struggling readers is more effective than a whole word approach (Adams, 1990; Chall, 1996; Snow, Burns, & Griffin, 1998), the most effective ways to develop fluency are less well understood. Although current research has given us some direction about effective methods for increasing fluency (National Reading Panel, 2000), further systematic research is needed to give us more comprehensive answers to questions concerning the best methodologies, types of materials, and length/intensity of interventions necessary for optimal gains. The purpose of this article is to suggest some techniques that are consistent with the research and have been found to be either clinically effective or logically appropriate.

What are automaticity and fluency?

Automaticity is defined as fast, accurate, and effortless word identification at the single word level. The speed and accuracy with which single words are identified is the best predictor of comprehension. Fluency, on the other hand, involves not only automatic word identification but also the application of appropriate prosodic features (rhythm, intonation, and phrasing) at the phrase, sentence, and text levels. Wood, Flowers, and Grigorenko (2001) emphasize that fluency also involves anticipation of what will come next in the text and that speeded practice alone is not sufficient. Anticipation facilitates reaction time and is particularly important for comprehension.

What are the relationships among phonemic awareness, phonics, and orthographic reading?

The ability to read fluently develops during Jeanne Chall's Stage 2 of reading, Ungluing from Print, which for most students occurs around 2nd to 3rd grade. (For a complete discussion of Chall's stage theory of reading acquisition, please see Chall, 1983.) This is the last stage where the student is developing skills related to "learning to read" and after this stage, the child will be required to shift to an emphasis on "reading to learn." The type of text being read shifts from being primarily narrative to expository and the language complexity of the written material begins to increase dramatically (including vocabulary level, sentence complexity, and text structure). The importance of background knowledge for comprehension also increases. Fluent reading at this point is essential.

Automatic reading involves the development of strong orthographic representations, which allows fast and accurate identification of whole words made up of specific letter patterns. English orthography is generally alphabetic in nature and initially word identification is based on the application of phonic word attack strategies (letter-sound associations). These word attack strategies are in turn based on the development of phonemic awareness, which is necessary to learn how to map speech on to print. It is important to keep in mind that prior to the stage where children read orthographically, they apply alphabetic strategies to analyze words (Frith, 1985).

Figure 4.2.1 illustrates the relationships among the processes involved in word identification. The bottom of the figure depicts a strong base in phonemic awareness upon which word identification skills are built. There is, however, a reciprocal relationship between the development of phonemic awareness and the development of phonic word attack strategies. As the child becomes more familiar with letters, phonemic awareness also improves. Ultimately, strong underlying orthographic patterns begin to emerge.

Most children go through this process relatively seamlessly, moving easily from the use of alphabetic strategies to the formation of strong orthographic representations that can be accessed automatically. There is, however, a percentage of "at risk" children (approximately 20–40% depending on the specific school demographics) who benefit from having phonemic awareness and phonic word attack strategies systematically taught. There is also a smaller percentage of children who will need more intensive work in this area (See Sanders 2001 for a more in-depth discussion). The children who struggle the most with learning to read also fail to develop adequate automaticity (orthographic reading) and need structured, systematic training in this area. It appears that early preventive intervention may be particularly important in the development of automaticity and fluency (Torgesen et al., 2001).

Figure 4.2.1.   **Relationships Among Phonemic Awareness, Phonics, and Sight Word Recognition Skills**

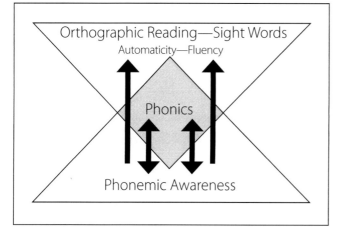

Word-level automaticity: How do we develop this automatic, orthographic reading ability in our students?

Figure 4.2.2. **The Six Syllable Types**

1. **closed**—*not*
   (closed in by a consonant—vowel makes its **short** sound)

2. **open**—*no*
   (ends in a vowel—vowel makes its **long** sound)

3. **silent e**—*note*
   (ends in vowel consonant e—vowel makes its **long** sound)

4. **vowel combination**—*nail*
   (the two vowels together make a sound)

5. **r controlled**—*bird*
   (contains a vowel plus r—vowel sound is changed)

6. **consonant-l-e**—ta/*ble*
   (at the end of a word)

In the Beginning—the Six Syllable Types

One of the most powerful tools to begin instruction in this area is the visual patterns inherent in the six syllable types (Steere, Peck, & Kahn, 1988). (See Figure 4.2.2.)

It is these letter (orthographic) patterns that signal vowel pronunciation. For example, while one or more consonants at the end of a syllable (closed syllable type) signals a short vowel sound, a vowel at the end signals a long vowel sound, etc. Highlighting, underlining, or enhancing the saliency of the visual pattern in some way is recommended to direct the student's attention to the critical components of the orthographic image. Students must become able not only to apply their knowledge of these patterns to recognize the syllable types, but to see these patterns automatically and ultimately read words as wholes rather than through the application of phonic word attack strategies. This need to move from decoding to automatic recognition was recognized years ago by Anna Gillingham when she incorporated the Phonetic Word Cards activity into the Orton-Gillingham lesson plan (Gillingham and Stillman, 1997). This activity involves having the student practice reading words (and some nonwords) on cards as wholes beginning with simple syllables and moving systematically through the syllable types to complex syllables and two-syllable words. The words are divided into groups that correspond to the specific sequence of skills being taught.

Accent

In addition to acquiring phonic word attack strategies, prosodic features at the word level such as stress on syllables are also important. At times, poor readers can accurately decode a word but true recognition of the word eludes them because they have not correctly accented one of the syllables. Dyslexic students often have difficulty hearing the accented syllable in a word, so teachers should first determine if a student is able to discriminate and identify through listening alone. If a student cannot hear differences, lessons should begin with listening practice and then move to oral production. Visual and tactile/kinesthetic strategies can be incorporated with listening if necessary.

A teacher can begin to practice listening for and producing accented syllables using the alphabet. The alphabet is presented in pairs and one letter of the pair is accented until a student is successful. The teacher begins presenting the accent only on the first letter until the student is consistent and then presents the accent only on the second letter. When a student can do both of those successfully, the teacher can then present mixed pairs to practice (e.g., A´B C´D E´F or GH´ IJ´ KL´ or M´N OP´ Q´R). Instruction should move as quickly as possible from using the alphabet to using real words. The teacher can begin with names to practice listening for accented syllables (e.g., *Court´ ney, Mich elle´, Ty´ ler, Je sus´*).

Mirrors can be used for visual reinforcement so students can see that their mouths open wider when they produce an accented syllable. If students need more reinforcement, they can place their hands along their jaw line and feel the jaw opening wider on the accented syllable. Visual signals such as bolding or accent marks can be used to indicate which syllable is accented. Manipulatives such as tokens or blocks can also be used to indicate accent placement by moving the token for the accented syllable higher than the tokens for the unaccented syllables (see Bell, 1997, for a complete description of this approach.)

Training and Linking the Orthographic Processor

Although most students learn to apply the rules of phonic word attack strategies and later of prefix, stem, and suffix through multisensory, structured, systematic teaching techniques and become quite accurate in their reading, many remain slow and laborious. They have trouble moving to the next level of automatic orthographic reading and thus comprehension suffers. Even adults who have seemingly compensated for their reading difficulties still require extended time when taking tests. These students need systematic training in the development of strong orthographic representations that will allow them to read quickly and effortlessly.

Approaches have been developed that use a variety of repeated reading strategies to strengthen these orthographic images. The automatic recognition of single graphemes is a critical first step to the development of the letter patterns that make up words or word parts (Adams, 1990). English orthography is made up of four basic kinds of words: 1) regular for reading and spelling (e.g., *mat, sprint*); 2) regular for reading but not for spelling (e.g. *boat, rain*–could be spelled "bote" or "rane," respectively); 3) rule based (e.g., *planning*–doubling rule, *baking*–drop *e* rule); and 4) irregular (e.g., *beauty*–it should be noted that most parts of an "irregular" word are actually regular and only the irregular part needs to be specifically addressed).

Students must learn to recognize all four types of words automatically to be effective readers; thus, techniques for developing strong orthographic representations for all types of words are essential. Extensive opportunity for repeated practice in pattern recognition is often necessary. In order to strengthen the letter patterns associated with the six syllable types and other rule-based orthographic patterns in English (such as *e, i,* and *y* signaling the pronunciation of *c* and *g*), Fischer (1994) has developed drills to "train the orthographic processor," which involve having the student mark the vowels long or short based solely on the letter patterns contained in the word. They do not actually read these words, but instead focus attention on the letter patterns. The next step is to "link the phonological and orthographic processors," which involves saying only the vowel sound of the words rather than reading the word. Again, the focus is primarily on the orthography. Other ways of emphasizing orthography would be card sorts where students sort different syllable types into appropriate categories as quickly as possible and then say the vowel sounds of each syllable type as quickly as possible.

Single Word-Level Word Drills—Regular and Irregular Words

Once these orthographic signals have become automatically recognized, the students complete speed drills in which they read lists of isolated words with contrasting vowel sounds that are signaled by the syllable type. For example, six to eight closed syllable and vowel-consonant-e words containing the vowel *a* are arranged randomly on pages containing about 12 lines and read for one minute. Individual goals are established and charts are kept of the number of words read correctly in successive sessions. The same word lists are repeated in sessions until the goal has been achieved for several sessions in a row. When selecting words for these word lists, the use of high-frequency words within a syllable category would increase the likelihood of generalization to text reading. (See the SPIRE program, Clark-Edmands, 1998, for word lists based on frequency.)

These same kind of speed drills can be used for irregular words as well as multi-syllable words that incorporate higher-level concepts of structural analysis (prefix, stem, and suffix). At the multi-syllable level, automatically recognizing both the visual patterns related to syllable division as well as prefixes, stems, and suffixes (larger chunks) can be very helpful. The syllable division rules around vccv and vcv syllable patterns can train the student to recognize visual patterns that signal pronunciation. The SPIRE program contains speed drills that at first mark these syllable breaks as well as prefixes and suffixes and then fade the cues as the student progresses through the drill.

Air Writing–Development of Symbol Imagery

In addition to repeated readings of words or word parts, specific techniques have been developed to strengthen the orthographic representations by the use of multisensory activities that link the motor and visual modalities to reinforce the auditory. Tracing, copying, and writing words have long been a part of many multisensory, structured language approaches. (e.g., See Gillingham & Stillman, 1997 and Raines, 1980 for a complete discussion of these techniques.) Sky writing, which involves using gross motor movements of the whole arm to form letters in the air, has also been used to help reinforce single letter formation by combining visual, auditory, and tactile-kinesthetic cues. More recently, an air writing technique has been included as a component of a program intended to improve symbol imagery, or the formation of orthographic representations (i.e., *Seeing Stars* (Bell, 1997)). This technique involves having the student look at a word or word part pronounced by the teacher, name the letters, and use his finger to write the word in the air directly in his visual field while looking at his finger. The student then reads the word from memory and the teacher questions him about the order and placement of specific letters in the word (e.g., "What is the third letter in the syllable?" "What is the second letter?"). The emphasis here is on enhancing the students' ability to "see" the letter patterns in their minds.

Text Level–Fluency

The lack of fluency in poor readers is evidenced by their slow, halting, and inconsistent rate; poor phrasing; and inadequate intonation patterns. Not only do good readers read fluently with adequate speed, but when they read aloud, they also use appropriate phrasing, intonation, and their oral reading mirrors their spoken language. Although practices that incorporate prosodic reading have not produced stronger fluency gains (Torgesen et al., 2001), application of appropriate phrasing and prosodic features is important for comprehension and should be directly addressed particularly with children who do not do this naturally. If fluency is a stepping-stone to comprehension, then it is necessary to help readers transition from decoding text to constructing meaning by connecting the prosodic features that are inherent in text to their established spoken language system. If their spoken language system is intact, making this connection allows a reader to self-monitor and self-correct, which in turn facilitates the comprehension of text.

Fluency training helps a student to connect the prosody of spoken language to the prosodic features of text that are signaled through punctuation. There are features present in spoken language that provide clues to a speaker's intent such as gestures, facial expression, intonation, and stress that are not present in printed text. The absence of these prosodic features in text inhibits some readers from chunking words (grouping by semantic and syntactic features) into meaningful units. Just as we teach students to make sound-symbol correspondences during decoding instruction, we also must teach readers to map the prosodic features of spoken language onto the printed text. Structured and systematic instruction in this area will facilitate spoken-to-print prosodic correspondences and enhance comprehension.

> "Not only do good readers read fluently with adequate speed, but when they read aloud, they also use appropriate phrasing, intonation, and their oral reading mirrors their spoken language."

Intonation/Punctuation

To begin to develop awareness of the prosodic features of language, teachers can introduce a short three-word sentence with each of the three different words underlined for stress (e.g. <u>He</u> is sick. He <u>is</u> sick. He is <u>sick</u>.). The teacher can then model the three sentences while discussing the possible meaning for each variation. The students can practice reading them with different stress until they are fluent. These simple three-word sentences can be modified and expanded to include various verbs, pronouns, and tenses (e.g. <u>You</u> are sick. <u>I</u> am sick. <u>They</u> are sick.).

This strategy can also be used while increasing the length of phrases and emphasizing the different meanings (e.g., <u>Get out</u> of bed. Get out of <u>bed</u>. Get out of bed <u>now</u>.). Teachers can also practice fluency with common phrases that frequently occur in text. Prepositional phrases are good syntactic structures for this type of work (e.g., on the _____, in the _____, over the _____, under the _____).

Teachers can pair these printed phrases to oral intonational patterns that include variations of rate, intensity, and pitch. Students can infer the intended meaning as the teacher presents different prosodic variations of a sentence. For example, when speakers want to stress a concept they often slow their rate of speech and may speak in a louder voice (e.g., "Joshua, get-out-of-bed-**NOW!**"). Often, the only text marker for this sentence will be the exclamation point (!) but the speaker's intent will affect the manner in which it is delivered. Practicing oral variations and then mapping the prosodic features onto the text will assist students in making the connection when reading.

This strategy can also be used to alert students to the prosodic features present in punctuation marks. In the early stages using the alphabet helps to focus a student on the punctuation marks without having to deal with meaning. The teacher models for the students and then has them practice the combinations using the correct intonational pattern to fit the punctuation mark (e.g., ABC. DE? FGH! IJKL? or ABCD! EFGHIJ? KL.).

Teachers can then move to simple two-word or three-word sentences. The sentences are punctuated with a period, question mark, and exclamation point and the differences in meaning that occur with each different punctuation mark (e.g., Chris hops. Chris hops? Chris hops!) are discussed. It may help students to point out that the printed words convey the fact that someone named Chris is engaged in the physical activity of hopping but that the intonational patterns get their cue from the punctuation mark. The meaning extracted from an encounter with a punctuation mark is dependent upon a reader's prior experiences or background knowledge to project an appropriate intonational pattern onto the printed text. Keeping the text static while changing the punctuation marks helps students attend to prosodic patterns.

Phrasing and Chunking Text

Students who read word for word may benefit initially from practicing phrasing with the alphabet rather than words since letters do not tax the meaning system. The letters are grouped, an arc is drawn underneath, and students recite the alphabet in chunks (e.g., ABC DE FGH IJK LM NOP QRS TU VW XYZ). Once students understand the concept of phrasing, it is recommended that teachers help students chunk text into syntactic (noun phrases, verb phrases, prepositional phrases) or meaning units until they are proficient themselves. Text can be formatted for the student or the student may write the phrases on an erasable sheet. There are no hard and fast rules for chunking but syntactic units are most commonly used.

Short phrases with familiar words can be introduced through chunking machines. A chunking machine is a tachistoscope that allows a student to pull the reformatted or chunked text through the window to increase speed of recognition. (See Figure 4.2.3 for an example of a chunking machine.) It is important to put comprehension questions at the beginning and end of this activity. Students benefit from an advanced organizer before reading to help them anticipate what they will be reading. The same series is read until students can pull the phrase strips through quickly and answer all of the questions correctly. Chunking machines are simple to make and allow the student to focus on small portions of text at one time. If teachers wish to emphasize one particular word that is important for comprehension, they may chunk it separately or underline it for stress. Once text has been reformatted, students can transfer these phrases to the cards and make chunking machines for each other.

Figure 4.2.3. The Chunking Machine

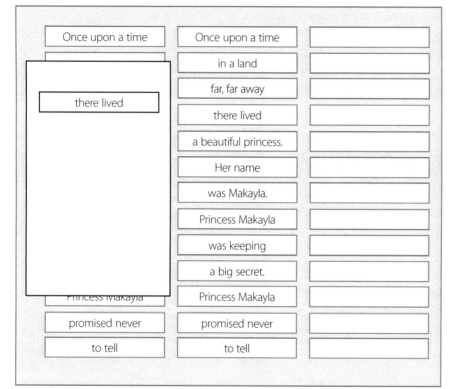

Slash Marks

For older or better readers, teachers can mark the phrasal boundaries with slashes for short passages. Eventually, the slashes are used only at the beginning of long passages and then students are asked to continue, "phrase reading" even after the marks stop. Marking phrases can be done together with students or those on an independent level may divide passages into phrases themselves. Comparisons can be made to clarify reasons for differences in phrasing.

Another way to encourage students to focus on phrase meaning and prosody in addition to word identification is to provide tasks that require them to identify or supply a paraphrase of an original statement. There are semantic paraphrases and syntactic paraphrases (Pearson & Johnson, 1978). Some examples follow:

Semantic Paraphrase
Jim jumped over the bushes.
Jim leaped over the hedge.
Syntactic Paraphrase
Jim flew the kite. (active voice)
The kite was flown by Jim.
    (passive voice)

Teachers can change the punctuation and vary intonation of paraphrases to increase student's ability to quickly adapt to changes. Discussion can focus on the differences between *jumped over the bushes* and *leaped over the hedge. Leaped* is a somewhat more interesting image so students might give it more stress during oral reading. They could then replace it with *bounded over the shrubbery* and discuss if this paraphrase changes the meaning and practice reading it. Because texts in different content areas tend to contain slightly different syntactic patterns, diverse reading of undemanding materials in different subjects and genres can be valuable during activities for improving fluency and comprehension.

Scooping

The incorporation of a multisensory component of scooping under syntactic chunks may benefit some students as they read at the text level, where the appropriate application of intonation and stress in conjunction with speed and accuracy are considered primary. Figure 4.2.4 offers a suggested progression for repeated readings of a paragraph that incorporates systematic work at the phrase and sentence levels.

Figure 4.2.4.   **Examples of Scooping**

1. Student reads the paragraph (after discussion of the content) orally (perhaps tape-recorded for comparison).

2. Student reads selected phrases from the paragraph while scooping under them with the finger or a pencil.

    in the tree   on the lawn

3. Student reads selected sentences from the paragraph individually while scooping phrases (with spaces between the phrases).

    Meg told Jim   her kite was stuck   in a tree.

4. Student reads the paragraph while scooping sentences within the passage (with spaces between the phrases).

    Meg told Jim   her kite was stuck   in a tree.   Jim ran

    on the lawn   to get his bike.   He rode his bike

    to find a ladder.   Jim used the ladder   to get the kite.

5. Student reads the paragraph as a whole without scooping and without spaces.

6. This reading is compared to the first reading in terms of fluency (accuracy, speed, and rhythm). In the beginning, timing a student as he or she reads connected text may not be as important as monitoring that he or she is applying prosodic features and chunking the text into syntactic units. Timing may be incorporated once rhythm has been clearly established. (See article by Marianne Meyer in this section for further discussion of Repeated Reading.)

Developing Anticipatory Set

As noted above, in addition to repeated readings and other sorts of speeded practice, it has been suggested that fluency is enhanced by being able to anticipate what is to come in the text, which in turn enhances comprehension. Wood et al. (2001) suggest that in addition to activities that involve developing automaticity, helping children to predict what is coming next is important. "Setting the stage" through activation of prior knowledge and reviewing what will be happening in the story can be instrumental in helping students predict text content. Summarizing the story and discussing the characters or previewing the pictures to get ideas of what the story may be about may serve the purpose of improving anticipatory set and thus enhance fluency. Other commonly used strategies such as reviewing the vocabulary and comprehension questions before reading the passage may also be helpful in this regard. (See the *J and J Language Readers*, Greene and Woods, 1993, for examples of these kinds of activities.)

Summary

Effective reading comprehension requires not only accurate reading skills but also automatic and fluent reading ability. Many struggling readers have difficulty moving to a level of automaticity and fluency that allows them to easily comprehend what they are reading. We have discussed the underlying processes involved in developing fluent reading as well as suggested some techniques for improving fluency. Research in the area of developing accurate decoding has consistently indicated that a systematic code based approach is important for teaching beginning reading skills. The best techniques for developing fluency, however, have not yet been clearly established. The suggestions here are based on clinical experience and more systematic research is needed to determine which methods or their components will be the most efficient.

Additional Resources

Carreker, S. (1999). Teaching reading: Accurate decoding and fluency. In J. R.Birsh (Ed.), *Multisensory teaching of basic language skills*. Baltimore: P. H. Brookes.

Honig, B., Diamond, L., & Gutlohn, L. (2000). *Teaching reading: Sourcebook for kindergarten through eighth grade*. Novato, CA: Arena Press.

References

Adams, M. J. (1990). *Beginning to read: Thinking and learning about print*. Cambridge, MA: MIT.

Bell, N. (1997). *Seeing stars*. San Luis Obispo, CA: Gander Educational Publishing.

Chall, J. (1996). *Learning to read: The great debate* (Third Edition). New York: McGraw-Hill.

Chall, J. (1983). *Stages of reading development*. New York: McGraw-Hill.

Clark-Edmands, S. (1998). *Specialized program individualizing reading excellence (SPIRE)*. Kennebunk, ME: Progress Learning, Inc.

Fischer, P. E. (1994). *Concept phonics*. Farmington, ME: Oxton House.

Frith, U. (1985). Beneath the surface of developmental dyslexia. In K.E. Paterson, J. C. Marshall, & M. Coltheart (Eds.), *Surface dyslexia: Neuropsychological and cognitive studies of phonological reading*. Hillsdale, NJ: Lawrence Erlbaum Associates.

Gillingham, A., & Stillman, B. W. (1997). *Remedial training for children with specific disability in reading, spelling, and penmanship*. Cambridge, MA: Educators Publishing Service.

Greene, J. F., & Woods, J. F. (1993). *J and J language readers*. Longmont, CO: Sopris West.

Lyon, G. R. (1995). Towards a definition of dyslexia. *Annals of Dyslexia, 45*, 3–27.

National Reading Panel (2000). Teaching children to read: An evidence-based assessment of the scientific research literature on reading and its implications for reading instruction. U.S. Department of Health and Human Services, National Institute of Child Health and Human Development, NIH Pub. No. 00-4754.

Pearson, P. D. & Johnson, D. D. (1978). *Teaching Reading Comprehension*. New York: Holt, Rinehart, and Winston.

Sanders, M. (2001). *Understanding dyslexia and the reading process: A guide for educators and parents*. Needham Heights, MA: Allyn and Bacon.

Snow, C. E., Burns, M. S., & Griffin, P. (1998). *Preventing reading difficulties in young children*. Washington, DC: National Academy Press.

Steere, A., Peck, C., & Kahn, L. (1988). *Solving language difficulties*. Cambridge, MA: Educators Publishing Service.

Raines, B. J. (1980). *Alphabetic phonics*. Cambridge, MA: Educators Publishing Service.

Torgesen, J. K., Rashotte, C. A., & Alexander, A. W. (2001). Principles of fluency instruction in reading: Relationships with established empirical outcomes. In M. Wolf (Ed.), *Dyslexia, fluency, and the brain*. Timonium, MD: York Press.

Wood, F. B., Flowers, L., & Grigorenko, E. (2001). On the functional neuroanatomy of fluency or why walking is just as important to reading as talking is. In M. Wolf (Ed.), *Dyslexia, fluency, and the brain*. Timonium, MD: York Press.

Repeated Reading
An Old Standard Is Revisited and Renovated

Marianne Meyer

As phoneme awareness deficits and resulting decoding weaknesses are increasingly addressed, there is heightened awareness of the role of fluency in reading. Recent research shows that improvement in decoding leads to only minimal gains in reading fluency for poor readers. Thus, despite enhanced word attack skills, these children and adults continue to read slowly and laboriously. These findings attest to the need to address fluency, defined as the ability to read connected text rapidly, smoothly, effortlessly, and automatically with little conscious attention to the mechanics of reading, such as decoding. Dysfluent reading often results in diminished motivation to read, avoidance of reading, reduced access to academic content, and, ultimately, poorer comprehension of text. In fact, the theoretical and actual link between fluency and comprehension is a compelling reason to focus on fluency because it is assumed that fluent reading allows the reader to focus on the meaning of text rather than on the mechanics of reading.

What could be the theoretical relationship between comprehension and fluency? One theory proposes that fluent reading allows the reader to focus his or her attention on the meaning of what is being read (the information processing model), while another theory holds that fluent reading allows the reader to hold large amounts of text in working memory (the verbal efficiency model) to facilitate comprehension. Still another holds that an underlying cognitive weakness, slow retrieval (slow naming speed), makes it difficult to rapidly and accurately access words, which could, in turn, have an adverse impact on comprehension. A fourth theory (the connectionist model) holds that fluency is only one component of a highly interactive process that includes proficiency in orthographic recognition, vocabulary/ morphological knowledge, and ability to use context. Two of the three programs discussed in the New Approaches section of this article test this latter model.

The interest in fluency and the techniques to remediate dysfluency are not new. In the 1970s Dahl and Samuels proposed that "Repeated Reading" could increase reading speech, transfer that improvement in speed to subsequent material, and enhance comprehension with each successive rereading of the text. And, just recently, after considering all the best intervention research, the National Reading Panel (NRP; 2000), concluded that this old technique of *guided repeated oral reading* (another term for Repeated Reading) is the most efficacious for improving fluency. In contrast, the NRP could not conclude that independent silent reading improved fluency.

Repeated Reading Method

The standard Repeated Reading (RR) method is simple and straightforward, emphasizing practice and repetition to improve fluency and accuracy. The procedure in the standard technique is as follows: 1) First the student reads aloud a passage at the appropriate instructional level several times until the desired rate of reading, measured in words per minute (wpm), is achieved. 2) After reaching the criterion rate, the student reads aloud another passage at the same level of reading difficulty until that rate is attained again. In some cases the child is given feedback on word recognition errors. 3) Results are graphed to document fluency gains and provide much needed motivation.

Variations of this standard technique include *assisted RR* where the child reads aloud and along with a fluent reader and *prosodic RR* where the child's attention is directed to the syntactic and rhythmic cues of the passage, usually by first listening to a model read in an expressive manner or, less often, using the "assisted" technique with the focus being on expressiveness. More recently, the old technique of reading a list of single words, as opposed to passages, has been revived using flashcards, page speed drills, and computer practice to increase fluency.

Research on the Efficacy of Repeated Reading

Research over the last 35 years provides convincing evidence that Repeated Reading is effective. Review of the literature indicates that RR improves reading rate and accuracy in both normal and poor readers with most studies being conducted with elementary school students. The majority of improvement in rate and accuracy occurs after three or four readings of the same passage; only minimal increases occur thereafter.

Expected reading rates are developmentally defined so that for most 1st graders, 30–50 wpm is satisfactory, for mid-2nd graders 100 ± 15 wpm is average, and by 5th grade 120–150 wmp is typical. Silent reading rates also improve incrementally (at least through high school) at a constant rate of about 10–20 wpm per year when reading level is at or below instructional level. By 9th grade, an average silent reading rate is about 200 wpm while college students' silent rates range from 250 to 300 wpm.

The type of RR (standard, assisted, prosodic, single-word reading) found most effective appears to vary with age, reading skill, and characteristics of the reader. For example, slow, but accurate, beginning readers profit from a "read along" technique using a prosodic approach where fluent, well-phrased reading is modeled. However, for older readers with a history of reading difficulties, actual reading of the text (standard or assisted) accounts for their improvement. In contrast, neither prosodic reading nor listening to text read aloud significantly improved the oral reading fluency in poor readers above and beyond that accounted for by actual reading of the text. Recently, there is accumulating evidence that practice reading single words can result in as much improvement in fluency as reading in context.

Both reader and text characteristics—and the interaction between them—affect fluency. Dysfluent readers may become overly reliant on decoding for word recognition and may slowly process graphological symbols (as measured by the Rapid Automatized Naming test—RAN) As a consequence, they do not rapidly and efficiently read single words, the factor that Torgesen finds accounts for the most variability in fluent reading of text. Students with a "Double Deficit" (those with weaknesses in both rapid naming and phonological awareness/decoding) are even more "at risk." Several text characteristics affect fluency. The more difficult the material and the closer a student is to his or her instructional level (approximately 1 in 10 words are difficult for the reader) and frustration level (more than 1 in 10 words are difficult for the reader), the more obvious dysfluency becomes. While most dysfluent readers experience significantly fewer problems with material on the easiest level (independent—95% accuracy) some do not, continuing to read in a slow, laborious manner. Increased curriculum demands also can affect fluency. Thus, after 3rd or 4th grade, when text becomes more complex, has less familiar (and often polysyllabic) words, and requires more advanced vocabulary knowledge, dysfluency can become more obvious. A final text-related factor is the number of shared words between texts; the fewer words shared between two texts, the more dysfluent readers struggle; conversely, the more words shared, the easier it is. Consequently, in subjects where content specific words are frequent (as in science and social studies), previewing words can improve fluency.

A complex, and still unanswered question is the relationship between fluency and comprehension. Although there is well-documented evidence of a high correlation (ranging from as high as .75 to .90) between fluency and comprehension, there is not a direct one to one causal relationship. For example, one study found that directing students' attention to either fluency or comprehension is critical. Students cued to attend to fluency showed significant improvement in fluency but not as much improvement in comprehension; whereas students cued to pay attention to meaning showed better comprehension and were able to better retell the story. Unraveling the fluency-comprehension connection is critical. It is addressed by several intervention programs based on the connectionist theory, discussed below in the New Approaches section. First, let us turn our attention to translating the current research results presented above so that RR can be used most effectively.

Research-Based Principles for Fluency Training Using RR

- In addition to instruction in decoding and word identification, fluency training is an *important component* of reading instruction for many students.
- Multiple readings of *continuous text* can lead to improvement in reading speed, accuracy, expression, and comprehension.
- Students should read text that can be read *accurately* (no more than 5–10% error rate). Material should be carefully selected so the student is not frustrated by reading text that is too difficult.
- Material should be read *three to four times* for optimal benefit.

- *Measures of rate and accuracy* are both important benchmarks of improvement in reading fluency.
- Multiple readings of *single words and phrases* can improve fluency.
- Fluency training can be combined with strategies to *enhance comprehension,* such as vocabulary development.
- *Short, frequent periods* of fluency practice should be scheduled on a regular basis.
- *Incentives* for reading practice as well as concrete measures of progress—graphs of changes in rate and accuracy and records of number of stories/passages read should be provided.
- Student characteristics should be taken into account. For *more impaired readers,* provide more adult guidance during reading; use more decodable text as reading material; practice words or phrases from the text before reading the text; practice reading short passages and model expressive reading.

New Approaches to Fluency Training

Three instructional programs, targeting early elementary students through young adults, illustrate new, innovative approaches to fluency training. They all incorporate traditional RR oral passage reading, but supplement it with other features, such as practice reading single words and phrases, chunking word parts to improve orthographic recognition, enhancing knowledge of word meanings to increase semantic awareness and flexibility, and using computers both to adjust reading speed requirements and to provide reinforcement and practice. The good news is that recent research attests to the efficacy of these interventions.

Great Leaps (Campbell and Mercer), a commercially available program with materials for K–adult can be implemented by a wide range of tutors (volunteers, paraprofessionals, peers, parents, in addition to teachers). Unlike traditional RR, it involves repeated reading not only of passages, but also lists of single words and phrases, a good addition to RR since there is now accumulating evidence that reading of single words is a beneficial fluency technique. It requires a minimum of 5–7 minutes daily taught in a one-to-one setting and is meant to supplement an existing reading program, preferably a systematic code program. For K–2 students, fluency tasks range from phonemic awareness to sound-symbol awareness to systematic decoding. Materials for older students are designed to be age-appropriate (i.e., high interest, low vocabulary).

Students read in 1-minute segments, first from a list of learned decodable words, next from a list of phrases, and finally from a story geared to the student's instructional level. Tutors pause as needed to review skills and/or model fluent reading. After each portion of instruction (decodable word reading, phrase reading, and text reading) the student's performance is graphed. When the expected rate per minute and accuracy goal is reached, the student "leaps up" to a higher-level passage.

Recent research (Mercer et al., 2000) on three groups of very reading disabled middle school students (with initial skills ranging from primer to beginning-2nd grade) demonstrates substantial improvement in fluency after Great Leaps training. Training was daily, running from 6 to 24 months, depending on the severity of the child's reading problem. At the conclusion students could read, on average, passages two to three grade levels higher and posted a 30 to 40 wpm improvement even on these higher-level passages. One can speculate that reading not only passages, but also single words and phrases increases the power of the RR approach. Note also that these results were obtained using a trained teacher assistant, highlighting the adaptability of this particular program.

RAVE-O (Retrieval-Rate, Auto-maticity, Vocabulary Elaboration-Orthography), based on the Double Deficit hypothesis of Wolf and Bowers and on connectionist theory, provides a comprehensive approach to fluency. RAVE-O emphasizes the five major components of written language: phonology, orthography, semantics, syntax, and morphology. In the semantic component, RAVE-O focuses on helping students understand word meanings through awareness of common meaning components (e.g., morphological units) and how words change in different contexts. Wolf and Bowers believe that fast, accurate retrieval of oral and written words is easiest when words are familiar and possess rich associations that arise from semantic, morphical and syntactic knowledge. The *O* component of RAVE-O—orthographic fluency—emphasizes systematic development of orthographic pattern recognition. Consequently, teaching children to chunk word parts (such as rimes, affixes, and consonant blends) is a key component since chunking allows more rapid recognition by helping form orthographic images of the words.

In this research-based program for early elementary age children, small groups of 2nd and 3rd grade children receive an hour of instruction from a certified teacher for a total of 140 sessions. The first half hour is spent on programs stressing phonetic decoding principles, either a systematic, sequential code approach that emphasizes phoneme analysis and blending (PHAB-Phonological Analysis and Blending) or WIST (Word Identification Strategy Training), another systematic, phonological-based program for decoding. The next half hour, the RAVE-O component, uses various game-like activities. These activities stress word meanings (such as the multiple meanings of the word *jam*); enhance rapid recognition of orthographic patterns in core words with rime patterns (*ock, ell, ung*); promote understanding about the interconnectedness of words (using word webs); and improve fluency (computer games to reinforce rapid recognition of learned words, repeated reading of 1-minute controlled vocabulary stories, etc.).

"Three instruction programs, targeting early elementary students through young adults, illustrate new, innovative approaches to fluency training."

Preliminary reports indicate that RAVE-O results in measurable broad-based gains in oral reading and fluency, in addition to gains in word identification and word attack related to the decoding programs. However, it is the statistically significant gains in comprehension on standardized measures that is particularly notable. As cited previously, comprehension does not automatically improve as fluency improves. RAVE-O's success suggests that the comprehensive nature of the program that focuses not only on speed and accuracy, but also semantic, lexical, and orthographic aspects, is the underpinning of this improvement in comprehension.

Landmark College, which specializes in educating young adults with learning disabilities, developed the *Decoding Pilot Program* (now known as the *Language Focus Community*) several years ago to address multiple aspects of reading in students with very low decoding skills, but with better oral language and verbal abilities. The goals of this comprehensive year-long program were to increase decoding skills, fluency, vocabulary, metalinguistic knowledge, and the quality and quantity of written output. Students received one-to-one tutoring using the Wilson Language Training materials; other classes, such as those emphasizing written expression and morphological knowledge, were taught in small classes. The fluency-training component used the Kurzweil Ultimate Reader-3000, a PC-based reading system with its own software system and scanner. Students wore headphones and initially read along silently as the computer read the text, or subsequently turned off the voice activated system and read text aloud to a partner, several times, obtaining feedback about errors. Fluency improvement was charted. The rate at which the PC presents material can be adjusted from 50 to 390 wpm and text can be highlighted by single words, phrases, sentences, or lines.

For young adults who completed the year-long program, significant growth occurred in phonological awareness and word attack, the initial focus of remediation. The most impressive growth, however, was in comprehension of orally read material, presumably related to growth in decoding skills for students whose initial skills were 4th grade or below. Oral reading accuracy also improved, but oral reading rate did not. This latter finding is not uncommon in adults with poor decoding skills whose focus on accuracy comes at the expense of rate.

However, it is reasonable to hypothesize when decoding is more automatic, that fluency would improve. Indeed, this hypothesis is confirmed by a recent Landmark College finding (Hecker, et al.) in which the Kurzweil 3000 computer program was used to treat students with ADHD who had proficient word identification and decoding, but poor fluency. Their findings are particularly interesting given that fluency training per se (using the RR technique) was not used—rather students read passages with and without the reading machine. Hecker et al. concluded that students with ADHD who benefited most from using the reading machine were slow readers who were easily distracted, had difficulty sustaining attention, and had poor comprehension on timed measures. This technology not only allowed the students to focus for longer periods on text, but also to increase their reading rate for both short and extended periods; comprehension also improved.

It is worth noting that as in the earlier Elkind report, the ADHD Landmark College study found that use of the reading machine was most effective in improving fluency for students with slower silent reading rates (about 175 to 190 wpm); fluency for those with significantly faster rates did not improve and some actually showed a decrement. However, both groups could read for longer periods of time and read more pages per minute. These findings, reader characteristics and the goals of intervention need to be considered when using computer technology.

Conclusion

In its most straightforward form, the Repeated Reading technique clearly improves fluency under a variety of conditions. It has the added advantages of easy implementation, applicability in a number of settings with a variety of students, and wide effectiveness using low tech or high tech materials. However, its efficacy depends on proper methodological use coupled with enough practice to ensure its transfer to other settings so that reading becomes less effortful, less laborious, and more fluent and, hence, pleasurable. Because of their comprehensive, integrated approach to a balanced reading program, the new approaches to fluency outlined above show considerable promise. Researchers and practitioners look forward to future reports, hoping to add techniques and methods to understand under what conditions and with which children fluency can improve and can have a positive impact on comprehension, the ultimate goal of reading.

One fact has become increasingly evident: It is much easier to prevent fluency problems than to remediate them. The enormous differences in reading practice that accumulate between normal readers and poor, dysfluent readers is well documented and as the old adage goes, "Those who read the best are those who read the most." Thus, the longer we wait to implement fluency training, the further behind dysfluent readers (or those "at risk" of dysfluency) become. The bottom line is that fluency instruction needs to be added to a balanced instructional program as early as kindergarten. Young students "at risk" of reading difficulties should receive formal fluency training in conjunction with a strong program of decoding, word recognition, and comprehension.

References and Suggested Readings

Listed below are new references not included in the article by Meyer and Felton (1999), "Repeated reading to enhance fluency: Old approaches and new directions." *Annals of Dyslexia, 49*, 283–306.

Campbell, K. U. (1998) *Great Leaps Reading Program.* Micanopy, FL: Diarmuid.

Cohen, E. A., Sevcik, R. A., & Wolf, M. (1999). The RAVE-O curriculum. *Perspectives. Spring, 25(2),* 9–14.

Elkind, J. (1998). Computer reading machines for poor readers. *Perspectives, Spring, 24(2),* 17–19.

Hecker, L., Gunther-Mohr, R., & Burns, L. (1999, November). *The Landmark College Decoding Pilot program.* Presentation to IDA Annual Conference.

Hecker, L., Burns, L., Elkind, K., Elkind, J., & Kaufmann, S. (2001, October). *Reading machine technology; Effect of reading performance on students with ADHD.* Presentation to IDA Annual Conference.

Kurzweil 3000 (1998). Kurzweil Educational Systems, Inc. Waltham, MA.

Lovett, M. W., Borden, S. L., Lacerenze, L., Frijers, J. C., Steinback, K. A., & DePalma, M. (2000). Components of effective remediation for developmental reading disabilities: Combining phonological and strategy-based instruction to improve outcomes. *Journal of Educational Psychology, 92(2),* 263–283.

Mercer, C. D., Campbell, K. U., Miller, M. D., Mercer, K. D., & Lane, H. B. (2000). Effects of reading fluency intervention for middle schoolers with specific learning disabilities. *Learning Disabilities Research & Practice, 14(4),* 179–189.

Report of the National Reading Panel: Teaching children to read (2000). Retrieved from www.nichd.gov/publicationss/nrp

Torgesen, J. K., Rashotte, C. A., & Alexander, A.W. (2001). Principles of fluency instruction in reading: Relationships with established empirical outcomes. In M. Wolf (Ed.), *Dyslexia, fluency and the brain.* Timonium, MD: York Press.

Wolf, M., Miller, L., & Donnelly, K. (2000). Retrieval, Automaticity, Vocabulary Elaboration, Orthography (RAVE-O): A Comprehensive, fluency-based reading intervention program. *Journal of Learning Disabilities. 33(4),* 375–386.

Vocabulary and Comprehension of Written Text

Nancy Hennessy

anguage serves thought and our words come alive in their contexts. Extracting and constructing meaning from an author's words has been defined as "thinking guided by print" (Perfetti, 1985). On the surface, comprehension may seem to be a straightforward construct. The "Simple View of Reading" describes reading comprehension as the product of word recognition and listening (language) comprehension (Gough & Tunmer, 1986). However, when one considers what lies below the surface of this formula, it becomes apparent that comprehension is anything but simple, dependent on multiple linguistic and cognitive processes that either impede or facilitate the reader from interacting with the text. Hollis Scarborough's reading rope analogy (2001) identifies the language comprehension competencies—vocabulary, background and literacy knowledge, verbal reasoning, and language structures—as necessary for the reader to work with text at the surface level (exact words, syntax), text base (underlying ideas), and to form a mental model of what has been read. Others have also written about the multiple levels of language processing necessary to create a coherent representation of written text. Cain & Oakhill (2007) describe the reader as having to decode and understand the meanings of words, work out the syntactic structure of each sentence while integrating information from different sentences, and incorporate background knowledge and ideas to make sense of details that are only implicitly mentioned.

For instruction to be informed, the practitioner must be knowledgeable in the areas of comprehension construct, contributors to reading proficiency, and effective practices. The authors seek to clarify the reader's understanding of comprehension and to increase the practitioner's ability to design and deliver effective instruction, particularly for those students who struggle with constructing meaning.

In "Making Sense of Text," Kate Cain discusses the meaning of comprehension, provides a theoretical background, and focuses on the importance of three text processing skills that are predictive of reading comprehension ability: 1) integration and inference, 2) comprehension monitoring, and 3) text structure. She provides instructional guidance, stating, "These text comprehension skills can be taught through both written and spoken language activities and fostered before reading instruction."

The article by the late Steven Stahl addresses vocabulary, a significant contributor to comprehension, and outlines a comprehensive, intensive multifaceted approach to vocabulary learning. He advises educators that "to have an impact on children's comprehension, instruction should be rich, intensive and full of interesting information."

The three articles on reading comprehension instruction in this section challenge the reader to think more deeply about the use and effectiveness of strategy instruction and an alternative approach. Danielle McNamara argues the importance of reading strategies and clarifies purpose by indicating that strategy instruction "builds on the notion that less skilled students should learn strategies that mimic those exhibited by skilled students or that compensate for processes exhibited by skilled students." She discusses the effectiveness of strategies that prompt the reader to actively process the text by engaging in "self-explanation." Margaret McKeown, Isabel Beck, and Ronette Blake compare an alternative approach to comprehension instruction, a focus on content rather than strategy, which directs students' attention toward the content of what they are reading. Through questioning and interactive discussion, students are encouraged to work through the text, make sense of it, and connect and integrate the information presented. The authors explain, "Getting students to focus on meaning is at the heart of the content approach." In a third article, McKeown and Beck advocate for an organized approach to framing questions that promotes the building of coherent representations of text. Teachers are encouraged to formulate queries that are designed toward thinking and understanding rather than more traditional questions that are often a "prescription of answers" related to the content reading.

Last, Gary Troia discusses specific tactics that help students use writing to express comprehension of content areas. Summary writing, one of the tactics described, has been validated as an effective strategy for increasing reading comprehension. The author indicates that the use of this and other tactics described in the article can "promote expository text comprehension and increase the likelihood that struggling learners will be successful in their content area learning efforts."

All of these authors provide critical insights into comprehension and instruction. Their work is an essential step toward teachers having the knowledge they need to help students today. But this area is also ripe for further study and reflections. The ending to the comprehension story has not yet been written for educators or students.

References

Cain, K., & Oakhill, J. V. (Eds.). (2007). *Children's comprehension problems in oral and written language: A cognitive perspective*. New York: Guilford Press.

Gough, P. B., & W. E. Tunmer (1986). Decoding, reading, and reading disability. *Remedial and Special Education,* 7(1), 6–10.

Perfetti, C. (1985). *Reading ability*. New York: Oxford University Press.

Scarborough, H. (2001). Connecting early language and literacy to later reading (dis)abilities: Evidence, theory and practice. In S. B. Neuman & D. K. Dickinson (Eds.), *Handbook of early literacy research* (pp. 97–110). New York: Guilford Press.

Making Sense of Text
Skills That Support Text Comprehension and Its Development

Kate Cain

Successful reading involves the acquisition of two broad sets of skills and knowledge: those that enable accurate and efficient word recognition and those that support comprehension. In this article, I focus on the skills and knowledge that support the latter. I consider how research on the development of reading comprehension and on children with specific reading comprehension difficulties can inform the teaching of reading and interventions for struggling readers.

Reading is a complex activity. Huey (1968) stated: "To completely analyze what we do when we read would almost be the acme of the psychologist's achievements, for it would be to describe very many of the most intricate workings of the human mind." The challenge to understand how children learn to read and comprehend text may be great, but the potential benefits for young and struggling readers are far greater. Learning to read is not an end in itself. It is a skill that opens doors and provides opportunities throughout one's lifetime. Successful comprehension of written text enables the reader to acquire and apply new knowledge, to experience other (fictional) worlds, to communicate successfully, and to attain academic success.

What Is Comprehension?

It is worth considering exactly what we mean by *comprehension* before examining some of the problems experienced by young readers and the skills that support the development of reading comprehension. Let us start with a short text:

James went to the beach for a picnic with his friends.
He trod on some broken glass.
His friends took him to hospital.

To understand this simple text, the reader must retrieve the meanings of the individual words and combine them into phrases and sentences. The result is a representation in which specific word meanings and the syntactic form of sentences are retained. This representation is not usually stored for any great length of time unless the precise wording is important, as for jokes (Kintsch, 1998).

When reading for meaning, skilled readers go beyond this surface level of representation. They construct a representation of the text's meaning in which the ideas and concepts expressed in separate clauses and sentences are related. In the above text, the pronoun *he* in the second sentence refers back to *James* who was introduced in the first sentence. The pronoun links the sentences and enables their meanings to be integrated. By integrating the meanings of successive clauses and sentences, readers achieve *local coherence.*

Integration between successive sentences is not always sufficient to understand the concepts and information contained in a text. Why did James go the hospital? The meaning and significance of sentence three is not clear, unless the reader goes beyond the details provided explicitly in the text and provides a reason for the hospital trip by making an inference from general knowledge: James cut his foot on the glass. By establishing how the ideas fit together as a whole, the reader achieves *global coherence.* This results in a representation of the situation described by the text, rather than a description of the text itself: a *situation model* (Graesser, Singer, & Trabasso, 1994; Kintsch, 1998). These meaning-based representations are enduring and can be retrieved several days after the information was presented. They are not unique to reading comprehension: successful comprehension of spoken discourse also results in a coherent situation model.

> "Learning to read is not an end in itself."

Text comprehension is a dynamic and interactive process involving several sources of information and knowledge. These include the information provided by the author, the reader's linguistic, pragmatic, and world knowledge, and the reader's memory for the text that has been read so far, the situation model. The latter provides the context for interpreting subsequent words, phrases, and events. If the second sentence read: "He ate a peanut butter sandwich," to understand the final sentence, the reader might infer that James had an allergic reaction.

Table 5.1.1. **Characteristics of Good and Poor Comprehenders at Ages 9–10 (14 Children in Each Group)**

Characteristics	Good comprehenders	Poor comprehenders
Chronological age	9, 08	9, 08
Sight vocabulary	34.20	34.00
Word reading accuracy in context	10, 06	10, 07
Reading comprehension	10, 07	7, 11

Notes. Chronological and reading ages are given as years, months. A reading age indicates a child's competence compared with the average competence of a group of typically developing children of the same chronological age. Therefore, the poor comprehenders have achieved a level of reading comprehension that is below-average for both their chronological age and their word reading level. The sight vocabulary measure has a maximum possible score of 45. It assesses children's ability to read and understand words presented in short phrases, by asking them to choose an appropriate synonym for a target word, which is underlined. For example: "a different sword" with the choices: weapon, practice, turn, team, spurt.

Children with Reading Comprehension Difficulties

Word reading is essential for reading comprehension: if a child cannot read any of the words on the page, he or she cannot comprehend the written text. An ability to read words does not, however, ensure adequate text comprehension. Approximately 10% of young readers acquire age-appropriate word reading skills but do not develop commensurate reading comprehension ability. These children are *unexpectedly poor comprehenders* because their reading comprehension is below the level predicted by their word reading ability and their chronological age (Cain & Oakhill, 2007). Their listening comprehension is also poor. Table 5.1.1 illustrates the typical characteristics of poor comprehenders in comparison with their peers.

> "Text comprehension is a dynamic and interactive process involving several sources of information and knowledge."

Poor comprehenders have weaknesses on many language and cognitive tasks that may influence their ability to construct a situation model of a text's meaning. Some poor comprehenders have weak semantic and syntactic skills, which will presumably affect their ability to construct representations of the meanings of phrases and sentences (Nation, Clarke, Marshall, & Durand, 2004). Other groups of poor comprehenders do not demonstrate significant difficulties with word or sentence processing, but have problems with text processing skills that may lead to difficulties with the construction of a situation model. These skills are integration and inference, comprehension monitoring, and knowledge and use of text structure (Cain & Oakhill, 2007).

Integration and Inference

Integration and inference making are crucial for good text comprehension. Children with poor reading comprehension are less likely than good comprehenders to integrate meanings across sentences and to combine information in the text with general knowledge for inference generation. Clearly, an inference can only be made if readers have the requisite knowledge. Research in which knowledge availability has been carefully controlled, rules out the possibility that knowledge deficits are the primary source of poor comprehenders' inference making difficulties.

Comprehension Monitoring

Skilled readers appear to monitor their comprehension as they read. They notice when an inference or additional processing is required to incorporate a new piece of information into their situation model. Children with poor reading comprehension do not monitor their comprehension consistently: they often fail to notice if two lines in a text state contradictory information. An example of a text used to assess comprehension monitoring is provided in Table 5.1.2. Good comprehenders are also more likely than poor comprehenders to engage in strategic processing, such as rereading previous text, to resolve comprehension failure.

Knowledge and Use of Text Structure

Knowledge about text macrostructure may aid comprehension by providing a framework for the identification and integration of important information. For example, narrative texts typically comprise a goal-directed sequence of events, which are causally related. A common method to assess knowledge and application of narrative text structure is to get children to produce their own stories, usually orally. When asked to tell a story about a general topic, such as *the holiday*, poor comprehenders produce poorly structured stories, which tend to comprise a list of events with no obvious goal. In contrast, good comprehenders are more likely to produce a narrative with a clear causal structure, in which events happen for a reason and characters develop goal plans to achieve their aims. Performance improves when picture sequences and informative goal-directed titles are used as prompts.

Memory

Text comprehension and the skills that support it are dependent on memory. *Short-term memory* enables the reader (or listener) to store and recall short pieces of information. It might be useful for processing sentences with long or complex structures. Although short-term memory is often poor in children with word reading difficulties, children with good word reading but poor reading comprehension typically do well on measures of short-term memory (Cain, 2006).

Working memory refers to the type of memory involved in the simultaneous processing and storage of information. Many comprehension processes rely on working memory, for example, the integration of two sentences requires the reader to maintain the meaning of one sentence while reading another. Children with reading comprehension difficulties do poorly on measures of working memory that involve the processing of verbal information (Cain, 2006).

Table 5.1.2. **Example of a Text with Contradictory Information Used to Assess Children's Ability to Monitor Comprehension**

Moles are small brown animals that live underground using networks of tunnels.

* Moles cannot see very well but their sense of smell is good.

They sleep underground in nests lined with grass, leaves, and twigs.

Moles use their front feet for digging.

* Moles can easily find food for their young because their eyesight is so good.

They mainly eat worms but they also eat insects and snails.

* These two lines contain contradictory information. The distance between them can be manipulated so that they are either adjacent or separated by other lines, as shown here.

Text Processing and Memory

Poor comprehenders have deficits in skills that may directly contribute to the construction of a situation model: integration and inference, comprehension monitoring, knowledge and use of story structure. All three are related to independent measures of working memory, suggesting that at least some of the difficulties experienced by poor comprehenders on these tasks may be due to working memory limitations (Cain, 2006). For example, poor comprehenders are particularly poor at spotting inconsistencies in text when several lines of text separate the two contradictory sentences (as in the example provided in Table 5.1.2). In this instance, the reader will only notice that something does not make sense if he or she tries to integrate the just-read information with the existing situation model, rather than with the previous sentence.

Which Skills Drive the Development of Reading Comprehension?

In a study with Jane Oakhill, I tracked the development of reading comprehension in young readers between the ages of 8 and 11 years to explore how skills that support the construction of situation models influence comprehension development (Oakhill & Cain, under review). We were particularly interested in the three skills found to be poor in children with reading comprehension difficulties: integration and inference, comprehension monitoring, and knowledge and use of story structure.

Similar to research with younger readers, we found that different skills explained the development of word reading and reading comprehension. Verbal ability, vocabulary, and phonological processing at ages 8 and 9 years helped to explain children's word reading ability at age 11. Early verbal ability and vocabulary knowledge were also important predictors of later reading comprehension. In addition, each of the three text processing skills was an important predictor of a child's level of reading comprehension at 11 years. A diagram of the skills that directly predicted reading comprehension is provided in Figure 5.1.1.

At each time point in the study, working memory was related to reading comprehension and the three text processing skills (i.e., integration and inference, comprehension monitoring, and use of story structure). However, working memory was not an independent predictor of children's reading comprehension development across time. One explanation for this finding is that working memory and its influence on reading comprehension was indirectly assessed by the three text processing skills.

Figure 5.1.1.   **Skills that Directly Predicted Reading Comprehension Level between 8 and 11 Years**

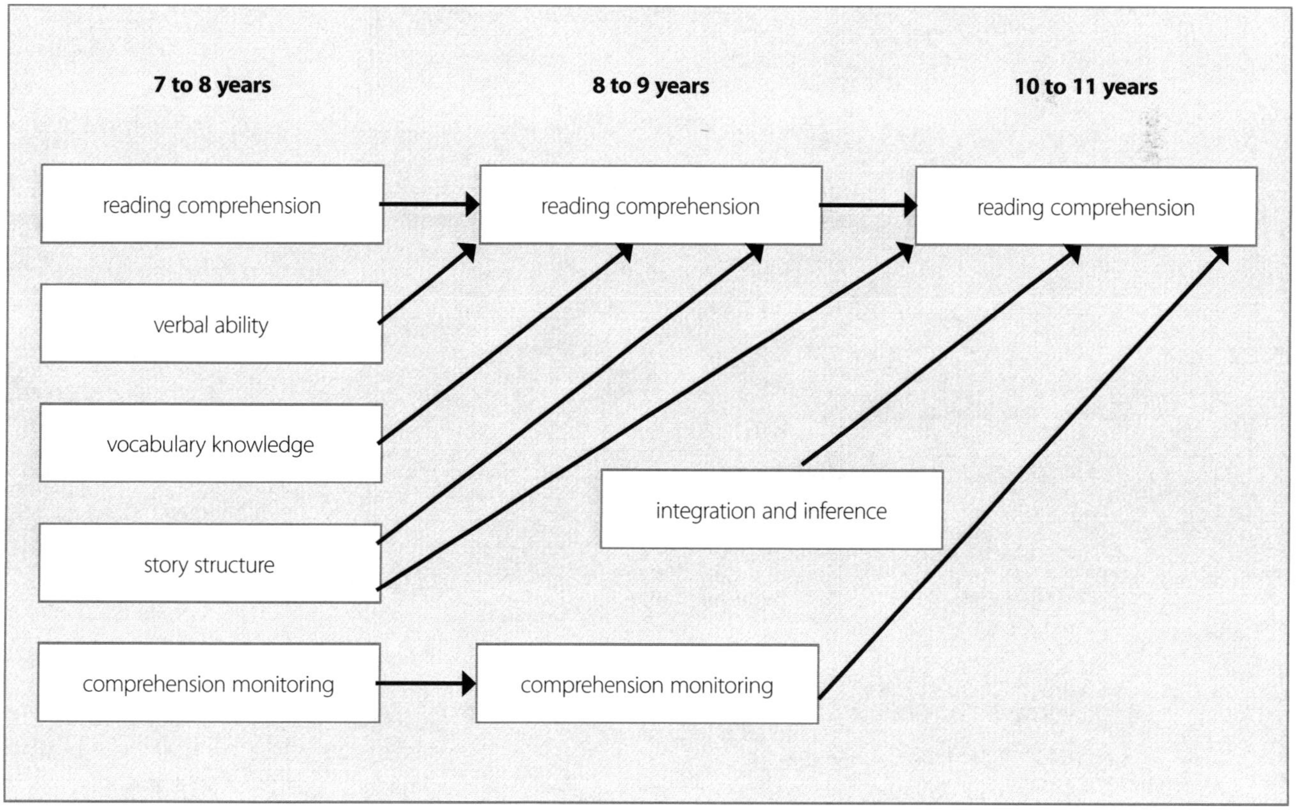

The Wider Consequences of Poor Comprehension

Many dyslexics experience literacy problems throughout the lifespan. The same may be true for poor comprehenders: they do not appear to grow out of their difficulties. In a study of 23 poor comprehenders who were identified at age 8, only one obtained an age-appropriate reading comprehension score 3 years later (Cain & Oakhill, 2006).

Poor comprehension may also have an impact upon language and literacy development more widely. Children who fail to understand adequately what they read may lack the motivation to read in their leisure time. As a result, they will get less practice in word reading and comprehension than their peers and have fewer opportunities to acquire new vocabulary and knowledge (Stanovich, 1986). Preliminary work indicates that their vocabulary development suffers over time. Poor comprehension skills may impair the ability to learn more generally. Children who have poor reading comprehension at 8 years obtain lower scores than their classmates on United Kingdom national assessments of English, maths, and science taken at age 11 (Cain & Oakhill, 2006). Thus, the consequences of unremediated reading comprehension difficulties may extend beyond literacy skills.

Implications for Teaching

Children with unexpectedly poor reading comprehension have difficulties with the skills needed to construct the meaning-based representation of a text. These difficulties are not restricted to visually presented text: they also have listening comprehension problems. Poor comprehenders do not appear to have a developmental delay and will probably require targeted interventions to remediate their comprehension difficulties.

How to Spot a Poor Comprehender

Children with unexpected comprehension difficulties comprise around 10% of school population in the United Kingdom but are rarely spotted by their teachers (Nation et al., 2004). It is easy to detect the child with word reading difficulties, because he or she will read slowly or inaccurately. Many children with unexpectedly poor comprehension probably go unnoticed by parents and classroom teachers because their accurate and fluent word reading skills hide their difficulties. Comprehension difficulties become apparent when these children are asked questions about texts that require more than recall of simple facts. For example, to answer the question "Why did James go to hospital?" for the text used earlier, the reader must generate an inference. Poor comprehenders will also produce poorly structured written and oral narratives.

What Should Be Taught?

There have been relatively few intervention studies with unexpectedly poor comprehenders, to date. Published studies indicate that instruction in text processing skills will alleviate poor comprehenders' difficulties. Teaching children to read effectively by learning how to summarize what has been read so far and to generate questions to test understanding, is an effective strategy (Brown, Palincsar, & Armbruster, 1984). Poor comprehenders have also successfully been taught how to make inferences from "clue" words in texts. This type of lexical inference involves identifying and using key words: for example, the words *steam, splash, soap,* and *towel* indicate a bathroom. A combination of training both lexical inference and question generation to test understanding leads to significant gains on standardized measures of reading comprehension (Yuill & Oakhill, 1991). Although poor comprehenders reliably demonstrate limited memory capacity, inference training is unlikely to lead to memory gains. Instead it might enable some poor comprehenders to compensate by using their memory resources more effectively.

When Should We Teach These Skills?

It is well established that the foundation skills for word reading develop before reading instruction begins. In a similar way, reading comprehension draws on skills and knowledge that develop before children are taught to read. Preschoolers generate inferences to understand spoken and televised narratives. Children under 3 years monitor their comprehension: they can detect when the order of events in a familiar storybook has been changed. An understanding of narrative develops before school, through listening to stories and making sense of events in everyday life. These crucial comprehension skills can be nurtured before reading instruction begins during storybook interactions and conversation.

Summary

Skilled readers construct a representation of a text's meaning that encodes the state of affairs described by the text. To do this, successful comprehenders engage in meaning-making processes in addition to word identification and sentence processing. They make links between the meanings of different sentences and fill in missing details, often by making inferences. Skilled comprehenders monitor their comprehension as they read, to check that the text makes sense. They use their knowledge of text structure to guide the construction of the representation of the text's meaning.

Children with unexpectedly poor comprehension have difficulties with these three text processing skills: integration and inference, comprehension monitoring, and knowledge and use of story structure. These skills contribute to growth in reading comprehension during middle childhood. Educators and researchers need to be aware that comprehension can be limited not just by word reading proficiency but by these other skills, as well. Importantly, these text comprehension skills can be taught through both written and spoken language activities and fostered before reading instruction begins.

References

Brown, A. L., Palincsar, A. S., & Armbruster, B. B. (1984). Instructing comprehension-fostering activities in interactive learning situations. In H. Mandl, N. L. Stein, & T. Trabasso (Eds.), *Learning and comprehension of text*. Hillsdale, NJ: LEA.

Cain, K. (2006). Children's reading comprehension: The role of working memory in normal and impaired development. In S. J. Pickering (Ed.), *Working memory and education* (pp. 62–91). San Diego: Academic Press.

Cain, K., & Oakhill, J. (2006). Profiles of children with specific reading comprehension difficulties. *British Journal of Educational Psychology, 76*, 683–696.

Cain, K., & Oakhill, J. (2007). Reading comprehension difficulties: Correlates, causes, and consequences. In K. Cain & J. Oakhill (Eds.), *Children's comprehension problems in oral and written language: A cognitive perspective* (pp. 41–75). New York: Guilford Press.

Graesser, A. C., Singer, M., & Trabasso, T. (1994). Constructing inferences during narrative text comprehension. *Psychological Review, 101*, 371–395.

Huey, E. (1968). *The psychology and pedagogy of reading*. Cambridge, Mass: MIT Press (originally published 1908).

Kintsch, W. (1998). *Comprehension: A paradigm for cognition*. New York: Cambridge University Press.

Nation, K., Clarke, P., Marshall, C. M., & Durand, M. (2004). Hidden language impairments in children: Parallels between poor reading comprehension and specific language impairment? *Journal of Speech, Language, and Hearing Research, 47*, 199–211.

Oakhill, J. V., & Cain, K. (under review). The precursors of reading ability in young readers: Evidence from a four-year longitudinal study.

Stanovich, K. E. (1986). Matthew effects in reading: Some consequences of individual differences in the acquisition of literacy. *Reading Research Quarterly, 21*(4), 360–406.

Yuill, N. M., & Oakhill, J. V. (1991). *Children's problems in text comprehension: An experimental investigation*. Cambridge: Cambridge University Press.

SCALY? AUDACIOUS? DEBRIS? SALUBRIOUS?
Vocabulary Learning and the Child with Learning Disabilities

Steven A. Stahl

The word *vocabulary* itself can be confusing. Sometimes educators talk about a "sight vocabulary" or a set of the most common words in English (e.g., Fry, Fountoukidis, & Polk, 1985). Although it is certainly important for children to recognize instantly a set of 100 or 300 or more words in print, especially since a small number of words (105 according to Adams, 1990) accounts for 50% of the words encountered in a typical passage, we are talking here about word meanings and will use the words *vocabulary* and *word meanings* as synonyms. Further, I will talk about other types of vocabularies—concepts, content area vocabularies, and so on. These different "vocabularies" have different demands and should be taught in different ways.

The Sheer Number of Words

Consider phonological awareness. At its root, phonological awareness is an awareness that spoken words can be thought of as a series of phonemes, which can be mapped unto letters of the alphabet (Stahl, McKenna, & Jones, 2003). This insight is one foundation of learning the written code. This is an area in which children with learning disabilities have particular difficulty (e.g., Stanovich, 2000), but is remediable with more or less difficulty for children with learning disabilities (e.g., Snow, Burns, et al., 1998). Phonics instruction generally involves the learning of a finite number of sound-symbol relationships and various forms of phonics instruction have been part of practice with children with learning disabilities. Comprehension instruction, intended for children with learning disabilities or normally achieving children usually involves a small number of strategies well taught (e.g., Rosenshine & Meister, 1994). Fluency instruction involves practice, structured or wide reading, in reading connected text (e.g., Kuhn & Stahl, 2003). There is, however, a point at which children have adequate fluency and may not greatly exceed that point (see Carver, 2000).

These traditional goals of reading instruction all present manageable goals, although more or less able to be achieved with individual children. Vocabulary knowledge is a goal that may never be fully achieved, even among intelligent adults. Even though we, as educated adults, know thousands of words (many will be discussed shortly), there are always words that we run into that we do not know. To tell on myself, a few years ago I was reading *Newsweek* and encountered the word *quotidian*. This is not a word that I had known previously and was surprised to see it in a mass-market magazine. Since then, I have run into it numerous times, but for some reason had not up until then. Once, when telling this story, a Spanish-speaking teacher told me that the word *quotidian* had a Spanish cognate and that it would be more likely to be known by a Spanish speaker.

Estimates of how many words are in English vary. The Oxford English Dictionary, which is the largest compilation of English words, modern, obsolete, archaic, contains upward of 1,000,000 words, with new words (such as *McJob* and *JPEG*) being added periodically. English is promiscuous in adding words, taking words from other languages, from slang, from compounding, from everywhere. This does not mean that children or adults need to know that many words, but they are out there.

A more reasonable estimate is that of Nagy and Anderson (1984). They estimated that Printed School English, or the number of different word families found in the books that children read from grades 1–12 was approximately 87,000. Many of these words are seen only once and may not have to be known. Other estimates suggest that an average high school senior may know 45,000 different words.

Forty-five thousand words are still a great many words. Consider the implications of that number. Assuming that a child enters 1st grade knowing roughly 6,000 different words, that means that the child will learn approximately 39,000 additional words over the next 12 years, or about 3,000 new words per year. Three thousand new words means that a person will learn roughly 10 new words each day. And there is research to suggest that the average child does learn roughly 3,000 words per year (White, Graves, & Slater, 1990).

This average does obscure some important differences. White and his colleagues found a range of growth between 1,000 words for low-achieving children and 5,000 for higher achieving children. This range is important. If one child's vocabulary grows only a fifth as much as another's, the differences between low achieving and high achieving children will only grow larger over time.

There are lower estimates of how many words children know and how many words children need to know (e.g., D'Anna & Zechmeister, 1991), some as low as 5,000 root words over the course of the school years. This would be a more manageable number to teach. Root words would not include, however, less common but still essential words such as (to pull a random sample from a book I am reading) *bridal, nonchalant, taxidermy, stamina* and so on. Since the children that we work with are generally intelligent and inquisitive, concentrating on basic words (although they are certainly important) would deny our children a source of pleasure in the "gift of words."

Where Words Come From

Ten words per day is more than can be taught directly. Typically, I have observed teachers teaching 10–12 words per week, but never that many per day, at least not successfully. Instead, most words come from exposure in context. Children's books contain a great many rare words and this is the source of word learning in both children with learning disabilities and normally achieving children. One problem that children with learning disabilities have is that although they can learn word meanings from children's books and at the same rate as other children, they read less (because they have reading problems) and they read less challenging books, resulting in them falling further and further behind their peers.

Stanovich (2000) has termed this the "Matthew Effect" after the passage in the Bible stating that the "rich will get richer and the poor will get poorer." The widening gap between children with learning disabilities and normally achieving children is an important secondary result of reading problems. Because children with learning disabilities tend to have lower vocabularies, mainly through a lack of exposure to words in challenging books and not through differences in abilities, they often have difficulty understanding oral discussions of content topics that contain challenging words. Since intelligence tests tend to weight vocabulary knowledge in their scores, often the measured IQs of children with learning disabilities tend to fall over time, resulting in a change of classification from learning disability, which requires average or above intelligence, to mild mentally handicapped. In many of these cases, the child's intelligence is unchanged, but the child appears less intelligent because of the lack of growth to vocabulary over the years.

These are the problems that vocabulary presents for children with learning disabilities. First, there are so many words to be learned that one cannot teach all of them. This is as true for normally achieving children as it is for children with learning disabilities, but it is especially problematic for children who have so many other needs.

In tutorial instruction, it is far more efficacious to target those other needs, needs that can be reasonably accomplished in the constraints of a tutorial situation. Second, because children with learning disabilities tend to read fewer books and fewer challenging books, they acquire fewer new word meanings. The fewer word meanings preclude them from more challenging materials, thus exacerbating differences between children with learning disabilities and normally achieving children. These differences may have secondary effects such as a "drop" in intelligence test scores.

What to Do—Read to Children

We typically view reading to children as an activity for pre-readers or primary aged children. Reading to older children is often used as a way of getting children interested in a book so that they would continue reading it on their own. However, reading to children can be a good source of word meanings, for all children, especially children with learning disabilities. Stahl, Richek, and Vandevier (1991) found that sixth grade children learned word meanings from a read aloud at the same rate that children typically learned words from written context. This suggests that listening to stories can be as rich a source of word learning as reading. Since most words are learned from context, listening to stories may substitute for some of the reading that children with learning disabilities do not do.

The books should be books that are intellectually challenging. The children that we work with need such stimulation. Consider the richness of language in a book such as *Freedom Summer* (Wiles, 2001), a book intended for 3rd or 4th graders, but rich enough to be used in upper grades:

> "Children with learning disabilities tend to have lower vocabularies mainly through lack of exposure to challenging books and not through differences in abilities..."

> John Henry's skin is the color of browned butter. He smells like pine needles after a good rain. My skin is the color of the pale moths that dance around the porch light at night. John Henry says that I smell like a just-washed sock. "This means war!" I shout. We churn that water into a white hurricane and laugh until our sides hurt. (Wiles, 2001, unpaged).

To deny children the richness of language because of difficulties in recognizing words would be wrong in itself. A more pragmatic reason would be that children's books are a major source of word meanings for all children. Hayes and Ahrens (1988) examined the vocabulary levels of various texts and found that children's books contain more uncommon words and richer vocabulary than television shows intended for children and even more than conversations between two college educated adults. Trelease (2001) is a wonderful source of books for reading aloud.

Listening to stories should not be a passive activity. Children should always be responsible for what they hear; this should not be a time to relax. Instead, children should be listening for a purpose, to discuss afterwards, to critically react, to generate a conversation about what they hear. I prefer that this active listening be done in groups. Since children with learning disabilities are at equal footing with others, this is a wonderful integrative activity. But even if tapes are used (e.g., Chomsky,

1978), children should be responsible for what they hear, even if that responsibility is limited to retelling to an adult or to answering questions. Studies have found that merely listening to tapes, without responsibility for what was on the tapes, does not improve achievement (e.g., Leinhardt, Zigmond, & Cooley, 1981; Haynes & Jenkins, 1986).

Scott (2003) talks about an active listening approach that she calls the "Gift of Words." In this activity, children are encouraged to listen for particularly poignant words or phrases, words that express feelings or meanings or descriptions particularly well. These are written down, put in a word bank, and used for writing later. After reading, children share their words or phrases, discuss what it was that made them strong or memorable. These "Gifts of Words" from the author are put in a word bank or on a word wall and referred to during student writing. Although Scott has a number of wonderful examples, I love the following fictional example from a Philip Roth novel:

> I was beginning to perspire profusely from the sun on my face, from the excitement of meeting Iron Rinn, and now from being on the spot, having to answer Mr. Ringold as though I were in class while I was sitting between two shirtless brothers well over six feet tall, two, big, natural men exuding the sort of forceful, intelligent manliness to which I aspired. Men who could talk about baseball and boxing, were talking about books. And talking about books as though something were at stake in a book, not opening up a book to worship it or to be elevated by it or to lose yourself to the world around you. No, *boxing* with the book.
> [This is the first paragraph of the longer excerpt in the original article.—Ed.]

Again, this is an activity in which a child with reading problems can participate in with no greater problem than that presented by the writing of the phrase, and a short phrase would present a relatively minimal problem.

Different Words, Different Teaching

All words are not the same. That goes without saying. But the differences between words make a difference in how they can be more effectively taught. Consider the following types of words:

- Words that a child knows a synonym for, such as *evil*, *crimson*, *speaking*, or *superior*
- Words that can be explained with a definition, examples, and the use in context, such as *challenge*, *pedal*, *harp*, or *betray*
- Words that represent complex concepts, such as *liberty*, *biome*, or *probability*

These different types of words can be taught differently, making vocabulary teaching a less time-consuming task.

One of the problems with vocabulary teaching is that it takes a great deal of time, time that could be spent doing more targeted instruction. One study, admittedly attempting to provide the "Cadillac" of vocabulary instruction, devoted about 20 minutes to the teaching of each word. The reality is much less than that, but, given the number of words to be taught, vocabulary instruction can be very time consuming.

Point of Contact Teaching

For words that a child knows a synonym for, the task is for the child to learn enough about the word to get through the passage. Such instruction probably will not have long-term effects on reading comprehension, but may be enough to support children through a particular passage. One study found that simply having children memorize a set of synonyms for words in a passage did not affect comprehension of that passage (see Stahl, 1998; Stahl & Fairbanks, 1986 for review). However, knowing that a *malefactor* is a bad person or that *crimson* is a form of red may be enough. This approach is best with words that may be relatively rare (*malefactor* is a good example) or not particularly important for understanding that passage. Given the literary language of children's books, even those intended for young children such as *Freedom Summer*, this point of contact teaching is important. Not every "hard" word has to be taught. This involves teacher judgment, but we observe teachers making this judgment all the time.

Point of contact teaching can be initiated by the teacher, either before reading a section of the text or during reading. If a word comes up that seems to be a puzzlement, the teacher can quickly say something like, "Flare means flame" and move on. Such a statement should be quick and non-disruptive of the meaning of the text. Such point of contact teaching should be minimal and restricted to once per page. Any more would be disruptive of the flow of the text. Since the purpose of reading should be comprehension, disruptions should be avoided.

Children could also initiate point of contact instruction. Awareness that one does not know a word is a meta-cognitive understanding (Baker & Brown, 1984). Children with learning disabilities often do not have this understanding and gloss over words that they do not understand. The awareness that they do not know a word, or that they need to know a word is an important one. A point of contact can be initiated with a hand signal during reading and the teacher or a peer can provide the word. This point of contact teaching should not be limited to children with learning disabilities, but can be taught to the entire class. This is minimal instruction, and possibly not really instruction at all. It is a way of helping children to get through a difficult text, with little disruption. It should be done, probably, no more than once a page and should not substitute for more extensive instruction, such as discussed below.

Students, of course, may initiate point of contact teaching of words other than obvious synonyms; such instruction needs to be more extensive. Such instruction is discussed below.

More Extensive Teaching

"Point of contact" teaching is not adequate for children to learn words, at least in a way that would substantially improve their comprehension or their vocabulary. Certainly, some of the words would "stick," and having even one exposure to a word and its synonym is better than nothing, but it is unreasonable to expect too much word learning from a short exposure. To teach words in a meaningful manner requires instruction that is more extensive, although probably not as extensive as the 20 minutes per word discussed earlier.

Stahl and Fairbanks (1986), in a review of vocabulary instructional studies found three principles that characterized effective vocabulary instruction:

- Effective vocabulary instruction provides both definitional and contextual information about a word.
- Effective instruction requires that the child engage in deep processing about each word, including generating information that ties the new word to already known information.
- Effective instruction involves multiple exposures to each word.

I will discuss these briefly in turn.

Definitional and Contextual Information

If you picture the traditional vocabulary instruction of your upper elementary and secondary years (and your instruction was somewhat like mine), you remember memorizing lists of definitions, with a test on Friday. If the test was in the morning, nearly all of the words were out of your head by lunch. Not only was this memorization boring, but it also did not lead to appreciable growth in vocabulary (Stahl, 1998; Stahl & Fairbanks, 1986, National Reading Panel, 2000).

There are two reasons for the sheer ineffectiveness of this approach. One is that passive memorization does not, itself, produce very strong results. But also a word's meaning is more than just a definition. Consider the word *swim*, used in its ordinary sense as "to move through water by one's hands and feet." It can, of course, be used as both a noun and a verb, but it also has multiple senses depending on the surrounding context, as in the following:

1. Melissa swam toward the wall.
2. The five year old swam across the kiddie pool on her belly, propelling herself by kicking and pushing herself forward, laughing as she did it.
3. The swim team began the meet with the sound of the starter's pistol.
4. The alligator swam through the swamp toward the girls' dangling feet.
5. Dad slowly swam across the pool to get an iced tea from Mom.

"A word's meaning is more than just a definition… Words as simple and well-defined as *swim* can change so much in different contexts."

The first sentence evokes a fairly typical swimming action. We do not know much about it without any additional context. The second sentence creates a picture of a beginner, the third of a vigorous competition, the fourth of stealth, and the fifth of a leisurely crawl. Each of these is *swim*, but each of these is distinctively different. Words as simple and well defined as *swim* can change so much in different contexts.

To learn a new word, one must not only learn how that word relates to other words (the definitional information), but also how the word changes in different contexts. Learning definitional information is more than just learning the definition (and definitions can be difficult to understand), but also learning about the following:

- *Synonyms*

- *Antonyms*—Antonyms force children to think about words differently. Obvious antonyms (*black/white, good/bad*) do not require children to think much about a word's meaning, but less obvious antonyms or *near-antonyms* can get children to think more about what a word means. For example, what is the antonym of *ponder*? *Not consider*? *Avoid*? Trying to come up with antonyms of unlikely words can force children to think about which features are important for a word's meaning and which are not.

- *Categories*—Part of definitional knowledge is knowing what category a word fits into. Knowing that *vehicle* is a form of transportation, that *accountant* is a type of job, or that *orca* is a type of whale, which in turn is a mammal, is an important part of the word.

- *Comparisons to other, similar words*—This can be a very powerful means of learning words. Consider the word *debris*. *Debris* is a form of trash, but not all trash is *debris*. *Garbage* actually means organic material, such as leavings from apple peels or leftover and unwanted food. *Debris* means trash left over from some sort of accident or catastrophic event, such as an automobile accident or a plane crash (and sometimes from a child's room).

Venn Diagrams can be used to make some of these comparisons, as can Silly Questions (see McKenna, 2004).

Definitions can be hard to understand (Scott & Nagy, 1997). This is especially true in my experience for children with learning disabilities. The children we work with tend to be focused on words and believe that the definition of the word is the word's meaning and that the task is to simply memorize that word's definition. As a result, I find that children with learning disabilities tend to be more confused with dictionaries than enlightened. This is usually the case with normally achieving children. Normally achieving children tend to have more flexibility, since their attention is not as focused on individual words as children with learning disabilities.

Definitions have a particular form and children do not often recognize it. Each definition presents the Category (Genus) to which the word belongs and how that word differs from other members of the category (Differentiae). Thus, for some randomly chosen words, "eider" is "a large sea duck of the northern hemisphere" (Genus = duck, Differentiae = large, sea, northern hemisphere) and "hagiography" is a "biography that treats its subject with undue reverence" (Genus = biography, Differentiae = with undue reverence).

The form of definitions can and should be taught, especially to children with learning disabilities. This can be done simply and directly, by analyzing dictionary definitions in the course of vocabulary instruction. A dictionary can be a useful tool. Another approach is to use an explanatory dictionary, such as the COBUILD dictionary. In this dictionary, the definitions are in sentence form. For example, the entry for "fissure" is "A fissure is a deep crack in something, especially in rock or in the ground." Other entries have longer explanations. For example, the entry for "plunge" is "If something or someone plunges in a particular direction, especially into water, they fall, rush, or throw themselves in that direction. At least 50 people died when a bus plunged into a river...He ran down the steps to the pool terrace and plunged in." Although the COBUILD includes examples from American English, it is a British dictionary and the usages and spellings do differ from those in the United States. This might confuse some children, so caution should be used.

Children not only need to know the logical relations between a new word and known words, or definitional knowledge, but also know how that new word fits into different contexts. This involves looking at words in contexts, but more importantly, generating contexts, or contextual knowledge.

- *Generating Sentences.* Generating sentences is a useful way of learning about word meanings, but the sentences need to be sentences that are good at expressing the meaning of the words. All too often, sentences become a meaningless time filler, perceived that way by both child and teacher. One way of avoiding this problem is to have three or four children come up with sentences and have the rest of the class rate how well they express the word. This can be done orally so that children with learning disabilities can participate equally.

- *Scenarios.* Having children (in groups) make up a scenario containing a word or (preferably given the amount of time this takes) a group of words can also be useful. Scenarios can bring words together, forcing children to not only put the words in context but also understand the relations between a set of words. Scenarios can be prose or plays that groups can put on.

- *Possible Sentences.* Possible Sentences is an activity that allows children to predict not only the meanings of the words to be learned but can be useful in having children predict the content of what they are going to read. In Possible Sentences, children are given a set of ten to twelve words taken from a passage they are about to read. Of these words, about four should be known and the rest unknown. Children are asked to make up sentences that might appear in the passage and contain two of the words from the list. Words can (and should) be reused and each sentence must contain two words from the list. For a passage on insects, words might include:

    antenna, butterfly, abdomen, thorax, grasshopper,
    wings, jointed, legs, spider, propulsion, feeling, ant

Students might come up with sentences such as:
Grasshoppers use their legs for propulsion. (Correct)
Spiders are not insects because they have eight legs. (Correct)
The thorax is the part of the ant that eats. (Incorrect)
Butterflies have pretty wings. (Correct)

Note the emphasis on rich contexts. Fill in the blanks, and having students generate short, quick sentences provide contexts to augment definitions and can be included in vocabulary instruction for expediency, but are not as effective. These activities also contain a substantial oral or collaborative component, allowing children with learning disabilities to participate equally in the learning process.

Generating Rich Connections

The second principle of effective vocabulary instruction is that children need to generate rich connections between the new word and already known information. This involves more than learning a simple association, as in the old-fashioned dictionary memorization activities of our youth. Merely comprehending the word in context, during wide reading alone or with point of contact teaching, leads to more learning, but not as much as having students process the word deeply, generating connections between the new word and different contexts and prior knowledge of other words.

As a contrast, consider the process of looking up a phone number. You go to the phone book, look up the number, rehearse it while picking up the phone, dial the number, and forget it once it rings through. Now consider the following scenario for the word *apprentice*.

The apprentice must rise before the master, before the first rays of the sun come out. At that time, the apprentice needs to put on the fire, heat up a pitcher for hot water to make the master's tea. Once breakfast is finished, the apprentice needs to prepare the tools for the morning's work. As the master sits down on his bench, the apprentice sits on the side, ready to provide the tools that the master needs, but otherwise watches closely. The master is ready to teach. The apprentice is ready to learn.

Preparing such a scenario requires that the children connect *apprentice* to *master*, *learn*, and *teach*, all crucial concepts. It also requires that the children connect the concept of *apprentice* to a more historical, rural context. Such a scenario could not have been produced without some preteaching by the teacher, but would lead to rich learning and might be a good prereading writing activity for a book involving an apprenticeship. Discussion is a powerful way of having children generate connections between new and known information (Stahl & Vancil, 1986; Stahl & Clark, 1987). Discussion makes children active thinkers, since they are trying to make contributions to the discussion. These connections, of course, only occur if the individual child believes that the contribution will be accepted and valued. Often this is not the case with children with learning disabilities, so a teacher needs to make a special effort to create a classroom community in which the contributions of all children are equally accepted. Some guidelines can be found in Saunders and Goldenberg (1999) for creating an environment in which this can happen. True discussion, in which all children can participate without intervention by the teacher, is a powerful tool for vocabulary learning, but considerable vocabulary learning can occur in recitation, in which the teacher monitors the turn taking.

Beck and McKeown, (2001, 2003) provide a wonderful example of rich, vocabulary instruction as part of their *Text Talk* approach to discussing new books for young children. Here they introduce the word *absurd* in the context of a new book:

The following is the activity provided for the word *absurd* from the story *Burnt Toast on Davenport Street* (Egan, 1997, cited in McKeown, 2003).

> **absurd:** In the story, when the fly told Arthur he could have three wishes if he didn't kill him, Arthur said he thought that was absurd. That means Arthur thought it was silly to believe a fly could grant wishes. When something is absurd—it is ridiculous and hard to believe. If I told you that your teacher was going to stand on his or her head to teach you—that would be absurd. If someone told you that dogs could fly—that would be absurd. I'll say some things, and if you think they are absurd, say: "That's absurd!" If you think they are not absurd, say: "That makes sense." I have a singing cow for a pet. (absurd) I saw a tall building that was made of green cheese. (absurd) Last night I watched a movie on TV. (makes sense) This morning I saw some birds flying around the sky. (makes sense) If I said "let's fly to the moon this afternoon," that would be absurd. Who can think of an absurd idea? (When a child answers, ask another if they think that was absurd, and if so, to tell the first child: "That's absurd!")

Notice how they provide a bridge from the example of the word's use in the book to examples in different contexts. Also notice that this lesson should be quick paced, probably no more than two minutes, with high participation. Children could respond chorally except to the last item. From this instruction, it is likely that the group would understand "absurd" fairly well in the short period of time.

Provide Multiple Exposures to a Word's Meaning

The third principle of effective vocabulary learning is to provide multiple exposures to a word's meaning. This does not mean mere repetition of the word and a synonym or a definition (*companion* means *friend*), but seeing the word in different contexts—in sentences, with a definition, with elaborated information. There is a limit to how many repetitions are needed; repetition can be overdone, but a child probably has to see a word more than once to firmly place it in long-term memory.

The picture I have been painting is of vocabulary instruction in a context of rich instruction about texts, rather than the sterile instruction that we remember from our youth. This instruction occurs in oral discussion and collaborative work that fully enables all children in the class to participate. This involves group work and the teacher providing an environment in which equal participation can occur.

Teaching Complex Concepts

Even this more extensive instruction is not enough to teach some words. Words such as *flock*, *herd*, *confine*, or *slaughter*, all taken from a Thanksgiving article on turkeys are relatively easy to define and put into various contexts, both having to do with the traditional bird and outside of that context. However, understanding the larger concept of factory farming (the point of the article) requires more than learning a definition and coming up with a few selected contexts. This example seems abstract, but children encounter many such complex concepts, such as ecosystem, liberty, circulatory system, representation, and so on. These concepts cannot be neatly defined, but instead must be developed through what Spiro et al. (1994) call "criss-crossing" the landscape.

Take, for example, the concept of *liberty*. This is a fairly common concept for children in the upper elementary grades. A dictionary definition might be *The freedom to think or act without being constrained by necessity or force* (Expedia, 2001). In this definition, the category to which liberty belongs is *freedom* and what differentiates it is that the *freedom* refers to being able to think or act without constraint. But is this *liberty*? Obviously, society puts constraints on one's liberty, beginning with the constraint not to commit common criminal acts from murder to speeding so that we can function as a society. When a constraint is needed to maintain a civil society and when it violates liberty is a useful source for discussion, even in a 5th grade class. *Liberty* can also be personal. Parents differ in terms of rules and constraints; these are variations in liberty as well. In both realms there are non-examples. Totalitarian states restrict personal and political liberties. Curfews and chaperones restrict personal liberties.

To understand *liberty*, then, one must understand that liberty is—

Category:	Freedom
What is different:	To think or act without constraint
Examples:	Personal
	Going to the mall by oneself
	Hanging with friends
	Ability to choose
	Political
	Ability to vote
	Freedom of speech
	Freedom of religion
Non-Examples:	
	Personal
	Parents' rules
	Curfews
	Not being able to talk in class
	Political
	Not being able to kill or steal
	Dictatorships
	Not being able to chose one's leader
	Not being allowed to criticize the laws

A class discussion that generated a list such as this would have looked at the concept of *liberty* from a variety of perspectives, not just going through the concept as a definition, but "criss-crossing" it from the personal and political perspectives, looking at what liberty is and what it is not, understanding the boundaries of the concept. In other words, developing a full and rich understanding of the concept.

The discussion needed to develop this rich understanding is more time consuming than the extended instruction discussed above and should be reserved only for concepts that need such instruction. This discussion should take place prior to reading, since it is needed to set the stage for unit or theme understanding. The examples above are generally content area examples, but I could see using this for literary themes, or even discussion of genre (e.g., narrative, exposition, textbook, or recipe).

McKenna (2004) has a number of examples of how to develop these concepts in content areas. I will only present one, a "four-square" vocabulary approach (Eeds & Cockrum, 1985). This approach uses either a printed diagram or, more simply, folding a piece of paper so that it has four squares, as in Figure 5.2.1.

Figure 5.2.1   **Folded Paper for "Four-Square" Vocabulary Approach**

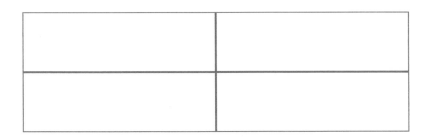

Into the first box, upper left, one writes a word to be learned, such as *prejudice*. In the second box, upper right, are written examples of the word, such as disliking someone because of his or her color or disliking someone because he or she does not speak English, or disliking someone because of how he or she dresses. In the next box, lower right, are put non-examples of *prejudice*, such as acceptance or reaching out to people different than oneself. Finally, in the last box, lower left, is put a definition of the word. Thus, the completed box might look like Figure 5.2.2:

Figure 5.2.2   **Example of "Four-Square" Vocabulary Approach**

prejudice	disliking someone because of his or her color…
hatred or dislike because a person is different	acceptance tolerance of differences

Four-square boxes can be done as whole class activities or by groups of children working together. Either way they provide an opportunity for children with learning disabilities to learn as equal participants in discussion. What I like about this activity is its ease and the possibility of spontaneous use to discuss a particularly gnarly concept that might arise during reading. It is flexible enough to use on less complex concepts, but adaptable to even fairly abstract ideas.

Learning About Words

In English, words come from everywhere. Words come from an original Anglo-Saxon, yes, but they all come from other languages as familiar as French (*chauffeur*) and as exotic as Icelandic (*mukluk*) or Chinese (*abacus*). Some come from the Army (*snafu*) or common songs (*Yankee Doodle*). But most of our words come from Latin and Greek. As learned scholars began to discover new concepts in the Renaissance and beyond, being trained in these "learned" languages themselves, they created neologisms (from the Greek, *neo-* [new], *logos* [word]) to describe those concepts. Thus, our language is full of words with *quad-*, *bio-*, *loq*, *fed-*, and so on.

Word part instruction can be the most boring instruction, full of memorization of lists of these parts with their definitions. It also can be a thoughtful exploration of the roots of English. Seeing the relations between, for example, *colloquial* and *elocution*, can be interesting. Teaching word parts in grades 3–5 can help children learn a great deal of words. Simple prefixes and suffixes can provide a significant amount of vocabulary growth in those grades (Anglin, 1993). See Blachowicz (2004) and Fisher (2004) for more extensive discussion.

Teaching Vocabulary to Children with Learning Disabilities (and Others)

To have an impact on children's comprehension, vocabulary teaching should be rich, intensive, and full of interesting information. It needs to cover a great many words and cover them well. This is too much to do in the hour sessions that our clinic conducts. Children with learning disabilities need to get their instruction in large and small groups, working cooperatively sometimes, in active discussion other times, and listening yet other times. Active vocabulary instruction should permeate a classroom, not just be a small segment at the beginning of a basal story. Vocabulary instruction is not just one of five important aspects of reading, but is a gift of words, one given generously to all in the class.

References

Adams, M. J. (1990). *Beginning to read: Thinking and learning about print*. Cambridge, MA: MIT Press.

Anglin, J. (1993). *Vocabulary development: A morphological analysis*. Monographs for the society of research in child development., Serial Number 238, Vol. 58, No. 10.

Baker, L., & Brown, A. L. (1984). Metacognitive skills and reading. In P. D. Pearson (Ed.), *Handbook of reading research* (pp. 353–394). White Plains, NY: Longman.

Beck, I. L., & McKeown, M. M. (2001). Text talk: Capturing the benefits of read aloud experiences for young children. *The Reading Teacher, 55*, 10–36.

Beck, I. L., & McKeown, M. M. (2003). Text talk: An approach to storybook reading in kindergarten. In A. v. Kleeck, S. A. Stahl, & E. B. Bauer, (Eds.). *On reading books to children: Parents and teachers* (10–35). Mahwah, NJ: Erlbaum.

Carver, R. P.(2000). *The causes of high and low reading achievement*. Mahwah, NJ: Erlbaum.

Chomsky, C. (1978). When you still can't read in third grade? After decoding: What? In S. J. Samuels (Ed.), *What research has to say about reading instruction* (pp. 13–30). Newark, DE: International Reading Association.

D'Anna, C. A., Zechmeister, E. B., & Hall, J. W. (1991). Toward a meaningful definition of vocabulary size. *Journal of Reading Behavior, 23*, 109–122.

Eeds, M., & Cockrum, W. A. (1985). Teaching word meanings by expanding schemata vs. dictionary work vs. reading in context. *Journal of Reading, 28*, 492–497.

Egan, T. (1997). *Burnt toast on Davenport street*. Boston: Houghton Mifflin.

Expedia Encyclopedia, (2001). Seattle, WA: MsWord.

Fry, E. E., Fountoukidis, D., & Polk, J. (1985) *The new reading teacher's book of lists*. Englewood Cliffs, NJ: Prentice Hall.

Hayes, D. P., & Ahrens, M. G. (1988). Vocabulary simplification for children: A special case of "motherese." *Journal of Child Language, 15*, 395–410.

Haynes, M. C., & Jenkins, J. (1986). Reading instruction in special education resource rooms. *American Educational Research Journal, 23*(2), 161–190.

Kuhn, M., & Stahl, S. (2003). Fluency: A review of developmental and remedial practices. *Journal of Educational Psychology, 95*(1), 3–21.

Leinhardt, G., Zigmond, N., & Cooley, W. W. (1981). Reading instruction and its effects. *American Educational Research Journal, 18*(3), 343–361.

McKenna, M. C. Teaching vocabulary to struggling older readers. *Perspectives, 30*(1), 13–16.

Nagy, W. E., & Anderson, R. C. (1984). How many words are there in printed school English? *Reading Research Quarterly, 19*, 303–330.

National Reading Panel (2000). *Report of the National Reading Panel: Teaching children to read*. Washington, DC: National Academy Press.

Rosenshine, B., & Meister, C. (1994). Reciprocal teaching: A review of the research. *Review of Educational Research, 64*, 479–530.

Roth, P. (1988). *I married a communist*. New York: Houghton-Mifflin.

Saunders, W.M., & Goldenberg, C. (1999). Effects of instructional conversations and literature logs on limited—and fluent—English proficient students' story comprehension and thematic under-standing. *Elementary School Journal, 99*(4), 277–301.

Scott, J. A., & Nagy, W. E. (1997). Understanding the definitions of unfamiliar verbs. *Reading Research Quarterly, 32*, 184–200.

Scott, J. A., Jamieson-Noel, D., & Asselin, M. (2003). Vocabulary instruction throughout the day in twenty-three Canadian upper elementary classrooms. *Elementary School Journal, 103*(3), 269–86.

Snow, C. E., Burns, M. S., & Griffin, P. (1998). *Preventing reading difficulties in young children*. Washington, DC: National Research Council.

Spiro, R. J., Coulson, R. L., Feltovich, P. J., & Anderson, D. K. (1994). Cognitive flexibility theory: Advanced knowledge acquisition in ill-structured domains. In R. B. Ruddell, M. R. Ruddell, & H. Singer (Eds.), *Theoretical models and processes of reading* (4th ed., pp. 602–615). Newark, DE: International Reading Association.

Stahl, S. A. (1998). Vocabulary Development. Cambridge, MA: Brookline Press.

Stahl, S. A., & Clark, C. H. (1987). The effects of participatory expectations in classroom discussion on the learning of science vocabulary. *American Educational Research Journal, 24*(4), 541–555.

Stahl, S., & Fairbanks, M. (1986). The effects of vocabulary instruction: A model-based meta-analysis. *Review of Educational Research, 56*, 72–110.

Stahl, S. A., McKenna, M. C., & Jones, J. (2003). The concurrent development of phonological awareness, word recognition, and spelling. Unpublished manuscript, Champaign, IL.

Stahl, S. A., Richek, M. A., & Vandevier, R. J. (1991). Learning meaning vocabulary through listening: A sixth-grade replication. In J. Zutell & S. McCormick (Eds.) *Learner factors/teacher factors: Issues in literacy research and instruction* (pp. 185–192). The Fortieth Yearbook of the National Reading Conference, Chicago, IL.

Stahl, S.A., & Vancil, S. J. (1986). Discussion is what makes semantic maps work. *The Reading Teacher, 40*, 62–67.

Stanovich, K. E. (2000). *Progress in under-standing reading: Scientific foundations and new frontiers*. New York: Guilford Press.

Trelease, J. (2001). *The read-aloud handbook*. Boston: Houghton Mifflin.

White, T. G., Graves, M. F., & Slater, W. H. (1990). Growth of reading vocabulary in diverse elementary schools: Decoding and word meaning. *Journal of Educational Psychology, 82*, 281–290.

Wiles, D. (2001). *Freedom Summer*. New York: Atheneum.

The Importance of Teaching Reading Strategies

5.3

Danielle S. McNamara

While the ability to read and furthermore, to understand what is written, is critical to success in our educational system, our nation's report card in reading achievement is lackluster at best. Moreover, comprehension problems become most apparent when students are faced with textbook material (e.g., Best, Floyd, & McNamara, 2008; McNamara, 2001).

Why Can't Students Understand What They Read?

Reading problems stem from several sources. First, the student may not be able to read the words themselves. Indeed, word decoding development and deficits are the concern of many researchers and educators, particularly for younger children and children with learning deficits. However, this concern has sometimes led to the neglect of the counterpart of word decoding: sentence comprehension. Numerous problems can occur for the reader at the comprehension level. Understanding how the words come together in each sentence can be a challenge. Or, the student may understand each word and even each sentence, but fail to understand the relationships between the sentences and the meaning of the text as a whole. Further, the stumbling block may not be sufficient reading ability to understand more familiar genres of text, but rather, the student may only falter when faced with challenging, knowledge demanding text. The reader may lack the requisite knowledge. More importantly, the student may lack the reading strategies necessary to overcome such challenges.

> "Understanding how the words come together in each sentence can be a challenge."

It is clear that many readers lack sufficient reading abilities and knowledge to understand the genre of texts that pervade their classroom lives. World knowledge is particularly helpful to understanding text genres such as narratives or novels. But students need domain-specific knowledge to understand their textbook material. Domain knowledge refers to knowledge about the topic of the text such as knowledge about science, history, or about specific topics, such as cell mitosis, heat exchange, or World War II. Textbook materials, in particular, tend to be challenging for most students because they often lack sufficient domain knowledge. Textbooks contain unfamiliar words, unfamiliar concepts, and have structures particularly germane to instructional textbooks. In addition, textbooks tend to have numerous cohesion gaps, posing additional hurdles for many students. Cohesion gaps occur when there is little conceptual overlap or explicit connections between sentences. Cohesion gaps force readers to access knowledge to make connections between sentences. Critically, making these connections requires both general and domain knowledge. Thus, the challenges posed by poorly written text are compounded for students with less knowledge about the domain (e.g., McNamara, Kintsch, Songer, & Kintsch, 1996; McNamara, 2001).

How Can We Help Poor Readers?

Readers may encounter any number of roadblocks in the path to comprehension. Regardless of the locus of the reading problems, teaching strategies is one of the most effective means of helping students to overcome them. Strategy instruction across a variety of domains builds on the notion that less skilled students should learn strategies that mimic those exhibited by skilled students or that *compensate* for processes exhibited by skilled students. The underlying assumption is that the processes or skills induced by the strategies become more automatic with practice. Strategies provide the means to tackle complex problems in more efficient ways and, with practice, the strategies lead to skills that become automatic and quick over time.

The importance of reading strategies is becoming increasingly recognized. This recognition is perhaps best exemplified by the inclusion of a Reading Strategies strand in English Language Arts College Board Standards for College Success™ published in 2006 by the College Board (see also, McNamara, Ozuru, Best, & O'Reilly, 2007). That this strand was adopted by the College Board underlines growing recognition that high ability students use reading strategies and these strategies are essential, not only to successful comprehension, but to overcoming reading problems and becoming a better reader and comprehender.

What Evidence Do We Have for the Importance and Effectiveness of Reading Strategies?

In the reading comprehension domain, there is abundant evidence that reading strategies improve reading comprehension (Bereiter & Bird, 1985; Fuchs, D. & Fuchs, L., 2005; King & Rosenshine, 1993; McNamara, 2007; Ozgungor & Guthrie, 2004; Palincsar & Brown, 1984). Indeed, strategy instruction is particularly needed and effective for those students who are struggling most, namely those with less domain knowledge or lower reading skills (McNamara, 2004; McNamara, 2007; McNamara, O'Reilly, Rowe, Boonthum, & Levinstein, 2007; O'Reilly & McNamara, 2007).

One such instructional technique is called Self-explanation Reading Training (SERT; McNamara, 2004). SERT was based on research showing the benefits of reading strategy instruction (e.g., Baumann, Seifert-Kessell, & Jones, 1992; Bereiter & Bird, 1985; Davey, 1983; Dewitz, Carr, & Patberg, 1987; Hansen & Pearson, 1983; Palincsar & Brown, 1984; Pressley, Harris, & Marks, 1992; Yuill & Oakhill,

1988). The purpose of SERT was to combine reading strategy instruction with a technique designed to induce overt active processing, called *self-explanation*. Self-explanation is the process of explaining orally or in writing, to oneself, the meaning of written text. Research by Chi and colleagues (e.g., Chi, de Leeuw, Chiu, & LaVancher, 1994; Chi, Bassok, Lewis, Reimann, & Glaser, 1989) indicates that self-explanation can improve deep-level comprehension of text; however, most readers do not naturally self-explain text and self-explain poorly if they are prompted to do so (e.g., Chi et al., 1994). The goal of SERT was to help readers improve their ability to self-explain by using reading strategies, and in turn, improve their use of reading strategies by using them in their self-explanations.

In SERT (e.g., McNamara, 2004), the participants are given training that includes a description of self-explanation and six reading strategies. After being introduced to and given examples of the strategies, the participants then practice using self-explanation. The six reading strategies are: 1) comprehension monitoring, 2) paraphrasing, 3) elaboration, 4) logic or common sense, 5) predictions, and 6) bridging. These strategies represent reading processes that are characteristic of effective self-explanation. Examples of the use of each of the strategies are provided in Table 5.3.1 (adapted from McNamara, 2004).

Comprehension monitoring is the process of being aware of understanding. In effect, the process of comprehension monitoring falls out of using effective reading strategies because to use a strategy the readers must be at least somewhat aware of their level of understanding. And, ideally, a reader's awareness of low understanding can often lead to the use of reading strategies to repair understanding. Usually, comprehension monitoring does not manifest in self-explanations, but when it does, the reader may say "I don't understand what that means," or, "I see what that means now."

Paraphrasing is the process of restating the text in different words, or in the reader's own words. It doesn't go beyond the information in the text, so it's not an explanation of the text. In the reading strategy literature, paraphrasing is often not recognized as an effective strategy. However, it is an important part of the explanation because many readers often paraphrase the sentence to begin an explanation (McNamara, 2004; Todaro, Magliano, Millis, McNamara, & Kurby, 2004). Paraphrases are important because they help the reader, particularly less skilled readers, to better understand the explicit information contained in the words and sentences of a text. Thus, paraphrasing can help the less skilled reader improve the basic understanding of the text, or textbase level understanding (McNamara, O'Reilly, Best, & Ozuru, 2006). Paraphrases also act as a jump start for self-explanations (McNamara, 2004; Todaro et al., 2006). Essentially, the act of paraphrasing externalizes the reader's understanding. This process can force the reader to fill in conceptual gaps and facilitates the activation of relevant concepts that are necessary to generate inferences (Best, Rowe, Ozuru, & McNamara, 2005).

Table 5.3.1. **Examples of Strategies Used by Participants in McNamara (2004) for Sentence 3 of Cell Mitosis:** "Mitosis guarantees that all the genetic information in the nuclear DNA of the parent cell will go to each daughter cell."

Strategy	Examples of Self-Explanation
Comprehension Monitoring	1. I don't remember what DNA stands for. 2. So I guess daughter cells are a part of a larger cell or came from a larger cell—I don't know.
Paraphrasing	1. So each daughter cell will receive a duplicate copy of the same strand of DNA from the parent cell. 2. Ok, through this process of mitosis all the genetic information belongs in the DNA of the parent cell and that is transferred over to the daughter cell.
Elaboration	1. Ok, so there's the daughter cell and then there's a parent cell—mitosis has to do with genetic information so when I'm thinking of cell division I'm thinking of maybe how a baby is made and how it's developing. 2. So, by mitosis it guarantees that the chromosomes will get passed on so that the traits or whatever will be able to live on or whatever.
Using Logic	1. Ok, what they're saying is that mitosis will make sure that equal amounts of genetic information will go to each of the cells—equal amount will go to each daughter cell that way. They will develop basically the same—multiply the same. 2. Ok, so the genetic information that must be the chromosomes because the chromosomes are going into each of the cells. And that is made up of the DNA. So a part of . . . a part of each of the . . . a part of genetic information which is the DNA goes into each of the two cells that come out of this.
Prediction	1. Ok, this is the separation of the cell—the DNA—the next one should be the RNA. 2. So, that's the first stage, now they'll give the second one.
Bridging Inference	1. So, mitosis—the first stage of cell division where each set of chromosomes goes to each daughter cell will contain DNA. 2. So, yeah, so all the genetic information is in the chromosomes and each cell gets a complete set, so that's mitosis—when each cell has just as much DNA as the first mother cell—main cell—parent cell.

The remaining four strategies are the heart of self-explanation because they are all strategies for generating inferences while reading. *Elaboration* is the process of making inferences that link what is in the text or sentence to related knowledge. For example, when reading the following sentence about heart disease, "Coronary artery disease occurs when the arteries become hardened and narrowed," the reader might make the link to prior knowledge that arteries supply blood to the heart muscle. The reader might also use general knowledge or logic to infer that narrowed arteries would reduce blood flow to the heart muscle, result in a lack of oxygen supply, and potentially lead to a heart attack. Thus, the two strategies, *elaboration* and *logic* are quite similar, but when learning to use the strategy, logic or *common sense*, the reader is encouraged to use whatever knowledge is available, because readers often don't have enough domain knowledge or directly related knowledge. Instruction to use logic or general knowledge was included in SERT because general knowledge helps readers understand that it is possible to make sense of the text, and go beyond the text, without knowing a lot about the topic (McNamara, 2004). This is an important aspect of SERT because its purpose is to help low-knowledge readers make sense of challenging, unfamiliar text.

> "... strategies are essential, not only to successful comprehension, but to overcoming reading problems and becoming a better reader and comprehender."

The *prediction* strategy involves thinking about what might be coming next in the text. For the most part, predictions are relatively uncommon (Magliano, Baggett, Johnson, & Graesser, 1993; McNamara, 2004) and may be more useful and more common when reading narrative texts than when reading science texts. Predictions are also more common and useful when the predicted outcomes are highly constrained or highly probable (Magliano, Dijkstra, & Zwaan, 1996; van den Broek, 1994). Though predictions are not likely to contribute a great deal to comprehension of science text, they are included in SERT because exposure to them indicates to the student to think ahead and more globally while reading. Predictions are also included because they may eventually enhance readers' ability to understand narrative texts.

Finally, making *bridging inferences* is the process of linking ideas and understanding the relations between separate sentences in the text. Deep comprehension requires more than merely interpreting individual sentences; the reader must also be able to integrate individual sentence meanings into a coherent text level representation (Kintsch, 1988; 1998). Making inferences is critical to text comprehension because texts normally do not (or cannot) state all of the relevant information (e.g., McNamara et al., 1996). Therefore, to successfully comprehend a text, the reader must generate inferences to fill in "missing" information and build a coherent mental model that incorporates information in the text (Zwaan & Singer, 2003). The meaning of a text can remain fragmented and disconnected without inferences. In sum, inferences that link sentences in a text combine the individual sentence meanings distributed across the text into a more coherent structure (Gernsbacher, 1997; Kintsch, 1988).

McNamara (2004) showed that SERT instruction helped readers to generate more effective self-explanations. In this study, all of the participants (SERT and control) were asked to self-explain a difficult text about cell mitosis. Those students who were prompted to self-explain (as in Chi et al., 1994) were compared to those who were provided with training to self-explain using the reading strategies (i.e., SERT). Those who received the additional training on reading strategies (i.e., SERT) showed significantly better comprehension than those who were merely prompted to self-explain. The effects of training on comprehension were also most evident for low-knowledge participants. Analyses of the self-explanations produced by the participants after training indicated that SERT's primary role was in helping the low-knowledge readers to use logic, common sense, or general knowledge to self-explain the text. Thus, the results showed that SERT helped the low-knowledge students to more effectively self-explain the text (using more effective strategies) and as a consequence they showed considerably better comprehension than the low-knowledge participants in the control condition who had not received training. Moreover, low-knowledge participants who received SERT showed comprehension performance comparable to the high-knowledge participants. Notably, these benefits only emerged on the text-based questions. The low-knowledge readers did not have sufficient domain knowledge to generate inferences to support a coherent deep understanding of the text, or situation model. Nonetheless, the use of paraphrasing along with the generation of inferences based on logic and general knowledge helped the readers to understand the basic ideas in the text and form a more coherent textbase level understanding.

Why Is SERT Effective?

One important aspect of SERT is that it is tightly aligned with theories of comprehension and theories of knowledge and skill acquisition. Theories of knowledge and skill acquisition prescribe that the learner benefits from the active generation of the to-be-learned information (e.g., McNamara, 1995). Hirsch (2006) argues that there are few reading strategy programs of instruction that are well aligned with theories of text comprehension. He further argues that strategy instruction has become reductionistic and isolated skill building is not well matched with the demands of reading for knowledge building. Reading strategies cannot be trained in isolation of each other or in contexts separate from the target content. Self-explanation, in contrast, encourages the reader to use a combination of strategies, all of which are induced by the process of attempting to explain the text. Moreover, the process of explanation is a natural activity that externalizes the understanding of the text and at the same time has an overt purpose. The task is made quite simple to the reader—the reader's objective is to understand the text to the level that it can be explained. This task in and of itself clarifies the purpose of reading. This is what successful comprehenders must do to learn from text.

Importantly, self-explanation is not enough. Readers must also understand how to effectively self-explain. SERT explicitly spells this out for the reader and gives examples of the various types of strategies that can be used to improve their self-explanations. Moreover, SERT does not just give examples. The student also learns to identify the various strategies, and most importantly, practices the strategies. No skill can be learned without practice, and thus the student practices the strategies during SERT and is encouraged to practice the strategies after SERT.

What Can Technology Do?

There are several problems that we encountered with SERT, particularly in studies where we tested it in the context of classrooms. First, it takes time to train those who administer SERT, and those who are trained often do so inaccurately, conveying their own misconceptions about the strategies. Second, if a teacher were to administer the training, that places an extra burden on the teacher to learn the strategies and how to teach them, and it takes time away from covering necessary content for the course. Third, it is difficult to adapt training to students' individual needs in a classroom context. And, fourth, it is difficult to set up opportunities for individual practice of the strategies (e.g., with students in pairs), particularly in schools where social dynamics rule peer interactions. The latter is a particular problem in schools where survival is key and academic success draws little respect from peers.

For these reasons, we developed an automated version of SERT, called iSTART (Interactive Strategy Training for Active Reading and Thinking; Levinstein, Boonthum, Pillarisetti, Bell, & McNamara, 2007; McNamara, Levinstein, & Boonthum, 2004). iSTART is an interactive tutoring system that uses full bodied, animated conversational agents to scaffold the learning of the SERT comprehension strategies (McNamara, Boonthum, Levinstein, & Millis, 2007; McNamara et al., 2004). The animated agents in iSTART provide three phases of training. The *Introduction Module* provides instruction on self-explanation and reading strategies. There is a trio of animated agents (an instructor and two students) that cooperate with each other, provide information, pose questions, and provide explanations of the reading strategies. After the presentation of each strategy, the trainees complete brief multiple-choice quizzes to assess their learning. In the *Demonstration Module*, two animated agents (cartoon characters who speak, gesture, and interact) named Merlin and Genie, demonstrate the use of self-explanation in the context of a science passage and the trainee identifies the strategies being used. The final phase is *Practice*, where Merlin coaches and provides feedback to the trainee while the trainee practices self-explanation using the repertoire of reading strategies. For each sentence in a text, Merlin reads the sentence and asks the trainee to self-explain it by typing a self-explanation. Merlin gives feedback and asks the trainee to modify unsatisfactory self-explanations.

iSTART interprets the trainees' contributions using computational linguistic algorithms. Feedback on the content and quality of the self-explanation is a critical component of practice. During the practice phase, the agents' interactions with the trainee are moderated by the quality of the explanation: more positive feedback is given for longer, more relevant explanations; whereas, increased interactions and support are provided for shorter, less relevant explanations. The computational challenge is for the system to provide appropriate feedback within seconds to the student concerning the quality of the self-explanations (McNamara, Boonthum, et al., 2007). Merlin's responses are based on the outcome of the computational algorithms. For example, if the self-explanation appears irrelevant, Merlin asks the student to add more information that is related to the sentence. Satisfactory explanations might get feedback such as, "That's really great!" or, "That's pretty good." Throughout the interaction, the module tracks the variety of strategies employed. Selected sentences in the practice texts have been identified as particularly appropriate for certain strategies. When explaining one of these sentences, the student may be encouraged to use that particular strategy if it has not been used during the practice.

Empirical studies on the effectiveness of iSTART have been positive. Studies at both the college (McNamara, 2004; O'Reilly, Sinclair, & McNamara, 2004b) and high school levels (O'Reilly, Best, & McNamara, 2004; O'Reilly, Sinclair, & McNamara, 2004a; Taylor, O'Reilly, Sinclair, & McNamara, 2006; O'Reilly, Taylor, & McNamara, 2006) have indicated that iSTART improves text comprehension and strategy use over control groups. Two studies have further confirmed that iSTART training is as good as and can exceed a live, classroom-based version of the training called SERT in effectiveness (Magliano et al., 2005; O'Reilly, Sinclair, & McNamara, 2004b).

Most students benefit from iSTART, but in different ways, depending on their prior skills and knowledge (Magliano et al., 2005; McNamara, O'Reilly, Best, & Ozuru, 2006; O'Reilly et al., 2004a). Those with less knowledge of reading strategies needed to learn how to develop a coherent understanding of the basic information conveyed in each sentence of the text. In contrast, those with more prior knowledge of reading strategies were able to make more bridging inferences and elaborations, which translated to better performance on the bridging inference questions. Thus, students tend to make progress in their area of proximal development. Readers need to first learn to form an adequate representation of the text-based information—essentially, the information presented in each individual sentence. Then, readers can learn how to understand the text at a deeper level by processing the relationships between the ideas conveyed across sentences and making links to world knowledge.

What Can a Teacher Do?

The heart of the SERT training is that the students learn to self-explain text, particularly when the going gets rough, and that the students learn reading strategies that help this process. A teacher can implement SERT by explaining and demonstrating self-explanation and elaboration, and encouraging the students to use these strategies. Paraphrasing is also important because it helps the students to start the explanation. Elaboration, of course, helps the student construct a more coherent understanding. Elaborations can be generated using a number of sources: previous text, general knowledge or common sense, and topic-specific knowledge. It's not necessarily important that the student distinguishes between these sources, but it is important that the student learns that when topic-specific knowledge deficits are encountered, elaborations can be made using general knowledge, logic, common sense, and information from previous sentences in the text. These general sources of knowledge are essential to the success of SERT for low-knowledge readers (McNamara, 2004).

It's also crucial that the students practice using the strategies. This could be achieved in a classroom in numerous ways. For example, the students could be placed in pairs and asked to take turns self-explaining a portion of the textbook. The teacher can also have the students self-explain as a class—calling on students to begin or continue self-explanations and asking the students to write out self-explanations for selected sentences in text. These simple exercises may have important benefits, particularly for the struggling students.

SERT is a relatively simple training that requires only a couple of hours. If the student then uses and practices the strategies, the potential benefit to performance in difficult, knowledge demanding courses is substantial. For many students, these strategies could translate to the difference of passing or failing the course.

References

Baumann, J. F., Seifert-Kessell, N., & Jones, L. A. (1992). Effect of think-aloud instruction on elementary students' comprehension monitoring abilities. *Journal of Reading Behavior, 24*, 143–172.

Bereiter, C., & Bird, M. (1985). Use of thinking aloud in identification and teaching of reading comprehension strategies. *Cognition and Instruction, 2*, 131–156.

Best, R. M., Floyd, R. G., & McNamara, D. S. (2008). Differential competencies contributing to children's comprehension of narrative and expository texts. *Reading Psychology, 29*, 137–164.

Best, R. M., Rowe, M. P., Ozuru, Y., & McNamara, D. S. (2005). Deep-level comprehension of science texts: The role of the reader and the text. *Topics in Language Disorders, 25*, 65–83.

Chi, M. T. H., Bassok, M., Lewis, M. W., Reimann, P., & Glaser, R. (1989). Self-explanations: How students study and use examples in learning to solve problems. *Cognitive Science, 13*, 145–182.

Chi, M. T. H., de Leeuw, N., Chiu, M., & LaVancher, C. (1994). Eliciting self-explanations improves understanding. *Cognitive Science, 18*, 439–477.

Davey, B. (1983). Think aloud: Modeling the cognitive processes of reading comprehension. *Journal of Reading, 27*, 44–47.

Dewitz, P., Carr, E., & Patberg, J. (1987). Effects of interference training on comprehension and comprehension monitoring. *Reading Research Quarterly, 22*, 99–121.

Fuchs, D., & Fuchs, L. S. (2005). Responsiveness-to-intervention: A blueprint for practitioners, policymakers, and parents. *Teaching Exceptional Children, 38*, 57–61.

Gernsbacher, M. A. (1997). Two decades of structure building. *Discourse Processes, 23*, 265–304.

Hansen, J., & Pearson, P. (1983). An instructional study: Improving the inferential comprehension of good and poor fourth-grade readers. *Journal of Educational Psychology, 75*, 821–829.

Hirsch, E. D., Jr. (2006). *The knowledge deficit.* Boston, MA: Houghton Mifflin.

King, A., & Rosenshine, B. (1993). Effects of guided cooperative-questioning on children's knowledge construction. *Journal of Experimental Education, 6*, 127–148.

Kintsch, W. (1998). *Comprehension: A paradigm for cognition.* Cambridge, England: Cambridge University Press.

Kintsch, W. (1988). The role of knowledge in discourse comprehension construction-integration model. *Psychological Review, 95*, 163–182.

Levinstein, I. B., Boonthum, C., Pillarisetti, S. P., Bell, C., & McNamara, D. S. (2007). iSTART 2: Improvements for efficiency and effectiveness. *Behavior Research Methods, 39*, 224–232.

Magliano, J. P., Baggett, W. B., Johnson, B. K., & Graesser, A. C. (1993). The time course of generating causal antecedent and causal consequence inferences. *Discourse Processes, 16,* 35–53.

Magliano, J. P., Dijkstra, K., & Zwaan, R. A. (1996). Predictive inferences in movies. *Discourse Processes, 22,* 199–224.

Magliano, J. P., Todaro, S., Millis, K. K., Wiemer-Hastings, K., Kim, H. J., & McNamara, D. S. (2005). Changes in reading strategies as a function of reading training: A comparison of live and computerized training. *Journal of Educational Computing Research, 32,* 185–208.

McNamara, D. S. (1995). Effects of prior knowledge on the generation advantage: Calculators versus calculation to learn simple multiplication. *Journal of Educational Psychology, 87*, 307–318.

McNamara, D. S. (2001). Reading both high and low coherence texts: Effects of text sequence and prior knowledge. *Canadian Journal of Experimental Psychology, 55*, 51–62.

McNamara, D. S. (2004). SERT: Self-explanation reading training. *Discourse Processes, 38,* 1–30.

McNamara, D. S. (Ed.). (2007). *Reading comprehension strategies: Theory, interventions, and technologies.* Mahwah, NJ: Erlbaum.

McNamara, D. S., Boonthum, C., Levinstein, I. B., & Millis, K. (2007). Evaluating self-explanations in iSTART: Comparing word-based and LSA algorithms. In T. Landauer, D. S. McNamara, S. Dennis, & W. Kintsch (Eds.), *Handbook of latent semantic analysis* (pp. 227–241). Mahwah, NJ: Erlbaum.

McNamara, D. S., Kintsch, E., Songer, N. B., & Kintsch, W. (1996). Are good texts always better? Text coherence, background knowledge, and levels of understanding in learning from text. *Cognition and Instruction, 14*, 1–43.

McNamara, D. S., Levinstein, I. B., & Boonthum, C. (2004). iSTART: Interactive strategy trainer for active reading and thinking. *Behavior Research Methods, Instruments, and Computers, 36,* 222–233.

McNamara, D. S., O'Reilly, T., Best, R., & Ozuru, Y. (2006). Improving adolescent students' reading comprehension with iSTART. *Journal of Educational Computing Research, 34,* 147–171.

McNamara, D. S., O'Reilly, T., Rowe, M., Boonthum, C., & Levinstein, I. B. (2007). iSTART: A web-based tutor that teaches self-explanation and metacognitive reading strategies. In D. S. McNamara (Ed.), *Reading comprehension strategies: Theories, interventions, and technologies* (pp. 397–421). Mahwah, NJ: Erlbaum.

McNamara, D. S., Ozuru, Y., Best, R., & O'Reilly, T. (2007). The 4-Pronged Comprehension Strategy Framework. In D. S. McNamara (Ed.), *Reading comprehension strategies: Theories, interventions, and technologies* (pp. 465–496). Mahwah, NJ: Erlbaum.

O'Reilly, T., Best, R., & McNamara, D. S. (2004). Self-explanation reading training: Effects for low-knowledge readers. In K. Forbus, D. Gentner, & T. Regier (Eds.), *Proceedings of the Twenty-Sixth Annual Conference of the Cognitive Science Society* (pp. 1053–1058). Mahwah, NJ: Erlbaum.

O'Reilly, T., & McNamara, D. S. (2007). The impact of science knowledge, reading skill, and reading strategy knowledge on more traditional "high-stakes" measures of high school students' science achievement. *American Educational Research Journal, 44,* 161–196.

O'Reilly, T. P., Sinclair, G. P., & McNamara, D. S. (2004a). iSTART: A web-based reading strategy intervention that improves students' science comprehension. In Kinshuk, D. Sampson, & P. T. Isaías (Eds.), *Proceedings of the IADIS International Conference: Cognition and Exploratory Learning in Digital Age: CELDA 2004* (pp. 173–180). Lisbon, Portugal: IADIS Press.

O'Reilly, T. P., Sinclair, G. P., & McNamara, D. S. (2004b). Reading strategy training: Automated versus live. In K. Forbus, D. Gentner, & T. Regier (Eds.), *Proceedings of the Twenty-Sixth Annual Conference of the Cognitive Science Society* (pp. 1059–1064). Mahwah, NJ: Erlbaum.

O'Reilly, T., Taylor, R. S., & McNamara, D. S. (2006). Classroom based reading strategy training: Self-explanation vs. a reading control. In R. Sun & N. Miyake (Eds.), *Proceedings of the 28th Annual Conference of the Cognitive Science Society* (pp. 1887–1892). Austin, TX: Cognitive Science Society.

Ozgungor, S., & Guthrie, J. T. (2004). Interactions among elaborative interrogation, knowledge, and interest in the process of constructing knowledge from text. *Journal of Educational Psychology, 96,* 437–443.

Palincsar, A. S., & Brown, A. L. (1984). Reciprocal teaching of comprehension-fostering and comprehension-monitoring activities. *Cognition and Instruction, 1,* 117–175.

Pressley, M., Harris, K. R., & Marks, M. B. (1992). But good strategy instructors are constructivist. *Educational Psychology Review, 4,* 1–32.

Taylor, R. S., O'Reilly, T., Sinclair, G., & McNamara, D. S. (2006). Enhancing learning of expository science texts in a remedial reading classroom via iSTART. *Proceedings of the Seventh International Conference of the Learning Sciences* (pp. 765–770). Hillsdale, NJ: Erlbaum.

Todaro, S. A., Magliano, J. P., Millis, K. K., McNamara, D. S., & Kurby, C. C. (2004). Intra-clause constraints in think-aloud protocols. In K. Forbus, D. Gentner, & T. Regier (Eds.), *Proceedings of the 26th Annual Cognitive Science Society* (p. 1642). Mahwah, NJ: Erlbaum.

van den Broek, P. (1994). Comprehension and Memory of Narrative Texts: Inferences and coherence. In M. A. Gernsbacher (Ed.), Handbook of Psycholinguistics (pp. 539–588). San Diego, CA: Academic Press.

Yuill, N., & Oakhill, J. (1988). Understanding of anaphoric relations in skilled and less skilled comprehenders. *British Journal of Psychology, 79,* 173–186.

Zwaan, R. A., & Singer, M. (2003). Text Comprehension. In M.A. Gernsbacher & A. C. Graesser (Eds.), *Handbook of Discourse Processes* (pp. 83–121). Mahwah, NJ: Lawrence Erlbaum Associates.

Reading Comprehension Instruction
Focus on Content or Strategies?

Margaret G. McKeown, Isabel L. Beck, and Ronette G. K. Blake

The importance of reading well has never been in dispute. Reading well not only provides practical tools for communication, for work, and, most importantly, for learning itself, it also helps citizens participate fully in the choices that govern communities and the nation. Yet, reports from research and the larger educational community suggest that too many students leave school without knowing how to read well.

Recent research on comprehension has certainly provided increased understanding of comprehension processes and broad and general knowledge of what makes for effective instructional practice. Knowing the effective practices at a general level may suffice to bring successful learning to many students. But helping readers who are struggling to achieve requires deep understandings of the kinds of instructional practices that affect students' comprehension.

A situation that raises the stakes on what goes on in schools is that struggling readers are least likely to spend time on reading outside of school (Cunningham & Stanovich, 1998). Further, students from lower socioeconomic status (SES) homes have the least amount of language interaction at home, providing them with less grist to enhance their language development (Hart & Risley, 1995; 1999). The consequence is that these students have little opportunity for development and practice of higher-level comprehension abilities, highlighting the need to provide the most effective school instructional practices.

Two Directions for Comprehension Instruction: Strategies and Content

Presently, comprehension instruction research has come to focus on teaching explicit comprehension strategies. A strategies approach is prominent in the literature on comprehension instruction and was featured in two major reports on reading: the National Research Council's (NRC) *Preventing Reading Difficulties in Young Children* (Snow, Burns, & Griffin, 1998) and the NICHD sponsored report of the National Reading Panel (NRP) (2000). However, although a large body of research on strategies instruction has accumulated, a great deal remains to be explained. One reason that much is still unknown is that the studies have varied so widely in the kind of instruction offered, and little appears in the reports of studies about actual interactions with text. Thus, what is it about a strategies approach that has brought about the positive results?

The issue of what makes strategy instruction effective seems to be reflected in comments that a number of reading scholars have made. The comments speak to the issue of what is essential for comprehension instruction. For example, Carver (1987) has suggested that the positive effects of strategies may spring from more time spent reading and thinking about text rather than from specific learning about strategies. Pearson and Fielding (1991) mused that strategies instruction might not be needed if student attention could simply be focused on understanding text content. Seeming to address this issue, Gersten, Fuchs, Williams, & Baker (2001) suggest moving from explicit strategies toward more fluid approaches to comprehension instruction, centered on getting students to read in more thoughtful ways. Similarly, Sinatra, Brown, and Reynolds (2002) question whether it may be more effective to teach students to approach reading with a problem-solving perspective rather than to explicitly teach comprehension strategies.

The notion of approaching comprehension instruction as just getting students to focus on meaning is at the heart of an alternative instructional approach. This approach, which we have labeled a content approach, aims to direct students' attention toward the content of what they are reading and encourage students to work through the text to make sense of it, connecting and integrating information as they proceed through the text. The goal of this process is a coherent mental representation of the ideas the text presents. In a content approach, working through text takes the form of an interactive discussion of text as reading proceeds.

"What is it about a strategies approach that has brought about the positive results?"

Relative to strategies instruction, fewer studies have been done that investigate a content approach, and none have compared strategies and content approaches. In this article, we report on a recently completed study in which we implemented standardized lessons on common texts for both a *strategies approach* and a *content approach* to comprehension instruction and compared their effects.

For a sense of how the two approaches operate, consider a group of students who have just finished reading a short segment of text. In a strategies approach, the teacher might ask the students to summarize the text and recall what kind of information goes into a good summary. She might follow up a student's summary by asking other students if it was a good summary and why or why not. In a content approach, the teacher might ask what the portion of text had been about, and as students respond, follow up by asking how pieces of information that students contributed fit in with what is being read or why the information is important.

Roots and Current Status of Strategies and Content Approaches

Strategies and content approaches have common features as well as distinctions. Both try to engender student engagement with reading and both approaches certainly intend that students understand the content of a text with which they are working. Both approaches can trace their roots to mental processing models—models of learning and thinking in the case of strategies and of text processing in the case of content.

The notion of providing instruction in strategies, individual routines for dealing with text, arose from work in developmental psychology that had established the active, strategic nature of learning that developed as children matured. Based on this developmental foundation, Brown and her colleagues researched strategies for general learning tasks, such as rehearsal, categorization, and elaboration (Brown, Bransford, Ferrara, & Campione, 1983), and followed by investigation of strategies for studying, such as note-taking and underlining (Brown, 1981; 1982b; Brown & Smiley, 1977). From their work, Brown and her colleagues surmised that strategies might be useful to improve comprehension of young or less able learners (Brown & Smiley, 1978). The eventual manifestation of this line of work in reading was Reciprocal Teaching, an approach that taught young students to apply strategies of summarizing, questioning, clarifying, and predicting (Palincsar & Brown, 1984).

Strategies instruction also finds roots in models of thinking. Pressley and his colleagues (Symons, Snyder, Cariglia-Bull, & Pressley, 1989) trace notions of strategy teaching to theories of Baron (1985) and Sternberg (1979; 1982), both of whom emphasize the role of efficient component processes in complex thinking such as problem solving. These subprocesses included identifying a goal, monitoring progress, and evaluating evidence. This line of thinking led researchers to provide young students with procedures they could employ while reading to facilitate comprehension. These roots led Pressley and his colleagues to develop Transactional Strategies Instruction, an approach in which the teacher explains and models strategies, and uses strategies to guide dialogue about text (Pressley, et al., 1992).

While models of thinking and general learning underlie strategies instruction, models developed to explain specifically how a reader processes text (see for example, Kintsch, 1974; Graesser, Singer, & Trabasso, 1994; Trabasso, Secco, & Van den Broek, 1984; Van den Broek, Young, Tzeng, & Linderholm, 1998) are the roots of a content approach to comprehension. Text processing models take the perspective that the mental processes in reading focus on the development of coherence based on organizing the meaningful elements of the text. From a text-processing perspective, a reader moves through text identifying each new piece of text information and deciding how it relates to information already given and to background knowledge (See Kintsch & van Dijk, 1978). The focus is on what readers do with text information to represent it and integrate it into a coherent whole. A text-processing perspective on comprehension suggests that comprehension enhancement might derive from a focus on continually striving for meaning as reading of the text moves along.

Overview of Study Comparing Strategies and Content Approaches

To conduct the study, we developed sets of standardized lessons for strategies and content around a common set of texts for fifth grade (McKeown, Beck, & Blake, 2008). The study ran for two consecutive years. In the first year the lesson materials were based on five narratives from the basal reader in use in the school district.

In the second year, these same story lessons were used again, and we added three expository texts.

The study included all fifth graders from one school in a low-performing urban district. This involved six classrooms and their teachers, two classrooms in which teachers taught strategies lessons, two classrooms in which teachers taught content lessons, and two classrooms in which lessons using the basal reader material were taught, serving as our comparison group. In this article we will confine our discussion to the results from the strategies and content classrooms. The content lessons were based on an approach that Beck and McKeown and their colleagues developed, Questioning the Author (QtA) (Beck, McKeown, Sandora, Kucan, & Worthy, 1996; Beck & McKeown, 2006).

To develop the strategies lessons, we first needed to identify the strategies to use. We considered which strategies had been highlighted as showing positive effects in the NRC (Snow, Burns, & Griffin, 1998) and NRP (2000) reports. The NRC report focuses on summarizing, predicting, drawing inferences, and monitoring for coherence. The NRP report lists comprehension monitoring, summarization, question-generation, question-answering, cooperative learning, graphic and semantic organizers, and multiple-strategy teaching. To select among these strategies, we considered which of those procedures might be most naturally called on as a reader works through a text to understand the content. Our thinking was that readers tend to summarize important information as they move through text; they develop a sense of what may be coming next; they need to draw inferences to create connections; and they may well form questions to check that they are on track. Additionally, effective readers monitor their understanding and take steps to remedy the situation if they do not understand. We thus selected summarizing, predicting, drawing inferences, question-generation, and comprehension monitoring as the strategies for our lessons. We developed the strategies instruction in a three-tiered process of design and feedback, with input from strategies experts in the field.

For lessons in the two instructional and the comparison conditions we followed a similar format that we scripted for the teachers. We chose stopping places in the text, which were very similar across the approaches, and developed questions for the teacher to pose (in the case of content and the comparison) and procedures to prompt students to implement a specific strategy for the strategies condition. The scripts also included suggestions on following up student responses, in case students did not address key information in their initial responses.

A stop in a strategies lesson, for example, might begin with the teacher saying, "This is a good place to stop and summarize." After a student responds, follow-up prompts suggested for the teacher include: "Was that a good summary?" to have other students evaluate and add or revise, and "What do we do when we summarize?" to have students review the thinking that goes into summarizing. At a stop in a content lesson a teacher might ask, "What just happened?" with a follow-up provided in case key information was not elicited, such as, "Why might that be important?" The lessons were presented over nine weeks.

The strength of our design was that instructional conditions were held constant except for the issue of interest. Thus, both the strategies and content conditions featured whole-class, teacher-led instruction with interspersed reading and discussion. Text was read aloud and student responses were elicited, acknowledged, and dealt with by the teacher to help students focus on both the task at hand of understanding the text and encouraging students to internalize a way of dealing with text. The key difference in the approaches was the kind of prompts that the teachers posed to students during reading. In the strategies condition the teacher focused on getting students to interact with the text by applying strategies, and in the content condition, teacher prompts focused on getting students to grasp important ideas and events in the text and how they were connected.

Measures and Outcomes

We used a variety of measures to assess the outcomes of the lesson conditions that were aimed to capture different aspects of the comprehension process. This included a comprehension test for each lesson's text based on Royer's sentence verification technique (SVT) (Royer, Hastings, & Hook, 1979), recall of texts used in the lessons, recall of a transfer text, and a comprehension-monitoring task.

The SVT required students to discriminate sentence-level paraphrases and inferences of text content from false instances of the content. Thus, the measure was more text-bound and called for recognition and matching of text content with assessment items. The text recall called for a constructed response, which requires a reader to bring forth information from memory, decide which information to include in the recall, and put that information into language.

Recall of the transfer text had similar requirements but also assessed the degree to which students were able to take advantage of the scaffolding of the reading process provided for lesson texts when directing their own processing. This task was designed to follow a sequence of lessons in which the teacher gradually released responsibility for scaffolding comprehension to the students. The final two lessons in the sequence, the fourth and fifth, provided for no discussion at all, but simply teacher prompts for students to deal with the text as they had been doing in lessons. Recall was taken on the fifth and final text. Finally the comprehension-monitoring task measured a specific aspect of comprehension, the ability to identify potential obstacles to comprehension, by presenting texts to students individually that contained anomalies and asking students whether segments of the text made sense or presented any confusing information.

The outcomes of our analyses showed no differences between students in the instructional conditions on the comprehension-monitoring task or the sentence verification task. Differences were found, however, in recall of both lesson and transfer texts in favor of the content group for both years of the study. At first blush, these differences may seem like inconsistent results, but we see them as offering a meaningful pattern.

First, consider the measures applied to the lesson texts: sentence verification and recall. Sentence verification requires recognition, a less cognitively demanding task than recall, which, as a productive measure, is usually considered to capture a higher level of comprehension. Also consider that scores on the SVT were relatively high for both strategies and content groups. We take this to mean that instruction in both conditions prompted adequate comprehension from students. This was to be expected, given that both conditions provided high-quality lessons and scaffolding. As we discussed, both strategies and content instruction have been found to be successful, and in our study the lessons were carefully designed to provide faithful versions of that instruction.

The comprehension-monitoring task showed no differences between conditions. This measure was presented as a pretest/ posttest comparison and did, however, show an overall pretest to posttest gain. Again, this would seem to reflect that students gained positive experiences in comprehension from both kinds of instruction, but the differences between conditions were not strong enough to bring about differential effects on texts that were well-removed from the classroom context of scaffolded lessons.

The differences in recall suggest that for higher levels of comprehension under conditions close to the learning condition, the kind of discussion fostered in the content lessons provided advantages for the students. Recall of lesson texts was directly influenced by the lesson discussion. The transfer task provided a measure of *proximal* transfer, in that it was not directly influenced by a structured lesson, but provided a similar but more generalized pattern of guidance.

Discussion

What are the roots of the benefits that occurred for the content group in text recall? An answer appears to lie in the nature of discussion prompted by the content lessons. Analysis of the discussions showed several features that may underlie the recall results. First, lesson discussions in the content classrooms included more information that was directly related to the text than the strategies discussions. Second, content students' contributions to discussions averaged twice as long as those in strategies classrooms.

Examination of transcripts of the discussions suggests how these differences may relate to the recall advantages. We consider aspects of discussions about two of the texts from one of the classrooms in each condition for that purpose. The first text is a story by Isaac Asimov, *The Fun They Had* (Asimov, 2005), about children in the future—the year 2157. In the first segment of the text, the children discover an old printed book and are stunned by it because "the words stand still" in contrast to the books they read on their television screens. In the strategies classroom, the teacher opens discussion of this segment by focusing on comprehension monitoring, asking if anything might be confusing. A student identifies a line of text that may offer confusion: "on the page headed May 17, 2157." When the teacher follows up by asking what the student could do to help herself understand 2157, the student replies with a strategic procedure: "Ask a question." Another student offers a way to address the confusion, but he frames it hypothetically: "Maybe you could, like, to tell if it's a date or what—just like if it's a date, you could see how many years from now it is."

Another student identifies a confusing aspect of the text, and when asked how he cleared up the confusion, the student also replies procedurally: "Ask a question, read on, reread." Although the students in this discussion select important concepts from the text, for the most part the concepts are not used for building meaning; rather they are treated as instances of how a strategy *could be* applied.

> "... the content class-rooms seem to provide a kind of external model of comprehension, charac-terized by going through text, selecting what is important, and connect-ing those ideas to build understanding."

In the content classroom, the discussion for this segment begins with the teacher asking, "So what's this all about?" A student provides a 96-word summary of the text segment in her own words, describing how the book the children found is different from those future children's experiences. Another student then weighs in, adding other relevant ideas, includ-ing that in this future time "They don't read books. They read, like, on television screens and they're shocked because the book is really old." As discussion proceeds, the teacher inte-grates student responses, and another student adds further elaboration.

In an example from another text, the classes are reading a story about a fifth grade girl who is running for president of her class (*Off and Running*, Soto, 2005). In the segment in focus, the girl is looking for someone famous to endorse her campaign, and her mother tells her about a rela-tive who was mayor of a Mexican town. The discussion in the strategies classroom begins with the teacher asking for a summary. When no student responds, the teacher asks what to do to form a summary. A student responds that it is the *who, what, when, where, why,* and *how* of the story. For the rest of the discussion the students respond to the teachers' prompts for the *who, what,* and *where* with brief, direct answers.

In the content classroom, the teacher asks, "What just happened?" A student begins to describe this new character who had been a mayor. Another student chimes in to clarify the woman's relationship to the girl. The first student contin-ues, providing a 55-word description of the events of the segment. The teacher then asks how this connects and a student responds appropriately and, again, at some length.

The discussions of the two texts show a similar pattern in that the strategies class focuses on aspects of strategy application while the content class focuses on text ideas and how they fit together. The pattern of discussion suggests that teacher questions that encourage students to express and integrate what they've understood from text supports the development of a coherent understanding, as evidenced by their higher quality recalls of text. As the foregoing examples typify, the discussions in the content classrooms seem to provide a kind of external model of comprehension, characterized by going through text, selecting what is impor-tant, and connecting those ideas to build understanding.

Strategy prompts create a path that is not directly into the text, but once removed. That is, rather than directing students' attention to the content of the text, strategy prompts may ask students to focus on components of a strategy, such as considering *who, what, when,* and *where* to create a summary. Or prompts may ask students to think about general ways to deal with text, such as that a reader might ask a question, or reread to resolve confusion.

The results of our study seem to bring into focus the question of what is the active processing that is at the heart of the rationale for both strategies and content instruction. For strategies instruction, active processing comprises conscious and deliberate attention to the process, while for content it is more of an active stance—consciousness that a process exists and that active effort is needed to bring about understanding. Our findings suggest that getting students to actively build meaning while reading does not necessitate knowledge of and focus on specific strategies, but rather it may simply require attention to text content in ways that promote selecting important ideas and establishing connections between them.

References

Asimov, I. (2005). The fun they had. In *Trophies distant voyages* (pp. 584–592). Chicago: Harcourt.

Baron, J. (1985). *Rationality and intelligence.* Cambridge, England: Cambridge University Press.

Beck, I. L., & McKeown, M. G. (2006). *Improving comprehension with Questioning the Author: A fresh and expanded view of a powerful approach.* New York: Scholastic.

Beck, I. L., McKeown, M. G., Sandora, C., Kucan, L., & Worthy, J. (1996). Questioning the author: A yearlong classroom implementation to engage students with text. *Elementary School Journal, 96*(4), 385–414.

Brown, A. L. (1981). Metacognition and reading and writing: The development and facilitation of selective attention strategies for learning from texts. In M. L. Kamil (Ed.), *Directions in reading: Research and instruction.* Washington, DC: National Reading Conference.

Brown, A. L. (1982b). Learning to learn how to read. In J. Langer & T. Smith-Burke (Eds.), *Reader meets author, bridging the gap: A psycholinguistic and social linguistic perspective.* Newark, NJ: Dell.

Brown, A. L., & Smiley, S. S. (1977). Rating the importance of structural units of prose passages: A problem of metacognitive development. *Child Development, 48,* 1–8.

Brown, A. L., & Smiley, S. S. (1978). The development of strategies for studying texts. *Child Development, 49,* 1076–1088.

Brown, A. L., Bransford, J. D., Ferrara, R. A., & Campione, J. C. (1983). Learning, remembering, and understanding. In J. H. Flavell & E. M. Markman (Eds.), *Handbook of child psychology* (4th ed., pp. 77–166). New York: Wiley Press.

Carver, R. P. (1987). Should reading comprehension skills be taught? In J. E. Readance & R. S. Baldwin (Eds.), *Research in literacy: Merging perspectives* (Thirty-sixth yearbook of the National Reading Conference, pp. 115–126). Rochester, NY: National Reading Conference.

Cunningham A. E., & Stanovich, K. E. (1998). What reading does for the mind. *American Educator, 22*(1-2), 8–15.

Gersten, R., Fuchs, L., Williams, J. P., & Baker, S. (2001). Teaching reading comprehension strategies to students with learning disabilities. *Review of Educational Research 71*(2), 279–320.

Graesser, A. G., Singer, M., & Trabasso, T. (1994). Constructing inferences during narrative text comprehension. *Psychological Review, 101,* 371–395.

Hart, B., & Risley, T. (1995). *Meaningful differences.* Baltimore: Paul H. Brookes.

Hart, B., & Risley, T. (1999). *The social world of children learning to talk.* Baltimore: Paul H. Brookes.

Kintsch, W. (1974). *The representation of meaning in memory.* Hillsdale, NJ: Erlbaum.

Kintsch, W., & van Dijk, T. A. (1978). Toward a model of text comprehension and production. *Psychological Review, 85*(5), 363–394.

McKeown, M. G., Beck, I. L., & Blake, R. G. K., (in press). Rethinking reading comprehension instruction: A comparison of instruction for strategies and content approaches. *Reading Research Quarterly*.

National Reading Panel (2000). *Teaching children to read: An evidence-based assessment of the scientific research literature on reading and its implications for reading instruction.* Washington, DC: National Institute of Child Health & Human Development.

Palincsar, A. S., & Brown, A. L. (1984). Reciprocal teaching of comprehension-fostering and comprehension-monitoring activities. *Cognition and Instruction, 2*, 117–175.

Pearson, P. D., & Fielding, L. (1991). Comprehension instruction. In R. Barr, M. Kamil, P. Mosenthal, & P. D. Pearson (Eds.), *Handbook of reading research* (Vol. 2, pp. 815–860). New York: Longman.

Pressley, M., El-Dinary, P. B., Gaskins, I., Schuder, T., Bergman, J. L., Almasi, J., & Brown, R. (1992). Beyond direct explanation: Transactional instruction of reading comprehension strategies. *Elementary School Journal, 92*(5), 513–555.

Royer, J. M., Hastings, C. N., & Hook, C. (1979). A sentence verification technique for measuring reading comprehension. *Journal of Reading Behavior, 11*, 355–363.

Sinatra, G. M., Brown, K. J., & Reynolds, R. (2002). Implications of cognitive resource allocation for comprehension strategies instruction. In C. C. Block & M. Pressley (Eds.), *Comprehension instruction: Research-based best practices* (pp. 62–76). New York: Guilford Press.

Snow, C. E., Burns, M. S., & Griffin, P. (1998). *Preventing reading difficulties in young children.* Washington, DC: National Academy Press.

Soto, G. (2005). Off and Running. In *Trophies distant voyages* (pp. 492–506). Chicago: Harcourt.

Sternberg, R. J. (1979). The nature of mental abilities. *American Psychologist, 34*, 214–230.

Sternberg, R. J. (1982). A componential approach to intellectual development. In R. J. Sternberg (Ed.), *Advances in the psychology of human intelligence*, Vol. 1. Hillsdale, NJ: Erlbaum & Associates.

Symons, S., Snyder, B. L., Cariglia-Bull, T., & Pressley, M. (1989). Why be optimistic about cognitive strategy instruction? In C. McCormick, G. Miller, & M. Pressley (Eds.), *Cognitive strategy research: From basic research to educational applications*. New York: Springer-Verlag.

Trabasso, T., Secco, T., & van den Broek, P. W. (1984). Casual cohesion and story coherence. In H. Mandl, N. L. Stein, & T. Trabasso (Eds.), *Learning and comprehension of text* (pp. 83–111). Hillsdale, NJ: Erlbaum.

Van den Broek, P., Young, M., Tzeng, Y., & Linderholm, T. (1998). The landscape model of reading: Inferences and the on-line construction of a memory representation. In H. van Oostendorp & S. R. Goldman (Eds.), *The construction of mental representations during reading* (pp. 71–98). Mahwah, NJ: Erlbaum.

Designing Questions Toward Thinking and Understanding Rather Than Answers

Margaret G. McKeown and Isabel L. Beck

Have you ever noticed when people say "that's a good question" they don't have a ready answer? We think that not having a ready answer may be very relevant to what makes a good question, and we will return to this notion later. But we begin by considering the status and potential of question-asking as an instructional technique.

Status of Question Asking

Question asking is one of the processing components that underlies comprehension, problem-solving, and other cognitive abilities (Otero & Graesser, submitted). The use of questions as an instructional device has a long history; as Tharp and Gallimore (1988) point out, Plato first argued that questioning is the sine qua non of teaching. Indeed, studies do show that asking questions can improve students' learning of text material. But results of such studies are mixed (Trabasso, van den

Broek, & Liu 1988), and the learning gains following questioning are often small (Pressley et al., 1992).

To understand why these results are so often unimpressive, let us begin with considering what questions in classrooms typically look like. Study after study, from at least 1908 through 1997, paint the same picture: the large majority of questions asked in classrooms follow the IRE pattern (Cazden, 1988); the teacher *Initiates* a question ("Where does the action take place?"), the student *Responds*, usually briefly ("near Chicago"), and the teacher *Evaluates* ("OK") and then goes on to ask another, not necessarily related, question. This format keeps things very orderly. Since students rely mostly on simple recall, they frequently get the answer correct and the teacher can judge instantly if the response is correct.

The Good Question

One big problem with the IRE is that the goal of a correct response can overwhelm the questioning enterprise. It often drives teachers to frame a question so tightly around an answer that students can't miss: "So Goldilocks went into the house owned by the three _____ ." That may help students deliver the answer, but it does not promote their understanding. This brings us back to our initial notion of a good question: When people say "that's a good question" they tend not to know the answer immediately. Rather, it often means that they need to think about the question. The point of asking students questions as part of instruction is not to have students get the answers right. It is to reveal where students are in what they know and to help them build understanding of what they don't know.

To build understanding, a reader needs to identify ideas, think through what they mean and how they connect to each other and to what the reader already knows, and then frame those ideas, connections, and knowledge into a coherent representation. If we ask the kind of questions that students "get right" with ease, then we are not promoting a thoughtful comprehension process, but asking them merely to report what they already know.

To be truly productive of students' comprehension of what they read, questions have to leave room for students to build meaning rather than too directly pointing them to the answers. An illustration of this "leaving room" occurred when we were doing some planning with junior high teachers for an upcoming story, The Tiger's Heart (Kjelgard, 1996), which is an interesting, ironic tale that begins with the line "The approaching jungle night was, in itself, a threat." The first two paragraphs in the story describe how strange and frightening the jungle became at night, and how well the village inhabitants knew every inch of the jungle during the day.

Consider the kind of student thinking prompted by the following questions: "How is the author comparing and contrasting the jungle at night and in the day?" in contrast to "What's this all about?" The first question already sets up that the author's intent is to contrast the jungle at night and during the day—but isn't that what we want students to build from reading this? So why give them that framework?

Framing questions so that students have to do more of the thinking brings us into messy territory. Rather than immediate, well-formed responses, what may surface is cognitive turmoil as students struggle with ideas. But it is students' un-restrained attempts at meaning-making that allow opportunities for understanding to grow. And from the teaching side, letting the process be messy puts student thinking into play where it can be facilitated.

Engaging Students with Questions

We entered this messy territory when we began to work on a project to develop ways to help students engage with what they read. The project resulted in Questioning the Author (QtA), an instructional approach aimed to help students build understanding by grappling with and responding to the ideas they read about (Beck, McKeown, Worthy, Sandora, & Kucan, 1996; McKeown & Beck, 1999).

QtA operates around open queries, such as "What is the author trying to say?" and "How does that connect to what we read about before?" Below we present an example from a QtA lesson in a 6th grade classroom. The class is reading Theodore Taylor's novel, *The Cay* (1995), in which a boy, Philip, and an old man, Timothy, have been shipwrecked on an island and Philip lost his sight during the accident. In the excerpt that follows, Philip is beginning to feel his way around the island, trying to conquer fear of his blindness.

> Timothy had fashioned a cane for me, and I was now using it to feel my way around the island. I fell down often, but unless I fell into sea grape, it did not hurt. Even then, I only got a few scratches.
>
> Slowly, I was beginning to know the island. By myself, keeping my feet in the damp sand, which meant I was near the water, I walked the whole way around it. Timothy was very proud of me.
>
> From walking over it, feeling it, and listening to it, I think I knew what our cay looked like. As Timothy said, it was shaped like a melon, or a turtle, sloped up from the sea to our ridge where the palms flapped all day and night in the light trade wind (p. 83).

The teacher, Mrs. C., opens with a question:
Mrs. C: Okay, what's the author's message in this little section that Makia read? Brian?

Brian gives a kind of literal replay of events, a common response we see to an initial question.
Brian: Um, he's like um… wondering what the island looks like just by um, feeling and walking around it.

Mrs. C. follows up, prompting for what the author is revealing to the reader and Carolyn responds by hinting at a change in Philip—that he's "walking around more," despite his blindness.
Mrs. C: What do you think the author means by telling us that now?

Carolyn: Like Brian said, he's walking around more and he can do that, even though he can't see, he can go around through feeling.

Mrs. C. recasts Carolyn's response as "adjusting to his blindness" and asks for a connection to earlier situations.

Mrs. C: So he's making adjustments to his blindness? How does that connect with how he was feeling before?

Makia: Before he was feeling like he couldn't do anything because he couldn't see, and now, since like he's been on that cay for a while and he's learned his way around, he's learning like that he can do things even though he's blind.

Makia does a pretty good job of articulating the connection between Philip's earlier feelings and his current acceptance of his blindness.

In this brief excerpt, discussion moves from a literal response to the meaning of Philip's actions in terms of the development of his character. This process was set in motion by the teacher's initial open question: "What's the author's message here?" Let us take the idea of open questions in a bit more detail.

Open questions are invitations to start grappling with ideas: "What's the author trying to say?" "What's the author setting up here?" "What's all this about?" "What's going on here?" This is all that is needed to kick things off. When more information is put into an initial question, it leaves students very little work to do. Considering the questions in Table 5.5.1 can illustrate why this is so. For example, suppose that a character held a small bird in her hand and that this was an important event in the story. Asking the first constrained question in Table 5.5.1 reduces the student's task by providing half the answer, that is, the character's having something in her hand is important to the story. Additionally, the answer to such a question is likely to be simply "a bird." In contrast, asking one of the open questions, such as "What's going on?" requires students to construct a response that explains the entire situation, such as: a character has found a wounded bird and is cradling it in her hand (see Table 5.5.1).

Table 5.5.1.   **Comparing Constrained and Open Questions**

Constrained Questions	Open Questions
What did she have in her hand?	What's this about? What's going on?
Where did the friends go?	What are they up to? So, what do you see happening here?
At the beginning she felt a little, what?	So, how does that connect with what we knew from before?
And is Lona happy about all this?	How is Lona taking this?
Where is this story taking place? Who is the story about?	How is the author starting us off here?

What Happens after Students Respond to Open Questions?

As the lesson excerpt presented earlier suggests, a teacher's role does not end with asking an open question to initiate discussion. An open question is posed to prompt students to think and formulate ideas, but those thoughts and ideas may not be complete or clear. The teacher's task, then, is to deal with the student thinking that comes forth and use it to further the discussion.

The importance of dealing with students' initial responses effectively has arisen in much recent work on teaching (Graesser, Person, & Magliano, 1995; Leinhardt , 1993; Mangano, 1986; Nystrand & Gamoran, 1991; Orsolini & Pontecorvo, 1992). The key element may be including some of the student's response in the teacher's follow-up. Studies have found that echoing students' language in subsequent questions positively affects the amount and quality of students' later responses (Nystrand and Gamoran, 1991; Orsolini & Pontecorvo, 1992). Leinhardt's research suggests that teachers can help move student thinking along by selectively and strategically following-up ideas that enter the conversation. In this way, teachers do not correct a student directly, but allow the student to self-revise by prompting rethinking of their ideas. The point is that the building of understanding is rarely complete with a response to a question; rather, an initial response sets the process in motion. Much of the work of meaning building occurs after that, in following up.

The teacher's task in following-up initial responses is to balance prompting students to do the thinking with maintaining a focus so that the talk is productive and directed toward a goal of building meaning. In the excerpt presented from *The Cay*, the teacher accomplished this by, for example, following a student's response with, "What do you think the author means by telling us that now?" This prompted students to consider why Philip's walking around the island was meaningful at this juncture in the story. The teacher then responded to the next student by recasting or revoicing the student's response to crystallize the idea that Philip's walking around even though he was blind meant that he was making adjustments to his blindness. This is what is meant by responding strategically and selectively to what students say. Mrs. C. did not simply repeat the response, nor did she simply turn to the next student for an additional comment. The key idea here is eliciting thinking that explains ideas in the text and how they connect, to move toward building meaning. With those features in mind, let us consider one more example.

The excerpt below is from a discussion of a social studies text's introduction of the French and Indian War. The 4th grade students are working to understand why the French, British, and Indians were moving toward war over some land. The following response from Olivia is rather garbled, but she does bring in a concept of land being hard to get:

> *Olivia:* Land was really hard to get before and like when. . . they probably like went in and they took the land and maybe Britain. . . like the British like named it and now the French and Indians are fighting.

The teacher's rejoinder recasts Olivia's response succinctly, selectively taking account of what Olivia has said, in order to give the discussion focus.

Mrs. W: Okay, so we see a conflict arising here over land.

Mrs. W. then invites Brittnay to join the discussion, but notice that Mrs. W. asks Brittnay if she "wants to add to what Olivia said." So again, the teacher is modeling that the discussion has a focus; it is not just random talk.

Mrs. W: Brittnay, do you want to add to what Olivia said?

Brittnay is then able to use the focus of a conflict over land and extend from Olivia's idea that land is hard to get, by considering how land was acquired:

Brittnay: I agree with Olivia because now you can go out and buy land. Then, you just couldn't go buy land, you'd have to go and then you'd have to fight for it.

And Mrs. W. responds, prompting for still further explanation:

Mrs. W: What do you mean you had to fight for it?

Thus, as students respond, the teacher takes account of the responses, entering their substance into the discussion, but turning the ideas back to students for further consideration. The focus of the enterprise remains on getting students to explain and to connect.

Effective Questions Need Organization

Our major point thus far has been that, in order to promote students' dealing with text ideas and making sense of them, questions should be open invitations rather than prescriptions of an answer. And we complicated that idea with the caveat that open questions often need to be followed up in ways that focus and extend an initial response.

Yet even optimal responses to open questions may not promote a coherent representation if those questions tap isolated information scattered across a text. Questions need to be organized and sequenced to promote coherent meaning building.

The notion of organization of questions was our starting point two decades ago when, after examining instruction in basal reading series, we developed the concept of the story map (Beck & McKeown, 1981). In our examination of basal instruction we found that the basals presented sets of questions for reading selections that were based on taxonomies. Taxonomies were developed to describe levels of thinking, from simple to complex, for example, beginning with literal, moving to inferential, evaluative, and appreciative (see for example, Barrett, 1967; Herber, 1970; Ruddell & Bacon, 1972). So, typically, questions for a reading selection would begin with several literal questions, move to inferential questions, etc.

The problem with this approach is that taxonomies do not encompass certain dimensions of the relationship between questions and a text, dimensions that could be critical to comprehension. One such dimension is the role within the text of information tapped by questions. Taxonomies assume that, for example, all questions requiring an inference are of equal value in promoting understanding. Taxonomies also fail to account for the relationship among the questions for a particular text.

With the limitations of taxonomies in mind, we established the concept of the story map to guide the development of questions that promote comprehension. The story map is defined as a unified mental representation of a story based on logical organization of central story events and ideas and their interrelationships. The idea of the story map is to develop questions that elicit information that matches the progression of ideas and events in a text.

A story map means knowing where you're going, that is, what the comprehension "looks like" that you want students to develop. For example, for the story of the three little pigs, a coherent representation would include that three pigs were being pursued by a hungry wolf, and to escape the wolf they built houses. The first two pigs hurriedly built houses of flimsy materials, and they had to run for their lives when the wolf blew in their houses. The third pig took time to build a sturdy house of bricks that saved him and the other two pigs. In fact, because the house was so wolf proof, the three pigs were able to capture the wolf when he climbed the roof seeking entrance through the chimney. By placing a boiling pot in the fireplace, the pigs did away with their wolf problem and gained a hearty dinner. This framework then suggests the ideas and events that need to be tapped for understanding to develop. Questions would tap, for example, what the pigs' problem was, how their choice of building materials connected to their problem, etc.

What we are suggesting here is that developing questions that are effective for enhancing students' comprehension takes some forethought about the understanding that is the goal of a text interaction, followed by development of questions that target key ideas and the connections between ideas. When a teacher enters a lesson armed with a goal and questions, she is well prepared to respond to students' spontaneous thinking in ways that move the discussion while keeping students in charge of the meaning building.

References

Barrett, T. C. (1967). Goals of the reading program: The basis for evaluation. In Thomas C. Barrett (Ed.) *The evaluation of children's Reading Achievement*, Newark, DE: International Reading Association.

Beck, I. L., & McKeown, M. G. (1981). Developing questions that promote comprehension: The story map. *Language Arts, 58*, 913–918.

Beck, I. L., McKeown, M. G., Worthy, J., Sandora, C., & Kucan, L. (1996). Questioning the author: A year-long classroom implementation to engage students with text. *Elementary School Journal, 96* (4), 385–414.

Cazden, C. B. (1988). *Classroom discourse: The language of teaching and learning*. Portsmouth, NH: Heinemann.

Dillon, J. T. (1988). *Questioning and teaching: A manual of practice*. New York: The Teachers College Press.

Graesser, A. C., Person, N. K., & Magliano, J.P. (1995). Collaborative dialogue patterns in naturalistic one-on-one tutoring. *Applied Cognitive Psychology, 9*, 495–522.

Herber, H. (1970). *Teaching reading in the content areas*. Englewood Cliffs, NJ: Prentice- Hall.

Kjelgard, J. (1996). The Tiger's Heart. In *Adventures for Readers, Book One* (pp. 170–177). New York: Holt, Rinehart & Winston.

Leinhardt, G. (1993). On teaching. In R. Glaser (Ed.) *Advances in instructional psychology*. Vol. 4, pp 1–54. Hillsdale, NJ: Erlbaum.

Mangano, N. (1986). *Transforming questioning behaviors into instruction: Implications from the research.* Paper presented at the Annual Meeting of the National Reading Conference. Austin, TX.

McKeown, M. G., & Beck, I. L. (1999). Getting the discussion started. *Educational Leadership, 57*(3), 25–28.

Nystrand, M., & Gamoran, A. (1991). Instructional discourse, students engagement, and literature achievement. *Research in the Teaching of English, 25*(3), 261–290.

Orsolini, M., & Pontecorvo, C. (1992). Children's talk in classroom discussions. *Cognition and Instruction, 9*(2), 113–136.

Otero, J., & Graesser, A. C. (submitted for publication) PREG: Elements of a model of question-asking.

Pressley, M., Wood, E., Woloshyn, V. E., Martin, V., King, A., & Menke, D. (1992). Encouraging mindful use of prior knowledge: Attempting to construct explanatory answers facilitates learning. *Educational Psychologist, 27*(1), 91–109.

Ruddell, R., & Bacon, H. (1972). The nature of reading: Language and meaning. In R. Hodges & E. H. Rudorf (Eds.) *Language and learning to read: What teachers should know about language.* Boston: Houghton Mifflin.

Taylor, T. (1995). *The Cay.* New York: Camelot.

Tharp, R. G., & Gallimore, R. (1988). *Rousing minds to life.* New York: Cambridge University Press.

Trabasso, T., van den Broek, P. W., & Liu, L. (1988). A model for generating questions that assess and promote comprehension. *Questioning Exchange, 2*(1), 25–38.

5.6

Tactics to Help Students Use Writing to Express Their Comprehension of Content Area Texts

Gary A. Troia

As students move through the grades, schools become increasingly grounded in disciplinary traditions and discourses (Donahue, 2003; Moje, 2002; Siskin, 1994). Specialization within each discipline increases as students move from elementary school classes (e.g., science) to high school classes (e.g., biology, chemistry, physics). Accordingly, students are expected to deepen and elaborate their content area knowledge as well as continue to develop and deploy a broader array of related skills and strategies as they gain competence in each discipline.

Attaining competence in any discipline requires a student to learn how knowledge is constructed, organized, and represented within that discipline. In science, for instance, the successful science student needs to understand the assumptions that guide scientists' work, the processes associated with scientific inquiry, what forms of evidence are valid for making scientific claims, and how scientists communicate about their work (Lemke, 1990). Thus, to become competent in science (or any other discipline), a student must possess adequate disciplinary literacy skills—he or she must comprehend science texts, talk about science in ways understood by other scientists and non-scientists, and present scientific information in various forms, including tables, graphs, diagrams, and other modes of visual representation (National Council of Teachers of Mathematics, 2000). Content area literacy is both a requisite for content area learning and a product of that learning. As students deepen their understanding of a subject, their ability to read, write, and speak about it begins to approximate how experts communicate about that subject.

Forces that Shape Content Area Literacy
Learner Characteristics

For students with disabilities, content area literacy is often an elusive goal due to at least three factors. First, these students exhibit poor reading and writing skills that are more pronounced over time, thereby widening the achievement gap between themselves and their peers without disabilities (e.g., deBettencourt, Zigmond, & Thornton, 1989; Stanovich, 1986). Simultaneously, they are asked to learn content, often from hard-to-read textbooks, with diminishing teacher support for acquiring competency in literacy (Schumaker & Deshler, 1984). For instance, according to secondary teachers, including English teachers, reading instruction is the province of elementary school educators and is not plausible given the demands of middle and high school curricula (Alvermann & Moore, 1991; Ericson, 2001; Konopak, Wilson, & Readance, 1994; Moje & Wade, 1997).

Second, students with poor reading and writing skills lack the requisite classroom survival tactics (e.g., concentration, perseverance, self-advocacy, time and task management, note-taking routines, study and testing strategies) needed to regulate and learn content information (Bender & Smith, 1990; Gregory, Shanahan, & Walberg, 1985). In particular, students with disabilities do not actively monitor and evaluate their task performance, reducing the likelihood that they will deploy effective strategies, such as repairing disruptions to text comprehension (e.g., Garner & Alexander, 1989; Simpson & Nist, 1997). Third, because classrooms tend to become more performance oriented across the grades, many students perceive demonstrated ability as more highly valued than effort or mastery (Midgley, Anderman, & Hicks, 1995; Eccles, Lord, & Midgley, 1991). This is particularly detrimental for students with disabilities, who view ability as fixed rather than malleable and for whom lack of success, which they have in abundance, signals limited ability. As a consequence of these factors, students with disabilities experience high rates of failure in mainstream content area classes (Donahoe & Zigmond, 1990). When faced with recurring academic failure, they become less bonded with school, which often is signified by increased absenteeism and behavior problems, and eventually drop out (deBettencourt et al., 1989; Sinclair, Christenson, Evelo, & Hurley, 1998).

Knowledge and Text Characteristics

Apart from these general factors, there are several components of content area literacy that exert a strong influence on the success with which students with and without disabilities learn to read and write in a particular discipline. These components include vocabulary knowledge, topic knowledge, text structure knowledge, and textual transparency. First, sufficient vocabulary knowledge is essential to comprehension of disciplinary information because many content area texts and lectures are heavily loaded with abstract general vocabulary (e.g., *correlate*), specialized common vocabulary (e.g., *dividend* in economics and *solution* in chemistry), and technical vocabulary terms (e.g., *ribosome*). Consequently, vocabulary knowledge is a powerful predictor of not only basic reading and writing achievement, but also content area learning (Baker, Simmons, & Kame'enui, 1998; Nagy & Scott, 2000). Students who struggle in content area classes know far fewer words, on the order of thousands, than their more successful peers (Nagy & Herman, 1985).

Second, prior knowledge of a topic introduced during content area instruction also is a strong predictor of students' comprehension (e.g., McKeown, Beck, Sinatra, & Loxterman, 1992). However, prior knowledge can be misleading and even interfere with the development of content knowledge when students tenaciously hold onto erroneous preconceptions or misinformed beliefs (Alvermann & Hague, 1989; Alvermann & Hynd, 1989; Anthony & Smith, 1984; Guzzetti, 1992). Nevertheless, it is crucial to help students develop relevant background knowledge about instructional topics and establish connections between their personal experiences and the content taught (Alexander & Kulikowich, 1991; Symons & Pressley, 1993). This aspect of instruction is most important when we consider that many students fail to activate their topic knowledge because of a tendency to compartmentalize and disassociate knowledge obtained in the "real world" from knowledge obtained in school (Pressley, 2000). Students with disabilities are at an even greater disadvantage because they often fail to activate the prior knowledge they possess and typically have limited or fragmented background knowledge about content area topics (Bos & Anders, 1990; Lenz & Alley, 1983).

Third, textual schemata help the reader and the writer anticipate, follow, locate, extract, and organize information presented in a text (Pressley, 2000); consequently, the ability to discern and use text structure knowledge is related to comprehension (e.g., Englert & Thomas, 1987). Anderson and Armbruster (1984) identified six basic expository text structures that are relevant to content area literacy: description, explanation, definition, sequential, compare-contrast, and cause-effect. However, most content area textbook passages use a hybrid of several of these structures. Proficient readers are aware of these structures and use them to build logical connections between ideas (Meyer, 1984). Students with disabilities, on the other hand, are less aware of them and thus are less capable of differentiating essential and nonessential information and formulating reasonable hypotheses based on textbook content (Kinder & Bursuck, 1991; Rupley & Willson, 1996; Wong & Wilson, 1984).

Last, textbooks serve as the primary vehicle for teaching content area knowledge to students (e.g., Bean, Zigmond, & Hartman, 1994; Tyson & Woodward, 1989). The degree to which content area texts are well designed (i.e., the most important information to be acquired is transparent to the reader) determines how well these texts are understood and the information within them recalled (Dickson, Simmons, & Kame'enui, 1998). Unfortunately, content area texts tend to be poorly written (e.g., Anderson & Armbruster, 1984; Beck, McKeown, & Gromoll, 1989;

Lovitt & Horton, 1991; Mastropieri & Scruggs, 1994). For example, many social studies and science textbooks use misleading titles and subtitles, lack explicit main ideas or guiding principles, omit critical information, and contain contradictory information (Chambliss & Calfee, 1989; Garner, Gillingham, & White, 1989; Pressley, Yokoi, Van Etten, & Freebern, 1997; Tyson & Woodward, 1989). They presuppose too much prior knowledge about topics and present numerous facts with little explanation (Beck et al., 1989; McKeown & Beck, 1990). In addition, they often are written at reading levels higher than the grade for which they are intended (Chall & Conrad, 1991; Wood & Wood, 1988).

Writing in the Content Areas

Classroom teachers often feel that devoting ample time to writing instruction is problematic given the voluminous content area information that must be covered in the typical curriculum (Troia & Maddox, 2004). Simultaneously, general and special education teachers sometimes struggle to identify relevant and stimulating writing topics and assignments that will help students develop their expertise as writers. One way to resolve these dilemmas is to integrate writing instruction with content area learning. Such integration has been shown to be beneficial to students with and without writing problems. For instance, Graham and Perin's (2007) meta-analysis of experimental and quasi-experimental writing intervention studies yielded a mean effect size of .82 for summary writing instruction (which means that, on average, the treatment groups outperformed the control groups by nearly 12 standard score points on measures of the accuracy and completeness of written summaries of content area information) and a mean effect size of .23 for instruction aimed at helping students use writing to learn subject matter information (which means that, on average, the treatment groups outperformed the control groups by nearly 3.5 standard score points on measures of academic achievement in a discipline). Successful disciplinary writing depends to a great degree on a student's ability to comprehend expository texts that often serve as source material for content area learning; comprehension rests on the capacity to summarize information, not merely for simple recall, but for knowledge transformation (Pressley, Brown, El-Dinary, & Afflerbach, 1995). Thus, in the remainder of this article, tactics for improving students' summarization of content area information will be described, as summaries represent the products of learning as well as serve as mechanisms for increasing subject matter knowledge.

General Tactics

To effectively summarize a text, students must be able to read the words in the text accurately and fluently. This is why readability must be evaluated and, if necessary, adjusted (e.g., through print-to-speech software or having students read the text in tandem with an audio version, providing students with a parallel text written at a lower readability level to read before reading the original text, giving students easier topic-related source materials that cover the most salient content to be learned (see Schumm & Stickler, 1991)). Students also must be able to maximize redundancies in the text to aid their understanding and, consequently, produce useful summaries.

So, it is important to help students identify text enhancements (e.g., indexes, headings and subheadings, bold and italicized typeface, labels and captions) and graphical aids (e.g., charts, tables, graphs, diagrams, illustrations), which often are used to organize, highlight, and elucidate topical information (Spyradikis & Standal, 1986). Because many students with language and learning problems struggle with the vocabulary associated with expository texts, there should be three aims in content area vocabulary instruction to enhance comprehension: 1) teach common (e.g., *robust*), specialized (e.g., *dividend*), and technical (e.g., *isotope*) terms that are critical to understanding the most essential information; 2) teach students to recognize common literary aids used by authors for expressing word meanings such as definition, analogy, and synonymy; and 3) teach signal words and phrases for relationships between ideas in informational writing, as noted below (Lorch, 1989; Lorch, Lorch, & Inman, 1993; Nagy & Herman, 1987):

- Causal: so, thus, therefore, because, consequently, as a result
- Sequential: to begin with, initially, next, then, not long after, finally
- Conditional: if, but, however, although, nevertheless, yet, regardless, irrespective
- Comparative: same as, alike, likewise, similarly, different, unlike, in contrast

Perhaps at the heart of producing a good summary is the ability to synthesize and translate (i.e., a summary is not a retelling or paraphrasing) main ideas, often encapsulated in topic sentences, and relevant supporting details from the source text. When topic sentences are present in a text, students should be able to identify them via their characteristics (e.g., most important sentence in a paragraph or segment, all other sentences refer to it and elaborate upon it, if omitted the paragraph or segment would not make sense). When topic sentences are not present, students must be able to invent them to serve as mental "hooks" for details (writing newspaper headlines and chapter titles can serve as practice exercises). Underlining important details associated with each main idea in the text will help students create an initial summary, once the main ideas and supporting details from the paragraphs or sections of text are combined. The deletion of trivial and redundant information and the substitution of superordinate category labels for subordinate items (e.g., *farm animals* for pigs, cows, and horses) will transform an initial summary that reads like a paraphrase into a true summary of the gist of the content. Of course, checking the summary against the original text helps ensure accuracy and completeness. This process reinforces and facilitates reading comprehension through written expression.

Specific Tactics

Graphic organizers can help students integrate and synthesize content knowledge from an expository text and can be accompanied by written summaries to demonstrate and extend their disciplinary understandings. One such example of this is **K-W-L-H +** (Carr & Ogle, 1987; Ogle, 1986), which is a method for activating background knowledge about a topic (**Know**), setting learning goals (**Wonder**), summarizing learning from text (**Learned**), and promoting continued investigation (How to Find Out More) and/or reflection (How Do I Know This). The plus (+) portion of the method is a written summary of what was learned and what additional things students would like to learn. This method can be used as a teacher-led, pre- and post-instructional exercise or as a small-group activity. For younger students in kindergarten and 1st grade or older students with severe writing problems who cannot easily generate text, teacher-led instruction can be combined with a class **K-W-L-H** chart and summary dictated by the students; likewise, each student in a small group can illustrate and caption a panel in a visual summary. A sample of a completed chart and summary is provided in Table 5.6.1. There are five steps to implementing **K-W-L-H +** :

1. The teacher asks students to brainstorm all that they know about the topic and list their responses under the **Know** column. This student-generated information should be organized into categories either by the teacher or the students with teacher guidance that will facilitate text comprehension.

2. The teacher lists under the **Wonder** column those things students would like to discover about the topic (which helps motivate them to read the text).

3. After reading, the teacher records under the Learned column what the students learned from the text, with particular attention to information that confirmed their prior knowledge, information that was inconsistent with what was anticipated, or new information. If appropriate, new categories are added.

4. Students write their summary paragraph based on the information listed in the Learned column.

5. Students identify how they would locate missing information in the **How to Find out More** column (e.g., use a Web browser to search for documents related to the topic), which can help motivate additional learning; alternately, or additionally, students can identify how they verified learned information in the How Do I Know This column (e.g., list page numbers where that information is provided in the text and other confirmatory sources).

A jigsaw content learning group (Aronson & Patnoe, 1997) is a cooperative learning activity for social studies and science instruction that can aid in preparing summaries for research reports. It can be coupled with double-entry journals (Cox, 1996) for an effective and efficient means of learning from multiple source materials on a topic. There are four steps to implementing a jigsaw activity:

1. Students are assigned to home groups and each person in a group reads a different source text (e.g., a magazine article about exercise and cardiovascular health, a newspaper clipping about new medical procedures and drugs that can help

reduce the risk of heart attacks, a consumer brochure outlining healthy eating tips for promoting cardiac health, and a textbook chapter about the human circulatory system).

2. Each student completes a double-entry journal while reading the assigned source text. A double-entry journal is a journal in which the student records an important piece of information from the source text on the left side of the journal page (with an accompanying page number) and a response, question, or evaluative comment on the right side.

3. After completing their double-entry journal entries, students disperse to an expert group, that is, a group whose members have all read the same source text. Members of the expert group share their journal entries and summarize the material using a graphic organizer (e.g., a Venn diagram or attribute chart). The double-entry journal could be expanded to a triple-entry journal by having students within the expert groups respond to each other's responses, questions, or evaluations in a third column.

4. Students return to their home groups to teach the other members about the content information they learned (using the graphic organizer) from their text and discuss how this information relates to that covered by the other texts, noting similarities and differences in their journals.

The story impressions method (McGinley & Denner, 1987), similar to exchange-compare writing (Wood, 1986), also uses a cooperative learning framework. Students are assigned to a group and given roles for writing a brief summary that predicts the content of a lesson or unit text based on key vocabulary provided by the teacher. Once the group has read the text, they rewrite their summary to reflect the actual content of the text and their improved understanding of the material. The six implementation steps for this method are as follows:

1. The teacher assigns students to heterogeneous groups and gives each student a role to perform based on his or her strengths:
    a. Researcher: consults secondary materials such as dictionary, encyclopedia, or other topic-related documents to help the group complete the composing task
    b. Scribe: records summary generated by group
    c. Content Editor: checks summary against text for accuracy of information
    d. Proofreader: checks summary for accuracy of writing mechanics and grammar usage
    e. Reporter: reads summary aloud to group for editing and to rest of class for discussion

2. The teacher lists and preteaches 10–15 key vocabulary words from the text (see vocabulary instruction techniques under "General Tactics").

3. Each group uses these words to predict the informational content of the unit

contained in the text to be read and writes a short collaborative summary (one or two paragraphs) in which each word is used.

4. Students read the text.

5. Each group rewrites the collaborative summary to reflect new understandings of the actual text content.

6. Each group reads its summary to the rest of the class for discussion and feedback.

Table 5.6.1.   **Completed K-W-L-H+ Graphic Organizer for Snakes and Accompanying Summary**

What We <u>K</u>now	What We <u>W</u>onder	What We <u>L</u>earned and Still Need to Learn	<u>H</u>ow We Find What We Still Need to Learn
Some are venomous	How does poison work?	Injected through fangs to paralyze their prey Sometimes can spit venom at a distance Some snakes squeeze their prey to death before eating it	Are there different kinds of venom? Look on Web or in an encyclopedia
No real legs	How do snakes move?	Most slide on their bellies	
Carnivores	Do snakes kill their prey before eating it?	Not always Swallow prey whole by unhinging jaws Use their tongues to sense odors	
Reptiles, so are cold-blooded	Do all snakes lay eggs?	No, some give birth to live babies	
Have scales and shed their skin	How often do they shed their skin?	3-6 times each year Their eyes are covered by clear scales Some snakes use color as camouflage or pretend to be poisonous	
	Where do they live?	Every continent except Antarctica Don't live on some islands like Hawaii, Ireland, Iceland, and New Zealand Some snakes spend most of their lives in the water or in trees	Do snakes live in our area? Look on Web or in an almanac

Categories of information:	Summary of What We Learned and Still Need to Learn:
• Physical characteristics • Locomotion • Habitat • Defenses • Eating habits • Reproduction	Snakes are cold-blooded reptiles with dry scales and no real legs— they usually slide on their bellies to move. They live all over the world on land, in water, and in trees, except where it is extremely cold (Antarctica) and some islands (Ireland, Iceland, and New Zealand). We don't know which snakes, if any, live in our area. Some snakes lay eggs while others give birth to live babies. They are carnivores and eat prey whole, often using their tongues to sense the odor of an animal. Some snakes use venom to paralyze their prey first before eating it, whereas others squeeze their prey to death before eating it. Poisonous snakes can either inject the venom through fangs or shoot the venom at a distance. We'd like to find out if there are different kinds of venom. Snakes can eat prey much larger than their heads because they can unhinge their upper and lower jaws. Snakes shed their scales 3-6 times per year, including the clear scales over their eyes. The scales might be very colorful if the snake is poisonous or is imitating a venomous snake; some snakes have colors that help camouflage them and blend in with their surroundings.

One last method for integrating content area reading with summary writing is the use of writing frames (Nichols, 1980), which help struggling writers use appropriate text organization for summarizing content area information that adheres to a basic structure (e.g., compare-contrast). The frames prompt coherent organization by providing partially completed sentences or transition words that, over time, can be faded as students become familiar with each frame. This instructional tactic is well suited for students who cannot write extended texts without substantial support. The two examples provided in Figure 5.6.1 can easily be adjusted to fit the contents of a particular source text.

Figure 5.6.1.   **Sample Writing Frames for Compare-Contrast and Chronological Sequence Expository Text Structures**

Compare-Contrast Frame:

_____ are different from _____ in several ways. First, _____, while _____. Additionally_____, whereas _____. They are alike in that _____and _____. So, it is evident that _____.

Chronological Sequence Frame:

At the end of _____, what happened was that _____ _____. Prior to this, _____. Before that, however, _____. This whole sequence of events began when_____. The most important event to occur was_____, because _____.

Conclusion

The use of these and other instructional tactics to promote expository text comprehension as demonstrated through and facilitated by written summaries increases the likelihood that struggling learners will be successful in their content area learning efforts. The accumulation of small successes as students grapple with difficult subject matter presented in often hard to read texts in turn is likely to improve their motivation and engagement as disciplinary novices. The tactics described here do not place heavy burdens on teacher time, and ultimately pay great dividends for content area teachers and other educators who lament the poor retention of information among their students. Likewise, these tactics can help students communicate their disciplinary understandings more effectively through writing. Although summaries are only one kind of writing used in subject matter instruction, they do serve as the "bread and butter" of most forms of writing undertaken in the sciences, social sciences, and mathematics. Reports, essays, articles, and the like all incorporate the synthesis of information gleaned from a variety of source materials. Thus, focusing instructional efforts on summary writing, identified by Graham & Perin (2007) as one of the most effective writing instruction elements, is well worth the effort.

References

Alexander, P. A., & Kulikowich, J. M. (1991). Domain knowledge and analogic reasoning ability as predictors of expository text comprehension. *Journal of Reading Behavior, 23,* 165–190.

Alvermann, D. E., & Hague, S. A. (1989). Comprehension of counterintuitive science text: Effects of prior knowledge and text structure. *Journal of Educational Research, 82,* 197–202.

Alvermann, D. E., & Hynd, C. R. (1989). Effects of prior knowledge activation modes and text structure on nonscience majors' comprehension of physics. *Journal of Educational Research, 83,* 97–102.

Alvermann, D. E., & Moore, D. (1991). Secondary school reading. In M. L. Kamil, P. B. Mosenthal, P. D. Pearson, & R. Barr (Eds.), *Handbook of reading research* (Vol. 2, pp. 951–983). New York: Longman.

Anderson, T. H., & Armbruster, B. B. (1984). Content area textbooks. In R. C. Anderson, J. Osborn, & R. J. Tierney (Eds.), *Learning to read in American schools: Basal readers and content texts* (pp. 193–226). Hillsdale, NJ: Erlbaum.

Anthony, C. W., & Smith, E. L. (1984). Children's preconceptions and content area textbooks. In G. G. Duffy, L. R. Roehler, & J. Mason (Eds.), *Comprehension instruction: Perspectives and suggestions* (pp. 187–201). New York: Longman.

Aronson, E., & Patnoe, S. (1997). *The jigsaw classroom: Building cooperation in the classroom* (2nd ed.). New York: Addison Wesley Longman.

Baker, S. K., Simmons, D. C., & Kame'enui, E. J. (1998). Vocabulary acquisition: Research bases. In D. C. Simmons & E. J. Kame'enui (Eds.), *What reading research tells us about children with diverse learning needs: Bases and basics* (pp. 183–217). Hillsdale, NJ: Erlbaum.

Bean, R. M., Zigmond, N., & Hartman, D. K. (1994). Adapted use of social studies textbooks in elementary classrooms. *Remedial and Special Education, 15*(4), 216–226.

Beck, I. L., McKeown, M., & Gromoll, E. W. (1989). Learning from social studies texts. *Cognition and Instruction, 6,* 99–153.

Bender, W. N., & Smith, J. K. (1990). Classroom behavior of children and adolescents with mild educational handicaps or learning disabilities. *Journal of Learning Disabilities, 23,* 298–305.

Bos, C. S., & Anders, P. L. (1990). Effects of interactive vocabulary instruction on vocabulary learning and reading comprehension of junior-high learning disabled students. *Learning Disability Quarterly, 13,* 31–42.

Carr, E., & Ogle, D. M. (1987). K-W-L plus: A strategy for comprehension and summarization. *Journal of Reading, 30,* 626–631.

Chall, J. S., & Conrad, S. S. (1991). *Should textbooks challenge students?* New York: Teachers College Press.

Chambliss, M. J., & Calfee, R. C. (1989). Designing science textbooks to enhance student understanding. *Educational Psychologist, 24,* 307–322.

Cox, C. (1996). *Teaching language arts: A student and response centered classroom*. Boston: Allyn & Bacon.

deBettencourt, L. U., Zigmond, N., & Thornton, H. (1989). Follow-up of postsecondary-age rural learning disabled graduates and dropouts. *Exceptional Children, 56,* 40–49.

Dickson, S. V., Simmons, D. C., & Kame'enui, E. J. (1998). Text organization: Research bases. In D. C. Simmons & E. J. Kame'enui (Eds.), *What reading research tells us about children with diverse learning needs: Bases and basics* (pp. 239–277). Hillsdale, NJ: Erlbaum.

Donahoe, K., & Zigmond, N. (1990). Academic grades of ninth-grade urban learn-ing-disabled students and low-achieving peers. *Exceptionality, 1,* 17–22.

Donahue, D. (2003). Reading across the great divide: English and math teachers apprentice one another as readers and disciplinary insiders: A teacher educator uses an apprentice reading project to teach new teachers about the ways they read in the content areas. *Journal of Adolescent & Adult Literacy, 47,* 24–41.

Eccles, J. S., Lord, S., & Midgley, C. (1991). What are we doing to early adoles-cents? The impact of educational contexts on early adolescents. *American Journal of Education, 99,* 521–542.

Englert, C. S., & Thomas, C. C. (1987). Sensitivity to text structure in reading and writing: A comparison of learning disabled and nonhandicapped students. *Learning Disability Quarterly, 10,* 93–105.

Ericson, B. (Ed.). (2001). *Teaching reading in high school English classes*. Urbana, IL: National Council of Teachers of English.

Garner, R., & Alexander, P. A. (1989). Metacognition: Answered and unan-swered questions. *Educational Psychologist, 24,* 143–158.

Garner, R., Gillingham, M., & White, C. S. (1989). Effects of "seductive details" on macroprocessing and microprocessing in adults and children. *Cognition and Instruction, 6,* 41–57.

Graham, S., & Perin, D. (2007). *Writing next: Effective strategies to improve writing of adolescents in middle and high schools—A report to Carnegie Corporation of New York*. Washington, DC: Alliance for Excellent Education.

Gregory, J. F., Shanahan, T., & Walberg, H. (1985). Learning disabled 10th graders in mainstreamed settings: A descriptive analysis. *Remedial and Special Education, 6*(4), 25–33.

Guzzetti, B. J. (1992). Promoting conceptual change in science: Can texts be used effectively? *Journal of Reading, 35,* 642–649.

Kinder, D., & Bursuck, W. (1991). The search for a unified social studies curriculum: Does history really repeat itself? *Journal of Learning Disabilities, 24,* 270–275.

Konopak, B., Wilson, E., & Readance, J. (1994). Examining teachers' beliefs, decisions, and practices about content-area reading in secondary social studies. In C. Kinzer & D. Leu (Eds.), *Multidimensional aspects of literacy research, theory, and practice* (pp. 127–136). Chicago, IL: National Reading Conference.

Lemke, J. L. (1990). *Talking science: Language, learning, and values.* Norwood, NJ: Ablex.

Lenz, B. K., & Alley, G. R. (1983). *The effects of advance organizers on the learning and retention of learning disabled adolescents within the context of a cooperative planning model.* Final research report submitted to the U.S. Department of Education, Office of Special Education.

Lorch, R. F., Jr. (1989). Text-signaling devices and their effects on reading and memory processes. *Educational Psychology Review, 1,* 209–234.

Lorch, R. F., Jr., Lorch, E. P., & Inman, W. E. (1993). Effects of signaling topic structure on text recall. *Journal of Educational Psychology, 85,* 281–290.

Lovitt, T. C., & Horton, S. V. (1991). Adapting textbooks for mildly handicapped adolescents. In G. Stoner, M. R. Shinn, & H. M. Walker (Eds.), *Interventions for achievement and behavior problems* (pp. 439–471). Silver Spring, MD: National Association of School Psychologists.

Mastropieri, M. A., & Scruggs, T. E. (1994). Text versus hands-on science curriculum. *Remedial and Special Education, 15*(2), 72–85.

McGinley, W. J., & Denner, P. R. (1987). Story impressions: A pre-reading/writing activity. *Journal of Reading, 31,* 248–253.

McKeown, M. G., & Beck, I. L. (1990). The assessment and characterization of young learners' knowledge of a topic in history. *American Educational Research Journal, 27,* 688–726.

McKeown, M. G., Beck, I. L., Sinatra, G. M., & Loxterman, J. A. (1992). The contribution of prior knowledge and coherent text to comprehension. *Reading Research Quarterly, 27,* 78–93.

Meyer, B. J. F. (1984). Text dimensions and cognitive processing. In H. Mandle, N. L. Stein, & T. Trabasso (Eds.), *Learning and comprehension of text* (pp. 3–51). Hillsdale, NJ: Erlbaum.

Midgley, C., Anderman, E., & Hicks, L. (1995). Differences between elementary and middle school teachers and students: A goal theory approach. *Journal of Early Adolescence, 15,* 90–113.

Moje, E. B. (2002). Re-framing adolescent literacy research for new times: Studying youth as a resource. *Reading Research and Instruction, 41,* 211–229.

Moje, E. B., & Wade, S. (1997). What case discussions reveal about teacher thinking. *Teaching and Teacher Education, 12,* 691–712.

Nagy, W. E., & Herman, P. A. (1985). Incidental vs. instructional approaches to increasing reading vocabulary. *Educational Perspectives, 23,* 16–21.

Nagy, W. E., & Herman, P. A. (1987). Breadth and depth of vocabulary knowledge: Implications for acquisition and instruction. In M. G. McKeown & M. E. Curtis (Eds.), *The nature of vocabulary acquisition* (pp. 19–35). Hillsdale, NJ: Erlbaum.

Nagy, W. E., & Scott, J. A. (2000). Vocabulary processes. In R. Barr, M. L. Kamil, P. B. Mosenthal, & P. D. Pearson (Eds.), *Handbook of reading research* (Vol. III, pp. 269–284). Hillsdale, NJ: Erlbaum.

National Council of Teachers of Mathematics (2000). *Principles and standards for school mathematics.* Reston, VA: Author.

Nichols, J. N. (1980). Using paragraph frames to help remedial high school students with writing assignments. *Journal of Reading, 24,* 228–231.

Ogle, D. (1986). K-W-L: A teaching model that develops active reading of expository text. *The Reading Teacher, 39,* 564–570.

Pressley, M. (2000). What should comprehension instruction be the instruction of? In R. Barr, M. L. Kamil, P. B. Mosenthal, & P. D. Pearson (Eds.), *Handbook of reading research* (Vol. III, pp. 545–561). Hillsdale, NJ: Erlbaum.

Pressley, M., Brown, R., El-Dinary, P. B., & Afflerbach, P. (1995). The comprehension instruction that students need: Instruction fostering constructively responsive reading. *Learning Disabilities Research & Practice, 10,* 215–224.

Pressley, M., Yokoi, L., Van Etten, S., & Freebern, G. (1997). Some of the reasons why preparing for exams is so hard: What can be done to make it easier? *Educational Psychology Review, 9,* 1–38.

Rupley, W. H., & Willson, V. L. (1996). Content, domain, and word knowledge: Relationship to comprehension of narrative and expository text. *Reading and Writing: An Interdisciplinary Journal, 8,* 419–432.

Schumaker, J. B., & Deshler, D. D. (1984). Setting demand variables: A major factor in program planning for the LD adolescent. *Topics in Language Disorders, 4,* 22–40.

Schumm, J. S., & Stickler, K. (1991). Guidelines for adapting content area textbooks: Keeping teachers and students content. *Intervention in School and Clinic, 27,* 79–84.

Simpson, M. L., & Nist, S. L. (1997). Perspectives on learning history: A case study. *Journal of Literacy Research, 29,* 363–395.

Sinclair, M. F., Christenson, S. L., Evelo, D. L., & Hurley, C. M. (1998). Dropout prevention for youth with disabilities: Efficacy of a sustained school engagement procedure. *Exceptional Children, 65,* 7–21.

Siskin, L. (1994). *Realms of knowledge: Academic departments in secondary schools*. Bristol, PA: Falmer Press.

Spyradikis, J. H., & Standal, T. C. (1986). Headings, previews, logical connectives: Effects on reading comprehension. *Journal of Technical Writing and Communication, 16,* 343–354.

Stanovich, K. E. (1986). Matthew effects in reading: Some consequences of individual differences in the acquisition of literacy. *Reading Research Quarterly, 21,* 360–407.

Symons, S., & Pressley, M. (1993). Prior knowledge affects text search success and extraction of information. *Reading Research Quarterly, 28,* 250–261.

Troia, G. A., & Maddox, M. E. (2004). Writing instruction in middle schools: Special and general education teachers share their views and voice their concerns. *Exceptionality, 12,* 19–37.

Tyson, H., & Woodward, A. (1989). Why students aren't learning very much from textbooks. *Educational Leadership, 47,* 14–17.

Wong, B. Y. L., & Wilson, M. (1984). Investigating awareness of a teaching passage organization in learning disabled children. *Journal of Learning Disabilities, 17,* 477–482.

Wood, K. D. (1986). How to smuggle writing into the classroom. *Middle School Journal, 17*(3), 5–6.

Wood, T. L., & Wood, W. L. (1988). Assessing potential difficulties in comprehending fourth grade science textbooks. *Science Education, 72,* 561–574.

6

Developing Written Expression

Karen E. Dakin

IN *Writing Next: Effective Strategies to Improve Writing in Middle and High Schools*, Steve Graham and Dolores Perin (2007) sound an alarm, bringing attention to the serious problem of adolescent writing difficulty. Low achieving students, some with diagnosed learning disabilities, will need intervention to meet classroom writing demands, as well as to meet the later writing demands of college and work. The authors carried out a meta-analysis of writing research that allowed them to identify the most effective instructional practices. Thus, although there is a crisis regarding poor adolescent writing, there is hope. This section presents articles by experts in the field regarding evidence-based approaches to writing instruction that are effective for teaching critical writing skills to all students, but especially struggling students.

In the first article, Charles Haynes and Terrill Jennings emphasize that the literacy skills of reading and writing are based on foundational oral language skills. Presenting multisensory techniques, the authors move from a word-level emphasis to sentence-level strategies, moving from simple to more complex sentence patterns while insisting that instruction be incremental and sequential. Finally, they instruct the reader in the language cueing and scaffolding that signify different types of paragraphs.

In their article, Dolores Perin and Steve Graham summarize the meta-analysis of research on writing instruction with students in grades 4–12, carried out for their *Writing Next* report. They remind educators that assigning writing alone without explicit instruction may just reinforce poor writing skills instead of improve these skills. They explain the 11 recommendations for effective writing instruction based on their meta-analysis, ordering them according to the strength of the effect.

Bruce Saddler's article addresses Drs. Perin and Graham's sixth recommendation, sentence combining. Dr. Saddler provides expert guidance in creating, sequencing, and introducing sentence combining exercises, and evaluating student responses.

Suzanne Carreker explains that the teaching of basic grammatical concepts is necessary to equip students to write complete, varied, and precise sentences, and to mature in their writing. She carefully guides the reader through the introduction of the parts of speech, using color-codes to make the abstract concepts of the parts of speech concrete. She then moves on to the important task of building paragraphs using a "sentence-by-sentence" process.

Finally, Charles MacArthur's article reviews research that supports the use of technology to aid planning, transcription, and revision. Dr. MacArthur emphasizes that students need instruction in strategies to maximize the power of technology and that researchers and teachers must collaborate to determine how to make best use of writing technologies through developing effective instructional methods.

The authors of these selected articles expertly guide the practitioner to the effective instructional practices necessary to improve adolescent writing skills. They include advice on how to manage the needs of students with weak language skills in the classroom and how to harness the power of assistive technology to support struggling writers. Taken together, this collection goes a long way toward addressing the serious national problem of low writing achievement in grades 4–12.

References

Graham, S., & Perin, D. (2007). Writing next: Effective strategies to improve writing of adolescents in middle and high schools-A report to Carnegie Corporation of New York. Washington, DC: Alliance for Excellent Education.

Listening and Speaking
Essential Ingredients for Teaching Struggling Writers

Charles W. Haynes and Terrill M. Jennings

Putting words onto paper is demanding even for naturally gifted writers—indeed, the great novelist and short story writer Ernest Hemingway reported that he revised the last page of Farewell to Arms thirty-nine times before he decided it was "good writing." For students with dyslexia and related language learning difficulties, the complex demands of writing pose a particularly daunting challenge (MacArthur, et al., 2006). This article describes practical strategies and techniques for teaching writing that can aid this group of students; the primary focus is on developing and exploiting listening and speaking skills in order to support the development of writing at the word, sentence, and paragraph levels.

Why teach oral language skills to students who need to improve their writing? Reading and writing are based on a foundation of oral language skills; preschool phonological awareness, semantic, syntactic, and discourse level skills predict with fairly high accuracy who will succeed or fail on both reading and composition tasks in grades 2 and 4 (e.g., Fey et al., 2004; Catts, Fey, & Tomblin, 2002). With systematic instruction in listening, speaking, reading, and writing, literacy skills develop interactively and synergistically. For example, instruction in phonological awareness enhances phonic reading/spelling skills, and vice versa. Similarly, systematic oral-aural teaching of sentence structures enhances children's ability to comprehend and compose sentences, and conversely, learning to write sentence patterns shapes the child's ability to understand and produce sentences orally. Following are examples of oral language based teaching principles and techniques that can enhance students' writing skills.

It is important to set the stage for language learning with a few Golden Rules for language management in the classroom. Efficient management of classroom discussion is critical for priming students' questions, vocabulary, and content for writing. Students with word retrieval and language formulation difficulties benefit from a classroom environment that supports and guides their verbal participation. Golden Rules for students should include the following:

- Giving other students opportunities to talk by taking turns and self-monitoring to avoid interrupting others
- Respecting others' efforts to express themselves (no teasing!)

When querying students for their points of view, *teachers* need to be acutely aware of students' retrieval difficulties, and self-monitor for the following:

> "…oral language based teaching principles and techniques…can enhance students' writing skills"

- Trying to fill the silence when a student searches for words
- Giving children the time they need to respond

In large-group classrooms, where maintaining the flow of discussion is important for keeping the class engaged, a helpful strategy is to provide a student with a question and return later for a response. This allows the student time to retrieve and formulate a response without interrupting the discussion.

Word-Level Strategies and Techniques

Forward and backward chaining are classic, word-level speech-language techniques designed to aid production of key multisyllabic vocabulary words. Students with dyslexia and related language learning difficulties often display core phonological processing deficits that impair their word retrieval. It is not unusual for a teacher to introduce a key multisyllabic vocabulary word only to see a student struggle to say the word and announce, "Forget it—that's a stupid word!" Responses like this can be eliminated by helping students become comfortable with pronouncing longer words through choral chaining of selected vocabulary. Forward chaining and backward chaining of a history class target word, *constitutionality*, are illustrated in Table 6.1.1.

Table 6.1.1.   **Examples of Chaining for a Multisyllabic Vocabulary Word**

Forward Chaining	Backward Chaining
"con-"	"-ty"
"consti-"	"-ity"
"constitu-"	"-ality"
"constitution-"	"-tionality"
"constitutional-"	"-tutionality"
"constitutionali-"	"-stitutionality"
"constitutionality"	"constitutionality"

Note that, depending on the technique employed, different parts of the word receive more practice. For both techniques, the teacher introduces pronunciation of syllables gradually and students repeat in unison at each step. This practice provides students with articulatory mastery, and thus ownership, of key vocabulary.

Phonetic spelling is another word-level technique that provides students with a method for managing difficult-to-spell words that may pose an obstacle to composition or may force students to switch to less specific, higher frequency words they can already spell (e.g., substituting *big* for *enormous*). One way to eliminate this obstacle is to employ a three-step phonetic spelling strategy:

Step One: Identify the number of syllables in the word (e.g., "enormous" = 3) and write a blank for each syllable: ___ ___ ___.

Step Two: Spell the phonemes in each syllable and spell each syllable in correct order; for example: <u>ee</u> <u>nor</u> <u>muss</u>

Step Three: Synthesize the spelling into one word: <u>eenormuss</u>

Later, the teacher can provide the correct spelling beside the student's phonetically spelled word: eenormuss <u>enormous</u>. Students who are cryptic (dysphonetic) spellers and tend to produce spellings that do not allow the reader to guess the target word (or prevent a spell-checker from predicting the word) benefit greatly from this phonetic spelling strategy and report that it allows them to employ a wider range of vocabulary and compose more fluently. Of course, phonetic spelling does not replace formal, structured teaching of spelling rules; rather, it is an interim strategy to enhance the richness and fluency of students' writing. In addition, phonetic spelling enhances phonemic awareness and strengthens sound-symbol association skills.

Two factors that aid vocabulary learning and recall are 1) the extent to which a learning activity requires integration of semantic and phonological information and 2) the presence of semantic associations among a set of vocabulary words. A helpful strategy for helping students strengthen their knowledge and retrieval of theme-related vocabulary is the use of an *"A-to-Z Vocabulary Sheet"* (Jennings & Haynes, 2002). Table 6.1.2 provides an example for how selected, thematic vocabulary around the topic of sailing can be reinforced using this approach.

Table 6.1.2. **Sample A-to-Z Vocabulary Sheet (Theme = Sailing)**
Adapted with permission from Jennings & Haynes (2002). From *Talking to Writing: Strategies for Scaffolding Expository Expression.* Prides Crossing, MA: Landmark School.

Grapheme-Phoneme Cue	Syllable # Cue	Semantic Cue
r _ _ _ _ _ _	(2)	Device used for steering a sailboat
s _ _ _ _ _ _ _ _	(2)	Right side of a boat
s _ _ _ _	(1)	Rear portion of a boat

Students discuss, and if necessary orally chain, the core vocabulary in class and then fill out the sheet for homework or for review at the beginning of the next class. Phonological cues are gradually extinguished as students gain mastery.

Students who have particular difficulty with word-retrieval may require *extrinsic* (teacher-provided) and *intrinsic* (self-provided) cues and/or cueing strategies. Types of extrinsic cues include, but are not limited to the following:
• Visual (picture)
• Gestural (mimed verb or action of target noun)
• Semantic (definitional)
• Phonologic/Graphemic (first sound or letter of a word)

Of the extrinsic cues, phonologic/graphemic cues are usually a last resort, because they cue the actual sound structure of the word and therefore tend to be easiest. Intrinsic cueing strategies are methods students can employ by themselves to help them find words. Examples include, but are not limited to the following:
• Visualizing (trying to envision the object or action)
• For concrete nouns, thinking about the object's function, typical location/circumstances, or typical time of day or season of year when the noun is used.

Students who are less strategic may need to memorize these intrinsic strategies and be taught to employ them when they are having retrieval difficulties.

Sentence-Level Strategies and Techniques

Once students are introduced to theme-related vocabulary and concepts, they are ready to learn to recognize and employ them in theme-centered sentences. Here are a few principles that can support student's learning at the sentence level:

1. Teach using a developmental sentence hierarchy.
2. After a student masters a basic set of simple to complex patterns, introduce flexibility and options.
3. Address sentence skill learning in all modalities:
   - Listening (monitoring/recognition)
   - Speaking (oral rehearsal)
   - Reading (monitoring what is written)
   - Writing (formulation)
4. Provide visual templates in early stages, then fade them as students gain mastery.

While slight differences in developmental sequence for sentence patterns have been suggested in the research literature and in commercial instructional programs, what is critical is that sentence instruction be incremental and sequential, moving from simple to more complex. Table 6.1.3 provides a sample sentence hierarchy. Because students with language impairment are often confused by formal grammatical terms (e.g., *noun phrase, predicate, temporal adverbial phrase*, simplified terms (*noun, verb, where*) can help them identify sentence parts and develop rudimentary syntactic awareness. As students become more facile with recognizing and producing sentences, conventional terms can be introduced, as appropriate.

Table 6.1.3. **Sample Sentence Hierarchy**
Adapted with permission from Jennings & Haynes (2002). From *Talking to Writing: Strategies for Scaffolding Expository Expression*. Prides Crossing, MA: Landmark School.

Structure	Example
Noun (N) + Verb (V)	Gulls screeched.
N + V + Where Prepositional Phrase (Where)	The captain leaned over the stern.
Adjective (Adj) + N + V + Where	Icy breezes blew against their cheeks.
Adj + N + V + Where + When phrase (When)	Three lads snoozed on the deck at dawn.
N + V + Where + and + N + V + Where	Pesky gulls screeched over the bow and waves lapped against the side of the sailboat.
N + V + Where + but + N + V	Dark clouds gathered in the East, but the sailors slept.
N + V + where + because + N + V	The boys sailed back to shore because clouds gathered in the East.
[When clause] + Noun + Verb	When the wind blew, the sails filled.
N + V + Object Noun + [who/which/that clause]	The boys spotted a whale that was surfacing nearby.
N + [who/which/that clause] + V + Where	Dolphins that had followed the boat disappeared.

After mastery is demonstrated, then students can experiment with moving elements around in sentences. For example, once students have learned the Noun + Verb + Where Phrase pattern (e.g., "The pioneers set camp next to a bend in the

Mississippi River."), they can play with moving the "where" phrase to the beginning of the sentence ("Next to a bend in the Mississippi River, the pioneers set camp.").

At each level of sentence complexity, it is important for teachers to engage students in listening, speaking, reading, and writing the target sentence pattern. Listening and reading tasks require students to monitor for the teacher's correct versus incorrect production(s), while speaking and writing tasks have students apply self-monitoring to their own production. Following are sample, theme-centered exercises for a Noun + Verb + Where sentence pattern:

A. Listening (Recognition/Monitoring) Task

Procedure: Teacher displays target sentence pattern: Noun + Verb + Where Phrase. Students listen to teacher's production of theme-centered sentences and identify correct ("C") versus incorrect ("X"). If incorrect, they indicate the part of the sentence that is missing.

Table 6.1.4.　　　**Listening Task**

Stimuli	Students' Response
(1) "Gulls flew."	X – Where phrase
(2) "The sailors jumped into a row boat."	C (correct)
(3) "The mast over the boat."	X – Verb

B. Reading (Recognition/Monitoring) Task

Procedure: Same as for task A, but with written stimuli

C. Speaking (Production) Task

Procedure: Teacher displays target sentence pattern and says thematic nouns. Students take turns orally producing sentences that follow the pattern:

Noun + Verb + Where Phrase
Examples: "Barnacles were embedded in the stern of the boat."
　　　　　"Waves….."
　　　　　"A whale….."

D. Writing (Production) Task

Procedure: Same as for task C, but requiring written formulation

This repeated practice with sentence patterns in multiple modalities helps students to internalize the forms, and the linking of recognition and production tasks prepares students to self-monitor their production at the multi-sentence level (see Jennings & Haynes, 2002). The use of theme-centered words provides students with opportunities to recognize and employ key vocabulary within sentences.

Sentence combining is an additional technique for teaching sentence formulation skills. As the name suggests, this method involves practice at merging smaller sentences, or parts of sentences, into larger sentences. For example, a student might be asked to combine "The teenager is steering the sailboat" with "The teenager is in the stern of the sailboat." The resulting sentence could be, "The teenager who is in the stern is steering the sailboat." While sentence combining has been found to increase the syntactic complexity of students' writing, its use in teaching has subsided since its introduction in the late '60's and early '70's, soon after Noam Chomsky proposed his seminal theory of transformational grammar (e.g., Strong, 1973). While this strategy may currently be out of vogue, it remains an effective method for aiding sentence production skills, particularly in the context of thematic instruction. At the paragraph level, sentence combining skills can help students to avoid redundant use of words and eliminate short, choppy sentences.

Students with deficits in language formulation often display concomitant difficulties with organizing writing on the page. An effective remedial strategy is to employ templates to visually scaffold oral and written production. Table 6.1.4 provides a simple example of how a template could be employed to scaffold an expanded kernel sentence: employ a template for teaching, observe that a student has mastered a given pattern using the template, and then be disappointed when the student fails to use the same pattern correctly in spontaneous writing. In such cases, it is important to remember that children with significant language impairment need gradual elimination of scaffolding (category headers, boxes). This same teaching principle—systematic application and removal of scaffolding—applies to any kind of cueing system that one employs to support language learning.

Table 6.1.4. **Sentence Template**

Article/Noun Pointer	Adjective	Noun	Verb	Where Phrase
The	oaken	rudder	sliced	through the waves.

Paragraph-Level Principles, Strategies, and Techniques

A main objective of teaching word- and sentence-level skills is the development of paragraph-level writing. Some key principles for teaching paragraph-level writing include the following:

1. Employ oral rehearsal prior to writing
2. Prepare students with theme-centered sentence expansion and/or sentence combining
3. Teach the sentence at the core of each paragraph type
4. Scaffold paragraph components (introductory and concluding sentences, paragraph body).

Principles 1 and 2 have already been discussed at length: when students struggle with paragraph-level writing, it is important for teachers to ensure that they have employed adequate oral rehearsal and sentence-level instruction prior to introducing paragraphs. With respect to principle (3), standard expository paragraph types (e.g., enumerative, comparison-contrast, descriptive, sequential-process) have at their core a specific type of sentence and logic. For example: comparison-contrast paragraphs have at their core sentences that denote contrast (e.g., while-, although-, …but-, …however); descriptive expository paragraphs typically contain sentences with pre-nominal adjectives (*nervous sailors, gray clouds, whistling breeze*) and adjective stacking (*three screeching gulls, icy turquoise waves, exuberant young captain*); and sequence-process paragraphs usually include words or phrases denoting temporal transition (*first, then, next, after that, finally*). Lastly, scaffolding (principle 4) is often needed to ensure that students learn to formulate appropriate sentences for initiating and ending their paragraphs (e.g., see discussion of Object Description Paragraph, following).

Scaffolding of paragraph components varies according to the type of paragraph. Figure 6.1.5 illustrates generic techniques for scaffolding an Object Description. This paragraph-level exercise—a description of a coyote—was part of a larger "Pioneers' Westward Expansion" theme:

Table 6.1.5.   **Sample Object Description Paragraph Scaffold**
Adapted with permission from Jennings & Haynes (2002). From *Talking to Writing: Strategies for Scaffolding Expository Expression*. Prides Crossing, MA: Landmark School.

Description of: coyote   Name: _____

Date: _____

Day: _____

Topic sentence: A coyote is a mammal with many important characteristics.

       Topic noun + category + Generic Attributes Phrase

Key features: ears, muzzle, coat, legs, paws, tail

Article	Adj.	Adj.	Noun	Function Verb
The	alert	triangular	ears	listen for danger.
A	sensitive	pointed	muzzle	sniffs for food.
A	thick	grayish	coat	protects it from the cold.
	Strong	thin	legs	carry the coyote quickly towards its prey.
The	padded	black	paws	pad silently across the snow.
A	long	bushy	tail	acts as a signal flag.

Concluding sentence: In conclusion, the coyote has many important features that help it to survive in its environment.

In the example above, the introductory sentence is cued by the scaffold: Topic Noun + is/are + Category + General Attributes Phrase; this pattern can be used to introduce a description for any complex animate or inanimate noun. See Table 6.1.6.

Table 6.1.6.   **Pattern to Introduce a Description**

Target Noun	→	Introductory Sentence
Ferrari	→	A Ferrari is a racing vehicle that has many important components.
Grandfather Clock	→	A grandfather clock is a time-keeping device that has many important components.
Tyrannosaurus Rex	→	The Tyrannosaurus Rex was a prehistoric reptile that had many important characteristics.

The body of this Object Description Paragraph is comprised of sentences that describe parts of the complex object. The first step in setting up the paragraph is to show students a picture of the target object and have them brainstorm key components. The component nouns are then inserted under the noun category in a series of sentence grids. The student completes each sentence with stacked adjectives describing the given noun as well as verbs explaining the noun's function.

The concluding sentence is a simple, generic frame: "In conclusion, the (Target Noun) has important components that are well-suited for (Action of Category)." For animals, the final part of the concluding sentence can refer to adaptation to that animal's environment. This pattern can be used reliably to conclude the description of any concrete object that is inanimate or animate. For example:

Table 6.1.7. Pattern to Conclude a Description

Target Noun	→	Concluding Sentence
Ferrari	→	In conclusion, the Ferrari has important components that are well-suited for racing.
Grandfather Clock	→	In conclusion, the grandfather clock has important components that are well suited for telling time.
Tyrannosaurus Rex	→	In conclusion, the Tyrannosaurus Rex had many important characteristics that helped it adapt to the prehistoric environment.

The Object Description Paragraph technique described here differs from typical paragraph templates in the number and types of supports it employs. When teaching at the paragraph level, it is critical to consider the different types of cues needed for a given student or group of students and then plan for how to systematically remove the supports as mastery is demonstrated.

In conclusion, oral language skills provide a foundation for reading and writing. While writing is a complex activity that can be daunting for students with dyslexia and related language learning difficulties, there are many ways in which oral language skills can be employed to support writing instruction. Given structured, systematic teaching that exploits synergies between listening, speaking, reading, and writing, struggling writers can learn to write independently and effectively at the word, sentence, and paragraph levels.

References

Catts, H., Fey, M., & Tomblin, J. (2002). A longitudinal investigation of reading outcomes in children with language impairments. *Journal of Speech, Language, Hearing Research. 45*(6), December, 1142–1157.

Fey, M., Catts, H., Proctor-Williams, K., Tomblin, J., & Zhang, X. (2004). Oral and written story composition skills of children with language impairment. *Journal of Speech, Language, Hearing Research. 47*(6), December, 1301–1318.

Jennings, T., & Haynes, C. (2002). *From talking to writing: Strategies for scaffolding expository expression.* Prides Crossing, MA: Landmark School.

MacArthur, C., Graham, S., & Fizgerald, J. (2006). *Handbook of writing research.* New York: Guilford Publications.

Strong, W. (1973). *Sentence-combining: A composing book.* New York: Random House.

Teaching Writing Skills to Adolescents
Evidence-Based Practices

Dolores Perin and Steve Graham

Students with a history of learning difficulty often continue to have uncomfortable experiences as they face academic writing assignments, even when reading has become easier. Faced with a writing task, these students may not know where to start. They may feel overwhelmed by the need to organize their thoughts, and they may not have at their disposal the means for translating their ideas into written words in a way that communicates them adequately to their audience. They may feel ill at ease when asked to revise something they have written. By adolescence, writing difficulties threaten students' potential to benefit from the types of curricular experiences that build knowledge and stimulate critical thinking. Increasingly common by middle and high school are subject-specific research projects that include writing tasks designed to help students extend their thinking about complicated topics. Teachers who assign these projects often take writing skills for granted. A major opportunity to expand one's intellectual universe is denied to students who lack these skills.

Extent of the Problem

Large numbers of middle and high school students display extreme difficulty with academic writing. In a national assessment, Persky, Daane, and Jin (2003) divided writing ability into "Basic," "Proficient" and "Advanced" levels at the 4th, 8th and 12th grade levels. For example, at the 8th grade level, Basic-level writers' compositions show an understanding of the nature of the writing task and the informational needs of the reader. Their papers also include supporting details in an organized way and use fairly accurate grammar, spelling, punctuation, and capitalization. These students' writing, however, does not include precise language, varied sentence structure, creativity, or analysis and evaluation of information. These qualities are found at the higher Proficient level, which is considered a minimal goal for writing attainment (Persky et al., 2003, p. 10). At all grade levels, the findings from this national assessment were discouraging. At the 8th grade level, for instance, 69% of students tested *below or at* the Basic level. Just 29% of students were at the Proficient level, whereas only 2% were at the Advanced level. These statistics suggest that there is a large gulf between what middle school students could accomplish intellectually through writing experiences, and how they are actually performing now.

Connections between Writing and Reading in Secondary Education

Writing is typically related to some type of reading activity in school settings. These connections become very close by the middle school grades. At this point, students must read and write to learn new information (Fitzgerald & Shanhan, 2000). Reading and writing fold into a larger endeavor called "writing-to-learn" (Bangert-Drowns, Hurley & Wilkinson, 2004) in which students read text and then use the content in some way by writing about it. For example, in a social studies class, the students may read historical documents and then write an essay arguing for one perspective or another on the events in question (De La Paz, 2005). Similarly, students in a science class may gather data about soil erosion and then write lab reports that describe their observations and reflect on how their understanding of the topic may have changed (Keys, 2000). Writing-to-learn can build students' critical thinking skills and lead to a transformation in their knowledge (Bereiter & Scardamalia, 1987). However, a foundation in writing skills is needed if students are to write for the purpose of learning.

Improving Writing Skills: Practice vs. Instruction

How can teachers and specialists promote better writing skills among middle and high school students? One point to note is that writing difficulties are not confined to individuals with diagnosed learning disabilities (LD). Persky et al. (2003) indicated that writing difficulties extend well into the "regular" middle school population. The magnitude of the problem as well as the critical importance of writing skills for learning subject matter indicate that writing instruction deserves a prominent role in secondary education.

It is important to distinguish between teaching students to write, i.e., explicit writing *instruction*, and giving students *opportunities* to write about content material – the contrast is between "learning-to-write" and writing-to-learn as described above. Many teachers assign writing to learn tasks under the misapprehension that students' writing will improve simply by involving them in the act of writing. However, assigning writing tasks without providing explicit instruction in component skills creates a situation where students, if they *do not* write well, may merely practice poorly-developed abilities rather than actually improve existing writing skill.

The component skills in proficient writing can be found in an influential model of skilled writing proposed by Hayes (2000). These skills include *reflection*, for example when a writer reflects on his or her ideas in order to plan to write; *text production*, which involves translating one's ideas to written text, and *text interpretation*, for example where the writer reviews what he or she has written, taking into consideration the ideas initially planned, and makes revisions accordingly. Text production has been divided into two types of skills (Swanson & Berninger, 1994), transcription, which involves handwriting, keyboarding, spelling, and mechanics; and text-generation, which involves expressing the ideas to be written. Implementing all of the skills involved in writing is accomplished through deployment of cognitive strategies that can be taught explicitly (Graham & Harris, 2005).

Focused, explicit instruction is needed to ensure that weaker writers are able to take advantage of opportunities they are given to write. The effects of learning-to-write activities may be assessed in terms of the quality of written compositions. For instance, a well-written essay is organized coherently, and contains well-developed and pertinent ideas, supporting examples, and appropriate detail (Needels & Knapp, 1994). How should writing be taught to middle and high school students, including those with LD? Over the last forty years, evidence has been accumulating about approaches that are effective in increasing the quality of secondary students' compositions. Such approaches hold considerable promise for improving the writing of middle and high school students.

Instructional Directions from a Meta-Analysis

Recently, we reviewed research on adolescent writing instruction with students in grades 4–12 (Graham & Perin, 2006). We conducted this review in the form of a meta-analysis, a procedure that provides a measure of the comparative strength or power of a specific intervention. In our review, we examined studies that compared one group that received a specific intervention to a control group that did not receive it. We limited our review to true experiments (students were randomly assigned to treatments) and quasi-experiments (students were not randomly assigned). Our decision to focus on this type of research does not distract from the valuable contribution made by other research methodologies, such as single subject design or qualitative studies.

Our meta-analysis incorporated findings for adolescent writing from previous meta-analyses (Bangert-Drowns, 1993; Goldring, Russell, & Cook, 2003; Graham, 2006; Graham & Harris, 2003; Hillocks, 1986), and we added more recent research. We extended the previous meta-analyses by reorganizing their instructional categories and examining the impact of treatments not included in the earlier work. We found that the majority of studies focused on students with a full range of ability (from low to high achieving) rather than testing the instructional approaches specifically with students with special learning needs.

The key statistic utilized in a meta-analysis is the "effect size," which indicates the magnitude and direction of an effect. Conventionally, an effect size of .2 is considered small, .5 medium and .8 or above large. When we calculated an average effect size for a treatment (based on four or more studies), we weighted the effect size for each study based on the number of participants, giving more weight to studies with larger samples.

Based on the meta-analysis, we were able to calculate a mean weighted effect size for 10 writing interventions that can be applied by classroom teachers as well as literacy and learning specialists (see Graham & Perin, 2006 for full details and methodology). Although these recommendations in themselves are not meant to constitute a full writing program, they do provide a catalogue of interventions that can make a difference in how well middle and high school students write. The recommendations are ordered according to the strength of effect, and the text in italics is quoted directly from Graham and Perin (2006); further details regarding instruction are provided in Perin (2006).

Effective Writing Instruction: Recommendations from the Meta-Analysis

1. *Strategy Instruction.* Teach adolescents strategies for planning, revising, and editing their compositions (mean weighted effect size = .82).

2. *Summarization.* Teach adolescents strategies and procedures for summarizing reading material, as this improves their ability to concisely and accurately present this information in writing (mean weighted effect size = .82).

3. *Peer Assistance.* Develop instructional arrangements where adolescents work together to plan, draft, revise, and edit their compositions. Such collaborative activities have a strong impact on the quality of what students write (mean weighted effect size = .75).

4. *Setting Product Goals.* Set clear and specific goals for what adolescents are to accomplish with their writing product. This includes identifying the purpose of the assignment, e.g., to persuade, as well as characteristics of the final product, e.g., addresses both sides of an argument (mean weighted effect size = .70).

5. *Word Processing.* Make it possible for adolescents to use word processing as a primary tool for writing, as it has a positive impact on the quality of their writing (mean weighted effect size = .55).

6. *Sentence Combining.* Teach adolescents how to write increasingly complex sentences. Instruction in combining simpler sentences into more sophisticated ones enhances the quality of students' writing (mean weighted effect size = .50).

7. *Process Writing with Training.* Provide teachers with training in how to implement the process writing approach when this instructional model is used with adolescents (mean weighted effect size = .46). Note: "process writing" refers

to opportunities for extended writing; writing for authentic audiences; cycles that include planning (e.g., pre-writing activities or free writing), translating ideas to text, and reviewing (e.g., evaluating, revising, and editing); personal responsibility and ownership of writing projects with the teacher serving as facilitator; high level of student interaction, supportive writing environment; writing portfolios and writing rubrics; conferencing and mini-lessons; and in some instances more systematic instruction).

8. *Inquiry Approach.* Engage adolescents in activities that help them develop ideas and content for a particular writing task by analyzing immediate and concrete data, e.g., comparing and contrasting cases or collecting and evaluating evidence (mean weighted effect size = .32).

9. *Pre-writing.* Engage adolescents in activities that help them gather and organize ideas for their composition before they write a first draft. This includes activities such as gathering possible information for a paper through reading or developing a visual representation of their ideas before writing (mean weighted effect size = .32).

10. *Use of Models.* Provide adolescents with good models for each type of writing that is the focus of instruction. These examples should be analyzed and students encouraged to imitate the critical elements embodied in the models (mean weighted effect size = .25).

In a companion document to Graham and Perin (2006), entitled *Writing Next*, to be published by the Alliance for Excellent Education with support from Carnegie Corporation, we also reported an additional finding, that using writing as a tool to facilitate adolescents' learning of content material was effective (average weighted effect size = .23). Although the impact of writing activity on content learning is small, it is consistent enough to expect some enhancement as a result of writing-to-learn activities.

Example of Instruction

Below we provide an example of instruction for each of the first four recommendations. As noted earlier, there is a shortage of writing intervention research with special-needs adolescents. Two of the four examples, however, involved students with LD.

Strategy Instruction (recommendation 1).

In De La Paz (2005), 8th grade students were taught writing strategies, based on collaboration between a language arts and a social studies teacher. The social studies teacher taught a historical reasoning strategy for 12 days, and the language arts teacher taught a strategy for writing argumentative (persuasive) essays over 10 days. Writing strategy instruction included the use of two mnemonics for planning a persuasive essay, STOP, Suspend judgment, Take a side, Organize ideas, Plan as you write; and DARE, Develop a topic sentence, Add supporting ideas, Reject an argument for the other side, and End with a conclusion. The language arts teacher discussed the structure of a five-paragraph persuasive essay on a historical topic, and showed students essays that presented arguments for different views of a topic. The teacher modeled the planning and writing of paragraphs of a persuasive essay on a relevant historical topic, using the mnemonics. The students worked in small groups to plan a persuasive essay on another, relevant historical topic. The students proceeded to plan and write essays on different historical topics under the teacher's guidance, and then wrote essays independently.

Summarization Instruction (recommendation 2).

In Bean and Steenwyk (1984), 6th grade students were directly taught how to write an effective summary. The teacher taught students six rules for writing a summary: delete unnecessary material, delete redundant material, compose a word to replace a list of items, compose a word to replace the individual parts of an action, select a topic sentence and invent a topic sentence if one is not available. Students practiced applying these rules when summarizing a variety of different paragraphs. An alternative to teaching the rules was also tested by Bean and Steenwyck (1984). With this procedure, students were shown one sentence from a paragraph and asked to retell the information using 15 words or less. Next, the teacher presented two more sentences from a paragraph and asked the students to write a 15 word sentence that summarizes these two sentences. The teacher repeated this process until students could summarize entire paragraphs.

Peer Assistance (recommendation 3).

In MacArthur, Schwartz, and Graham (1991), 4th, 5th and 6th grade students with LD were taught to work in pairs to apply a revising strategy. This approach was designed to help youngsters revise compositions they had previously written on a word processor. One student was appointed as the Author and the other as the Editor. Each role was associated with specific activities for revising and editing essays, including receiving or giving feedback, respectively. The teacher taught students how to apply these procedures before peers began working together. The initial instruction used a videotape showing student actors applying these procedures, as they gave and received feedback on their compositions. The teacher then modeled the procedures, and students practiced applying them with example essays, before applying them to their own writing. Then, the teacher divided the students into pairs for peer-collaboration. The videotape was shown again, and the pairs practiced the peer revising procedures, receiving teacher assistance until they could use them without help.

Setting Product Goals (recommendation 4).

In Page-Voth and Graham (1999), 7th and 8th grade students with LD wrote persuasive essays. Before writing a paper, students were familiarized with basic elements of a persuasive paper: premise, supporting reasons, refutation of claims that can be made against the premise, and conclusion. The teacher also introduced and discussed the value of goal setting. Before writing an essay, each student participated in a writing conference, where he or she was assigned a writing topic and selected a goal (e.g., refute a specific number of claims that ran counter to the premise of the argument). The student recorded the goal and was encouraged to use a six-part strategy to accomplish it: (1) read the essay topic and state an opinion, (2) brainstorm and write down enough ideas to satisfy the goal, (3) write the essay, including the ideas brainstormed, (4) check whether all ideas are included in the essay, (5) modify the essay to add any ideas not included, and add any new ones, and (6) check to see if the goal has been met and return to step 5 if it has not. After writing the essay using these procedures, a post-writing conference was held, where students shared their essay (read it aloud), and the teacher provided feedback regarding the extent to which the goal was achieved.

Discussion

Our meta-analysis, which covers intervention research on adolescent writing from the 1960s to the present, revealed a number of effective instructional approaches. However, three absences are notable in the findings. First, the meta-analysis did not find traditional grammar instruction to be effective, although a method to teach grammar, sentence-combining (recommendation 6) was effective. Although it is clear from assessments such as Persky et al. (2003) that low-achieving adolescent writers need to improve their grammar, instruction needs to move away from traditional approaches.

Second, a recommendation that is frequently made in the hopes of improving writing is to increase the time allocated to writing activities (e.g., National Commission on Writing, 2003). However, for a variety of reasons (see Graham & Perin, 2006), we were not able to compute a mean weighted effect size for this recommendation. Our current opinion on this issue is that as much writing time as possible should be provided to students, but it is what happens during this time that is important. Since most of the treatments that were effective in our meta-analysis involved explicit instruction, we recommend that writing time include a research-based instructional component rather than leaving students to their own devices.

The third absence in the meta-analysis was an examination of the effectiveness of instruction in basic writing skills, such as spelling and handwriting. These skills remain poorly developed in a significant proportion of middle and high school students. Probably because difficulty with these skills is typically associated with younger students, there is very little experimental research on the impact of such instruction on the quality of adolescents' writing. This is not to say that these skills should be ignored. In fact, an instructional principle that receives support in the research literature is that instruction in lower-level literacy skills should be combined with instruction in higher-level skills, providing immediate opportunities to practice skills such as handwriting and spelling in a meaningful context (Berninger et al., 1995).

Another issue concerns the serious consequences that writing difficulties have for learning in the content areas, especially from the middle school grades on up. Different organizational structures or formats for writing instruction exist in secondary schools. Writing instruction traditionally occurs in the context of the language arts or English classroom, or with learning specialists such as special education teachers. Instruction tends to focus on developing students' writing skills using generic materials. However, because writing difficulties are so common and can impact adolescents' academic knowledge development, it is possible that writing instruction should be systematically connected to subject-matter, and/or that content area teachers should also assume some responsibility for providing explicit instruction in writing skills (see Shanahan, 2004).

There are several options for combining writing instruction with content instruction. Perin (2001) identified several formats in community college basic English instruction that can be considered for secondary education. With an "applied academics" format, the language arts or English teacher, or a learning specialist, could use subject matter such as science or social studies as the content of writing instruction. For example, strategies for writing persuasive essays might be taught using text read in a concurrent social studies class. In an "infused content" format, a content-area teacher could teach writing skills in the course of teaching subject matter, as encouraged by content-area literacy educators such as Alvermann and Phelps, (2002). In the "learning community" format, a content-area teacher and the English or language arts instructor could align their curricula, giving students assignments that systematically connect writing and content instruction. De La Paz's (2005) study described above, used this format. However, since further research is needed to identify effective formats for adolescent writing instruction, any recommendation that writing instruction be organized in one way or another remains tentative.

There is still much research to be done regarding effective methods of teaching writing to middle and high school students. Additional strategies need to be tested, and research needs to verify that strategies that are effective with the general population are effective with students with special needs (it should be noted that strategy instruction was even more effective with struggling writers than students in general). We also need to do a better job of helping teachers become aware of evidence-based practices, encouraging them to adopt new approaches that both meet the needs of their students and are feasible, given the realities of their specific educational setting.

Acknowledgements

This article is based on a meta-analysis funded by Carnegie Corporation of New York, reported in Graham and Perin (2006).

References

Alvermann, D. E., & Phelps, S. F. (2002). *Content reading and literacy: Succeeding in today's diverse classrooms* (3rd ed.). Boston, MA: Allyn and Bacon.

Bangert-Drowns, R. (1993). The word processor as an instructional tool: A meta-analysis of word processing in writing instruction. *Review of Educational Research, 63*, 69–93.

Bangert-Drowns, R. L., Hurley, M. M., & Wilkinson, B. (2004). The effects of school-based writing-to-learn interventions on academic achievement: A meta-analysis. *Review of Educational Research, 74*, 29–58.

Bean, T. W., & Steenwyk, F. L. (1984). The effect of three forms of summarization instruction on sixth graders' summary writing and comprehension. *Journal of Reading Behavior, 16*, 297–306.

Bereiter, C., & Scardamalia, M. (1987). *The psychology of written composition.* Hillsdale, NJ: Erlbaum.

Berninger, V. W., Abbott, R. D., Whitaker, D., Sylvester, L., & Nolen, S. B. (1995). Integrating low- and high-level skills in instructional protocols for writing disabilities. *Learning Disability Quarterly, 18*, 293–309.

De La Paz, S. (2005). Teaching historical reasoning and argumentative writing in culturally and academically diverse middle school classrooms. *Journal of Educational Psychology, 97*, 139–158.

Fitzgerald, J., & Shanahan, T. (2000). Reading and writing relations and their development. *EducationalPsychologist, 35*, 39–50.

Goldring, A., Russell, M., & Cook, A. (2003). The effects of computers on student writing: A metaanalysis of studies from 1992-2002. *Journal of Technology, Learning, and Assessment, 2*, 1–51.

Graham, S. (2006). Strategy instruction and the teaching of writing: A meta-analysis. In C. MacArthur, S. Graham, & J. Fitzgerald (Eds.), *Handbook of Writing Research* (pp. 187–207). New York: Guilford.

Graham, S., & Perin, D. (2006). A meta-analysis of writing instruction for adolescent students. Manuscript submitted for publication.

Graham, S., & Harris, K. R. (2003). Students with learning disabilities and the process of writing: A metaanalysis of SRSD studies. In L. Swanson, K. R. Harris, & S. Graham (Eds.). *Handbook of research on learning disabilities* (pp. 383–402). New York: Guilford.

Graham, S., & Harris, K. R. (2005). *Writing better: Effective strategies for teaching students with learning difficulties.* Baltimore, MD: Paul H. Brookes.

Hayes, J. R. (2000). A new framework for understanding cognition and affect in writing. In R. Indrisano & J. R. Squire (Eds.). *Perspectives on writing: Research, theory and practice* (pp. 6–44). Newark, DE: International Reading Association. Originally published in C. M. Levy, & S. Ransdell (Eds.) (1996). *The science of writing: Theories, methods, individual differences, and applications.* (pp. 1–27). Mahwah, NJ: Erlbaum.

Hillocks, G. (1986). *Research on written composition: New directions for teaching.* Urbana, IL: National Council of Teachers of English.

Keys, C. W. (2000). Investigating the thinking processes of eighth grade writers during the composition of a scientific laboratory report. *Journal of Research in Science Teaching, 37*, 676–690.

MacArthur, C., Schwartz, S., & Graham, S. (1991). Effects of a reciprocal peer revision strategy in special education classrooms. *Learning Disability Research and Practice, 6*, 201–210.

National Commission on Writing (2003, April). *The neglected R: The need for a writing revolution.* Available from www.collegeboard.com

Needels, M. C., & Knapp, M. S. (1994). Teaching writing to children who are underserved. *Journal of Educational Psychology, 86*, 339–349.

Page-Voth, V., & Graham, S. (1999). Effects of goal setting and strategy use on the writing performance and self-efficacy of students with writing and learning problems. *Journal of Educational Psychology, 91*, 230–240.

Perin, D. (2001). Academic-occupational integration as a reform strategy for the community college: Classroom perspectives. *Teachers College Record, 103*, 303–335.

Perin, D. (2006). Best practices in adolescent writing. In S. Graham, C. MacArthur, & J. Fitzgerald (Eds.). *Best Practices in Writing.* New York: Guilford (manuscript submitted for book in preparation).

Persky, H. R., Daane, M. C., & Jin, Y. (2003). *The nation's report card: Writing 2002.* (NCES 2003529). U.S. Department of Education. Institute of Education Sciences. National Center for Education Statistics. Washington, DC: Government Printing Office.

Shanahan, T. (2004). Overcoming the dominance of communication: Writing to think and to learn. In T. L. Jetton & J. A. Dole (Eds.). *Adolescent literacy research and practice* (pp. 59–73). New York: Guilford.

Swanson, H. L., & Berninger, V. (1994). Working memory as a source of individual differences in children's writing. In E. C. Butterfield (Ed.). *Children's writing: Toward a process theory of the development of skilled writing* (pp. 31–56). Vol. 2 of J. Carlson (Ed.). *Advances in cognition and educational practice.* Greenwich, CT: JAI Press.

Sentence Combining

Bruce Saddler

Writing places many demands on a writer. Consider the sentence for instance. Depending on a writer's intent and ability, a composition could contain many types of sentences. In any given piece, for example, a writer could use a very short sentence to emphasize a point, write a more complex construction to elaborate an idea, or repeat certain elements for a specific effect.

By varying sentences in this manner a writer can create a rhythm and flow that makes reading the composition more enjoyable. Likewise, by filling each sentence with the words that precisely convey an idea, a writer makes the reading more understandable. But deciding which words to use in a specific type of sentence can test the ability of any writer, and according to Henry David Thoreau, it is a singular event when it does occur:

> *A perfectly healthy sentence, it is true, is extremely rare. For the most part we miss the hue and fragrance of the thought; as if we could be satisfied with the dews of the morning or evening without their colors, or the heavens without their azure.*

While our students may never craft a sentence as transcendent as Thoreau's, they need success with the process of sentence creation to effectively convey their thoughts. Learning these skills is important to all writers, as sentence generation (along with planning and revising) is a critical component of the writing process (Hayes & Flower, 1986). Sentence generation is the ability to convert mental ideas and intentions into syntactically correct written form. If writers struggle with this skill, they may not be able to accurately translate their thoughts into text or revise their ideas, making the text more difficult for others to read and appreciate. Lacking these skills could lead to less than desirable consequences. For example, if a student submits a writing assignment with poorly constructed sentences, his or her overall grade could be reduced, because a teacher's evaluation of the quality of a student's writing product can be strongly influenced by sentence structure.

Although sentence generation is a critical skill, it is not an easily mastered skill. The process of constructing creative sentences is quite complex, as a writer must handle several demands, including word choice, syntax, textual connections, clarity, and rhythm. Understandably, this process requires considerable effort.

Our young writers usually begin this process by creating simple, or kernel, sentences that may be very similar to the sentences they are reading in their primary readers. For example, a first grader might produce the following story:

A Nice Day
The girl sang. The boy danced. The dog ran.

However young writers must quickly add other sentence structures to their repertoire because too many simple sentences make a story less interesting to read:

A Dull Tale
The sentences were short. The sentences were simple. The story was boring.

In time, most students move away from simple sentences to create more syntactically complex structures, largely as a result of reading more sophisticated material and being exposed to more mature writing forms during writing instruction. However, for some students, this process progresses very slowly.

There are effective writing interventions that can help writers with the process of controlling and manipulating syntax. One of these, called *sentence combining*, has been systematically investigated by multiple researchers for many years. Sentence combining is a simple approach that prompts students to write and rewrite sentences to better convey intended meaning by learning and then practicing syntactic options. For example, if a student writes stories filled with simple kernel sentences such as "My cat is hairy" and "My cat is white," he or she can learn through sentence combining practice to change these sentences into more syntactically complex and mature sentences, such as "My hairy cat is white" or "The cat has white hair," depending on his or her intent.

No other writing activity has been as well researched. Over 80 studies conducted since the early 1960s have shown that sentence combining is an effective method to help students produce more syntactically mature sentences, improve the overall quality of their writings, and improve revising skills.

Recently, two high-profile reports clearly documented the effectiveness of sentence combining. First, a meta-analysis of the effect of grammar teaching on writing development by Andrews and colleagues (2006) indicated that there was little evidence to suggest that teaching grammar is effective, but sentence combining had a much more positive effect on writing. In addition, in *Writing Next: A report to the Carnegie Corporation* (Graham & Perin, 2007), sentence combining was found to have a positive effect on writing and was listed among the effective practices recommended for inclusion in effective writing programs.

Although conceptually simple, sentence combining is a powerful intervention because it offers writers a systematic method to explore language that initially does not require them to generate content or ideas. The exercises can provide a non-threatening, scaffolded venue for playing with words and ideas while also providing purposeful, stimulating language experiences that can accelerate a writer's use of syntactic patterns. Through mindful practice opportunities, students can work with sentence patterns they may not currently use in their writing. If this practice is frequent and systematic, they can gain familiarity and comfort with these structures. Such practice is particularly valuable for students with written language difficulties, because these children likely need to establish control over sentence production (Graham & Harris, 1988) and increase their repertoire of sentence options (Englert, 1991).

Creating Exercises

Becoming aware of different ways to put words together through a variety of syntactic options provides our students with greater control over their own language and makes it easier for them to express their ideas in a way that is meaningful and enjoyable to a reader (Saddler & Preschern, 2007). The first step in this journey is creating exercises. Although there are a few published sentence combining workbooks on the market, you can actually create exercises from a literature series or other classroom books by reducing or decombining a passage into kernel sentence clusters. Activities from the lives of your students or other school events can also be sources, along with newspapers and magazines. Content area textbooks are particularly valuable sources for decombining to create exercises, as these offer information about a new concept or reinforce an idea while the students practice writing.

Although these exercises are the best place to start, you should try to use the student's own work as quickly as you can. Having students work with their own writing allows practice in controlling and manipulating the syntactic options available in their actual writing *(Strong, 1986).* In addition, when students rework their own pieces, the challenges they encounter with expressing ideas within a current piece of writing can be addressed, making the knowledge they are gaining immediately usable.

Sequencing Exercises

Although there are many possibilities, Table 6.3.1 provides a list of various combinations to teach your students. Although the list is not exhaustive, it does provide sufficient options to help students write a variety of interesting sentences.

Table 6.3.1.   **Possible Sequence of Sentence Combining Exercises**
Note: For a more detailed discussion on sequencing sentence combining exercises, see Cooper (1973) and Lawlor (1983).

1.   Inserting adjectives and adverbs
Examples: The man drank the soda. / The man was <u>thirsty</u>. / The thirsty man drank the soda.
2.   Producing compound subjects and objects
Examples: Maren wanted to play. / <u>Bruce</u> wanted to play. / Maren and Bruce wanted to play.
3.   Producing compound sentences with *and* and *but*
Examples: Linda wanted to read. / Sam wanted to play games. / Linda wanted to read, <u>but</u> Sam wanted to play games.
4.   Producing possessive nouns
Examples: I like the dog. / It is <u>Frank's</u> dog. / I like Frank's dog.
5.   Producing sentence with adverbial clauses, using connecting words (*because, after, until,* and *when*)
Example: We went to school. / We wanted to learn to read. / We went to school <u>because</u> we wanted to learn to read.
6.   Producing sentences with relative clauses.
Example: The student will be last in line. / The student <u>is the slowest</u>. / The student who is the slowest will be last in line.

Introducing Exercises

Because your students may never have attempted anything in writing like the sentence combining exercises, it is helpful to explain that the purpose of the exercises is to assist them in crafting more interesting sentences, paragraphs, and stories that readers will appreciate and enjoy. Students need to know that reworking sentences is something that all good writers do, even very skilled professional writers. Tell them that you anticipate mistakes because many of the constructions will be different from those they typically write. You also can say that there is usually more than one possible sentence that can be created from a pair or cluster of simple sentences.

It is best to begin instruction in sentence combining by demonstrating how you would combine a pair of kernels. An overhead, document camera, or SMART Board will work equally well for this activity. Create two simple kernel sentences. Read each sentence and then combine the kernels. Share your thinking as you combine the sentences. In particular, share that when combining you might move words around, eliminate words, or change words. Then, discuss why the new combination sounds better. You may want to circle the omitted words to highlight exactly what was changed.

You can follow up this direct modeling by supporting the students while they practice either alone or in pairs. You can place several kernel sentence clusters on the overhead for students to practice. After allowing the students some time to work, have them share several of the possible solutions they discovered, either orally or by having them write responses on the overhead or board. Allow the students to discuss which options sound better and why. A discussion of language gradually develops an awareness of language and its use; this is a very positive outcome of this practice and can help you create a wonderful community that is comfortable engaging in this type of critical dialogue.

Bear in mind that some students will pick up on the process of sentence combining right away, while others might need more direct support in choosing how best to make effective changes. Other students may need a more tactile approach involving words placed on index cards that they can move around and manipulate.

One fun way to incorporate movement into your practice sessions is to write words on very large cards and have one word assigned to each student. Next, ask the students to align themselves into the two kernel sentences. The class can then suggest how the students can be rearranged to create a new sentence. However you choose to differentiate your instruction, it is helpful during these practice sessions to initially have all of the students working on the same sentence. This will provide an opportunity for all students to discuss and find solutions to the same rhetorical problem, while at the same time offering various solutions for comparison and discussion.

Evaluating Responses

Although language does have grammatical rules, it is best not to explain the technical aspects (e.g., dangling participles) when rating the quality of the new sentence.

Belaboring grammatical terminology will do little but confuse most students. It is better to rely on the effectiveness of the new sentence to convey accurately the writer's intention and meaning to assess the sentence.

This emphasis on *effectiveness* rather than *correctness* alludes to the idea that there is usually no right or wrong answer in sentence combining practice. Instead, some sentence combinations simply sound better or are more effective representations of the writer's intent and meaning. To explain *effectiveness* to your students, you can use the standards of clarity and directness of meaning, rhythmic appeal, and intended audience (Nemans, 1995). Initially, you will want to model the application of these standards to combinations you create and then, through discussion, guide your students to rate each other's responses. These criteria should be included in your rubrics for writing assignments.

> "This emphasis on effectiveness rather than correctness alludes to the idea that there is usually no right or wrong answer in sentence combining practice."

Conclusions

Improvements in writing take time, patience, and persistence. Sentence combining should be one component of a well-rounded writing program and should not replace instruction in the writing process. Instead, look at sentence combining sessions as focused writing experiences that will support other writing assignments. Keep your sentence combining sessions short and fun, but engage in the practice often. Your discussions about the varied complexity of sentences is one key to developing student awareness of language and an understanding of how to use language to convey meaning and purpose in writing. Who knows, one of your students might write a transcendent sentence of his or her own!

References

Andrews, R., Torgerson, C., Beverton, S., Freeman, A., Locke, T., Low, G., et al. (2006). The effect of grammar teaching on writing development. *British Educational Research Journal, 32*, 39–55.

Cooper, C. R. (1973). An outline for writing sentence combining problems. *English Journal, 62*, 96–102.

Englert, C. S. (1991). Making strategies and self-talk visible: Writing instruction in regular and special education classrooms. *American Educational Research Journal, 28*, 337–372.

Graham, S., & Harris, K. R. (1988). Instructional recommendations for teaching writing to exceptional students. *Exceptional Children, 54*, 506–512.

Graham, S., & Perin, D. (2007). *Writing next: Effective strategies to improve writing of adolescents in middle and high schools – A report to Carnegie Corporation of New York.* Washington, DC: Alliance for Excellent Education.

Hayes, J. R., & Flower, L. S. (1986). Writing research and the writer. *American Psychologist, 41*, 106–113.

Lawlor, J. (1983). Sentence combining: A sequence for instruction. *Elementary School Journal, 84*, 53–62.

Nemans, B. S. (1995). *Teaching students to write.* New York: Oxford University Press.

Saddler, B., & Preschern, J. (2007). Improving sentence writing ability through sentence-combining practice. *Teaching Exceptional Children, 39(3)*, 6–11.

Strong, W. (1986). *Creative approaches to sentence combining.* Urbana, IL: ERIC Clearinghouse on Reading and Communication Skills and the National Council of Teachers of English.

Thoreau, H. D., A perfectly healthy sentence. Retrieved March 15, 2009 from http://thinkexist.com/quotation/a_perfectly_healthy_ sentence-it_is_true-is/261348.html

The Parts of Speech
Foundation of Writing

6.4

Suzanne Carreker

When I ask people if they remember learning the parts of speech in school, there are two typical responses—affirmative nods or exasperated groans. When I then ask why they were taught parts of speech, even among the most enthusiastic responders to question one, few are able to answer this question. I, myself, thoroughly enjoyed learning the parts of speech but never understood why, never even thought to ask. Simply stated, the parts of speech are the foundation of writing.

The parts of speech provide the building blocks for teaching students how to write sentences, which are the building blocks for teaching students how to write paragraphs, essays, and other forms of written discourse. As students learn the parts of speech, they learn that some parts of speech are essential for a sentence to be complete. They learn that other parts of speech add additional information or interest to a sentence that help the writer convey the clearest and most precise message or viewpoint to the reader.

Knowledge of the parts of speech plays a valuable role in reading. It aids word recognition, comprehension, and fluency by enabling students to predict what will come next in a sentence, group words into meaningful units, and better monitor their reading (Rego & Byrant, 1993; Tunmer, Herriman, & Nesdale, 1988).

Introducing the Parts of Speech

There are compelling reasons to teach the parts of speech. Instruction should be direct and systematic. When introducing the parts of speech, there are four tasks:

1. Confirm the idea that no word is born a part of speech. A word is a part of speech according to the function it serves in a sentence.
2. Establish the need to know the parts of speech. What would happen if a particular part of speech did not exist?
3. Make the abstract concept of the parts of speech concrete. For example, the parts of speech can be marked with different symbols or colors. This article will present the use of color-codes to mark the parts of speech.
4. Connect the parts of speech to students' writing. How will knowledge of the parts of speech make them confident and competent writers?

The introductions for each part of speech are outlined below. The color-codes for the parts of speech and definitions are summarized in Table 6.4.1 (Carreker,

1992). Introductions take three to five minutes. Depending on the readiness and needs of students, introduction of all the parts of speech may take several days, several weeks, or an entire school year.

Table 6.4.1.   **Parts of Speech**

Part of Speech	Color-code	Definition
Nouns	Yellow	Nouns name a *person, place, thing,* or *idea.* Almost every sentence has a noun.
Pronouns	Yellow	Pronouns take the place of nouns.
Verbs	Orange	Verbs show action. Every sentence must have a verb.
Adjectives	Blue	Adjectives describe nouns. They tell *what kind, how many,* or *which one.*
Articles (adjectives)	Red	Articles warn that a noun is coming. The articles are *a, an,* and *the.*
Prepositions	Green	Prepositions show the relation between a noun or pronoun and another word.
Adverbs	Purple	Adverbs can modify a verb and tell *how, when,* or *where.* An adverb can modify an adjective or an adverb and tell *to what extent.*
Conjunctions	Brown	Conjunctions join words or groups of words together.
Interjections	No color	Interjections express strong emotion.

Nouns and Pronouns

The word *noun* comes from the Latin word for *name.* Nouns name a *person, place, thing,* or *idea.* To establish the need to know nouns, the teacher presents four yellow objects and says, *"Give me the yellow."* Students attempt to choose the "correct" yellow. Of course, they will be unable to choose the "correct" object, and this will lead to their understanding of the need to learn nouns. If there were no nouns, it would be difficult to know who or what someone was talking about. It is easy to choose the correct object if it is given a name.

Road signs such as crossing signs are yellow. These signs carry important information (e.g., be cautious as children may be crossing the road). Nouns are important; almost every sentence has a noun. Nouns are color-coded yellow. As students identify nouns in printed sentences, they underline them in yellow.

A noun that tells who or what the sentence is about is called the *subject noun.* The noun that receives the action of the verb is the *direct object* and is found after the verb. The direct object completes the predicate. As students are learning the concept of the direct object, the interim term *completer noun* can be used. This term better clarifies the concept.

Because pronouns take the place of nouns, they are color-coded yellow. If a sentence does not have a noun, it will have a pronoun. There are different classes of pronouns. Personal pronouns are the most helpful in the early introduction of the parts of speech. They include the *nominative case pronouns* that take the place of subject nouns (*I, he, we*). Those personal pronouns that take the place of direct objects are called *objective case pronouns* (*me, her, us*). Other pronouns such as reflexive (*myself, themselves*), relative (*who, which*), demonstrative (*this, that*), and indefinite (*all, each*) pronouns can be introduced later.

Articles

There are three words in English that are called articles –*a, an, the*. They are adjectives, but they do not provide the vivid images that adjectives such as *beautiful* or *enormous* provide. Knowledge of articles helps students identify nouns in sentences. Articles are color-coded red, a warning color. An article warns that a noun is coming, or in traditional grammatical terms, it modifies a noun. Students underline an article in red and draw a red arrow to the noun it modifies.

Verbs

Verbs show action, being, or state of being. Action verbs are the easiest for students to understand. The teacher establishes the need to know verbs by writing this sentence on the board: *I can ____.* Students generate words that complete the sentence. The generated words show action. Verbs are necessary; without verbs, no one could do anything.

Some road signs such as detour signs are orange. They carry very important information (e.g., the bridge is out, so take another route). Verbs are very important; every sentence must have a verb. Verbs are color-coded orange. As students identify verbs in sentences, they underline them in orange.

When students are secure with action verbs, linking and auxiliary verbs can be taught. Linking verbs connect the subject with the predicate and include *appear, be, become, feel, prove, remain,* and *seem*. Auxiliary verbs, also known as helping verbs, include *be, can, do, have, may, must, should, will,* and *would*. All verbs are color-coded orange.

Adjectives

The teacher presents four items that are identical except for color, such as four pens. The teacher says, *"Give me the pen."* Students attempt to give the "correct" item. Students will be unable to choose the "correct" item, and this will help them understand the need for adjectives. Adjectives describe or modify nouns, so with the addition of an adjective such as green or red, students would be able to choose the correct item.

Adjectives are blue. They describe or modify a noun and tell *what kind, how many,* or *which one*. Students underline an adjective in blue and then draw a blue arrow to the noun it describes or modifies.

Adverbs

The teacher establishes the necessity of adverbs by asking students to write their names on a piece of paper. After students have written their names, the teacher says,

"Did you do that "now"? Did you write your names "there"? Did you write your names "neatly"? That is not what I had in mind, but I did not tell when, where, or how." An adverb modifies a verb and tells *how, when,* or *where.* Without adverbs, it would be difficult to know *how, when,* or *where* to do something. An adverb can also modify an adjective or an adverb and tell to what extent.

Because the function of adverbs is similar to the function of adjectives, adverbs will be color-coded in a color that is similar to adjectives, which are blue. Adverbs will be purple. Students underline an adverb in purple and draw a purple arrow to the verb, adjective, or adverb it modifies.

The little boy ran <u>fast</u>.

The <u>very</u> little boy ran.   The little boy ran <u>extremely</u> fast.

Prepositions

To introduce prepositions, the teacher presents a cut-out picture of a squirrel named Preppy and a separate picture of a tree. The teacher moves the squirrel in various relations to the tree and states, *"Preppy runs up the tree, down the tree, to the tree, from the tree, around the tree....All the words that show Preppy's position to the tree—up, down, to, from, around—are called prepositions."* Prepositions show the position or relation between a noun or pronoun and another word. Where would Preppy run without prepositions? Prepositions are color-coded green to remind students of the leaves on the tree that Preppy runs *up, down, to, from,* and so on.

Prepositions always occur in phrases that begin with the preposition and end with a noun or pronoun. The noun or pronoun at the end of the phrase is called the *object of the preposition.* Prepositional phrases act as adjectives or adverbs. Students underline the preposition in green, circle the prepositional phrase in green, and then draw a green arrow to the word it modifies.

The children (on the bus) sang. (An adjective, answer which children)

The children sang (on the bus.) (An adverb, answering where)

Conjunctions

The teacher establishes the need to know conjunctions by writing this sentence on the board: *Dogs and cats play.* The teacher asks, *"Who is this sentence about? Yes, the sentence is about dogs and cats, not just dogs nor just cats. The word* and *is a conjunction. It joins the words that make up the subject together."* A conjunction (from the Latin, meaning *to join together*) joins words, phrases, or sentences and is brown like a wooden peg that joins the legs of a table to the top.

Coordinating conjunctions join single words or groups of words together and include *and, but, for, or,* and *nor.* Subordinating conjunctions join groups of words together and include *as, after, because, before, if, when,* and *while.* Knowledge of these conjunctions aids students' understandings of different sentence structures and comma usage.

Interjections

The word *interjection* comes from the Latin, meaning to throw in between. Interjections are thrown in here and there to express strong emotion. To introduce interjections, students compare two sentences: *I am insulted* and *Well, I am insulted.* The two sentences convey the same message, but the second sentence is stronger in its message with the addition of the interjection *well;* however, the word *well* has no relation to other words in the sentence. Interjections include *well, wow, oops, oh,* and *ugh.* Because they do not relate to other words in the sentence, they are colorless.

Sentence Structures

A *complete sentence* is a group of words that has a subject and a predicate. The *subject* tells who or what the sentence is about, and the *predicate* tells what is said about the subject. A complete sentence has a yellow part—the subject—and an orange part—the predicate. If a group of words does not have a yellow part and an orange part, it is not a complete sentence. Sentences may have one or more subjects and one or more predicates.

Simple Sentences

A *simple sentence* contains only one subject and one predicate. When students have been introduced to nouns and verbs, they are ready to write simple sentences, which may have only two words (e.g., *Geese migrate, Flowers blossom, Elephants trumpet*). The one word in a sentence that tells who or what the sentence is about is the *simple subject,* and the one word that tells what is said about the subject is the *simple predicate.*

As students learn more parts of speech, the lengths of their sentences grow as well as the lengths of the subjects and the predicates within the sentences. The *complete subject* contains the simple subject and all its modifiers, and the *complete predicate* contains the simple predicate and all its modifiers and complements. In printed sentences, students highlight the complete subject in yellow because it is connected to a subject noun or a nominative case pronoun. They highlight the complete predicate in orange because it is always connected to a verb.

Compound and Complex Sentences

To relieve the monotony that can be created with exclusive use of simple sentences, students need to learn other sentence structures. Once students have learned to write simple sentences and have learned conjunctions, they are ready to learn the structures of compound, complex, and compound-complex sentences.

Students first must understand that a *clause* is a group of words that has a subject and a predicate. A clause may be an *independent clause* (i.e., a simple sentence) that can stand alone, or it can be a *dependent clause* that cannot stand alone (e.g., *before I go, while he waited, because she studied*). Even though a dependent clause has a yellow part and an orange part, it is contingent upon another complete sentence that makes it make sense.

A compound sentence has two or more independent clauses joined by coordinating conjunctions. A complex sentence has one independent clause and at least one dependent clause joined by a subordinating conjunction. A compound-complex sentence has two independent clauses and at least one dependent clause.

Activities

As needed, students practice information about parts of speech and sentence structures using two kinds of activities. One kind of activity reinforces the functions of the parts of speech, and the second kind connects the parts of speech to students' writing. A sampling of activities is listed below.

Activities that Reinforce the Functions of the Part of Speech

1. *Color-Coding Sentences* – The teacher distributes a page with five or six sentences. The sentences contain words that exemplify the parts of speech that have been previously introduced. Using colored pens or pencils, students color-code each sentence. They underline the parts of speech in the appropriate colors, draw appropriately colored arrows from modifiers to the words they modify, and highlight the complete subject in yellow and the complete predicate in orange.

2. *Sentence Dictation* – The teacher gives each student a set of one-inch squares of colored paper. In the set are three squares of each color that represent the parts of speech that have been previously introduced. The teacher dictates a sentence. Students repeat the sentence and arrange their squares to match the arrangement of words in the sentence. When all the squares have been arranged, students touch each square as they say the sentence. They then touch each square and identify the part of speech that is represented by each square. The sentences can be related to a topic or theme that is part of students' course of study.

Activities that Connect to Student's Writing

1. *Sentence Pattern Cards* – On 10 large cards, the teacher arranges colored stickers or draws colored squares in patterns. Most of the patterns will represent complete sentences, but some will represent incomplete sentences. The teacher shows each card to students. Students identify whether or not the pattern represents a complete sentence. If it does not, students determine what is needed to make the sentence complete. If the pattern represents a

complete sentence, students take turns orally composing sentences that follow the pattern. Students then write sentences that follow the pattern. The teacher can suggest a topic or theme for students to incorporate as they write their sentences.

2. *Analyzing Sentence Structures and Editing* – The teacher gives students a short paragraph. (See Figure 6.4.1.) Students analyze the sentence structures of the paragraph. They color-code the initial word in each sentence, highlight the simple subject and the simple predicate, and underline any conjunctions. They then answer these three questions:
   - Do the sentences begin with a variety of colors?
   - Are the simple subjects and simple predicates located after the first three or four words in some of the sentences?
   - Is there any brown or, in other words, are there any conjunctions?

   If the answer to any of the questions is "no," students realize that the paragraph does not contain diverse sentence structures. Rewriting, reorganizing, and/or combining some of the sentences will make the paragraph more appealing to the reader, so students edit the paragraph by combining two sentences with a coordinating conjunction and two other sentences with a subordinating conjunction. As students write and edit their own work, they should ask themselves the same three questions and make a conscious effort to include conjunctions.

Figure 6.4.1.   **A Sample Paragraph for Students to Analyze and Rewrite**

> Tuesday was a horrible, terrible day for my sister. Sally spilled her milk during breakfast. She had to clean it up. She was late for the bus. She had to run to catch it. Sally left her homework on the bus. She had to do it at recess.

Building Paragraphs Sentence by Sentence

Good sentence writing supports the writing of paragraphs. Struggling writers benefit from practice in writing different kinds of paragraphs sentence by sentence. Figure 6.4.2 illustrates the steps for writing a persuasive paragraph sentence by sentence (Carreker & Birsh, 2005). Students write eight sentences, one sentence at a time. They edit each sentence and then write the sentences in paragraph form.

Sentence-by-sentence writing allows students to focus on the content without worrying about conventions of paragraph writing such as indenting and attending to margins. This sentence-by-sentence process also helps students learn the structure and order of different paragraph structures. The formulaic construction of the paragraphs yields to more natural expression as students gain proficiency in writing.

Figure 6.4.2. **Sentence-by-Sentence Writing of a Persuasive Paragraph**
Chart from Carreker, S., & Birsh, J. R. (2005). Composition: Writing persuasive paragraphs. *Multisensory teaching of basic language skills activity book* (p. 116). Baltimore: Paul H. Brookes; adapted by permission.

1. Give your opinion.
2. Give a reason for your opinion.
3. Give an example of that reason.
4. Give a second reason for your opinion.
5. Give an example of that reason.
6. Give the most compelling reason for your opinion.
7. Give an example of that reason.
8. Restate your opinion.

Summary

The teaching of the parts of speech is necessary. This article has demonstrated the teaching of basic grammatical concepts that 1) enable students to write complete and varied sentences, 2) provide the underpinnings for understanding more complex ideas about syntax that help students mature in their written discourse, and 3) support students' reading. So, take the time to teach... those very important parts of speech!

References

Carreker, S. (1992). *Multisensory grammar and written composition*. Bellaire, TX: Neuhaus Education Center.

Carreker, S., & Birsh, J. R. (2005). *Multisensory teaching of basic language skills activity book*. Baltimore: Paul H. Brookes.

Rego, L. L. B., & Byrant, P. E. (1993). The connection between phonological, syntactic, and semantic skills and children's reading and spelling. *European Journal of Psychology of Education,* 8, 235–246.

Tunmer, T. E., Herriman, M. L., & Nesdale, A. R. (1988). Metalinguistic abilities and beginning reading. *Reading Research Quarterly, 23,* 134–158.

Assistive Technology for Struggling Writers

Charles A. MacArthur

This article reviews ways in which technology can support the writing efforts of students with learning disabilities (LD) and other struggling writers. A wide range of computer applications have been developed to support writing, and many of them are especially helpful for struggling writers. Word processing, spelling checkers, word prediction, and speech recognition offer support for transcription and revision. Outlining programs and concept mapping software can help with planning. This article includes a summary of the research for each of these tools and recommendations for practice. At the end, new forms of writing on the Internet are briefly discussed. Research on these new tools is very limited, but it is critical to teach students with LD to use online communication tools because of the increasing importance of the Internet in our society.

Word Processing

Word processing is the one aspect of writing technology that is supported by a substantial research base. Reviews of research studies that compared writing instruction with and without word processing have found positive effects on the quality of compositions with larger effects for low achieving students. The most recent review (Graham & Perin, 2007) found moderate effects for writers in general but a larger effect for low achieving writers.

The most often mentioned advantage of word processing is the ease of revision. For struggling writers, word processors make it possible to revise repeatedly without recopying and making new errors. However, our research suggests that simply having access to word processing does not help students with LD to revise effectively. For example, in one study (MacArthur & Graham, 1987) with students with LD who were familiar with word processing, we found no differences between handwritten and word processed essays on any of our measures, including length, grammar, vocabulary, spelling, or overall quality. Word processing makes revising easier and, thus, may increase motivation for learning about revision. However, it does not directly help students learn how to evaluate their writing, diagnose problems, or fix those problems.

Students need instruction in strategies for revision in combination with word processing. Our research group has conducted three studies on this combination, one that evaluated a revising strategy for individual students and two that investigated peer revising strategies (for a review, see MacArthur, 2006). In all three studies, instruction had positive effects on the number and quality of revisions and the quality of the students' final papers. The results illustrate the general point that positive effects of technology depend on instruction that is designed to help students take advantage of the power of technology.

In addition, of course, spelling checkers provide significant support for students with spelling problems, but it is important for teachers and students to recognize the limitations of this tool. For example, in one study with middle school students with LD (MacArthur, Graham, Haynes, & De La Paz, 1996), we found that students corrected 37% of their errors with a spelling checker compared to just 9% on their own—an improvement, but far from adequate. One significant limitation is that spelling checkers fail to detect spelling errors that make the word a correctly spelled different word, such as homonyms and other similarly spelled words (e.g., *were* for *wear*). Another important limitation is that the correct spelling may not appear in the list of suggestions, especially when words are severely misspelled. Students need to learn to proofread to find errors that the spelling checker does not find, and they need to learn strategies for generating more suggestions, if needed, such as trying a phonetic spelling.

One important practical issue in using word processors is typing. Typing fluency is connected to writing quality, as is handwriting skill. Russell (1999) compared word processing and handwriting for middle and high school students taking a statewide writing test and found that effects depended on typing skill. Students who typed at least 20 words per minute (wpm) did better with word processing, but students who typed less than about 8 wpm did better with handwriting. The practical implications

> ".. positive effects of technology depend on instruction that is designed to help students take advantage of the power of technology."

are clear; students need typing instruction to use word processing effectively. In my experience, typing instruction software is an effective way to develop a student's skill.

Another important issue is access. Although word processing is probably the most widely available and commonly used computer application, few schools have sufficient technology to permit students to do most of their writing on a computer. Students cannot get the real benefit of word processing unless they use it for the entire writing process from drafting through revision and publication. Typing text already written by hand should be avoided, especially for struggling writers who find the process very difficult. Practical solutions include shared computer labs devoted to writing instruction or inexpensive laptops dedicated to word processing.

The Computers and Writing Instruction Project (MacArthur, Graham, Schwartz, & Shafer, 1995) evaluated a yearlong writing curriculum for students with LD that integrated three components: First, students participated in a writers' workshop that emphasized meaningful writing, peer collaboration, teacher conferencing, and publishing of student work. Second, students learned strategies for planning and revising for narrative and informative writing. Third, students had ample access to computers for word processing and received typing instruction. Students in 12 experimental classes made greater gains in the quality of their narrative and informative writing than students with LD in 10 control classes.

Tools to Support Transcription

For some students, word processing and spell checking are not enough. Other tools, including word prediction and speech recognition, can be helpful to students who struggle with spelling or fluent production of text.

Word Prediction

Consider the following entry from the journal of a ten-year-old boy with LD:
> "The Redr was my farvt croms past. It a ras car Im go to red the sooc old tree to the little kers. good bay" [The red Rocket was my favorite Christmas present. It's a race car. I'm going to read *The Spooky Old Tree* to the little kids. Good bye.]

Word prediction is one potential solution for students who need more intensive support for both reading and writing. Word prediction software predicts what word the user intends to write based on the first few letters. For example, if I have typed, "My best f," the program might offer a list of predictions including "food," "friend," and "family." If I continue by adding "r" to the "f," the program would update the list. When the intended word appears in the list, I can insert the word in the text by clicking on it. Most word prediction systems also provide speech synthesis to help students read the list of words. Depending on the sophistication of the program, predictions will be based on spelling alone or in combination with syntax and words or phrases recently used by the writer.

My research (e.g., MacArthur, 1998) has found that word prediction provides significant support to students with severe spelling problems. Across two studies, most students made dramatic improvements in the legibility of their writing and spelling when using word prediction. Spelling errors decreased from 25–58% of words with just word processing to less than 10% with word prediction. This research focused on students with severe spelling problems, but I have talked with many teachers who reported success using word prediction with students with less severe spelling problems, claiming that it increased motivation and helped them use more varied vocabulary. Further research is much needed.

Speech Recognition

Speech recognition in its ideal form would be the ultimate assistive technology for writers who struggle with transcription. Speech recognition permits writers to compose by dictating, yet unlike dictating to a tape recorder, it also lets them see their developing text and reread as needed. Speech recognition software is far from ideal; it still makes errors in deciphering the user's speech and requires clear speech and dictation of punctuation. However, the research shows that it can have substantial positive effects for struggling writers (for a review, see MacArthur, 2006).

In one study, we (MacArthur and Cavalier, 2004) investigated speech recognition as a test accommodation for high school students with LD. We provided 6 hours of training in speech recognition to 10th grade students with and without LD and then had them compose essays with handwriting, speech recognition, and dictation to a scribe. All 31 students, except one who dropped out, were able to use speech recognition to compose and edit essays with acceptable accuracy. Students with LD made fewer errors using speech recognition than handwriting. Most important, students with LD produced higher quality essays using speech recognition than handwriting, and even better essays when dictating to a person. Speech recognition provided no benefit to students without LD. We interpreted the results to support the validity of speech recognition as a test accommodation.

Speech recognition has great potential for some struggling writers, but there are many practical issues. It does not work well in school classrooms because the software requires a relatively quiet environment for accuracy and because dictation is too public a process, especially for struggling writers. However, it is quite realistic to consider its use in a resource room setting or at home. College students with LD, in particular, are likely to benefit from speech recognition because they need to produce substantial amounts of writing with few errors. Training the software to recognize an individual's speech is a relatively quick process and accuracy will continue to improve with practice. The learning experience involves several important tasks: First, the student must learn to speak clearly without excessive pauses. Second, students must learn new processes for editing; the software never misspells a word, but it regularly uses the wrong word, and these errors can be challenging to find at first. Third, it takes time to learn to think and compose via speech at the same time. It's very important to develop an outline or other plan before starting to dictate.

> "…word prediction provides significant support to students with severe spelling problems."

Support for Planning with Concept Mapping

A variety of computer tools are available to help with the process of planning and organizing content. Planning is critical to effective writing, and many struggling writers do not know how to plan effectively. The most common software tools for planning are outlining and concept mapping programs (e.g., *Inspiration*). A concept map is a graphic organizer that visually represents the connections among ideas.

One way that teachers can use concept maps is to provide students with templates that represent common ways to organize text; graphic organizers such as these are commonly used in writing strategies. When concept maps are created on the computer, they can be easily revised and expanded. In addition, they can be converted automatically into outlines, which can be exported to a word processor.

> "Students wrote more complex essays when they created concept maps."

Anderson-Inman and her colleagues (e.g., Anderson-Inman & Horney, 1998) have conducted a number of qualitative studies of concept mapping as a tool to support reading and studying by students with LD. They have reported on processes for using concept mapping to take notes from textbook reading and then using those notes to study and write content-area papers. My colleagues and I recently completed a study of an instructional method for using concept-mapping software to support writing (Karchmer-Klein, MacArthur, & Najera, 2008). Students learned to use concept mapping to plan a compare-contrast essay. They converted their maps to outlines, added text in the outline format, and then exported their outlines to a word processor where they added more text and polished their essays. Students wrote more complex essays when they created concept maps. Further research is needed on these commonly available tools.

New Directions

This article is about the use of technology to support the development of traditional writing skills and the production of written documents. However, technology is having and will have a broader impact on literacy through the development of new environments for writing and forms of written communication. Internet communication tools, such as e-mail, blogs, wikis, and social networking sites are becoming increasingly common, especially among adolescents. Research has barely begun to investigate these tools, and I know of no research with students with LD. It is impossible to know with certainty how they will affect struggling writers. They may offer new opportunities, but they will certainly also create new challenges.

New Internet tools for reading and writing differ from print in several important ways. First, the Internet integrates text and audiovisual media. Audiovisual features offer another channel for learning for students who struggle with reading, but they may also encourage over-reliance on nonverbal information. Second, the Internet provides access to a vast amount of information, but the access comes with a price, especially for struggling readers who may have difficulty with searching, skimming, and evaluating that information. Finally, the Internet, especially the newest software, is a highly interactive environment that encourages users to communicate in writing and provides access to new audiences. These opportunities may encourage struggling writers to write more, but the interactivity also creates valid concerns about privacy and safety, and the writing may be too informal to reinforce skills needed for academic writing.

Regardless of the effect of the Internet on traditional writing skills, educators need to help students learn to communicate effectively using the Internet. It is impossible to know what literacy skills will be needed in the future, but it seems clear that skills such as searching for information online, reading information critically, integrating multimedia in writing, networking, and writing online will be important.

In summary, technology offers a wide range of applications that can support struggling writers. Research provides clear support for the value of word processing. Although less research has focused on assistive technology, enough research has been done to show that applications like word prediction and speech recognition can be beneficial for some students. Planning tools, such as concept mapping and outlining, are probably beneficial for all students. In my view, the major research need is for more studies in which researchers and teachers collaborate to develop effective instructional methods. For most writing technologies, the main question is not whether they work but how to design effective instruction to make the best use of them.

References

Anderson-Inman, L., & Horney, M. A. (1998). Transforming text for at-risk readers. In D. Reinking, M. C. McKenna, L. D. Labbo, & R. D. Kieffer (Eds.), *Handbook of literacy and technology* (pp. 15–44). Mahwah, NJ: Erlbaum.

Graham, S., & Perin, D. (2007). *Writing next: Effective strategies to improve writing of adolescents in middle and high schools*. New York: Carnegie Corp.

Karchmer-Klein, R., MacArthur, C. A., & Najera, K. (2008, December). *The effects of concept mapping software on fifth grade students' writing*. Paper presented at the annual meeting of the National Reading Conference, Orlando, FL.

MacArthur, C. A. (1998). Word processing with speech synthesis and word prediction: Effects on the dialogue journal writing of students with learning disabilities. *Learning Disability Quarterly, 21*, 1–16.

MacArthur, C. A. (2006). The effects of new technologies on writing and writing processes. In C. A. MacArthur, S. Graham, & J. Fitzgerald (Eds.), *Handbook of writing research* (pp. 248–262). New York: Guilford.

MacArthur, C. A., & Cavalier, A. (2004). Dictation and speech recognition technology as accommodations in large-scale assessments for students with learning disabilities. *Exceptional Children, 71,* 43–58.

MacArthur, C. A., & Graham, S. (1987). Learning disabled students' composing under three methods of text production: Handwriting, word processing, and dictation. *Journal of Special Education, 21*, 22–42.

MacArthur, C. A., Graham, S., Haynes, J. A., & De La Paz, S. (1996). Spelling checkers and students with learning disabilities: Performance comparisons and impact on spelling. *Journal of Special Education, 30*, 35–57.

MacArthur, C. A., Graham, S., Schwartz, S. S., & Shafer, W. (1995). Evaluation of a writing instruction model that integrated a process approach, strategy instruction, and word processing. *Learning Disability Quarterly, 18*, 278–291.

Russell, M. (1999). Testing writing on computers: A follow-up study comparing performance on computer and on paper. *Educational Policy Analysis Archives, 7*(20). Retrieved February 1, 2009, from http://epaa.asu.edu/epaa/v7n20/

Moving Targets in Adolescent and Adult Literacy Instruction

John R. Kruidenier

The articles in this anthology demonstrate convincingly that reading is a complex process and teaching reading is, necessarily, a complex undertaking. The articles in this section underscore the fact that neither the process nor the teaching of reading becomes any simpler as children mature into adolescents and adults. Jeanne Chall (1983) helped popularize the notion of a fourth grade slump: after children have learned the fundamentals of reading (decoding), some then have difficulty when they begin to use reading to comprehend content area texts such as social studies and math books. As it turns out, the shift in content that occurs around the fourth grade is only the first such shift. The articles in this section describe the growing focus on content-area reading at the high school level, and on workplace literacy, family literacy, and health literacy later in life. Each shift presents unique challenges for teachers and learners. In addition, national assessments of reading have consistently shown that a large number of adolescents and adults have still not mastered the basic reading skills that enable comprehension: phonemic awareness, decoding, reading fluency, and meaning vocabulary. The articles in this section all address the complex task of boosting the reading achievement of those who are still struggling to learn to read while, at the same time, helping them read and understand increasingly difficult and important texts.

It is important to assess each of the components of reading to understand older, struggling readers. In the first article in this section, Donald Dreshler, Michael Hock, and Hugh Catts demonstrate the use of a profile of the reading skills of adolescents as a way to understand their unique needs. The authors of this article show how they use this profile as a basis for a continuum of literacy instruction that schools can provide. In addition to recognizing the need for adolescents to master entry level reading skills, the initial level on the continuum focuses on ensuring that all students master critical content regardless of reading level.

In the second article, Mary Beth Calhoun focuses on reading skill rather than content, exploring the best mix of instruction in the components of reading to use when teaching struggling adolescent readers, including phonological awareness, spelling, vocabulary, and comprehension. James McPartland, Robert Balfanz, and Nettie Legters shift their focus in the third article to literacy and English teachers and how they can be supported in their efforts to use effective reading instruction in their classrooms. They demonstrate how traditional supports, derived from practical experience, can be tested through research, including intensive workshops, availability of complete and extensive instructional materials, and continuous coaching for teachers. In the fourth article, Rebecca Moak, Tanya Shuy, and Peggy McCardle summarize the articles on adolescent literacy from the Summer 2006 issue of *Perspectives* by examining the common myths about basic skills instruction and content-area reading that they dispel.

The last two articles in this section address adult literacy. There is a clear shift in the content of the material that adults read to obtain information. According to a review of adult reading assessment and instruction conducted by the NIFL/NCSALL Adult Literacy Research Working Group (a joint effort of the National Institute for Literacy and the National Center for the Study of Adult Learning and Literacy), there is also still a need for instruction in basic reading skills. The review by this group of experts in adult education and literacy research and practice is summarized in my article (and recently updated in Kruidenier, MacArthur, & Wrigley, 2010). Like Dreshler, Hock, and Catts, authors of this review find that creating profiles of reading abilities across the components of reading is an effective way to understand learners' needs and help design effective instruction. There is much less research with adults on basic skills instruction in reading, but current research suggests that many of the approaches used with children and adolescents to improve decoding, fluency, vocabulary, and comprehension are also effective with adults. These approaches need to be modified to take into account the unique instructional needs of adult learners, including the content of adult reading material as reflected in the types of adult education programs offered (basic education, secondary education, English for speakers of other languages, and family, workplace, and health literacy, for example).

The final article, which I wrote with Sherry Mee Bell, summarizes articles on adult literacy from the fall 2007 issue of *Perspectives on Language and Literacy*, including one that describes the lifelong impact that dyslexia has on adults who have difficulty accessing print-based information. It also describes additional efforts by the NIFL/NCSALL Adult Literacy Research Working Group and some of its members to provide adult educators with research-based tools for teaching reading, including a comprehensive teacher's guide to adult reading assessment and instruction, an interactive assessment website, and a norm-referenced, standardized tool to use in assessing adult educators' knowledge of effective approaches to reading instruction, designed to aid in professional development.

The articles in this section provide practitioners with a wealth of information about research-based methods and material for teaching struggling adolescent and adult readers. They address the need for explicit and systematic instruction in the components of reading and for the accurate assessment of these components to determine the right mix of instruction when working with older learners. These learners' profiles, or their patterns of strengths and needs across the components of reading, may vary considerably depending on the severity and type of reading disability and other factors such as motivation and English language ability. The articles also address the difficult dilemma that teachers and program directors face when learners' poor reading prevents them from efficiently acquiring essential information from text that becomes both more difficult and more important as they get older (from content area texts in high school and college to work, family, and health oriented texts in adulthood). Finally, these articles present general approaches as well as specific resources that can be used to support teachers in their challenging work with adolescents and adults with a reading disability.

References

Chall, J. (1983). *Stages of reading development*. New York: McGraw-Hill.

Kruidenier, J. R., MacArthur, C. A., & Wrigley, H. S. (2010). Adult education literacy instruction: A review of the research. Washington, DC: National Institute for Literacy. Retrieved from http://lincs.ed.gov/publications/publications.html

Enhancing Outcomes for Struggling Adolescent Readers

Donald D. Deshler, Michael F. Hock, and Hugh W. Catts

> *"There is a need for a solid understanding of basic skills. I have never met the guy who doesn't know how to read and do math who created software."*
>
> ~Bill Gates

This statement highlights the challenges and educational needs of individuals preparing to enter and successfully compete in the global economy described by Thomas Friedman (2005) in his book, *The World is Flat: A Brief History of the Twenty-First Century*. According to Friedman, our world has become flattened because the Internet has enabled people, regardless of their location or status in life, to share their ideas and engage others on a playing field that has been leveled (flattened) by innovations associated with technology. Foundational to ensuring that the Western world can successfully respond to the challenges and opportunities presented by a flat world is its ability to develop students who have the skills and knowledge necessary to compete in a global economy. The ability to read, comprehend, and apply knowledge to novel learning situations is essential. In fact, if individuals cannot read well, much knowledge will be beyond them (Adelman, 2006).

During the past few years, a spate of reports detailing the challenges facing secondary school has been released (e.g., Alliance for Excellent Education, 2004; Kamil, 2003; National Governors Association, 2005). Running throughout most of these reports is a dual challenge for secondary teachers and administrators. Namely, raise standards so graduates of secondary schools are better able to compete in the world economy and close the achievement gap for the growing number of struggling adolescent learners who do not possess sufficient literacy and numeracy skills to respond to demanding course requirements.

More specifically, as students leave high school during the first decade of the 21st century, they must be prepared to compete for jobs that require markedly different skill sets than most currently possess. In the last quarter century, the economy could provide students who lacked a high school diploma with relatively well-paying jobs in the manufacturing sector. However, between 2000-2010 more than two thirds of all jobs will require some postsecondary education (Carnevale & Desrochers, 2003). The jobs requiring the most education and offering the highest pay are the fastest growing. In light of these trends, it is important for students to be taking rigorous classes that prepare them to enter into and successfully compete in this new environment. In light of limited time and financial resources, high

" ...the time and place to build a strong literacy foundation so students can benefit fully from a challenging high school curriculum is in the late-elementary and middle school years."

schools can't afford to deal with the large numbers of students who arrive in the 9th grade without the fundamental literacy skills and at the same time raise standards.

In short, the likelihood of successfully "raising the bar" for high school graduates is extremely remote unless a way is found to "raise the floor" for the large number of middle-school students who are entering high school lacking the necessary literacy skills. It is logical that the time and place to build a strong literacy foundation so students can benefit fully from a challenging high school curriculum is in the late-elementary and middle school years (Deshler, 2006).

The Reading Skills of Adolescent Readers

The magnitude of the challenge that high school educators face if the achievement gap is not closed prior to students becoming 9th graders is underscored by recently collected data on 346 urban high school freshmen. This descriptive study (Hock, Brasseur, Deshler, Catts, & Marquis, 2005) identified a profile of the reading skills adolescents have and have not mastered. Adolescents in this study were administered a battery of reading assessments to determine their reading proficiency in decoding, fluency, comprehension, vocabulary, and motivation for reading.

Findings indicated that approximately 57% of the adolescent readers in this sample had an overall reading skill profile at or below the 40th percentile and need intensive word-level interventions in addition to comprehension interventions. These students scored significantly below expectations in decoding, word recognition, vocabulary, fluency and reading comprehension on multiple measures of reading skills (Hock, et al. 2005). Specifically, they scored at the 1st to 7th percentile in all reading skills measured by the GORT-4 (Weiderholt & Bryant, 2001). In contrast, highly proficient adolescent readers had acquired both word-level and comprehension skills but still needed higher-level reading comprehension instruction. They scored just above average in reading comprehension, which does not make them competitive in a rapidly changing flat world. Thus, it seems likely that in some schools (especially those in inner-city urban areas) large numbers of struggling adolescent readers may require both word-level and comprehension interventions in order to make it over the fourth-grade hump (Chall, 1983; Pressley, 2002) and those who have acquired word level skills would benefit from reading comprehension instruction. The case for balanced reading instruction is strengthened by this initial analysis of the descriptive data set, particularly for adolescents who struggle with reading comprehension.

Performance on the Woodcock-Johnson Learning Proficiency Battery subtests for reading comprehension, Woodcock (1991), listening comprehension, letter/word identification, word attack, and vocabulary defined the general reading profile of the adolescents assessed in this study. While the reading skills of those students assessed increased from lower levels of proficiency to higher levels as expected, the standard scores of the struggling readers remained significantly below expected mean scores, generally by more than one standard deviation. These standard scores place the readers in the 8th to 19th percentile across all reading component skills assessed. Clearly, these students will require a markedly different instructional focus, intensity, and balance than students in the Proficient and higher groups. If proficient reading requires foundational skill, in word level reading, as characterized in the National Reading Panel (2000), these skill deficits must be addressed if reading comprehension achievement gaps are to be significantly narrowed.

A Theory of Adolescent Reading: A Simple View of a Complex Process

To help us understand how to best close the achievement gap that struggling adolescent readers face, it is important to ground the way we conceptualize and offer instruction in a theoretical formulation of the reading process for older students (see Figure 7.1.1).

Figure 7.1.1. **Adolescent Reading Theoretical Model**
KU-CRL Hock & Deshler, 2006

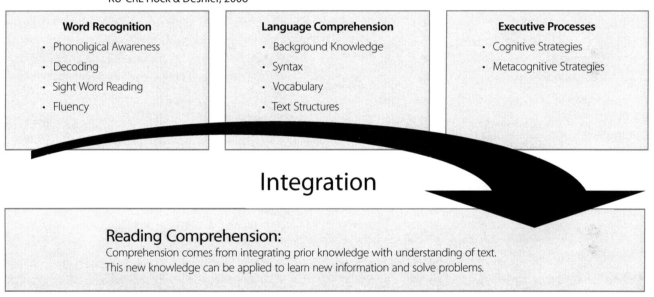

Over the last 15 years considerable knowledge has been gained about the nature of reading and its development. Much of this work has focused on skilled adult readers or young beginning readers (e.g., Lyon, Alexander, & Yaffee, 1997; McCardle & Chhabra, 2004). However, recent efforts have also examined literacy in adolescent populations (Catts, Hogan, & Adlof, 2005). This work has shown that reading comprehension involves a complex combination of word recognition, language comprehension, and executive process abilities. Research indicates that skilled readers are efficient at sight-word recognition and decoding of new words. Such efficiency leads to fluent reading of text-length material and provides the substance for comprehension (Stahl & Hiebert, in press).

Beyond word reading, skilled readers rely on language and metacognitive executive skills to derive meaning from text. Walter Kintsch's Construction-Integration theory of reading (1998) provides a useful framework for understanding these comprehension processes. Kintsch argues that skilled readers use their knowledge of word meaning, grammar, and text structure to build an initial understanding of text. This understanding consists of links between words and larger meaningful units (e.g., propositions). It is often incomplete but may be sufficient to enable readers to provide a short retell or answer questions like those found at the end of chapters in textbooks. Kintsch makes a distinction between this type of understanding and the deep understanding that is needed for "learning from text."

For readers to achieve a deep understanding, the material in a text must be integrated with their prior knowledge and experience with the topic. This integration results in what Kintsch calls a situation model, a mental model of the situation described in the text. This model often goes beyond the verbal domain and may include such components as visual imagery, emotions, or personal experiences. Constructing a situation model may proceed automatically, but often involves conscious, effortful mental activity, much like solving a problem.

Skilled readers are strategic and use executive or metacognitive processes. For example, they begin reading with a plan, monitor their understanding, deploy repair strategies when necessary, and critically evaluate text material (Pressley & Hilden, 2005). The resultant situation model reflects a much deeper understanding of the text, one that allows for true learning to take place such that new knowledge is created and can be assessed easily and used in novel situations.

Adolescents with reading difficulties are frequently reported to lack good reading comprehension strategies (Swanson & Hoskyn, 1999; Vaughn, Gersten, & Chard, 2000). First, struggling adolescent readers may lack fluency in word reading. Although it is often assumed that by adolescence readers have acquired adult-like decoding and word recognition abilities, recent work suggests that many struggling adolescent readers lack sufficient fluency in decoding and word recognition, and can benefit from intervention targeted at word reading strategies (Hock, et. al, 2005). Second, struggling readers may not have vocabulary, grammar, or text-level language knowledge to form an initial understanding of the text. Such limitations may be the result of a lack of language experience (i.e., English as a second language) or a developmental language impairment (August & Shanahan, 2006; Catts, et. al, 2005). A further obstacle might be the lack of relevant background knowledge. As noted above, this knowledge is critical to building a deep understanding of the text. Adolescents without knowledge of the subject matter would be expected to gain far less from reading a text than those with such knowledge. A likely problem for comprehension is the lack of efficient strategies for relating the text to past knowledge and experience. Finally, struggling adolescent readers lack knowledge of and fluency with critical processes that allow for effective monitoring and problem solving during the reading process.

Defining Features of Effective Programs for Struggling Adolescent Readers

The primary and very obvious function of schools is to ensure that all students learn critical skills and content; however, the energies and time of many secondary administrators are devoted to activities other than instruction (e.g., facilities, staffing, scheduling). While these things are necessary, they sometimes end up becoming the primary focus and ends rather than means to ends. Elmore (2005) has stated, "until leaders and teachers relentlessly focus on things that are core to the instructional process, student outcomes will not improve markedly." The key to transforming students from struggling to competent learners is to put in place programs that bring a "laser-like focus" on teaching and learning (Deshler, 2006). The following are features considered foundational to effective programming for struggling adolescent learners.

A Continuum of Literacy Instruction

Because the literacy needs of struggling adolescent readers are so diverse, the most effective literacy programs offer instruction at various levels of intensity, are comprehensive, and are well coordinated. For example, some students benefit when teachers use graphic organizers to help them master critical subject-matter content; others need learning strategies embedded in content material, explicit strategy instruction, or instruction in basic skills or even the basic language elements that are the foundation of literacy competence. A framework for conceptualizing literacy instruction in secondary school settings, called the Content Literacy Continuum (Lenz, Ehren, & Deshler, 2005) posits that some students require more intensive, systematic, explicit instruction of content, strategies and skills, and that there are unique but very important roles for each member of a secondary staff relative to literacy instruction. Figure 7.1.2 provides a summary of the five levels of this continuum.

Figure 7.1.2. **A Continuum of Literacy Instruction**

Level 1:	Enhance content instruction (mastery of critical content for *all* regardless of literacy levels)
Level 2:	Embedded strategy instruction (routinely weave strategies within *and* across classes using large group instructional methods)
Level 3:	Intensive strategy instruction (mastery of specific strategies using intensive-explicit instructional sequences)
Level 4:	Intensive basic skill instruction (mastery of entry level literacy skills at the 4th grade level)
Level 5:	Therapeutic intervention (mastery of language underpinnings of curriculum content and learning strategies)
Tutoring:	Strategic Tutoring (extending instructional time through before or after school tutoring)

Instruction that is especially intensive and focused is necessary for students reading several years behind grade level (at or below the 3rd-grade level). Classes of no more than 15 students that meet for at least one hour per day are generally required. A highly skilled teacher would use a combination of whole-class and small-group and one-on-one instruction. These classes should have computer technology to provide supported reading practice and quality feedback and error correction. The focus of instruction should be on word recognition, fluency, vocabulary and strategies for encouraging persistence in reading. As students master the basic skills of reading, the instructional focus needs to shift to comprehension strategies with continued emphasis on vocabulary building. Finally, it is important to provide well-supplied classroom libraries of leveled/high-interest materials that capture student interest and increase the amount of reading students do (Torgesen, 2005).

Systems for Managing Student Behavior Effectively

The climate that exists within secondary schools needs to be conducive to student learning. Regrettably, it is not unusual for the behavior in classes and common areas in secondary schools to be unruly and out of control (Public Agenda, 2004). In the absence of effective school-wide and classroom management systems, quality instruction and focused learning cannot occur. Evidenced-based management systems built on the principles of positive behavioral supports have been effective in creating school and classroom climates conducive to learning (e.g, Sprick, 2006).

Screening System

A school-wide screening instrument(s) administered to all students as they enter a middle school can be helpful in identifying those students most in need of literacy instruction. Such a screening should provide information on word analysis skills, fluency, and comprehension. With predetermined cut-points, these data can be used to assign students to instructional programs best designed to meet their needs.

High Quality Teaching Practices

Teachers who achieve the greatest gains with students who have literacy deficits are those whose instruction is consistently responsive, systematic, and intensive (Deshler, Schumaker, & Woodruff, 2004). These factors are central to much of what is embodied in effective instruction, regardless of whether a student is being taught subject-matter content, or a learning strategy or skill to facilitate the learning of subject matter content. Swanson's (1999) meta-analysis on effective components of explicit cognitive learning strategy instruction (e.g., advance organizer, skill review, demonstration, modeling, guided practice, independent practice, and corrective feedback) underscores some of the defining features of highly effective teaching practices.

Progress Monitoring

Remedial education is very costly in economic (e.g., smaller class sizes, highly skilled teachers) and non-economic (e.g., increased sense of hopelessness by adolescents who continue to fail) terms. Hence, it is important to carefully monitor students' responses to instruction and their progress toward meeting benchmarks. Adjustments in the instructional program are made in response to the data collected. Monitoring probes in key skill areas should ideally be taken at least four times per year.

Access to Engaging, Leveled Reading Materials

Making engaging and leveled reading materials readily available to struggling adolescent readers can help capture and/or reignite their interest in reading. One of the reasons many struggling readers don't read is lack of interest in the materials available to them to read (Guthrie, Wigfield, & Perencevich 2004). Well-supplied classroom and/or school libraries are key to increasing the volume of student reading and ultimately to independent, self-motivated reading.

Create a "Culture of Growth and Achievement"

The prevailing culture within a secondary reading classroom should, among other things, focus on: student goal setting, holding students accountable for achieving outcome goals, good habits of learning (e.g., using time wisely, working hard to achieve goals, building reading endurance, etc.), high expectations for each student, and personalized, respectful, caring interactions between teachers and students.

Structures that Support Instruction

High quality instruction does not take place in a vacuum. One of the most important roles that school leaders can play is to create conditions that enable it. As Elmore (2005) states: "The schools that succeed in changing practice are those that start with the practice and modify school structure to accommodate it" (p. 4). In other words, form should follow function. One of the structures that can promote improved student outcomes is the opportunity for teachers to plan together for the purpose of coordinating instruction across classes so that critical reading strategies are modeled, prompted, and practiced in each class. This can reduce the fragmentary learning that most secondary students experience. School administrators can provide leadership in creating decision-making teams (teams of 6-8 teachers that discuss students who are having difficulty meeting standards, identify ways to alter instruction to address identified needs, and review data on student progress), and ensure that school schedules are sufficiently flexible to enable students to move seamlessly from one instructional level to the other with ease (see description of the Content Literacy Continuum above). In short, student learning can become the overriding focus of attention only if teachers have the necessary instructional supports to teach students and to work with other teachers to address each student's needs.

High Quality Professional Development

The degree to which a school staff is successful in improving outcomes for students is directly tied to the capacity of members of that staff to effectively teach research-based practices with fidelity. This capacity is developed through a program of high quality professional development which is characterized by being coordinated, targeting major learning needs of students, grounded in principles of adult learning, and directly linked to the accountability system for teachers and administrators. While districts generally make substantial annual investments in professional development, a recent study has shown that often these funds are not clearly tied to directly improving student outcomes and are not a part of the accountability system in the district (Deninger, Curtis, & McIntyre, 2005).

Instructional Coaching

When properly used, instructional coaches serve as central partners in the instructional change process. Their sole role should be to assist teachers to improve the quality of their instruction so student outcomes are directly improved. There is evidence, however, that instructional coaches often end up being used to perform non-instructional roles, such as overseeing the school's state assessment program or administrative support duties for the principal (Knight, in press). Working one-on-one with teachers, instructional coaches can make it easier to adopt instructional methods that make a difference in student outcomes. They can also serve as members of teacher decision-making teams to facilitate instruction on targeted student benchmarks (Knight, in press).

Final Comments

An interesting metric is being used by some secondary schools to determine the likelihood that a student will graduate from high school: the "on-track indicator" (Allensworth & Easton, 2005). This research has shown that students who remain on track (that is, earn at least five credits and get no more than one semester F in their freshman year) are three and one-half times as likely to graduate from high school than students who do not stay on track. This study underscores how devastating freshman-year failure can be. Namely, just one semester F decreases the likelihood of graduating from 83% to 60%; a second semester F decreases the likelihood to 44%; and an alarming 31% of students with three semester F's graduate from high school.

These data highlight the vital importance of making certain that middle school students enter high school prepared for the rigorous course demands that they will face. The key to transforming students from struggling to competent learners is to put in place programs that are grounded in sound learning theory and embody the features described above that bring a "laser-like focus" to teaching and learning.

References

Adelman, C. (2006). *The Toolbox Revisited: Paths to Degree Completion From High School Through College*. Washington, D.C.: U.S. Department of Education.

Allensworth, E. M., and Easton, J. Q. (2005). *The on-track indicator as a predictor of high school graduation.* Chicago: University of Chicago.

Alliance for Excellent Education (2004). *Reading Next: A vision for action and research in middle and high school literacy*. Washington, DC: Author.

August, D., & Shanahan, T. (2006). *Developing literacy in second language learners. Report of the national literacy panel on language-minority children and youth*. Mahwah, NJ: Lawrence Earlbaum Associates, Inc.

Carnevale, A. P., & Desrochers, D. M. (2003). *Standards for what? The economic roots of K-12 reform*. Princeton, NJ: Educational Testing Service.

Catts, H. W., Hogan, T. P., & Adlof, S.M. (2005). *Developmental changes in reading and reading disabilities*. In H. W. Catts & A. G. Kamhi (Eds.), The connections between language and reading disabilities (pp. 25-40). Mahwah, NJ: Lawrence Erlbaum Associates.

Chall, J. S. (1983). *Stages of Reading Development*. New York, NY: McGraw-Hill.

Deninger, M., Curtis, R., & McIntyre, J. (2005). *Professional development spending in the Boston Public Schools*. Boston: Institute for Professional Development.

Deshler, D. D. (2006). Building a strong literacy foundation for high school excellence. In D. Clark (Ed.). *The challenge of high school reform*. Washington, DC: The Aspen Institute.

Deshler, D. D., Schumaker, J. B., & Woodruff, S. K. (2004). Improving literacy skills of at-risk adolescents: A schoolwide response. In D. S. Strickland and D. E. Alvermann (Eds.) *Bridging the literacy achievement gap grades 4-12*. New York: Teachers College Press.

Elmore, R. F. (2005). *School reform from the inside out: Policy, practice, and performance*. Cambridge, MA: Harvard Education Press.

Friedman, T. L. (2005). *The world is flat: A brief history of the twenty-first century*. New York, NY: Farrar, Straus and Giroux.

Guthrie, J. T., Wigfield, A., & Perencevich, K. C. (2004). *Motivating reading comprehension: Concept oriented reading instruction*. Mahwah, NJ: Lawrence Erlbuam.

Hock, M. F., Brasseur, I., Deshler, D. D., Catts, H., & Marquis, J. (2005), *What is the nature of adolescent struggling readers in urban high schools?* Lawrence, KS: Research Report No. 1, University of Kansas Center for Research on Learning.

Kamil, M. (2003). *Adolescents and literacy: Reading for the 21st century*. Washington, DC: Alliance for Excellent Education.

Kintsch, W. (1998). *Comprehension: A paradigm for cognition*. Cambridge, United Kingdom: Cambridge University Press.

Knight, J. (in press). *Instructional coaching: A model for professional development and school change*. New York: Corwin Press.

Lenz, B. K., Ehren, B., & Deshler, D. D. (2005). The content literacy continuum: A school-wide framework for improving adolescent literacy for all students. *Teaching Exceptional Children*, 60–63.

Lyon, G. R., Alexander, D., & Yaffee, S. (1997). Progress and promise in research in learning disabilities. *Learning Disabilities: A Multidisciplinary Journal, 8*, 1–6.

McCardle, P., & Chhabra, V. (2004). *The voice of evidence in reading research*. Baltimore: Brookes.

National Governors Association (2005). *Reading to achieve: A governor's guide to adolescent literacy*. Washington, DC: Author.

National Reading Panel. (2000). *Fluency in teaching children to read: An Evidence-based assessment of the scientific research literature on reading and its implications for reading instruction*. Bethesda, MD: National Institutes of Health, National Institute of Child Health and Human Development.

Pressley, M. (2002). *Reading instruction that works: The case for balanced teaching*. New York: Guilford.

Pressley, M., & Hilden, K. (2005). Toward more ambitious comprehension instruction. In E. R. Silliman & L. C. Wilkinson (Eds.), *Language and literacy learning in schools* (pp. 151–174). New York: Guilford Press.

Public Agenda (2004). *Teaching interrupted: Do discipline policies in today's public schools foster the common good*. New York: Public Agenda.

Sprick, R. S. (2006). *Discipline in the secondary classroom: A positive approach to behavior management*. San Francisco: Jossey-Bass.

Stahl, S. A., & Hiebert, E. (in press). The assessment of fluency and other component skills and knowledge: Contributions to comprehension. In S. G. Paris & S. A. Stahl (Eds.), *Current issues in reading comprehension and assessment*. Mahwah, NJ: Erlbaum.

Swanson, H. L. (1999). Instructional components that predict treatment outcomes for students with learning disabilities: Support for a combined strategy and direct instructional method. *Learning Disabilities Research and Practice. 14*(3), 129–140.

Swanson, H. L., & Hoskyn, M. (1999). Definition X treatment interaction for students with learning disabilities. *School Psychology Review, 28*, 644–658.

Torgesen, J. K. (2005). *Recommendations for actions to accelerate the reading development of struggling adolescent readers in Florida's middle schools*. Tallahassee: Florida State Department of Education.

Vaughn, S., Gersten, R., & Chard, D. J. (2000). The underlying message in LD intervention research: Findings from research synthesis, *Exceptional Children, 67*(1), 99–114.

Weiderholt, J. L. and B. R. Bryant (2001). *Gray oral reading tests*. Austin, TX, Pro-Ed.

Woodcock, R.W. (1991). *Woodcock language proficiency battery-Revised*. Itasca, IL: Riverside Publishing.

Rethinking Adolescent Literacy Instruction

Mary Beth Calhoon

How best to teach reading to middle school (6th–8th grades) students with reading disabilities (RD) is a challenge faced daily by thousands of special education teachers. The 2005 National Assessment of Educational Progress (NAEP) reveals that in eighth grade 34% of boys and 24% of girls cannot read at the basic level. Furthermore, 67% of our adolescents with disabilities are reading below the basic level (NAEP, 2005). These current NAEP scores demonstrate a growing trend in reading underachievement for adolescents (NAEP, 2005; McCray, 2001). Additionally, this trend shows the leading reading crisis in our country is not one of 1st through 4th graders, but of older middle school students (McCardle & Chhabra, 2004). Without remedial reading instruction these adolescents are at risk for falling further and further behind in reading each year (Stanovich, 1986). For this reason it is imperative that effective research-based instructional techniques be identified, that can be used in middle school special education classrooms, that not only increase reading skills, but also normalize students reading compared to their same age non-disabled peers.

Reading Processes

The goal of all reading instruction is to create accurate and fluent readers who comprehend what they read. Reading, however, is a complex task requiring the coordination and procedural sequencing of a multitude of sub-skills (Fuchs, Fuchs, Hops, & Jenkins, 2001). A breakdown in mastery of any of the sub-skills that comprise the reading process can have a direct impact on reading fluency (Wolf, Bowers, & Biddle, 2000) and comprehension. It has been determined that these sub-skills are hierarchical in nature, and theory suggests (LaBerge & Samuels, 1974; Reynolds, 2000; Samuels & Kamil, 1984) automaticity of the lower level sub-skills (consonants, vowels, syllables, grammatical endings, meaningful parts, and the spelling units that represent them) allows attention to be allocated to the acquisition of higher-level sub-skills (fluency and comprehension) (LaBerge & Samuels, 1974).

Adolescent Literacy
Phonological Impairments

Most adolescents with RD appear to have a core linguistic impairment at the lower sub-skill level in the sound structure of language (Ehri, 1991) leading to deficits concentrated in the areas of word identification and phonological processing (Fletcher et al., 1994). Research has also shown that phonological decoding skills are teachable (Torgesen et al., 2001) and students lacking prerequisite awareness of sounds, symbols, and word meanings can improve their reading if these critical linguistic skills are directly, systematically, and actively taught (Lovett et al., 2000; Torgesen et al., 2001). Because of this severe deficit in phonological decoding skills, adolescents with RD might need more practice in mapping sounds onto letters in *isolation* to acquire mastery of these skills.

Comprehension Impairments

Comprehension has been deemed the essence of reading (Durkin, 1993). It used to be thought that comprehension was "caught rather than taught" (Pearson & Johnson, 1978). However, research has convinced most educators that reading comprehension can be taught. Strategy instruction, instruction where teachers demonstrate, explain, model, implement, and scaffold strategies, has emerged as an appropriate method for teaching reading comprehension (National Reading Panel, 2000). Research has shown the most important comprehension skills students need to learn are questioning, clarifying, summarizing, and predicting (Adams, Treiman, & Pressley, 1996).

Few studies have examined the teaching of higher-level reading comprehension skills with older students with RD (Pearson & Fielding, 1991; Talbott, Lloyd, & Tankersley, 1994). Peer Assisted Learning Strategies (PALS), which

> "The challenge for teaching adolescents with reading disabilities, is not how to appropriately teach each individual reading sub-skill, but how best to sequentially balance each sub-skill... to maximize the responsiveness..."

teaches strategies for questioning, discovering the main idea, summarizing, and predicting, has demonstrated improvement in reading comprehension scores for middle and high-school students with RD (Fuchs, Fuchs, & Kazdan, 1999; Mastropieri, Scruggs, Mohler, Beranek, Spencer, Boon, & Talbott, 2001). Additionally, research on direct instruction of main idea summarization has shown favorable results for middle school students (Jitendra, Hoppes, & Xin, 2000; Jitendara, Cole, Hoppes, & Wilson, 1998).

While studies have answered many questions concerning specific instructional techniques that are necessary for the remediation of each individual reading sub-skill, they do not provide information concerning the most effective sequencing and balancing of each reading sub-skill to know how to maximize reading levels of these students with RD (Torgesen et al. 2001; Swanson, 1999). The challenge then for teaching adolescents with reading disabilities, is not how to appropriately teach each individual reading sub-skill, but how best to sequentially balance each sub-skill (phonemic decoding, spelling, reading fluency, and reading comprehension) to maximize the responsiveness of these students (Mathes et al, 1998; Lovett, et al., 2000; Torgesen et al., 2001).

Early Literacy Instruction

Scientifically based research on early literacy instruction suggests that teachers should provide students with a variety of experiences relating to all aspects of reading. Students should be exposed to oral language activities promoting concept and vocabulary development, such as story reading, accompanied by verbal discussions, as well as phonics lessons, word-recognition instruction, spelling, and writing activities (Chard & Osborn, 1999). The reading of connected text built on previously mastered phonological skills should be added as quickly as possible, allowing for practice of learned skills in context (Mathes, Howard, Allen, & Fuchs, 1998). This sequential balancing of sub-skill introduction allows for instruction within each lesson to integrate the phonological, orthographic and semantic systems, which have been shown to be interactively connected within the reading process (Plaut & Booth, 2000; Plaut, McClelland, Seidenberg, & Patterson, 1996).

Current Adolescent Literacy Instruction

Remedial reading programs for older students who were either resistant to early literacy programs or received inadequate reading instruction typically follow the same sequential introduction of sub-skills as their early literacy counterparts. Most remedial programs incorporate a skill *integrated design* consisting of instruction in phonological awareness, spelling, vocabulary, fluency, and comprehension taking place within a single lesson. Yet research on a remedial program for students with RD indicates that while these programs do accelerate reading growth, they do not significantly close the reading gap and normalize reading skills for middle school students with RD to the level of their non-disabled peers (Hanushek, Kain & Rivkin, 1998; Kavale, 1988; Swanson, 1999; Zigmond, 1996).

Three possible reasons exist for the use of this *integrated approach*, 1) it is assumed that most middle school students in need of remedial programs already have some phonological and orthographic knowledge; therefore, the singular introduction of sub-skills is considered to be over burdensome and too time consuming, 2) the singular introduction of sub-skills would adversely affect the connection between single word decoding and context reading comprehension, or 3) the idea of teaching reading to adolescents a different way has not been conceived. Results from existing research on remedial reading programs for adolescents has led some researchers to question whether the *integrated approach* is the best way to accelerate reading skill acquisition in older students with RD.

Sequential versus Integrated Balancing of Reading Sub-Skills

Therefore to think differently or "Outside of the Box," a remedial phonological skills program, Linguistic Skills Training (LST); (Calhoon, 2003), was recently created specifically for adolescents to examine how best to sequentially balance each reading sub-skill to maximize responsiveness to instruction. The LST program was designed to accompany the existing PALS (Fuchs, Fuchs, Phillips, Hamlett, & Karns, 1995) reading comprehension program. Thereby combining into one program, LST/PALS has several elements research demonstrates effective for teaching adolescents with RD –i.e., small grouping sizes, directed questioning and responses, guided practice, explicit and direct instruction in phonological skills, extended practice opportunities with feedback, breaking down tasks into component parts, reading fluency, reading comprehension strategies, and contextual reading (Swanson 1999, 2001; Swanson & Hoskyn, 1998; Vaughn, Gersten, & Chard, 2000). More importantly, however, the LST and PALS programs were designed to provide intensive *segregated* phonics instruction *alternated* with a separate reading comprehension program allowing for a *sequential segregated* remedial reading program instead of an *integrated* remedial reading program.

Program Descriptions
Linguistic Skills Training (LST)

Based on the Direct Instruction (DI) model of program design, LST provides a systematic approach to the delivery of procedures for building and maintaining the basic cognitive skills necessary for learning letter sound correspondence. The LST program utilizes an intense and explicit linguistic system comprised of written signals (i.e., c = consonant, ^ = peak, _ = lax sound for the letter *e*, _ = tense sound for the letter *e*) for each linguistic skill. The signaling system enables students to identify the actual sounds letters or letter clusters make as well as recognize the seven basic rules the LST program is created around.

Developed based on knowledge of the structure of the English language, LST explicitly teaches (a) phonetics (i.e., speech sound identification, vowel and semivowel patterns, phoneme counting, phonetic transcription); (b) phonology (i.e., phonemes and minimal pairs, phonetic variation, systematic variation in speech sound production, sequencing, syllables [vcv, vccv, x, ble]; and (c) English orthography (i.e., historical layers of English orthography, Latinate ending, romance language spellings, orthographic conventions). These skills are reported to be essential for the learning of the English language (Moats, 2001). Furthermore, the core instructional technique used in LST employs a form of segmenting and telescoping developed by Carnine, Silbert, Kame'enui, & Tarver (2004) to teach phonemic awareness coupled with the idea that phonological awareness training needs to be anchored with print (letter-sound correspondence) to impact reading skills for older students (Adams, Treiman, & Pressley, 1998; Ehri, 1991; Share & Stanovich, 1995).

Moreover, research has shown that students with RD are able to decode letters in the initial position of words; however, middle and final positioned letters are more difficult and remain elusive for these students (McCandliss, Beck, Sandak, & Perfetti, 2003). LST focuses on the smallest spelling-to-sound units while training recognition of larger syllabic units, specifically the rime. LST attempts to promote generalization of word identification by systematically remediating the core sound and blending deficits through the teaching of a set of specific rule-based strategies and the skills necessary to implement them (see Calhoon, 2005).

Partner Comprehension Strategies (PCS)

PCS is the PALS (Fuchs et al., 1995) program renamed for middle school students to make it more age-appropriate. PCS is a program that incorporates three essential reading activities: partner reading (Simmons & Kame'enui, 1990), paragraph shrinking (similar to summarization) (Baumann, 1984), and prediction relay (Palinscar & Brown, 1984). Even though tutoring roles are reciprocal, the coach reads first for each activity to serve as a model for the partner. Each session begins with echo reading, which is designed to improve student's reading accuracy and rate. After both students have read, the partner then retells for 2 minutes the sequence of events in the text just read. After partner reading, students complete paragraph shrinking, which is designed to develop comprehension through summarization and main idea identification (Fuchs et al., 1995). The final activity is prediction relay, which extends paragraph shrinking to larger chunks of text, and asks students to make and confirm or disconfirm predictions.

Pilot Study

A recent study (Calhoon, 2005) examined the effect of LST/PCS with 38 middle school students with RD. Teachers were randomly assigned to one of two remedial reading programs, LST/PCS disabilities or Saxon Phonics Intensive plus SRA Skill Acquisition (SPI/SRA). LST was implemented three days a week allowing for approximately 51 hours of instruction. LST was coupled with PCS, which was implemented two days a week for 34 hours of separate comprehension instruction time.

Saxon Phonics Intensive plus SRA Skill Acquisition program follows the more traditional remedial reading program format by integrating reading sub-skills in a single lesson. SPI combines explicit teaching of decoding skills with spelling, vocabulary, reading fluency, and reading comprehension in the same lesson. SPI was implemented three days a week allowing for 21 hours of decoding, 10 hours of spelling, 5 hours of reading fluency, 5 hours of vocabulary and 10 hours of reading comprehension instruction. SPI was coupled with the SRA, a reading comprehension program, which teaches comprehension by having the students read a passage and then answer questions about the content of the passage, and was implemented two days a week allowing for 34 hours of instruction. Added with the comprehension training during SPI, the total comprehension instruction time for the treatment group was 44 hours. Table 7.2.1 shows the instructional design for the pilot study.

Table 7.2.1.   **Instructional Schedule for Pilot Study**
Note: LST – Linguistic Skills Training; PCS–Partner Comprehension Strategies; SPI – Saxon Phonic Intervention; SRA – SRA Skill Acquisition

31 weeks					
	Monday	Tuesday	Wednesday	Thursday	Friday
Group A	LST	PCS	LST	LST	PCS
Group B	SPI	SRA	SPI	SRA	SPI

Students were pre-, and post-tested on the word identification, word attack, passage comprehension, spelling, and reading fluency subtests of the Woodcock-Johnson Achievement Test – III. An ANOVA on pretest scores showed no significant difference on any subtests. A Repeated Measures ANOVA across time (pre-, post-) demonstrated a significant difference between groups with the LST/PCS significantly outperforming the SPI/SRA on letter word identification, word attack, and passage comprehension. No significant difference between groups was found for reading fluency and spelling. A one-way ANOVA to assess overall growth from pre- to posttreatment was also conducted. Significant growth for the LST/PCS treatment group was seen in letter word identification, word attack, and passage comprehension. Large effect sizes were found for letter word identification, $ES = 1.27$, word attack, $ES = .84$, and passage comprehension, $ES = .96$. No significant differences were found between the groups for growth for reading fluency or spelling.

Results from these findings demonstrated students with RD who received intensive *isolated* phonics instruction *alternated* with a separate reading comprehension program increased word recognition and word identification skills over the more traditional sub-skill *integrated* reading program. Furthermore, the LST/PCS group produced substantially stronger growth in passage comprehension with only 34 hours of comprehension training compared to 44 hours for the SPI/SRA group. The acquisition of nonword reading, word identification, and reading comprehension demonstrates a generalization across skills for the LST/PCS program. Lack of growth in reading fluency and spelling for both programs was disappointing, especially since the SPI/SRA group were explicitly taught each of these skills.

Examination of the study poses a number of new questions concerning sequential balancing of sub-skills. The significant gains produced with the LST/PCS program for word attack, word identification, and passage comprehension suggests the need for further research to expand upon and confirm these results as well as improve upon the instructional schedule. One way to expand the current design is to integrate and sequence explicit spelling and reading fluency skill instruction into the LST/PCS instruction. The question, however, is, how best to add these skills to the LST/PCS instruction?

Extension Study

A current study examining the sequential integration of spelling and reading fluency instruction into the LST/PCS program using two different instructional schedules is being conducted. The study is being conducted for a total of 28 weeks and examines three differently sequenced instructional combinations of basic reading sub-skills. All three treatment groups will receive the same amount of instructional time, approximately 45 minutes per day, five days per week, regardless of the combination of skills taught. See Table 7.2.2 for the instructional schedule and total hours of instructional time for each condition and reading sub-skill. The three instructional combinations were as follows:

Group A is receiving LST three days per week and PCS reading comprehension two days per week consistent with the successful pilot program instructional schedule. This schedule is acting as the control allowing investigation of changes to the current instructional schedule.

The second treatment group, Group B, is receiving spelling (SP) and reading fluency (FL) training integrated into each LST lesson. This instructional schedule is based on the more traditional instructional schedule, which *integrates within a single lesson* different reading sub-skills. Group B is receiving LST+SP+FL three days a week and PCS reading comprehension two days per week.

One of the purposes for this study is to examine *the effects of sequential integration* of reading skills instruction to determine maximization of responsiveness of adolescents to instruction. Therefore with this instructional schedule, Group C introduces and integrates each reading sub-skill one at a time. Group C begins by receiving the LST program five days a week for the first seven weeks, then during the second seven weeks SP is integrated with the LST program. During the third seven weeks, FL is integrated with LST + SP. Finally, during the fourth seven weeks LST will be discontinued and PCS is integrated with SP + FL five days a week.

The primary hypothesis is that middle school students with RD will benefit the most from the sequential integration of reading skill instruction, Group C. Therefore, we hypothesize that Group C, the sequential integration condition, will be more effective compared to Group B, the integrated condition, and Group A, the control condition. Also we are exploring the addition of spelling and reading fluency instruction to the LST/PCS program and its effect on middle school students with RD.

Table 7.2.2   **Instructional Schedule for Adolescent Remedial Reading Project**
Note: LST – Linguistic Skills Training; PCS – Partner Comprehension Strategies;
SP – Spelling; FL – Reading Fluency.

	1st 7 weeks					2nd 7 weeks					3rd 7 weeks					4th 7 weeks					Total Hours of Instruction
	M	T	W	T	F	M	T	W	T	F	M	T	W	T	F	M	T	W	T	F	
Group A	LST	PCS	LST	LST	PCS	LST	PCS	LST	LST	PCS	LST	PCS	LST	LST	PCS	LST	PCS	LST	LST	PCS	LST = 63 hrs PCS = 42 hrs
Group B	LST + SP + FL	PCS	LST + SP + FL	LST + SP + FL	PCS	LST + SP + FL	PCS	LST + SP + FL	LST + SP + FL	PCS	LST + SP + FL	PCS	LST + SP + FL	LST + SP + FL	PCS	LST + SP + FL	PCS	LST + SP + FL	LST + SP + FL	PCS	LST = 42 hrs SP = 14 hrs FL = 7 hrs PCS = 42 hrs
Group C	LST					LST + SP					LST + SP + FL					SP + FL + PCS					LST= 64 hrs SP = 17.5 hrs FL = 6 hrs PCS = 26 hrs

Implications for Teachers

Consensus in the research community has demonstrated that most reading disabilities are due to a specific impairment within the language process (e.g., Adams, 1990; Stanovich & Siegel, 1994). Language processing deficits consist of the inability to efficiently and accurately process the phonological, semantical, and syntactical building blocks of the English language into the written units of print that represent them. Research has shown that while teachers are literate and may even have years of experience (Moats & Lyon, 1996), they do not possess enough of an in-depth, broad-based, complex understanding of the spoken and written language structure (i.e. phonemes, graphemes, morphology) to provide the extensive instruction in linguistic constructs that older students with RD require (Bailet, 1990; Moats, 1995). Furthermore without this knowledge, teachers of students with RD will not be able to present linguistic concepts accurately, interpret errors, provide appropriate examples and relate spoken to written language (Moats & Lyon, 1996).

Implications from the pilot and extended study are beginning to demonstrate that teachers need know more than just a cursory knowledge of the English language. This comprehensive knowledge may be even more important for teachers of adolescents with RD. Incremental skill development (i.e., decoding, spelling, fluency, comprehension) may allow for these older students to develop a more foundational in-depth knowledge base of each reading sub-skill, as opposed to the more shallow, splintered skill base acquired through current integrated remedial reading programs. The most successful teachers for students with RD will extensively know their content, know effective teaching strategies, know the structure of language and understand the linguistic characteristics of the English language (Moats, 2000).

Acknowledgements

Preparation of this manuscript was supported by a grant from the National Institute of Children's Health and Human Development (NICHD) Grant #1R03HD04 8988-01. Thanks to team members Jennifer Johnson, Amanda Wooten, Alexia Sandow, Angela King, and Megan Klein.

References

Adams, M. J. (1990). *Beginning to read: Thinking and learning about print.* Cambridge, MA: MIT Press.

Adams, M. J., Treiman, R., & Pressley, M. (1996). "Reading, writing and literacy". In I. Sigel, A. Renninger (Eds.), *Handbook of child psychology, Volume 4: Child psychology in practice.* New York: Wiley.

Adams, M., Treiman, R., & Pressley, M. (1998). Reading, writing, and literacy. In P. Mussen, J. Flavell, & E. Markman (Eds.). *Handbook of child psychology, Volume 3: Cognitive development.* New York: Wiley.

Bailet, L. (1990). Spelling rule usage among students with learning disabilities and normal achieving students. *Journal of Learning Disabilities, 23*, 121–128.

Baumann, J. F. (1984). The effectiveness of a direct instruction paradigm for teaching main idea comprehension. *Reading Research Quarterly. 20*(1), 93–115.

Calhoon, M. B. (2003). *Linguistics Skills Training Reading Program.* Unpublished Manual.

Calhoon, M. B. (2005). Effects of a peer-mediated phonological skill and reading comprehension program on reading skill acquisition for middle school students with reading disabilities. *Journal of Learning Disabilities, 38*(5), 424–433.

Carnine, D. W., Silbert, J., Kame'enui, E. J., & Tarver, S. G. (2004). *Direct reading Instruction* (4th ed.). New Jersey: Merrill Prentice Hall.

Chard, D. J., & Osborn, J. (1999). Phonics and word recognition instruction in early reading programs: Guidelines for accessibility. *Learning Disabilities Research and Practice, 14*(2), 107–117.

Durkin, D. (1993). *Teaching them to read.* (6th ed.). Boston, MA: Allyn & Bacon.

Ehri, L. C. (1991). Development of the ability to read words. In R. Barr, M. L. Kamil, O. B. Mosenthal, & P. D. Pearson (Eds.). *Handbook of reading research:* Vol. II (pp. 383–417). New York, Longman.

Fletcher, J. M., Shaywitz, S. E., Shankweiler, D. P., Katz, L., Liberman, I. Y., Stuebing, K. K., Francis D. J., Fowler, A. E., & Shaywitz, B.A. (1994). Cognitive profiles of reading disability: Comparisons of discrepancy and low achievement definitions. *Journal of Educational Psychology, 86*, 6–23.

Fuchs, L. S., Fuchs, D., Phillips, N. B. Hamlett, C. L., & Karns, K. (1995). Acquisition and transfer effects of class wide peer students with varying learning histories. *School Psychology Review, 24*(4), 604–20.

Fuchs, L. S., Fuchs, D., & Kazdan, S. (1999). Effects of peer-assisted learning strategies on high school students with serious reading problems. *Remedial and Special Education, 20*(5), 309–318.

Fuchs, L. S., Fuchs, D., Hops, M. K., & Jenkins, J. R. (2001). Oral reading fluency as an indicator of reading competence: A theoretical, empirical, and historical analysis. *Scientific Studies of Reading, 5*, 241–258.

Hanushek, E. A., Kain, J. F., & Rivkin, S. G. (1998). *Does special education raise academic achievement for students with disabilities?* National Bureau of Economic Research, Working Paper No. 6690, Cambridge, MA.

Jitendra, A. K., Cole, C. L., Hoppes, M. K., & Wilson, B. (1998). Effects of a direct instruction main idea summarization program and self-monitoring on reading comprehension of middle school students with learning disabilities. *Reading and Writing Quarterly, 14*(4), 1057-35–69.

Jitendra, A. K., Hoppes, M. K., & Xin, Y. P. (2000). Enhancing main idea comprehension for students with leaning problems: The role of a summarization strategy and self-monitoring instruction. *The Journal of Special Education, 34*(3), 127–139.

Kavale, K. A. (1988). The long-term consequences of learning disabilities. In M. C.Wang, H. J. Walburg, & M. C. Reynolds (Eds). *The handbook of special education: Research and practice* (pp. 303–344) New York: Pergamon.

LaBerge, D., & Samuels, S. J. (1974). Toward a theory of automatic processing in reading. *Cognitive Psychology*, 6, 293–323.

Lovett, M. W., Borden, S. L., Lacerenza, L., Frijters, J. C., Steinbach, K. A., & De Palma, M.. (2000). Components of effective remediation for developmental reading disabilities: Combining phonological and strategy-based instruction to improve outcomes. *Journal of Educational Psychology, 92*(2), 263–83.

Mastropieri, M. A., Scruggs, T. E., Mohler, L. J., Beranek, M. L., Spencer, V., Boon R. T., & Talbott, E. (2001). Can middle school students with serious reading difficulties help each other and learn anything? *Learning Disabilities: Research and Practice, 16*(1), 18–27.

Mathes, P. G., Howard, J. K., Allen, S. H., & Fuchs, D. (1998). Peer-assisted learning strategies for first-grade readers: Responding to the needs of diverse learners. *Reading Research Quarterly, 33*(1), 62–94.

McCandliss, B., Beck, I. L., Sandak, R., & Perfetti, C. (2003). Focusing attention on decoding for children with poor reading skills: Design and preliminary tests of the word building intervention. *Scientific Studies of Reading, 7*, 75–104.

McCardle, P., & Chhabra, V. (2004). *The voice of evidence in reading research.* Baltimore: Brooks Publishing.

McCray, A. D. (2001). The intermediate grades: Middle school students with reading disabilities. *The Reading Teacher, 55*(3), 298–300.

Moats, L. C. (1995). *Spelling: Development and disability.* Timonium. MD: York Press.

Moats L. C., & Lyon, G. R. (1996). Wanted: Teachers with knowledge of language. *Topics and Language Disorders, 16*(2), 73–86.

Moats, L. C. (2000). *Speech to Print: Language essentials for teachers.* Baltimore: Brooks Publishing.

Moats, L. C. (2001). When Older Students Can't Read. *Educational Leadership, 58*(6), 36–40.

National Assessment of Educational Progress (2005). Available from http://nces.ed.gov/ nationsreportcard/about/

National Reading Panel. (2000). Report of the National Reading Panel. Retrieved January 28, 2004, from http://www.nichd.nih.gov/publicatio ns/nrppubskey.cfm

Palinscar, A. S., & Brown, A. L. (1984). Reciprocal teaching of comprehension-fostering and comprehension monitoring activity. *Cognition and Instruction, 2*, 117–175.

Pearson, P. D., & Fielding, L. (1991). Comprehension instruction. In R. Barr, M.L. Kamil, P. Mosenthal, & P. D.Pearson (Eds), *Handbook of reading research*, 2, 815–860. White Plains, NY: Longman.

Pearson, P. D., & Johnson, D. D. (1978). *Teaching reading comprehension.* Orlando, FL: Holt, Reinhart & Winston.

Plaut, C. A., & Booth, J. R. (2000). Individual and developmental differences in semantic priming: Empirical findings and computational support for a single-mechanism account of lexical processing. *Psychological Review, 107*(4), 786–823.

Plaut, D. C., McClelland, J. L., Seidenberg, M. S., & Patterson, K. (1996). Understanding normal and impaired word reading: Computational principles in quasi-regular domains. *Psychological Review, 103*, 56–115.

Reynolds, R. E. (2000). Attentional resource emancipation: Toward understanding the interaction of word identification and comprehension processes in reading. *Scientific Studies of Reading, 4*(3), 169–95.

Samuels, S. J., & Kamil, M. L. (1984). Models of the reading process. In P. D. Pearson, R. Barr, M. L. Kamil, & P. Mosenthal (Eds.), *Handbook of reading research*, 185–224. New York, NY: Longman.

Share, D. L., & Stanovich, K. E. (1995). Cognitive processes in early reading development: Accommodating individual differences into a model of acquisition. *Issues in Education, 1*, 1–57.

Simmons, D. C., & Kame`enui, E. J. (May, 1990). The effect of task alternatives on vocabulary knowledge: A comparison of students with and without learning disabilities. *Journal of Learning Disabilities, 23*(5), 291–97.

Stanovich, K. E. (1986). Matthew effects in reading: Some consequences of individual differences in the acquisition of literacy. *Reading Research Quarterly, 21*, 360–406.

Stanovich, K. E., & Siegel, L. S. (1994). Phenotypic performance profiles of children with reading disabilities: A regression-based test of the phonological-core variable difference model. *Journal of Educational Psychology, 86*, 24–53.

Swanson, H. L., & Hoskyn, M. (1998). Experimental intervention research on students with learning disabilities: A meta-analysis of treatment outcomes. *Review of Educational Research, 68*(3), 277–321.

Swanson, H. L. (1999). Reading research for students with LD: A meta analysis of intervention outcomes. *Journal of Learning Disabilities, 32*, 504–532.

Swanson, H. L. (2001). Searching for the best model for instructing students with learning disabilities. Focus on Exceptional Children, 34(2), 1–15.

Talbott, E., Lloyd, J. W., & Tankersley, H. (1994). Effects of reading comprehension interventions for students with learning disabilities. *Learning Disability Quarterly, 17*, 223–232.

Torgesen, J. K., Alexander, A. W., Wagner, R. K., Rashotte, C. A., Voeller, K. K. S., & Conway, T. (2001). Intensive remedial instruction for children with severe reading disabilities: Immediate and long-term outcomes from two instructional approaches. *Journal of Learning Disabilities, 34* (1), 33–58, 78.

Vaughn, S., Gersten, R., & Chard, D. J. (2000). The underlying message in LD intervention research: Findings from research syntheses. *Exceptional Children, 67*(1), 99–114.

Wolf, M., Bowers, P. G., & Biddle, K. (2000). Naming-speed processes, timing, and reading: A conceptual review. *Journal of Learning Disabilities, 33*(4), 387–407.

Zigmond, N. (1996). Educational intervention research and students with learning disabilities. *Learning Disabilities: A Multidisciplinary Journal, 7* (2), 69–73.

Supporting Teachers for Adolescent Literacy Interventions

James McPartland, Robert Balfanz, and Nettie Legters

Many of the frequently recommended instructional interventions for narrowing and closing reading gaps for adolescent learners are very demanding of teachers. This paper outlines the instructional challenges of five categories of classroom interventions and describes different ways that teachers can be supported for strong implementations. Evidence is drawn from experiences with the Talent Development model for reading instruction that is being developed and evaluated by Johns Hopkins University for middle and high schools (Kemple, Herlihy, & Smith, 2005; McPartland, Balfanz, & Shaw, 2004).

Classroom Practices for Adolescent Literacy

Most adolescents who are poor readers need to improve the fluency with which they can handle diverse texts and their comprehension skills to properly understand and interpret what they have read. Some also need to upgrade their word attack skills (Kamil, 2003). Five categories of instructional interventions drawn from research target these needs and pose different implementation challenges to teachers: modeling, vocabulary building, cooperative learning, self-selected reading, and focused tutoring.

Modeling

Students can learn reading comprehension strategies by observing an expert reader who verbally demonstrates various techniques and by practicing these approaches. Teachers can use a "read-aloud/think-aloud" activity to model reading comprehension strategies during which they read aloud from a short selection and pause regularly to verbalize what they are thinking, and what comprehension strategies they are using as they read. Thinking along with the author will include visualizing, predicting, questioning, and summarizing, as well as guessing unknown words from the context. Teachers can also model metacognitive strategies of checking for understanding and dealing with confusion by allowing the story to progress or re-reading for clarification (Bereiter & Bird, 1985; Kingery, 2000; Palinscar & Brown, 1984; Schoenbach, Greenleaf, Cziko, & Hurwitz, 1999).

Teachers should not be satisfied with dramatic oral reading alone. While this may engage students, it does not always focus on comprehension strategies of "reading between the lines" by reflecting out loud on a mental conversation with the author and monitoring one's own understanding. Even when teachers do include regular "think-aloud" pauses during modeling, they may focus on only one or two strategies, which limit the learning opportunities, or they may fail to label each strategy so that students can recall equivalent strategies across different daily lessons. Teachers should also give students the chance to practice and discuss different comprehension strategies through their own participation in "read-aloud/thinkaloud" activities.

> "The Talent Development model for adolescent literacy has developed three seperate and complementary approaches for supporting teachers... intensive workshops, complete instructional materials, and ongoing coaching."

How can we support teachers so that they model reading comprehension strategies that include multiple approaches for thinking along with the author, and checking oneself for understanding with good instructional practices to clearly label specific strategies and actively involve their students?

Building Vocabulary

Students can build reading fluency by expanding their word recognition vocabulary so that they do not stumble over many new words as they process different texts. Teachers can help their students build their recognition vocabulary by pulling problematic words from upcoming assignments for practice with students before reading. Students will then be better able to read with ease (Beck, McKeown & Kucan, 2002; Dole, Sloan & Trathen, 1995).

Vocabulary building occurs not only by choosing new words that students encounter in a reading passage, but also by how the meaning of new words is learned. Using dictionary definitions may be helpful, but other ways to engage students may be more effective for mastering new vocabulary. Asking students what they guess the meaning is, is a good start, followed with possible probes about word family roots or prefixes and suffixes. After initial clarification of definitions, practicing each new word in a "meaningful sentence" can be critical. An acceptable sentence should be specific enough that the targeted word cannot be easily replaced without losing meaning.

How can we support teachers to identify new words to be learned for reading assignments, and to draw students into learning activities that will result in strong, internalized vocabulary?

Cooperative Learning

Students can learn reading comprehension strategies through focused discussions of readings they have shared with their peers (Greenleaf, Schoenbach, Cziko, & Mueller, 2001; NICHD, 2000; Samway & Whang, 1996). Getting feedback and hearing others' views of the same material can help each student develop a deeper understanding of how to draw meaning from different writers. But, the student discussions have to delve deeper into the reading materials than the brief opinions in many adolescent conversations. Student team discussions should go beyond information recall and consider character and plot development in fiction, arguments on alternatives in nonfiction, and other implications and interpretations appropriate to the selection. How can we support teachers to pose good questions and focus student discussions for deep comprehension?

Also, readers need to have relevant background information and a purpose for undertaking the topic, to comprehend well and use what they have read. How can we support teachers to supply or activate background information as context for a reading assignment and to generate reasons for approaching the selection that will motivate students?

Self-Selected Reading

Student fluency is a function of how much practice students have had; reading complete works and reading diverse fiction and non-fiction can provide such practice. Providing regular class time for students to read silently from a book or article of their own choosing can supply some of the added practice needed for increased fluency (Curtis & Longo, 1999; Parr & Maguiness, 2005; Wilhelm, 1996).

The instructional challenges of self-selected reading opportunities include both matching student interests and skills with available material, and following reading with activities for accountability and reflection. The classroom library from which students choose readings should include a variety of materials to appeal to various gender and race-ethnic groups at multiple reading levels so all students can read without frustration. The student selection process should have guidance or benchmarks to match both individual interests and current reading abilities. After reading, activities should be available to record student's completion and understanding of the selection, and to encourage further thought on the value or usefulness of this reading experience. How can we support teachers to assemble materials and to facilitate the student selection and feedback processes for the most effective reading practice through self-selected reading opportunities?

Focused Tutoring

Adolescent readers will profit from personal attention from their teacher to assess current individual learning needs and address them (Biancarosa & Snow, 2004; Hock, Schumaker, & Deshler, 1995). Formal progress monitoring of students' reading progress using standardized assessment tools can be combined with informal teacher conferences with students to identify individual needs for extra help. Such informal face-to-face teacher conferences with small student groups or with individuals where students read aloud and discuss the material can give teachers insights into current skills and specific needs of each learner. Further work at this level can provide focused tutoring for students who still have decoding and word attack problems or who struggle with other aspects of reading. Sometimes assignments should follow. Students can work to strengthen word skills or to enhance fluency with books-on-tape. How can we support teachers to schedule class time for student conferences or tutoring with appropriate activities for different students?

Supporting Teachers Through Intensive Workshops, Complete Instructional Materials, and Ongoing Coaching

The Talent Development model for adolescent literacy has developed three separate and complementary approaches for supporting teachers with implementing recommended classroom practices. These approaches involve different costs and resource availability. An ongoing evaluation is designed to examine the cost-efficiency of these three broad approaches for teacher support: intensive workshops, complete instructional materials, and ongoing coaching.

Intensive Workshops

A traditional approach to professional development for implementing reforms, such as including literacy instruction in all content subjects or expanding language arts courses to cover comprehension strategies for both fictional and informational texts, is to gather participating teachers for intensive workshops that demonstrate and practice the recommended materials and methods.

For our Talent Development model in partnership secondary schools, intensive workshops for adolescent literacy teachers occur for two or three full days before the beginning of the fall term, and for one full day between the fall and spring terms. The workshops cover each of the five instructional approaches discussed above. Workshops begin with a full discussion of fluency and comprehension of adolescent literacy. Then each of the recommended instructional approaches is covered for its research rationale and with its practical challenges and solutions.

Each approach is taken on separately, as workshop participants first play the roles of students, while an expert teacher conducts a lesson. This simulated classroom experience allows each workshop member to observe an expert demonstration of the approach and to appreciate how a student might respond. Then participants watch and critique videotapes of actual classrooms of teachers attempting each approach. They delve into some of the nuances of superficial or expert implementations. Finally, teams of workshop teachers practice the approaches and discuss implementation challenges and best practices.

The mid-year follow-up workshop gives teachers a chance to share experiences, renew their understanding of the rationale for each instructional component, and refresh their training of implementation methods. Follow-up workshops are sometimes scheduled much more frequently, such as one day per month or for shorter after-school periods each month, depending upon district needs and resources.

Complete Instructional Materials

Providing complete daily lessons with extensive instructional materials may also be a powerful way to support teachers in implementing various adolescent literacy approaches. When intensive workshops are backed up by complete daily lessons, more teachers may feel prepared and confident enough to use the recommended classroom approaches. In our work with Talent Development middle and high schools, we have found that some of the implementation challenges can be addressed with detailed instructional materials.

For teacher modeling, lesson materials can indicate specific reading selections that are well suited for Read-aloud/Think-aloud demonstrations, and can point to appropriate places to pause to verbalize specific strategies. The placement of Post-It® reminders designates spots for particular pauses with a strategic comment.

For vocabulary practice, lesson materials with assigned readings can identify key new words and suggest meaningful sentences to assist teachers.

For cooperative learning, lesson materials can provide background information to motivate students, and offer discussion questions for student teams that address several levels of understanding and comprehension issues.

The Talent Development reform model has produced more than 250 Partner Discussion Guides (PDGs) for various novels, short stories and nonfiction selections (Maouyo, 2006). Each guide indicates background information and provides discussion questions for student teams and their shared reading.

For self-selected reading, lesson materials can indicate how a classroom library can organize books and articles by broad topic and reading level, and how teachers can help students make the best choices. Materials for follow-up activities for student accountability and reflection can be included.

For tutoring opportunities, lesson materials can help teachers with student conference assessment criteria and suggest different workstations where students can practice word skills or address other needs.

Complete daily lessons to support teachers with adolescent literacy interventions can be supplied by existing reform models such as Talent Development, or developed and distributed by school or district teams working on instructional materials.

Continuous Coaching

The most expensive support for adolescent literacy teachers is providing expert coaches who regularly visit teachers in their classrooms, following up on workshops and assisting with using lesson materials. Additional individual coaching may be required for some novice teachers or others who have not had much training in reading instruction.

Literacy coaches in many of the Talent Development sites fill full-time positions. They visit every English teacher in one or two schools for at least one class period per week. Additional coaching time can be scheduled for any teachers who need extra assistance in classroom management or other elements of implementing the recommended practices. Coaches are not part of the teacher evaluation process, and all interactions are confidential, so a collegial relationship of trust can be established.

Coaches can model-teach, or co-teach a lesson. Coaches will discuss instructional approaches that have proven successful in other classrooms, or those that usually should be avoided. Coaches will make sure all required materials and facilities for the lessons have been provided. Improvements in materials or lessons can be considered by the teacher and coach for feedback to the school or reform partner.

Coaches strengthen implementation through their expertise and technical assistance, and by being reminders and observers of the recommended practices.

Evaluating Supports for Literacy Teachers

Most of the guidelines for supporting literacy teachers are derived from practical experiences rather than strong scientific evaluations, which are largely missing in this area (Guinney, 2001; Neufeld & Roper, 2003; Sturtevant, 2003). But we are conducting a major randomized field experiment to provide direct empirical evidence on the effects of different ways of supporting ninth-grade English teachers in implementing the classroom instructional approaches discussed above. This study concentrates on struggling readers entering Grade 9, but reading between the fourth- and seventh-grade levels on tests.

A large sample of 108 ninth-grade teachers in 54 schools involving approximately 3,000 students is needed for the statistical power to detect any modest effect sizes that may apply for differences in teacher supports. The 54 schools are randomized across three different conditions of teacher supports. The first condition is Workshops Only, where the participating teachers receive an intensive two-day reading workshop before the start of the fall term, and a one-day refresher workshop between the two terms. The second condition is Workshop and Daily Lesson Materials, where in addition to workshops of the same duration, participating teachers receive complete lesson materials using the same recommended practices for each day of instruction. The third condition is Workshop, Daily Lessons, and Expert Coaching. An expert literacy coach visits participating teachers at least once per week to offer technical assistance. These teachers also receive the same Workshops and Daily Lesson Materials provided in the other experimental conditions. The recommended classroom literacy approaches are the same across the three experimental conditions, involving teacher modeling, vocabulary building, cooperative learning, self-selected reading, and focused tutoring, as described above. The experimental conditions vary in terms of the supports provided to the English teachers.

Implementation effects will be analyzed by comparisons among the experimental conditions of the degree to which teachers are using the recommended classroom practices. We are measuring classroom implementation by direct observations and by survey reports. Trained observers, who themselves have been experienced middle or high school classroom instructors, visit each teacher for a full period at three points during the school year to carefully record the instructional practices being used. Observers report the length of time each different practice is used, and the number of students who are fully engaged, as well as a rating on the quality of each practice. The observation protocol covers traditional practices such as teacher lectures and individual practice drills, as well as recommended practices such as teacher modeling and student team discussions. A quality rating rubric has been developed that specifies different teacher activities for low, medium and high manifestations of each type of classroom practice. Inter-rater reliability is established by all observers of the same classrooms and through joint debriefings soon after study observations. Additional measures of classroom implementations are collected from student and teacher surveys, where all participating individuals report the frequency of use of 22 classroom activities that include both traditional and recommended practices. Through these analyses, we will be able to fine-tune the results by studying the implementation of each component of the recommended practices as well as an overall summary scale. Thus, we can find out if particular recommended practices, such as teacher modeling or student discussions, are particularly in need of daily lessons or regular coaching as supports for powerful implementations.

Learning effects will be analyzed by comparison among the experimental conditions of student gains on the Gates-McGinitie reading test, which is administered at the beginning of the fall term and at the end of both the fall and spring term. In addition, the use of different reading strategies is measured by students' answers to questions about two reading selections from the Comprehensive Assessment of Reading Strategies, and by a student self-report survey of "How I Read," developed for this study.

Besides evaluating direct effects on classroom implementations and student learning from comparisons of teacher support categories, we will also study interaction patterns with teacher training or differences in student background. We will test whether novice teachers or those with the least prior training in reading instruction respond with stronger classroom implementations of recommended practices than other teachers when they receive daily lesson materials or coaching in addition to workshops. Likewise, we will estimate if the learning impacts are greater for the students who began with weakest preparations when the recommended practices are well implemented under different teacher support conditions. In this way, the study can detect any realistic complexities where teacher or student backgrounds set the context for different impacts of workshops, lessons, or coaching to support literacy instruction.

The study will be in the field for three school years to reach the full number of schools and teachers for impact analyses, with about 18 schools and 36 teachers being randomly assigned to study conditions each year. We are completing the first wave of schools during 2005–2006. Two additional waves are scheduled before our final results are due in 2008. The findings are expected to provide scientific evidence on the impacts of different ways of supporting teachers for adolescent literacy instruction.

References

Beck, I. L., McKeown, M. G., & Kucan, L. (2002). *Bringing words to life: Robust vocabulary instruction.* New York: Guildford Press.

Bereiter, C., & Bird, M. (1985). Use of thinking aloud in identification and teaching of reading comprehension strategies. *Cognition and Instruction, 2*, 131–156.

Biancarosa, G., & Snow. C. E. (2004). *Reading next—A vision for action and research in middle and high school literacy: A report from Carnegie Corporation of New York.* Washington, DC: Alliance for Excellent Education.

Curtis, M. E., & Longo, A. M. (1999). *When adolescents can't read: Methods and materials that work.* Cambridge, MA: Brookline Books.

Dole, J. A., Sloan, C., & Trathen, W. (1995). Teaching vocabulary within the context of literature. *Journal of Reading, 38*(6), 452–460.

Greenleaf, C., Schoenback, R., Cziko, C., & Mueller, F. (2001). Apprenticing adolescent readers to academic literacy. *Harvard Educational Review, 71*(1), 79–129.

Guinney, E. (2001). Coaching isn't just for athletes: The role of teacher leaders. *Phi Delta Kappan 82*, 740–43.

Hock, M. F., Schumaker, J. B., & Deshler, D. D. (1995). Training strategic tutors to enhance learning independence: A new conceptualization of the tutoring process. *Journal of Developmental Education, 19*(1), 18–27.

Kamil, M. L. (2003). *Adolescents and Literacy: Reading for the 21st Century.* Washington, DC: Alliance for Excellent Education.

Kemple, J. J., Herlihy, C. M., & Smith T. J. (2005). *Making progress toward graduation: Evidence from the talent development high school model.* New York: MDRC.

Kingery, E. (2000). Teaching metacognitive strategies to enhance higher-level thinking in adolescents. In P. E. Linder, E. G. Sturtevant, W. M. Linek, & J. R. Dugan (eds.) *Literacy at a New Horizon* (pp.74–85). Commerce, Texas: College Reading Association.

Maouyo, A. (ed.) (2006). *Student team literature partner discussion guide catalog.* Baltimore, MD: Talent Development Schools Program, Johns Hopkins University, 3003 N. Charles Street, Suite 200, Baltimore MD 21218.

McPartland, J., Balfanz, R., & Shaw, A. (2004). The talent development literacy program for poorly prepared high school students. In D. S. Strickland & D. A. Alvermann (eds.) *Bridging the literacy achievement gap grades 4–12* (pp. 252–265). New York, NY: Teachers College Press.

National Institute of Child Health and Human Development (2000). Report of the National Reading Panel: *Teaching Children to Read; Report of the Subgroups.* Washington, DC: Author.

Neufeld, B., & Roper, D. (2003). *Coaching: A strategy for developing instructional capacity.* Providence, RI: The Annenberg Institute for School Reform.

Palinscar, A. S., & Brown, A. L. (1984). Reciprocal teaching of comprehension-fostering and comprehension-monitoring activities. *Cognition and Instruction, 1*(2), 117–175.

Parr, J. M., & Maguiness, C. (2005). Removing the silent from SSR: Voluntary reading as social practice. *Journal of Adolescent and Adult Literacy, 49*(2), 98–107.

Samway, K. D., & Whang, G. (1996). *Literature study circles in a multicultural classroom.* York, Maine: Stenhouse.

Schoenbach, R., Greenleaf, C., Cziko, C., & Hurwitz, L. (1999). *Reading for Understanding: A Guide to Improving Reading in the Middle and High School Classrooms.* San Francisco: Jossey-Bass.

Sturtevant, E. G. (2003). *The literacy coach: A key to improving teaching and learning in secondary schools.* Washington, DC: Alliance for Excellent Education.

Wilhelm, J. (1996). *You gotta be the book: Teaching engaged and reflective reading with adolescents.* New York, NY: Teachers College Press.

Myths and Realities of Adolescent Literacy

Rebecca J. Moak, Tanya Shuy, and Peggy McCardle

Over the last several years the discouraging results of the National Assessment of Educational Progress and the greater emphasis on standardized assessments have spotlighted the need for greater understanding of what adolescents need in order to be successful readers. Upon entry into middle school, adolescents not only face increasingly difficult and dense expository texts, but they also encounter subject matter specialists rather than the generalists of earlier schooling. While teachers in secondary school are not usually considered teachers of reading, adolescents need increasingly complex literacy skills to comprehend, interpret, integrate, and demonstrate through oral discussion and writing their understanding of academic content, whether it is literature, science, history, or math.

Much of the message regarding adolescent literacy has been negative and frightening. Although the issues for adolescents are more complex than those encountered by younger beginning readers, we are beginning to understand more about what works and what can be done to support and enhance the literacy skills of these young people. By challenging some of the prevailing myths of adolescent literacy, the authors present realities that the classroom instructor can use when working with this age group.

Myth 1: Students are not interested in reading.

Motivation plays a key role in readers of all ages. Adults, primarily, read for two reasons: 1) it is required for their livelihood or 2) it is of interest as a leisure activity or for accessing information. Adolescents are required to read texts on subjects that they may not see as having any relevance to their lives. Moje (2006) reports that many of the students who are considered lacking in literacy abilities may be capable readers and writers in contexts that value their skills and allow them to draw on other text forms. Teachers are challenged by many different types of adolescent readers in secondary school classrooms, from youth who cannot decode but have high levels of knowledge, to youth who can decode and read with fluency, but fail to comprehend the challenging texts of different content areas. Students are often more interested in gaining knowledge from text than is initially apparent.

Myth 2: All teachers should be reading teachers.

Literacy is more complex than just reading; reading is more complex than just decoding. Without reading, students cannot become literate. Without decoding skills, students cannot read, but to comprehend they need vocabulary, background knowledge, and fluency. All teachers can use strategies that teach vocabulary and background knowledge. Deshler, Hock, and Catts (2006) discuss the complexities of adolescent readers. These authors present a framework for conceptualizing literacy instruction in secondary school settings, called the Content Literacy Continuum, which proposes that some students require more intensive, systematic, explicit instruction of content, strategies, and skills and that there are unique but very important roles for each member of a secondary staff relative to literacy instruction. So while all teachers are not and need not be reading teachers, all teachers do need to recognize the role of literacy in their own content areas and should be teaching strategic skills to enable students to gain knowledge from the types of text they will encounter in that particular content area.

Myth 3: Adolescents don't need decoding instruction.

A broad range of challenges confront adolescent readers, and it is not uncommon to find that struggling readers lack some of the basic skills needed to progress to more complex aspects of reading. Some need therapeutic intervention in these basic skills, as is illustrated by Calhoon (2006), who shares her research of students with reading disabilities. She shares insights on integrated design programs that accelerate adolescents' reading growth and the value of linguistically based instruction. Using an instructional model that provides intensive decoding instruction alternating with a separate reading comprehension program, she shows student growth on letter word identification, word attack, and passage comprehension.

Myth 4: Reading coaches are the key.

To support teachers in developing adolescent literacy skills, many school divisions are hiring reading coaches. While we know that teachers are grateful for and often benefit from various types of professional development, and that coaching can be a strongly supportive way to help teachers implement in the classroom what they may be exposed to in professional development workshops, at this point we do not have the empirical evidence to prove that the use of reading coaches is the best approach, or even that it is a generally successful strategy in raising literacy skills of adolescents. Is coaching alone enough? Or should it be combined with other supports to be most effective? An on-going research study using the Talent Development Model, is looking at varying degrees of teacher support to determine what is most effective for impacting student outcomes. McPartland (2006) outlines the instructional challenges of five categories of classroom interventions and describes different ways that teachers can be supported for strong implementation of reading instruction. Evidence is drawn from experiences with the Talent Development Model for reading instruction that is being developed and evaluated by Johns Hopkins University for middle and high schools. While coaches most likely contribute to reading improvement, the reality is that we need more evidence as to the best ways to use them, and the combinations of supports that will best enable teachers to address the literacy instructional needs for today's adolescent students.

References

Calhoon, M. B. (2006, Summer). Rethinking adolescent literacy instruction. *Perspectives, 32*, 31–35.

Deshler, D. D., Hock, M. F., & Catts, H. W. (2006, Summer). Enhancing outcomes for struggling adolescent readers. *Perspectives, 32*, 21–25.

McPartland, J., Balfanz, R., & Legters, N. (2006, Summer). Supporting teachers for adolescent literacy interventions. *Perspectives, 32*, 39–42.

Moje, E. B. (2006, Summer). Motivating texts, motivating contexts, motivating adolescents: An examination of the role of motivation in adolescent literacy practices and development. *Perspectives, 32*, 1–14.

Note: The assertions and opinions contained in this article are those of the authors and do not purport to represent the policies of the National Institutes of Health or the U.S. Department of Health and Human Services.

A Review of the Adult Reading Assessment and Instruction Research

John R. Kruidenier

The National Institute for Literacy (the "Institute"), in collaboration with the National Center for the Study of Adult Learning and Literacy, established the Adult Literacy Research Working Group to identify research-based practices for reading instruction and to disseminate information about these practices to those who provide reading instruction in adult education programs. This action is part of a larger effort by the federal government, beginning in the 1990s and continuing through the current administration, to build professional education cultures that value and use evidence-based principles for reading instruction with children, adolescents, and adults.

Reviewing adult reading instruction research is a key function of the Working Group whose other functions are described in detail in an article by John Comings and June Justice Crawford (2007). The Working Group's summary of results from studies of adult readers and adult reading instruction provides the basic content for its dissemination efforts as well as the basis for its efforts to identify or develop useable and practical research-based resources for adult education professional development. Some of these resources are described in two other articles: "Relating Reading Research to Practice: Two Resources for Adult Education Teachers" (McShane, 2007) and "Adult Educators in the United States: Who Are They and What Do They Know About Teaching Reading?" (Ziegler, McCallum, & Bell, 2007).

Although a large body of evidence-based principles exists for reading assessment and instruction of children in kindergarten through high school (K–12), not all of it applies to low-literate adults or adult education settings. For example, adult learners

> "A classroom full of adult literacy students may be filled with learners at just about any reading level, from beginners to those studying for their high school equivalency exam."

may not be able to devote as much time or be as consistent in their attendance as school children (Comings, Parella, & Soricone, 1999; Comings, Cuban, Bos, & Porter, 2003) making some proven instructional methods unworkable in adult education settings. Likewise, some evidence-based principles developed for adult struggling readers may not benefit children who are learning to read. For example, adults' interests and experiences may contribute to vocabulary and prior knowledge in ways that make adult literacy instructional methods less relevant for use with children. The needs of adults and children, and their teachers, are different: children who are learning to read are from all ability levels; adults who are learning to read may be predominantly those who have experienced difficulty academically because of a learning disability or for other reasons. Somewhat paradoxically, students reading at roughly the same grade level, or within a fairly narrow range, fill an elementary school teacher's classroom at the beginning of the school year. A classroom full of adult literacy students, however, may be filled with learners at just about any reading level, from beginners to those studying for their high school equivalency exam.

Thus, as a starting point for building an evidence-based education culture among adult literacy providers, the Working Group needed to identify and evaluate the existing research specifically related to adult reading instruction and assessment. At the same time, it realized that the relatively small size of the adult reading instruction research base would make it necessary to fill in the gaps with carefully selected studies of children learning to read. This article presents highlights from the Working Group's findings. For the complete findings and related instructional products, see the Working Group's publications (Kruidenier, 2002b; Curtis and Kruidenier, 2005) or visit the Institute's website (*www.nifl.gov/ partnershipforreading/publications/ adult. html*). The Working Group is in the process of completing an update to *Research-Based Principles for Adult Basic Education Reading Instruction* (Kruidenier, 2002b).

Methods

In order to accomplish its goal, the Working Group established a three-step process: 1) select the major topics to review, 2) conduct literature searches to locate studies that fit these topics, and 3) evaluate the studies using a set of evidence-based methodological standards. The Working Group began with topics and evaluation standards from two influential reports on K–12 reading, and modified them to reflect the differences between adult and childhood reading education and research. A report of the National Research Council of the National Academy of Sciences summarized past research that identified the essential components of reading and the importance of teaching them (Snow, Burns, & Griffin, 1998). *The Report of the National Reading Panel* summarized research in K–12 reading instruction and provided an initial set of methodological standards for use in the review of research (National Reading Panel [NRP], 2000a, 2000b).

Major Topics

The framework for the review is based on the major components of the reading process and reading instruction: alphabetics (including phonemic awareness and word analysis), vocabulary, fluency, and comprehension (see 7.5.1 "Major Components of the Reading Process and Reading Instruction"). After years of research, cognitive scientists have agreed that these subprocesses or components of reading are essential to the reading process and to reading instruction (Snow et al., 1998).

It is important to remember that these reading subprocesses take place in memory within individuals who have different goals and abilities and that they develop over time as students learn to read. It is also useful to remember that these basic processes are expressed through reading practices in specific contexts among groups of individuals (reading memos in the workplace, for example; Kruidenier, 2002a, p. 89).

With this in mind, the Working Group identified several subtopics that are important for reading instruction (see Table 7.5.1). Many of these topics are especially important to adult educators. First, the Working Group decided to separate studies that evaluated instruction from assessment studies, which looked at how well adults or specific groups of adults performed on reading tasks (e.g., all adults, adults with learning disabilities [LD], and English language learners).

Next, the Working Group recognized that differences in *Learner Characteristics*, *Goals and Settings*, and *Instructional Practices* were important subtopics to address within each major topic. They grouped studies that had common *Learner Characteristics* by reading levels, English language abilities, learning disabilities, and motivation to learn. Studies that had populations with similar *Goals and Settings* were sorted into three subtopics: general literacy, workplace literacy, or family literacy. Finally, they grouped studies with similar *Instructional Practices* by teaching strategies, instructional materials, intensity and duration of instruction, or type of teacher preparation indicated in each.

Figure 7.5.1.   **Major Components of the Reading Process and Reading Instruction**
Note: Individual researchers have focused on different aspects/components of the reading process and defined them in various ways. Researchers and writers may also use different terms to refer to the same skill.

Alphabetics
English is an alphabetic language where the 26 letters of the alphabet can be used to represent any words spoken in the language. Alphabetics, then, is the use of letters in an alphabet to represent spoken words. It consists of phonemic awareness, or knowledge of the basic speech sounds (phonemes) in the language, and word analysis or knowledge of the connection between written letters and the sounds they represent. Word analysis instruction could, for example, include decoding instruction or phonics as well as instruction in larger word parts like roots and affixes.

Fluency
Fluency is the ability to rapidly apply phonics knowledge and other reading skills, the ability to read with speed, ease, and expression.

Vocabulary
Vocabulary knowledge is simply knowledge of individual word meanings.

Comprehension
Comprehension is the ultimate goal for reading and it involves all of the components working together in order to understand or construct meaning from a text that is read. In order to comprehend, words must be decoded and associated with their meanings, ideas from phrases and sentences must be combined into a coherent whole that approximates what the writer intended, and all of this must be done quickly so that ideas from one sentence are not lost because of struggles with decoding on the next.

Table 7.5.1.

Table 7.5.1.   **Topics and Subtopics for Reading Instruction**

Note: Topic areas are shaded. LD = Learning Disability; ESOL Adults = Adults in English for Speakers of Other Languages programs; Vocab = Vocabulary; Comp = Reading Comprehension; Tech = Computer Technology.

SUBTOPICS	ASSESSMENT PROFILES	ALPHABETICS	FLUENCY	VOCAB	COMP	TECH
Assessment of Component						
All adults						
Adults with LD						
ESOL Adults						
Instruction						
Goals and Settings						
General literacy						
Workplace literacy						
Family literacy						
Instructional Practices						
Teaching strategies						
Instructional materials						
Intensity and duration						
Teacher preparation						
Learner Characteristics						
Functional reading level						
ESOL						
Learning disability						
Motivation						

Studies Included in the Review

The Working Group located studies that fit the major topics and subtopics through a literature search using social science databases, bibliographies, and expert recommendations. They included both experimental and non-experimental studies because so few studies of adult reading instruction and assessment exist, although experimental studies were given greater weight. They also categorized K–12 research from the *Report of the National Reading Panel* to help to fill in the gaps in the adult education research, keeping in mind the important differences between adults and children. For a more detailed description of the selection criteria, see *Research-Based Principles for Adult Basic Education Reading Instruction* (Kruidenier, 2002b).

Evaluation Standards

Approximately 70 studies of adult readers, most of which had non-experimental results, met the Working Group's criteria for inclusion in this review. Because of the small number of experimental studies within each topic area, the Working Group did not conduct a formal meta-analysis using statistical effect sizes, but instead identified emerging principles, trends, ideas, and comments for each major topic.

The Working Group looked for common themes in studies that addressed similar topics and subtopics. If they found two or more experimental studies with compatible results, they made a short statement summarizing the research findings, which they called *emerging principles*. A *true principle* would be based on a relatively large number of studies—enough so that the results have been replicated to ensure that the first time a result was found, it was not just a lucky accident. Only a few principles in this summary had a sufficiently large number of experimental studies to be called *true principles*.

Rather than overlook credible but unreplicated studies, the Working Group reported findings based on just one experimental study as *trends*. In addition, they relied on non-experimental studies to provided corroborating evidence or support for the emerging principles and trends. The Working Group referred to K–12 research that supplemented the adult literacy research as *ideas* when the findings were strong, and as *comments* when the research base was less robust.

Findings

The Working Group identified 18 emerging principles and 32 trends based on the relatively small body of adult literacy research in all topics. Some of the strongest principles, in terms of the number of studies used to support them, were assessment principles that described how well adult learners performed in each of the major components of reading (alphabetics, fluency, vocabulary, and comprehension). Very little of the research, however, distinguished subgroups within the adult education population (i.e., LD, English language learners).

From the K–12 research, the Working Group identified 22 ideas and 10 comments pertaining to reading instruction. These were useful in filling some of the gaps in the adult literacy research. The adult research, on the other hand, covered some areas not covered by the K–12 research that are especially important to adult education, including topics such as assessment, workplace and family literacy, the intensity and duration of instruction, and the effects of motivation and reading self-efficacy on reading achievement. It was encouraging to note that when studies with adults and children covered the same instructional topic, the results were not contradictory. Overall, much more research is needed with adults; there is ample opportunity for important contributions to the evidence base in the future.

Highlights from Assessment Findings

A broad principle that emerged from the assessment research was that adult readers' abilities are very diverse, and so assessments that measure only one component of reading give instructors insufficient information about learners' abilities and instructional needs. For example, if two hypothetical adult learners, Richard and Mary, each obtained a grade equivalency score of 4 (GE 4) on a norm-referenced reading comprehension test, such as the TABE (Test of Adult Basic Education, CTB/McGraw-Hill, 2000), many instructors would assume that they have similar instructional needs. However, if an instructor also knew what Richard's and Mary's word analysis, word recognition, spelling, oral reading, and oral vocabulary scores were (see Table 7.5.2), they would be more likely to differentiate instruction.

Table 7.5.2. **Two Hypothetical Reading Profiles**
Note: Scores are Grade Equivalent (GE) Scores. Maximum score is GE 12 for all except Word Analysis, which has a maximum of GE 3.

	STUDENTS	
COMPONENTS	**Richard**	**Mary**
Reading Comprehension	4	4
Word Analysis	1.5	2.5
Word Recognition	2	5
Spelling	1	5
Oral Reading	4	5
Oral Vocabulary	6	4

The maximum possible word analysis score for the test used was GE 3. Consequently, Mary's GE 2.5 word analysis score was pretty good, as her word recognition and spelling scores suggested (the maximum GE for all scores except word analysis is 12, or roughly the high school level). On the other hand, Mary's oral vocabulary (GE 4), which was measured orally so that it was not directly dependent on reading ability, seemed to be limited and may be the reason for her poor reading comprehension. Richard's instructional needs were very different from Mary's. He needed to significantly improve his word analysis skills and his word recognition skills to take advantage of his relatively good knowledge of word meanings (GE 6, oral vocabulary).

Studies that examined adults' alphabetics skills yielded a couple of strong principles. Adult non-readers and beginning readers demonstrated almost no phonemic awareness or knowledge of the basic sounds in our language. Adults without reading disabilities develop phonemic awareness as they develop other reading abilities until word analysis abilities are established. Assessment trends also suggested that important differences exist between adults and children who are beginning the process of learning to read, and that these should be kept in mind when using K–12 results with adults. For example, one might assume than an adult's vocabulary is better than that of a child reading at the same level, simply because adults have much more experience than children. Surprisingly, this assumption may not be true for adults and children who are learning to read when word recognition is above about the 4th-grade level.

Another difference between children and adults that one might expect is that adults' sight word knowledge (that is, their ability to recognize words quickly as opposed to sounding them out) is better than children's. In this case, the research trends support our expectations. Adult beginning readers' sight word knowledge seems to be better than that of children who are reading at the same level. The implication for phonics instruction in adult basic literacy is this: An instructor cannot use common sight words that might be used with children to teach an adult how to break a word down and sound it out. For example, *tax* is a word that might be included in a child's phonics lessons that adults would too frequently recognize on sight.

Highlights from Instruction Findings

The principles and trends in adult literacy research, combined with strong K–12 findings, suggest some specific approaches to teaching reading to adults. According to the research, an important principle for alphabetics instruction is that direct and explicit instruction, in contrast to incidental instruction, is best for teaching word analysis. The research also indicates that fluency improves with reading instruction that incorporates repeated, oral readings of texts. Although the research does not support a principle for vocabulary instruction, a trend suggested using engaging, adult-oriented contexts, such as family and workplace contexts, for teaching vocabulary. Direct instruction in reading comprehension strategies is an emerging principle for improving comprehension achievement among low literate adults.

Alphabetics instruction

The research suggests that adults can be taught phonemic awareness. Additional evidence, though not as strong, indicates that adults can also be taught word analysis skills. The instructional implications for these two emerging principles are that adult literacy educators should provide a significant amount of alphabetics instruction for beginning adult readers, and use direct and explicit instruction to teach word analysis skills.

K–12 research supports the principles for adult alphabetics instruction. In addition, the research with children suggests that instruction in phonemic awareness should focus on a few specific skills, especially blending and segmenting (putting phonemes together to make words and breaking words into individual phonemes). In addition, when teaching phonics skills, instructors should teach letter-sound correspondences in a systematic, direct, and explicit manner.

One caveat from the research is that adults with a learning disability may have an especially difficult time with phonemic awareness tasks. The research seems to suggest that these adults, like children who are struggling with their reading, may need to be taught phonemic awareness with written materials, in the course of phonics instruction, as opposed to being taught exclusively with oral tasks. For example, rather than being asked to imagine what the word *cat* becomes when the first sound is removed, they are shown a written version of the word as they manipulate the sounds.

Fluency instruction

The research indicated that fluency, the ability to read with speed, ease, and expression, can be taught to adult beginning readers. Furthermore, when adults increase their fluency, they also increase their overall reading achievement. This research, along with a much larger body of K–12 research, indicated that instructional practices that included repeated oral readings of text with guidance from a teacher were the best way to improve fluency. Although several variations to repeated readings exist, they all include reading the same text aloud many times. *Guided* means a teacher monitors the oral reading to keep track of speed, help out with difficult words, decide how many times to read, model fluent reading, and so on. Guided repeated oral reading is useful for all readers, including those with reading problems, and we can speculate that it is likely to be motivational because it leads to learners experiencing quick increases in reading rate and accuracy on the texts read. Quick success may be especially important for adult learners to maintain their motivation to improve their reading skills.

Vocabulary instruction

The Working Group found no emerging principles for adult basic education vocabulary instruction and relatively less K–12 research on this topic than on others. One trend in the adult research indicated that vocabulary could be improved in general functional literacy settings, although another trend suggested that vocabulary instruction might be more effective when conducted in family literacy or workplace settings. These trends were compatible with the ideas from K–12 research that engaging contexts with opportunities for repeated exposure to new concepts are effective for teaching vocabulary.

Comprehension instruction

The Working Group found that adult literacy researchers were only beginning to identify ways to improve reading comprehension through specific instructional practices. One emerging principle suggests that effective instructional approaches provide direct, rather than incidental, instruction in comprehension strategies, and another suggested focusing instruction on more than one component or aspect of reading during instruction. Another trend indicated that enabling settings or approaches were effective for comprehension instruction (adding classroom aides, for example, or addressing issues of reading self-efficacy).

The K–12 research supported the idea of multicomponent instruction (e.g., instruction in alphabetics, fluency, and vocabulary), indicating that it leads to improved reading comprehension. In addition, adult learners may benefit from direct instruction in a variety of strategies that include question answering, question asking, and cooperative learning. The best approach, based on the NRP review, is one that teaches multiple strategies, how to use two to three strategies flexibly.

One additional topic addressed by the K–12 research that may be of interest to adult educators is teacher preparation. A relatively small set of studies examined by the NRP suggests that teachers can learn how to teach reading comprehension to students and that their students can become aware of comprehension strategies, use them, and improve their reading. Although this is encouraging, the NRP also notes that even experienced teachers may have trouble implementing strategy instruction. This finding may be especially important for adult basic education settings, where teachers are frequently less experienced than their counterparts at the K–12 level.

Computer-assisted instruction

One particular method of instruction, computer-assisted instruction (CAI), is especially relevant for many educators and so was treated as a separate topic. CAI was shown to be at least as effective with adults as non-CAI reading instruction. Moreover, CAI that focuses on reading comprehension was demonstrated to be effective. The Working Group also noted a trend indicating CAI's effectiveness in word recognition instruction. Trends in the K–12 research support CAI for phonemic awareness and vocabulary instruction. Another trend cites speech-synthesis as an effective CAI feature because it allows computer-based text to be converted to speech for a student who is learning to read.

Summary

The Working Group found a relatively small base of adult literacy research, and that much more research is needed in almost all of the major topics and subtopics of adult literacy assessment and instruction. In the absence of a robust research base, findings from K–12 research were needed to support and fill in the gaps in adult education principles, keeping in mind the difference between adults and children who are learning to read. Studies of adult reading abilities (assessment studies) indicated that adult beginning readers are a very diverse population, and that assessments using only one measure of reading ability are insufficient for understanding their instructional needs. Studies of adult reading instruction generally indicated that adults can be taught alphabetics through direct and explicit instruction, vocabulary in meaningful contexts, fluency through repeated readings, and comprehension through explicit strategies instruction. In addition, computer-aided instructional methods were at least as effective as other methods. Perhaps more significant than any of these findings is the fact that education researchers need to conduct more experimental studies of adult literacy assessment and instruction. Partly as a result of the work of the Working Group and others, the Institute, the Departments of Education and Health and Human Services, and the National Institute of Child Health and Human Development are currently supporting at least six long-term studies of effective approaches to adult literacy instruction (http://www.nifl.gov/nifl/nat_research. html). This is a crucial first step toward providing the research base so critical to the success of adult learners and their teachers.

References

Comings, J., & Crawford, J. (2007, Fall). Introduction to the Adult Literacy Research Working Group. *Perspectives*, *33*, 11–13.

Comings, J., Cuban, S., Bos, J., & Porter, K. (2003). *As long as it takes: Responding to the challenges of adult student persistence in library literacy programs.* New York: MDRC.

Comings, J., Parella, A., & Soricone, L. (1999). *Persistence among adult basic education students in pre-GED classes* (Tech. Rep. No. 12). Cambridge, MA: Harvard University Graduate School of Education.

CTB/McGraw-Hill. (2000). *TABE forms 9&10: Tests of adult basic education.* Monterey, CA: Author.

Curtis, M. E., & Kruidenier, J. R. (2005). *Teaching adults to read: A summary of scientifically based research principles.* Washington, DC: National Institute for Literacy.

Kruidenier, J. R. (2002a). Literacy assessment in adult basic education. In J. Comings, B. Garner & Cristine Smith (Eds.), *The annual review of adult learning and literacy* (Vol. 3, pp. 84–151). San Francisco, CA: Jossey-Bass.

Kruidenier, J. R. (2002b). *Research-based principles for adult basic education reading instruction research.* Washington, DC: National Institute for Literacy.

McShane, S. (2007, Fall). Relating reading research to practice: Two resources for adult education teachers. *Perspectives*, *33*, 43–46.

National Reading Panel (2000a). *Report of the National Reading Panel: Teaching children to read.* Washington, DC: National Institute of Child Health and Human Development.

National Reading Panel (2000b). *Report of the National Reading Panel: Teaching children to read – Reports of the Subgroups.* Washington, DC: National Institute of Child Health and Human Development.

Snow, C. E., Burns, S. M., & Griffin, P. (Eds.) (1998). *Preventing reading difficulties in young children.* Washington, DC: National Academy Press.

Ziegler, M., McCallum, R. S., & Bell, S. M. (2007, Fall). Adult educators in the United States: Who are they and what do they know about teaching reading? *Perspectives*, *33*, 50–53.

7.6 Adult Reading Assessment and Instruction
Highlights from the Activities of the NIFL/NCSALL Adult Literacy Research Working Group

John R. Kruidenier and Sherry Mee Bell

The National Center for Education Statistics (NCES) completed a comprehensive assessment of adults' reading ability in 2003, administering a reading test to a representative sample of more than 19,000 people over the age of 16 in households (and prisons) in the United States. Applying its findings to the total adult population (222 million in 2003), the NCES concluded that 27 to 31 million adults are "Below Basic" readers and lack the skills needed for simple, everyday literacy activities. *Below Basic* readers are unable to consistently read and understand information in short, commonplace texts and simple documents, such as news articles, pamphlets, bus schedules, and food labels. This is roughly the level at which the average high school graduate reads. Many of these adults are unable to complete even simpler

> "...the NCES concluded that 27 to 31 million adults are 'Below Basic' readers and lack the skills needed for simple, every-day literacy activities."

reading tasks like locating specific information in short, commonplace texts (Kutner, Greenberg, & Baer, 2005).

According to the NCES, another group of 50 to 60 million adults is able to perform these tasks with varying degrees of consistency. The best readers in this "Basic" group can read at the high-school level. However, they have difficulty reading texts that are more dense and complex. Summarizing, making inferences, determining cause and effect, and recognizing an author's purpose are all difficult tasks for *Basic* readers (Kutner et al., 2005).

These findings are very troubling for a number of reasons. Low literacy correlates with a host of difficulties, such as low income (Barton & Jenkins, 1995), poor job prospects (Reder & Vogel, 1997; White, Strucker, & Bosworth, 2006), poor health (Baker, Parker, Williams, & Clark, 1997; Kutner et al., 2005; Kutner, Greenberg, Jin, & Paulsen, 2006), and even longevity (Baker et al., 2007). Those who track the needs of employers know that the vast majority of jobs now require workers who are able to read at the high-school level or better (White et al., 2006).

The U.S. Department of Education provides funding to states for adult education programs that include literacy instruction for adults who did not graduate from high school. Out of a total target population of about 40 million adults, states provide services for about 2.5 million (Lasater & Elliott, 2005). The 25–30 million adults with severe reading difficulties identified by NCES, along with a large group of immigrants whose first language is not English, make up the bulk of those in the target population who are eventually served in literacy programs for adults who read anywhere from a beginning level up to a 12th grade level. A significant proportion of this group includes those who have a learning disability, mostly in reading. Three to four percent, or roughly 7 to 9 million adults, report having a learning disability. Four percent of the NCES *Below Basic* readers report having a learning disability (Kirsch, Jungeblut, Jenkins, & Kolstad, 1993; Kutner et al., 2005).

To help address this vast problem of adults with low literacy skills, the National Institute for Literacy (the "Institute") in collaboration with the National Center for the Study of Adult Literacy and Learning (NCSALL) established the Adult Literacy Research Working Group. This group of approximately 40 experts in adult education and reading has met a number of times to work on identifying and disseminating effective research-based practices for the assessment and instruction of adults in adult literacy programs. The International Dyslexia Association's fall 2007 issue of *Perspectives on Language and Literacy* highlights some of the activities of the Working Group and several of its members.

In the introductory piece, John Comings and June Crawford (2007) provide context by describing the Working Group in detail and how it relates to the Institute's and NCSALL's missions. They also describe U.S. government supported resources identified for dissemination or actually developed by the Working Group. These include four of the resources described in this issue: a summary of the scientific research in adult reading instruction (Kruidenier,

2002); a professional development resource based on these findings (McShane, 2005); a website for teachers on assessing adult readers in preparation for instruction (Davidson, Strucker, & Bruce, 2003); and a tool designed to assess adult educators' knowledge of validated reading assessment and instruction practices (Ziegler, Bell, & McCallum, in press).

Following the introductory selection by John Comings and June Crawford (2007), Daryl Mellard, a member of the Working Group, and Kari Woods (2007) present data on the life-long impact of learning disabilities, particularly dyslexia, noting effects on postsecondary education, employment, and income. Importantly, they address implications for instruction. John Kruidenier (20007) next presents an overview of evidence-based adult reading assessment and instructional practices, based on the Working Group's comprehensive review of the literature, *Research-Based Principles for Adult Basic Education Reading Instruction.*

Following John Kruidenier's article are two selections that focus on the application of research-based assessment and instruction practices. First, Barbara Van Horn, a member of the Working Group, and Priscilla Carman (2007) describe both formal and informal assessment techniques that are appropriate for adults. They emphasize the need for multiple assessments to obtain information about learners' skills in the various areas of reading. Next, Susan McShane (2007) discusses issues related to linking research to practice and describes two resources that developed, at least in part, from the activities of the Working Group: (a) the *Assessment Strategies and Reading Profiles* website, which allows educators to enter assessment data and obtain diagnostic information and (b) the book she authored, *Applying Research in Reading Instruction for Adults: First Steps for Teachers*, which features practical, applied instruction and assessment strategies. Both are available through NIFL and have been identified as resources for dissemination as a part of the Working Group's dissemination efforts. Readers will find Susan McShane's article informative and the reference materials invaluable.

Finally, Mary Ziegler, Steve McCallum, and Sherry Mee Bell (2007) describe the population of adult educators in the United States and discuss what they seem to know about reading instruction, based on results of a recently standardized professional development tool, the *Assessment of Reading Instructional Knowledge-Adults* (in press), developed as a part of the Working Group's product development efforts. The issue concludes with a set of tips (from Bell & McCallum, 2008) for effective assessment of adults' reading skills.

We are pleased that IDA chose to highlight adult literacy in the Fall 2007 issue of *Perspectives*. The issue will, of course, be of special interest to those who work with older adolescents and adults who struggle with reading. We believe the information, resources, and references will also be of significant interest to educators and researchers committed to providing access to literacy for all individuals.

References

Bell, S. M., & McCallum, R. S. (2008). *Handbook of reading assessment.* Boston: Allyn & Bacon.

Baker, D. W., Wolf, M. S., Feinglass, J., Thompson, J. A., Gazmrarian, J. A., & Huang, J. (2007). Health literacy and mortality among elderly persons. *Archives of Internal Medicine, 167*, 1503–1509.

Baker, D. W., Parker, R. M., Williams, M. V., & Clark, W. S. (1997). The relationship of patient reading ability to self-reported health and use of health services. *American Journal of Public Health, 87*(6): 1027–1030.

Barton, P. E., & Jenkins, L., (1995). *Literacy and dependency: The literacy skills of welfare recipients in the United States.* Princeton, NJ: Educational Testing Service.

Comings, J., & Crawford, J. (2007, Fall). Introduction to the Adult Literacy Research Working Group. *Perspectives, 33*, 11–13.

Davidson, R., Strucker, J., & Bruce, K. (2003). *Assessment strategies and reading profiles: Research-based practice for the adult education classroom.* Retrieved from the National Institute for Literacy website: http://www.nifl.gov/readingprofiles

Kirsch, I. S., Jungeblut, A., Jenkins, L., & Kolstad, A. (1993). *Adult literacy in America: A first look at the results of the National Adult Literacy Survey.* Washington, DC: U.S. Government Printing Office.

Kruidenier, J. (2002). *Research-based principles for adult basic education reading instruction.* Washington, DC: National Institute for Literacy.

Kruidenier, J. (2007, Fall). A review of the adult reading assessment and instruction research. *Perspectives, 33*, 22–26.

Kruidenier, J., & Bell, S. M. (2007, Fall). Adult reading assessment and instruction: Highlights from the activities of the NIFL/NCSALL Adult Literacy Research Working Group. *Perspectives, 33*, 7–8.

Kutner, M., Greenberg, E., & Baer, J. (2005). *National Assessment of Adult Literacy (NAAL): A first look at the literacy of America's adults in the 21st Century.* Washington, DC: National Center for Education Statistics.

Kutner, M., Greenberg, E., Jin, Y., & Paulsen, C. (2006). *The health literacy of America's adults: Results from the 2003 National Assessment of Adult Literacy.* Washington, DC: National Center for Education Statistics.

Lasater, B., & Elliott, B. (2005). *Profiles of the adult education target population.* Washington, DC: Division of Adult Education and Literacy, U.S. Department of Education.

McShane, S. (2005). *Applying research in reading instruction for adults: First steps for teachers.* Washington, DC: National Institute for Literacy.

McShane, S. (2007, Fall). Relating reading research to practice: Two resources for adult education teachers. *Perspectives, 33*, 43–46.

Mellard, D. F., & Woods, K. L. (2007, Fall). Adult life with dyslexia. *Perspectives, 33*, 15–18.

Reder, S., & Vogel, S. A. (1997). Lifespan employment and economic outcomes for adults with self-reported learning disabilities. In P. J. Gerber, & D. S. Brown (Eds.), *Learning disabilities and employment.* Austin, TX: PRO-ED.

Van Horn, B., & Carman, P. (2007, Fall). Assessment of reading components in adult education programs. *Perspectives, 33*, 35–39.

White, S., Strucker, J., & Bosworth, B. (2006). *Adults with basic and below basic literacy levels: Findings from NAAL and implications for practice.* Webcast retrieved from http://www.nifl.gov/lincs/lincs_media.html

Ziegler, M., Bell, S. M., & McCallum, R. S. (in press). *Assessment of reading instructional knowledge-adults.* Washington, DC: National Institute for Literacy.

Ziegler, M., McCallum, R. S., & Bell, S. M. (2007, Fall). Adult educators in the United States: Who are they and what do they know about teaching reading? *Perspectives, 33*, 50–53.

The
International
DYSLEXIA
Association®

Promoting literacy through research, education, and advocacy.™

www.eida.org